Advance praise for *Green at Work: Revised and Expanded Edition*

Sue Cohn's book *Green at Work* addresses some of the most important questions concerning how people in business can make choices that create economic activity while conserving the natural resources that are the basis for our health and survival. It shows how each individual can use myriad skills and creativity to make professional choices that reflect personal values and concern for the planet's welfare.

I believe that there are many opportunities for individuals to work toward a greener world and to educate people about the choices they make. My company has done it. . . . We have environmental principles that govern our manufacturing and the selection of products and services that we offer to our customers. We look to nature for ways to be innovative in our no-waste philosophy of reduce, reuse, and recycle.

The business world needs leaders who include environmental considerations in all of their management decisions. Environmental responsibility can be a competitive advantage for business and . . . *Green at Work* is a great resource for people who are starting to ask questions about how their actions impact the environment and how their choices can indeed make a difference. This book will inspire people to seek to combine their education and creativity to participate in and use business as a positive force in sustaining a biologically diverse planet and a healthier environment for generations to come.

Horst Rechelbacher
Founder & CEO, Aveda Corporation

GREEN AT WORK

About Island Press

Island Press is the only nonprofit organization in the United States whose principal purpose is the publication of books on environmental issues and natural resource management. We provide solutions-oriented information to professionals, public officials, business and community leaders, and concerned citizens who are shaping responses to environmental problems.

In 1994, Island Press celebrated its tenth anniversary as the leading provider of timely and practical books that take a multidisciplinary approach to critical environmental concerns. Our growing list of titles reflects our commitment to bringing the best of an expanding body of literature to the environmental community throughout North America and the world.

Support for Island Press is provided by The Geraldine R. Dodge Foundation, The Energy Foundation, The Ford Foundation, William and Flora Hewlett Foundation, The James Irvine Foundation, The John D. and Catherine T. MacArthur Foundation, The Andrew W. Mellon Foundation, The Pew Charitable Trusts, The Rockefeller Brothers Fund, The Tides Foundation, Turner Foundation, Inc., The Rockefeller Philanthropic Collaborative, Inc., and individual donors.

GREEN AT WORK

Finding a Business Career That Works for the Environment

Revised and Expanded Edition

SUSAN COHN

ISLAND PRESS

Washington, D.C. ○ Covelo, California

Library of Congress Cataloging-in-Publication Data

Cohn, Susan, 1959–
Green at work : finding a business career that works for the environment / Susan Cohn.—Rev. and expanded ed.
p. cm.
Includes bibliographical references (p. –) and indexes.
ISBN 1-55963-333-6. — ISBN 1-55963-334-4 (pbk.)
1. Job hunting—United States. 2. Green movement—Vocational guidance—United States. 3. Environmental protection—Vocational guidance—United States. 4. Corporations—United States—Directories. 5. Nonprofit organizations—United States—Directories. I. Title.
HF5382.75.U6C64 1995
650.14—dc20 96-47939
CIP

Printed on recycled, acid-free paper

Manufactured in the United States of America
10 9 8 7 6 5 4 3 2 1

Contents

Foreword

The ordinariness of everyday life can make the past and present blend into each other in ways that seem as if little has changed. Days pass, weeks fly by, months are spent on mundane cares—work, study, shopping, friends—and only rarely do we pause to compare life today with what we had, say, twenty years ago. It quickly becomes clear that society has changed considerably in the last couple of decades. Of the many changes, one is directly connected with the book you are holding in your hands. And it concerns the place of the "green" world in our collective consciousness, and in society in general.

It was not unheard of to hold international conferences on the problems of ecology and the environment twenty years ago, but at that time the number of scientists and social activists in the world whom we would today call green probably amounted to no more than a few hundred. Today many tens of thousands of people are involved in environmental issues, and, what is more, environmental science has become a discipline in its own right. Environmental biology, environmental chemistry, ecotoxicology, and applied ecology are only some of the specialties that have cropped up in the field. Moreover, every branch of the sciences—from mathematics to microbiology—is, at least in part, related to the problems of environmental conservation. I would guess that not less than 20 percent of all scientific research is directly connected with these issues. Whereas twenty years ago green scientists could be found working only in the area of biology, today green scientists can include leading mathematicians, physicists, and chemists.

The changes in industry are even more remarkable. There is not a major firm or enterprise in the world today that does not have a department dedicated to dealing with environmental issues, and there is thus an increasing flow of environmentally aware engineers and leaders in the field entering the managerial ranks of industry. Even most major banks have whole departments of people whose work focuses on environmental concerns, and their general activities are, perforce, becoming increasingly green.

The greening of the political arena is even more striking than that in the industrial sphere. Over the past two decades, not only have scores of national green parties sprung up all around the world, but in each major party, bar none, there are groups of politicians who are associated with environmental issues. I think that if a summit of ecopoliticians were to be convened at this time, it would be necessary to invite tens of thousands of active political figures, beginning with the vice-president of the United States and the prime minister of Norway, and including the former president of the Soviet Union.

There are many reasons why contemporary society has become, if not green, at least "greenified." All spheres of society—industry, service, culture, science, education, politics, and even the military—are undergoing an intensive shift toward environmental awareness and are thus becoming increasingly ecofriendly. I do not intend to list the reasons for this, but I do want to note that all of the specific environmental issues that underlie this general movement, or at least the majority of them, are going to be factors to contend with for a long time to come. This means that greater numbers of environmentally aware people will be working in every sector—in business, in the sciences, and in politics.

Green at Work is, first and foremost, written for the young person who has decided to choose a profession that is in some way connected with the conservation and recovery of the environment. Until now, the choices for such a person were limited to a career in the organic sciences or in professional activism. This book, alternatively, introduces us to a broad range of professional options in literally all areas of business. It is also written for supervisors and leaders in those firms and companies that still perceive noisy environmentalists as a threat and fear that change will ultimately cause business to suffer. To these people I say: Don't worry! Not only is environmental awareness not a threat, but business could even stand to gain from becoming just a little "greener." Last, *Green at Work* is written for environmentalists themselves, to show them the full spectrum of the things that they can do in their various fields, and to indicate to them the potential for important and stimulating work that exists out there for them to undertake. This book provides concrete examples of how people can begin to ask the right questions, and it acts as a road map for understanding how our actions affect the environment. I recommend this important and inspiring resource in the hope that it may help encourage the greening of the world. We need it!

Alexey V. Yablokov
Russian Federation National Security Council Interagency Commission on Ecological Security

Introduction: The New Edition

The first edition of *Green at Work* contained tools and strategies for launching an environmental career and was intended to help present and future business leaders find or create green jobs. I chose that focus because environmental literacy can be a competitive advantage in the marketplace and in one's career, and because business is in a unique position to improve our quality of life and to help sustain a healthy environment. As business provides jobs and goods and services, it may develop leaders, new technology, more efficient processes, and more environmentally sound choices.

The second edition of *Green at Work* also offers tools and strategies for launching a green career, but I have expanded the scope of this edition beyond business to include many more career profiles, company listings, and resources; it covers people and organizations making "green" work in different ways across a range of professional fields. Just as it expands its scope, this edition also expands its definition of "environment." It uses the term to refer not to a separate entity from which we derive our resources, but rather to a process that influences our day-to-day lives in ways we may not even recognize. We are not observers outside the process; we are part of the ongoing system. As it goes, we go.

When we reframe win-lose "environmental" questions and integrate them into a view of a whole system of quality of life, environmentalism becomes not just a point of contention but a point of view based on interrelationships beyond traditionally defined categories. Issues such as resource consumption and waste disposal are not separate. They intersect with each other and with issues not traditionally considered environmental, such as poverty, urban violence, and human rights. To design effective solutions, we must recognize those interrelationships and understand them in the context of culture, history, attitudes, traditions, and available resources. This requires a variety of abilities, perspectives, and approaches, both conceptual and practical. Society needs people in all careers who recognize the value of environmental integrity, and who work along different routes to improve our approaches to solving our environmental problems. There are not always clear paths to greening a career, but the career profiles in this book provide examples that illustrate the variety of abilities, perspectives, and approaches that are possible.

Both editions of *Green at Work* have the same underlying theme: Rather than wait for people to tell you what to do, see from your own unique perspective what needs to be done and design a way to do it. Recognize and create alternatives beyond traditional fields. *Green at Work* offers strategies to help you make choices, tools to help you take action, and a community of people to help you find inspiration and information. It encourages you to envision a future that is cleaner and greener and to make decisions that can make a positive difference in the quality of all our lives.

My interest in greening careers comes out of my experience working in Alaska, in small Eskimo villages above the Arctic Circle, from 1982–1985. I went to Alaska to work for the Mauneluk Association, a nonprofit arm of Northwest Alaska Native Association, to run gardening programs and to work on renewable resource development projects in agriculture and fisheries. The projects were intended to improve native commercial and subsistence fishing, to provide jobs for village youth, and to produce a more varied diet of greens for village residents. My work involved creating employment opportunities for the Inupiaq that did not interfere with their subsistence activities.

Living in those villages, I learned to draw my water for laundry, drinking, and cooking from the river in buckets. In the fall and spring men on snow machines bring caribou to the villages, where I helped the women cut and dry the meat. I went to fish camps where families lived along the Mauneluk River during the spawning period in late summer and fall and helped cut hundreds of fish to be dried and put away for winter use. During this time, we also hiked along the tundra to pick salmonberries, cranberries, and blueberries to store for the rest of the year. While the women picked berries and cut and dried fish, men went out onto the tundra and often came back with caribou, moose, or bear. Every day we ate salmon, whatever fresh meat might have been caught, and berries with condensed milk for dessert. At night we slept in canvas tents with wood-burning stoves. The temperatures dropped below freezing even in the fall, and before bed we would eat some dry fish dipped in seal oil, which would provide calories to keep us warm during nights bright with northern lights.

In their subsistence activities, the Inupiaq wasted very little. They would invent ingenious ways to reuse materials when possible. Paper was used to start fires in wood stoves; five-gallon plastic containers became "honey buckets," or toilets; 55-gallon drums became wood stoves. They took only what they needed. The only waste I found there was introduced to the villages in over-packaged commodities flown in from Anchorage to the village general store.

In the village of Shungnak, residents explained to me their belief that work is central to a person's sense of power. Subsistence hunting and fishing had been their work; now rapid modernization created a need for money and employment. People needed jobs to support life in the oncoming Western culture and to pay for products they needed or desired, such as motor boats for fishing and hunting, satellite television hook-ups, and gas and electricity.

The dozen villages in the northwest region of Alaska have many government-subsidized houses, built with no attention to the knowledge and practices of the people there. The Inupiaq live successfully in one of the harshest climates on the planet, but architects and planners did not consult local inhabitants before building. The result was poor design: prefabricated structures that are not energy efficient, and that shake in the wind because their construction materials aren't appropriate to the terrain. In summer, the weight of any construction can thaw the top layers of permafrost, the permanently frozen subsoil that stretches across the tundra, and make buildings unstable. Indigenous knowledge of sod houses or cabins would have been useful in the design and construction of structures for that environment.

Living in Eskimo villages for almost three years, I saw clearly the value of both economic development and ecological conservation. Economic development was necessary for meeting basic needs in a rapidly changing economy. Conservation was critical to the Inupiaq, whose history, values, and basic needs were intricately tied to their environment. Any economic development in that region had to be evaluated against its potential effect on the ecosystem. To destroy the land was to destroy the main food supply and threaten Inupiaq culture. I have spent many years since my time in Alaska asking questions about how to create jobs while preserving ecological integrity. How do we move toward minimizing waste and valuing nature as we meet our daily needs and wants in industrial society?

In the two years since the first edition of this book was published, there has been progress toward environmental efficiency in the marketplace. Nevertheless, a choice is often presented between preservation of the environment and preservation of the livelihoods of human beings. We need to move beyond such polarized win-lose positions to explore new categories of questions and find common ground from which to define win-win objectives. We need both a healthy environment and jobs. We need both clean air and paychecks. "Quality of life" means that economic questions are environmental questions.

To find viable solutions, we have to see beyond entrenched positions toward a clearer view of our role in shaping and designing our environment. We must recognize the short-term and long-term consequences of our choices. The reality of our environmental problems does not fall into neatly defined categories. To create effective solutions, we need to consider a wide spectrum of approaches, not just prefabricated answers, which, like prefabricated houses, do not efficiently improve or appropriately preserve environmental integrity and quality of life.

I welcome letters, thoughts, and ideas from my readers. Please address any correspondence to Green at Work, c/o Susan Cohn, 61 East 8th Street, Suite 160, New York, NY 10003.

Acknowledgments

Green at Work is the result of the cooperation of hundreds of people in corporations, entrepreneurial ventures, and organizations who provided information on their environmental programs and initiatives. This book could not have been completed without their help. So to all those listed in the Company and Resource directories and their assistants, I thank you.

I would like to acknowledge Karen Serieka, my research assistant and preproduction editor, for her commitment, enthusiasm, and the thorough attention and suggestions given to this project; Jane Ratcliffe Clark for her unceasing attention to administrative detail, her organizational expertise, and her excitement about the book; those people listed in the Career Profiles section for their willingness to share their lives and educate readers about this subject; Jill Mason, Christine McGowan, and Bill LaDue for their meticulous final editing of *Green at Work;* my husband, Bob Schulz, for his patience and love; all the people who provided counsel, information, and encouragement, including my family, Bert and Barbara Cohn, Diana Cohn, Amy Liss, Piet Vermeer, Michael Silverstein, Joel Makower, Bhaskar Krag, Ted Mooney, Laura Myntti, Andy Yoder, Barbara Todd, David Dowd, Cate Strumbos, John Danzer, Mark Sammons, Joe Ingram, Sam Dorrance, Barbara Youngblood, and Richard Lanier; Wendy Newton, from the Trust for Mutual Understanding, who superbly translated Alexey V. Yablokov's foreword; Tom Waller of Computers Unlimited in Bridgehampton, New York; Bob Schulz, especially for his patience and love; and the people of northwest Alaska—in particular, Martha Ramoth, Jennie Melton, Mildred, Napoleon, and Wynona Black, Caroline Tickett, Sophie Cleveland, the late George Cleveland, and Reggie Joule—who shared their culture and ways of the land with me.

Building a Greener World

As business uses natural resources, spreads technology across the globe, and creates trade, it also has the power to lead social change. As business continues to develop and strengthen its global links, it has an important opportunity to exert environmentally prudent leadership both in the United States and in many developing countries where the environment is still a low priority for business despite serious environmental degradation.

Environmental management makes business sense, as greener and cleaner products and processes meet consumer demands, result in enhanced product marketability, decrease future environmental liabilities, and, ultimately, lower costs. Environmental management fosters a competitive business advantage through efficiency in production, minimum generation of waste, and a more productive and healthy work force. Companies used to be more concerned with "end of the pipe" solutions to environmental compliance regulations. Now, as Sandra Woods, vice president of Environment, Health & Safety Systems of Coors Brewing Company, quotes Chairman of the Board Bill Coors, "All waste is lost profit." Coors sells its spent grain as fertilizer and recycles its aluminum scraps and cans at its subsidiary, Golden Recycling.

Businesses can create partnerships with government, academic institutions, and nonprofit organizations to work toward solutions to environmental problems. You can find examples of such partnerships in the "Company Directory" (page 219).

Sustainable development requires international cooperation to manage the air, water, and other natural resources that comprise our global commons; and it requires responsible individual choices in all aspects of our lives at work and at home. It requires that all of us—activists, artists, designers, consumers, farmers, manufacturers, and ordinary citizens—realize that we are the real environmental decision-makers. We are the key to sustainable development. When the people lead—people who understand the connections between business development, human development, and the environment—leaders in policy and business will follow.

When people understand their connections to nature, their decisions may be better suited to the system of which we are all a part. This requires us to ask ourselves about the rules by which we work and the lifestyles we choose. Individuals and businesses have the power to value the environment as a priority and, in so doing, to create both ecological health and economic wealth.

Environmentally Conscious Design

Seeing beyond prefabricated answers means being aware of design. An awareness of the concept of design helps us to recognize patterns and then to question those patterns and our perceptions of them. From social change to industrial processes to career planning, it is important to see the big picture. Awareness of the concept of design helps us to see interrelationships and the interactions of patterns and gives us a clearer view of the role we may play within them.

Planning and design are critical to solving many environmental problems facing us. Many of our environmental problems, such as air pollution, traffic congestion in our cities and on our roads, energy problems related to building construction, and toxins in our water are partly a result of poor design. The future of our health and stability lies in redesigning, with our environment in mind, the processes through which we produce our goods and services and the processes through which we name our priorities and make our choices.

Design literacy enables us to recognize the influence of design in our day-to-day lives. In the practice of design, we define a problem, identify possible partners (companies, nonprofits, government, individuals), plan goals, and create alternatives to solve the problem.

More and more companies are looking to natural processes for effective models of how materials are transformed, reused, and designed for optimum efficiency and no waste. There is no waste in nature. Environmental guidelines modeled on natural processes enable companies to be cleaner and more effective while producing better quality and often less expensive products. Effective design enables companies to more efficiently plan, manufacture, and improve their products. For example, the IBM Center for Natural Systems studies nature's systems for ways to improve computer efficiency. Now IBM computers "hibernate," that is they shut down when not in use and can be reactivated by hitting a key. This uses less energy than turning the computer off and on.

Each of us is a designer. We can design a career, a daily schedule, and ways to integrate environmental concerns into the work we do. The practice of design enables us to outline priorities based on our values and make conscious choices consistent with those priorities. It enables us to figure out where we want to be and to take steps to get there. Just as there are many ways to solve the same problem, there are many ways to green our careers and our lives. It is up to each of us to discover the route we want to take and, in that process, learn what works and what doesn't. As you read about the greening of different job sectors, you may begin to see how people are designing new products and approaches in their respective industries.

The Greening of Job Sectors

The following is a rough overview that lists a cross-section of professional fields and a sampling of ways that environmental concerns are influencing them. These categories of professional fields intersect, and many are rapidly changing. The field of environmental justice is one example. It is part public health, part law, part communications, part finance, part community development, and part nonprofit work as it addresses such issues as crime, violence, and the disproportionate number of toxic sites located in or near poor and minority communities.

Opportunities exist in many different categories: on the international, national, state, and local levels; in the private, public, and nonprofit sectors; within different fields and industries; and in different organizations and job functions. One area of expertise will intersect with others as more and more environmental issues demand interdisciplinary groups of problem solvers possessing diverse sets of skills.

Here is a sample of industries that are being affected by environmental legislation, consumer demands, and environmental management practices:

Agriculture & Food Processing. More and more people are becoming interested in petrochemical-free, pesticide-free food and fabrics. This has increased the demand for organically grown fruits, vegetables, and grains; fibers such as cotton; and niche products such as baby food, and chocolates made from organic cocoa. Opportunities in these fields range from nontoxic pest management to retail of organic food and clothing.

Banking & Finance. Many banks are integrating environmental priorities into their internal operations, investment criteria, and financial services. Many are structuring corporate environmental policies to promote internal energy efficiency and reduce waste. They are factoring environmental assessments into loan and investment criteria. Banks are also performing debt-for-nature swaps with countries containing threatened land areas (such as rain forests) and offering investment funds and portfolios screened for environmental performance.

Chemicals. Top management in the chemical industry continues to prioritize environmental issues because profits depend on remaining in compliance with environmental regulations. Monsanto, DuPont, Dow, Kodak, and others spend several million dollars per year meeting environmental regulations. As a result, almost all top and middle managers in the chemicals industry may be said to have an environmental component in their job descriptions. Environmental engineers, compliance administrators, and product and marketing managers who have and can communicate environmental knowledge are in demand by chemical firms.

Communications. As the communications field continues to grow with telecommunications, cable networks, and on-line computer networks (including eco-net, bio-net, and others), there is a demand for people who can translate environmental information to the general public. Opportunities for public relations managers, researchers, writers, journalists, and media personalities who gather, analyze, and disseminate environmental information exist in both publication businesses and corporations. People with computer skills, a CD-ROM design background, and/or electronic publishing experience can use those skills in translating technical data and environmental information to the general public.

Consulting. Many consultants help companies become more efficient in areas ranging from energy use to packaging design to manufacturing processes to employee training and development. For example, as companies begin to provide more environmental information to their stakeholders and to the public, accounting firms will be needed to develop green audits and full-cost accounting systems to quantify and track environmental management and performance in company operations. Consulting continues to present opportunities for people interested in environmental management, especially for those with some technical background and management skills.

Consumer Products. As consumers educate themselves and demand cleaner and greener products, companies will look for ways to green their product lines to meet that demand. Product managers need to stay informed about environmental regulations affecting the packaged goods industry. They need to know trends in recycling and packaging design for products ranging from laundry detergent to toothpaste.

Design & the Arts. As our natural ecosystems become more threatened and our technologies more advanced, design becomes essential to how we define our material culture. Designers are problem solvers who have an opportunity to plan and provide blueprints and concepts that offer creative solutions to our environmental problems. Architects, industrial designers, graphic designers, and fashion designers have a choice of many different structures, forms, processes, and materials for their products. Until recently, many designed products were intentionally designed for obsolescence. Today, designers have an opportunity to create products that are more energy efficient and use fewer natural resources in manufacturing or construction. Additionally, artists such as Mierle Laderman Ukeles, Jean Blackburn, Mel Chin, Meg Webster, Michael Singer, Alan Sonfist, and others are offering powerful critiques of the relationship between art and nature. Artists are working with city agencies and offering innovative and inventive solutions to urban environmental problems.

Education. Education is in part the reason environmental concerns permeate all facets of life, and as we realize how little we understand the interconnectedness of all living things, we become increasingly aware of how much we have to learn. The ever increasing amount of new data and theories continually increase our need for education. Opportunities, in growing demand in the 1990s, will stem from the importance of environmental literacy and expertise in daily life and work. Teachers, trainers, and program developers will be needed to educate our present and future workforce about environmental issues.

Energy. Programs ranging from EPA's Green Lights to conservation programs from public utilities are reframing perspectives on energy use to include energy conservation practices. Opportunities for communications specialists, planners, and technical experts will grow as our energy needs are evaluated for office buildings and commercial real estate, mass transit, and households. Opportunities for the construction trades and for architectural design firms to better serve client energy conservation needs will also grow in coming years.

Entrepreneurs & Small Business. Small firms and start-ups may be better able to fill niches and adapt to rapidly changing markets.

People are creating their own consulting companies, products, and services to meet consumer demands and solve environmental problems. Opportunities hinge on the creativity, access to capital, and management skills of the entrepreneur. From technology to eco-furniture design, from retail to health services, opportunities for environmental entrepreneurship are growing.

Environmental Services. Environmental cleanup, including maintenance services of municipalities and the growth of recycling programs, along with the development of prevention technologies for industry, will provide employment opportunites for people with skills as varied as finance, water monitoring and testing, accounting, and marketing of new products. From cleanup of Superfund sites to pollution control, asbestos abatement, and solid-waste disposal, opportunities in existing companies and for start-ups are tremendous.

Health. Health issues ranging from lead poisoning to problems with off-gassing from petrochemicals in office carpeting have prompted health officials to look more closely at the relationship between health and the environment. From air pollution in cities such as Los Angeles, Mexico City, and Denver to water-quality problems, tainted fish from polluted seas, and synthetic hormones fed to or injected into livestock, a myriad of environmental problems present growing opportunities for health professionals to conduct research, disseminate information, and help create public policy.

International. As the borders of the former Soviet Union open onto the acute environmental degradation there, opportunities exist for people who can provide technological cleanup and waste prevention technology. This holds true for many developing countries as well. International environmental problems will demand work across most professional fields: consulting, engineering, management, environmental services, education, and health. People with language skills and environmental knowledge will have opportunities to work in most existing and new markets.

Law. Many environmental issues are regulated nationally—on federal, state, and local levels—and many are approached internationally, with agreements like the Montreal Protocol. This field will be important to every functional area of the workforce, from accounting, marketing, finance, and management to public policy and grassroots organizing. Therefore, almost everyone will benefit from a general understanding of environmental law. (See Michael Gerrard's overview of the field in the accompanying box.) Opportunities in the field itself

Environmental Law for the Layperson

Michael B. Gerrard

The Evolution of Environmental Law

Ever since British common law—the basis for the U.S. legal system—first evolved in the Middle Ages, courts have had to grapple with environmental disputes. For centuries judges have been faced with complaints regarding smoke, noise, dirt, water, and the disposal of garbage, ashes, and offal. Today the courts still apply the doctrines of nuisance and trespass that developed in those early days.

In the United States, legislative bodies became involved slowly. Congress enacted the Rivers and Harbors Act in 1899, barring certain kinds of dumping in the water, and the first Oil Pollution Act in 1924, imposing liability for oil spills. From the 1940s through the 1960s, laws concerning air and water pollution were enacted, but they mostly called for studies, grants, and advisory bodies; they had few teeth.

It is no coincidence that the modern era in environmental law began in 1970, the year of the first Earth Day. On January 1, 1970, President Nixon signed the National Environmental Policy Act (NEPA), which requires the preparation of environmental impact statements for major federal actions that significantly affect the human environment. That year he also created the Environmental Protection Agency (EPA) and signed into law the first Clean Air Act. The next six years saw the enactment of most of the other major federal environmental statutes: the Clean Water Act; the Noise Control Act; the Endangered Species Act; the Toxic Substances Control Act; the Federal Insecticide, Fungicide and Rodenticide Act; and the Resource Conservation and Recovery Act (RCRA).

The next watershed year in environmental law was 1980, when the disposal and cleanup of hazardous waste moved to the forefront. Horrified by reports of the contamination of the Love Canal neighborhood of Niagara Falls, New York, Congress passed the Comprehensive Environmental Response, Compensation and Liability Act (CERCLA), also known as the Superfund law, requiring the investigation and cleanup of old dump sites. EPA also promulgated the first important regulation under RCRA, aimed at preventing the creation of new dump sites. With the inauguration of Ronald Reagan in 1981, legislative progress stalled, as the administration was less sympathetic to environmental concerns than some of its predecessors.

Congress fought back by passing enormously detailed amendments to CERCLA and RCRA to limit the administration's discretion.

Still, some progress was made in the 1980s. In 1986, in the wake of the terrible tragedy in Bhopal, India, where a cloud of gas from a pesticide factory killed more than 2,000 people, Congress passed the Emergency Planning and Community Right-to-Know Act (EPCRA). Another environmental disaster—the *Exxon Valdez* oil spill in Alaska—led to the Oil Pollution Act of 1990. That year also saw a major strengthening of the Clean Air Act and the massive twentieth-anniversary celebration of Earth Day. While no major new federal laws have been enacted for nearly five years, as this book goes to press Congress is considering heavy revisions to several existing laws.

This very brief overview shows that two kinds of events have tended to drive the development of federal environmental laws: disasters and major upswings in public interest. The resulting laws, in turn, have a pervasive impact on every sector of the economy.

The Types of Environmental Laws

Most U.S. environmental laws fit within one or more of the following four categories. *Command and control laws* are very specific about what companies must and must not do. For example, the Clean Air Act, the Clean Water Act, and RCRA specify that factories that generate air or water pollution, or treat hazardous waste, must use certain technologies and comply with strict standards as to how much pollution they can release. Violations of these requirements can lead to heavy fines (often several thousand dollars a day) and, sometimes, to criminal penalties for company officials who knowingly caused the violations. *Information laws* require that companies and government agencies release certain information to the public. Examples include the environmental impact statements of NEPA and the plans and reports mandated by EPCRA. *Economic-incentive laws* allow companies to emit pollution, but charge them a fee or a tax to encourage them to pollute less. Certain portions of the Clean Air Act use this method. Many economists favor greater use of these incentives, but Congress has not been very receptive. And finally, *liability-bestowing laws* force companies that have made a mess in the past to clean it up. The chief example is CERCLA, which is retroactive—actions that were perfectly legal when performed can later be a basis for liability. CERCLA also makes landowners liable for contamination on their property, regardless of whether they were personally responsible for creating the pollution.

Role of Government

Anyone who is investigating the legality of some action that could affect the environment must look at the laws of every level of government—international, federal, state, and local. All fifty states have one or more environmental agencies and their own sets of environmental laws. In most instances, states are free to enact laws that are more (though not less) stringent than federal laws, and many states have done so. Many also have authority from EPA to implement key federal programs, such as those under the Clean Water Act and RCRA, within their borders. Municipalities can also enact their own laws. Many cities have special laws on solid waste and recycling, for example.

International Law is becoming increasingly important. Several treaties, such as NAFTA and GATT, have environmental requirements. The United States has signed a number of international agreements that require the signatory countries to assume certain environmental obligations, like controlling the export of hazardous waste, preventing ocean dumping, banning the manufacture of certain substances that deplete the ozone layer, and prohibiting the importation of certain endangered species.

Effect on Business

Environmental laws affect virtually every kind of business. The following are just some of the kinds of companies and organizations that need to know about environmental law:

- Real estate developers that require government approvals for new projects or that are concerned about the environmental liabilities that may accompany new property acquisitions.
- Financial institutions determining whether to invest in, or foreclose on, real property.
- Trucking, shipping, and railroad companies called upon to transport hazardous materials.
- Hospitals and other health-care providers needing lawful ways to dispose of medical waste.
- School systems faced with rapidly expanding requirements to abate hazards, such as asbestos and lead pipes, in school buildings.
- Investment banking firms called upon to finance such projects as resource-recovery plants, refineries, sewage-treatment plants, and factories.
- Construction contractors building facilities subject to heavy environmental regulation (for example, power plants, dams, highways, and landfills).

- Agricultural, food processing, and forestry businesses seeking to understand the impact that restrictions on pesticide application, irrigation management, storm-water runoff, and disposal of plant, animal, and wood by-products may have on their operations.

Government agencies also need to know about environmental laws for their operations. Drinking-water plants and sewage-treatment plants, which are usually operated by cities, are subject to extensive environmental regulation. So are highways, airports, and municipal landfills. Many military facilities have histories of dumping and are increasingly subject to environmental laws.

People working in any of these areas can unwittingly get their organizations, or themselves, into a great deal of trouble if they are unaware of environmental law. The greatest perils arise in facilities that handle hazardous materials; what might seem like a minor spill can have considerable legal consequences if it is not promptly reported and cleaned up. Investments in real estate can be wiped out, or possibly lead to liabilities that are much greater than the sale price, if there is hidden contamination. The opening or ongoing operation of a large factory can be jeopardized by noncompliance with an obscure regulation.

Conversely, environmental laws also create tremendous career opportunities. Private industry spends tens of billions of dollars a year on environmental compliance; governments spend many billions more. Each major new regulation carries with it business opportunities as well as dangers, and therefore the fortunes of a large company can rise and fall with the development of these laws, and with the company's preparedness for their implementation.

Keeping Up

Environmental laws change rapidly, and it is important to keep up with new developments. Most companies have environmental lawyers, either in-house or with outside law firms, who track the new laws, and who should be consulted whenever a question about environmental law arises. However, nonlawyers throughout the corporate ranks should stay familiar with developments in the field as well, and newspapers, magazines, journals, seminars, and conferences are the primary sources of up-to-date information.

Michael B. Gerrard has practiced environmental law since 1978. He is a partner with the New York City law firm of Arnold and Porter, and an adjunct professor at Columbia University Law School.

range from lobbying for nonprofit organizations to creating government policy to working in environmental divisions of corporations.

Nonprofit. Nonprofit organizations range from public interest groups to foundations, think tanks, labor unions, and trade associations. Each of these groups hires analysts and communicators to study, question, track progress, and plan strategy on national and international environmental issues. Since 1970, thousands of nonprofit groups have been established. Most of them need well-rounded professionals, not only those who have scientific and legal skills, but also those who can market, manage, and control the growth and maintenance of these organizations. Many people with skills in advertising, public relations, administration, and fund-raising may choose to use them in these areas.

Public Sector. Although the "Company Directory" does not list federal, state, and local government entities, the public sector has key environmental people in positions as varied as consultants, attorneys, accountants, public relations managers, information specialists, scientists, and computer specialists. Contact state and federal EPA offices and local departments of environmental protection, conservation, and sanitation for more information on public sector opportunities.

Seeking Green Employment

If you want a green job, you must first recognize the career development process of which any employment is a part. This book offers a framework through which you can begin to address both your career goals and your green concerns, and this chapter briefly considers some essentials to planning your search for green employment within the context of your career: careful research; consideration of your career goals; study of issues in the field and the industry; networking; a thorough evaluation of opportunities; and effective interviewing skills. (For books that discuss job and career questions in more detail, please refer to both the "Publications" section of the "Resource Directory" and the "Recommended Reading" list at the back of the book.)

Before you can market yourself for employment, you must first evaluate yourself. Ask yourself what motivates you. What do you want to contribute? Seek employment with this focus. Decide what areas you are most committed to. For example, do you want to work on clean air and water issues, rain forest issues, or waste reduction? What do you see that needs to be done? Can you do it?

Ask yourself what you most enjoy doing. What is your passion? Do you enjoy, for example, writing, designing, managing people, managing money, or marketing products or services? Asking these questions and following through on your answers will help you narrow your career search to specific fields and organizations. It will also help keep you focused and on track through rough times, which are inevitable in any career. When you are clear about your interests, that knowledge can help to inspire, guide, and support you both in your current job and when you are in the midst of a career transition.

No matter how much interest you have in the environment, however, to create a green job you need to define the skill base that makes you valuable to organizations in which you are interested. Know your skills and talents and determine how you can use them to contribute to those organizations. Assessing your skills in light of your understanding of an organization's goals and employment needs will help you sell yourself to that organization. It will also help you to understand how your career goals fit with the goals of that organization. For instance, having skills in editing and publishing could meet the needs of a nonprofit environmental research and publishing group or the needs of a public relations department for a major corporation. You must also be aware of your professional goals. You need to ask yourself what vision you have for your career, where you see yourself in the next five-to-ten years, and how your career fits into your personal and financial vision. These questions need to be continuously readdressed as you grow and develop professionally.

Once you have evaluated your interests, skills, and career goals, you must research companies and areas of interest to you, meet people in your area of career interest, pursue interviews, and network to obtain employment.

Researching Companies

To test your career goals against the realities of the marketplace, you will need to do research. Know what people and which companies are taking the lead in areas of interest to you. Research individual companies to further define your job search and to prepare yourself to build a network. Understand the needs of companies you've targeted. Know what their strengths are and how they differ from their competitors. You can do this by reading newspaper and magazine articles about the organization, reading the organization's annual reports—its 10-K filings—which disclose environmental challenges the company faces and the company's expenditures to meet those challenges, and talking to the organization's employees. Know the structure of the company. Know how it works. Know its problems.

Once you accomplish this research, you will be better able to assess yourself in relation to a company and to the position you seek. When you approach a company, do so with an idea of what service you want to contribute to improve the organization's performance. Evaluate how your experiences, skills, accomplishments, and education qualify you for the position you seek. To complete this process successfully, assess your level of commitment to the company you've researched. Ask yourself where your values coincide with the values of a potential employer, and where they don't coincide.

The "Company Directory" (page 219) is a first-stop resource to help you research how a company approaches environmental management, what environmental initiatives it is undertaking, and whom to call for further information.

Interviewing People

The informational interview supplements the information gained from research with a firsthand account of what someone does on the job. Whether you choose to call or write to initiate an interview depends on how you were referred to a person. When in doubt, write a letter and follow up with a phone call to arrange a time to meet. Most people are flattered to talk with someone interested in their career and will share their knowledge and experience with you. Remember that you are requesting information and ideas, not asking for a job. An effective informational interview will prepare you to better understand the demands of a position when you have a job interview. Interviewing people to gather information also helps you to better define your career goals as you explore different career areas and companies; and it may increase your network.

When meeting a contact, make the best use of his or her time. Be prepared. Know what questions you want answered. Remember that you are the one who initiated the interview: It is your job to know what information you seek and to keep the flow of information coming.

Here are some questions you may want to ask in an informational interview:

- Could you describe your career path? How did you enter this field?
- What is a typical workday like for you?
- What do you like about your job?
- What do you dislike about your job?
- How would you describe your work environment?
- What skills are valuable in a position like yours?
- Where do you see your career options after this position?
- What kind of entry-level positions are there in this field?
- What trends do you see in your field that are important to be aware of?
- Do you have any advice for people interested in succeeding in this field?
- What areas may be important to stress in my background?
- Could you suggest other areas of industry, companies, and jobs I might consider with my background?

Ask whether there is anyone else in the company with whom you might speak, or whether your interviewee can suggest other industry contacts. Follow up on every lead. Be sure to send thank-you notes and letters to inform people in your network of your progress in your job search and in your career.

Networking

Networking is critical to finding "green" employment. Eighty-five percent of all jobs are found through what is called the hidden job market; positions obtained through advertisements, executive search firms, and other sources account for only 15 percent of all jobs. Chances are, if you aren't networking, you aren't working.

When you build a network, you are building relationships, a support system of contacts. Each person can strengthen that system. Think of your network as you do the earth. Environmentalism values interrelationships. The interconnectedness of natural systems sustains and supports life on earth much like the people you connect with can support and sustain you if you are honest, straightforward about your intentions, and respectful of each person who assists you in your career. The best way to start building your network is to identify a list of sources. Be inventive. Everyone knows someone who can assist them in their job search. Here are a few suggestions:

- college friends and other alumni, faculty and student groups, and college placement services;
- friends and work colleagues;
- people in organizations you belong to, such as churches, synagogues, volunteer groups, political and environmental groups, membership organizations, and adult education classes;
- family, relatives, and their friends;
- people who are featured in or have written for newspapers, magazines, and directories or authored books;
- people who attend or speak at lectures, conferences, and events that have an environmental focus.

To build your green network, keep up with the issues. Read and clip newspaper articles and obtain names of people involved in your fields of interest. You may also make contacts through volunteer work.

The many ways to green your career may involve making your way through a web of individuals until you find someone who can answer your questions. Create a tracking system for organizing your contacts. Be sure you have accurate names, addresses, and phone numbers. This system will record your networking process and can highlight avenues that have been successful for you.

The Green Job Interview

If your networking has been successful, you will identify job openings and even be offered a job interview. The best candidates in interviews are those people who know themselves and are able to be themselves. So be who you are, be ready to talk about your experiences and about how they are relevant to a company, to a position, and to your future goals.

Communicate your understanding of a company's environmental liabilities and your ideas about how the company can respond to the challenges it faces. If you are aware of media coverage of a company's environmental programs or initiatives, let the interviewer know. This shows that you are knowledgeable about what the company is doing.

The environment can be a sensitive issue. Do not put the interviewer on the defensive during your first meeting by drilling her or him on the company's past environmental problems. If you are aware of the company's environmental performance, tell the interviewer. Look for opportunities to praise changes; express a desire to participate in future change.

Here are some questions about environmental management that you may wish to ask in your interview:

- What environmental concerns are being addressed in your line of business (for example, packaging issues, waste minimization, recycling)?
- What is the company doing to reduce waste, water pollution, and air pollution in its operations?
- Has the company initiated joint projects with government, university, or nonprofit environmental organizations?

Summary

The following are key issues for a strategic career search:

- Assess your skills, values, and interests. Decide how you can best use your talents and where you want to use them.
- Educate yourself about the environment. Read magazines, newspapers, and environmental publications. Stay current on developments in areas of interest to you. Intern with environmental organizations. Attend conferences.
- Research organizations and determine how you want to contribute to them.
- Interview people to gather information so that you can better understand a company, its structure, its culture, job responsibilities, and potential openings in areas of interest to you.
- Network, network, network! View it as an opportunity to meet interesting people and to learn. Do not be intimidated. Follow up with your contacts.
- In a job interview, know why you, not someone else, should be the prime candidate for a position there.
- Persist, persevere, and be patient. Remember, the environmental field is growing. Create your opportunities. Identify a need and demonstrate how you can meet it.

Remember that the career process requires time and constant evaluation. Aligning your career goals with your vision requires hard work. As you read the diverse career profiles in the next section you will find many different ways that people have created opportunities and pursued careers to work toward achieving their vision.

It's Your Turn

Four catalysts to find answers to the environmental challenges facing us are empowerment, education, employment, and creativity. From empowerment we take courage to use our voices, to be self-determined, and to act. Through education, we learn skills necessary both to a productive work force and to making informed choices about how our lives and actions affect our environment and how that environmental affects our lives. Employment may give us a vehicle to express our talents and to derive meaning, self-worth, and dignity. Creativity helps us to turn a question on its head, to transcend the habitual and the conventional, to create visions and work toward them. As we dare to do so, we create our world.

When creativity is combined with courage, it is a force for action in a world that needs a wake-up call to halt environmental degradation. Life, like art, is a work continually in progress; risking on the frontier is what most artists do. We are artists of our own life work. We must master certain skills, forms, techniques, and knowledge; make them ours; and then have the courage to go beyond them, beyond structures and preconceptions that may now define us.

This book attempts to help us find our way, create solutions to problems that face us, foster visions for a better quality of life on both the community level and the international level, and work toward those visions. With every person who undertakes this process of self-education, the world gains another person who is finding answers.

In the spring of 1994, I flew to Moscow to attend a symposium called "Women, Politics and Environmental Action." My experience there heightened for me the importance of educating ourselves and understanding how environmental considerations affect both our career fields and our lives.

The former Soviet Union is now confronting both economic crisis and serious environmental problems such as water pollution, nuclear wastes, and toxic industrial wastes. According to Chairman of the Commission on Ecological Security, National Security Council of the Russian Federation, Alexei Yablokov in a lecture entitled "The State of the Environment in Russia, Time for Action," 70 percent of the water in Russia cannot be used for human consumption and Russian forests are being cut at such a rate that, in the next five years, they will be lost altogether if something isn't done; these forests are as crucial to our planet as rain forests for circulation of oxygen.

While on the plane to Russia, I sat next to Dr. Ludmilla Zhirina, a professor from the Bryansk Pedagogical Institute. She is a committed environmentalist who lives with her two children in the Bryansk Oblast region of Russia, where the Chernobyl nuclear plant meltdown has contaminated water and agricultural systems. Dr. Zhirina teaches people in her region preventative measures to mitigate contamination: She instructs them to minimize the risk of toxins in food by washing and peeling all fruit and vegetables; and she instructs homeowners to water down the dust in the play areas for their children so that the children do not breathe toxins present in the soil.

Environmental degradation created by Chernobyl and by industrial pollution in the water and the air are contributing to alarming statistics of weakened health, toxicity in mothers' breast milk, and high mortality rates among children. With this knowledge, Ludmilla continues to live in this region as an environmentalist and as a mother. After listening to her speak about her work, I asked her whether she would ever leave the region. She responded that it was her home, where her family and children lived. People like Ludmilla are committed to making this region as livable as possible for its residents.

I took away from my trip to Moscow a bleak glimpse into the reasons partnerships need to be developed and international agreements formed to create solutions to environmental problems. There are no real borders when it comes to environmental issues. We are all affected. The challenges are enormous. It will take vision and action, perseverance and strength to tackle the problems, and it will not be easy. Today we need to recognize that environmental health is a human right. The environmental movement in Russia isn't just trying to save Siberian forests and tigers; people are fighting for their families and children. Russia's ability to clean up and rebuild—or deteriorate from lack of assistance and political instability—may portend our future. A world aching under environmental degradation, compromised human health, and proliferation of nuclear weapons faces us all. As individuals, we can make a difference by being responsible in our careers and in our life choices. Action begins with the self. To live to our potential we need a healthy environment. How do we create a society that prioritizes health and human potential?

The environmental challenges facing us require interdisciplinary thinking in design, engineering, marketing, strategic planning, and policy and across all other disciplines. The reality of many of our environmental problems negates both the geopolitical boundaries and the conceptual boundaries traditionally assigned to them. We can look to the boundaries for a sense of terrain, a sense of where we have been, but then we must have the courage to jump from the known forms to create something new.

Much of the exciting work to be done lies beyond known boundaries. That is where many new jobs will be created, new communities formed, and new hope generated. People need to educate themselves by reading, talking to others, taking classes, asking questions, being curious, and following their instincts. As our environmental problems become more harmful to human health and ecosystem stability, we need all people to be environmentally literate. As we examine global environmental problems, we may begin to use the catalysts of empowerment, education, employment, and creativity to ensure that environmental integrity becomes a human right.

We cannot wait for someone to tell us what to do. We create our opportunities and make a difference in our lives and in our society. The rapidity of environmental degradation demands that each of us ask which choices and which actions can help ensure our future, because the perils of the planet have less to do with Mother Nature than with human nature. At present, we are at a crossroads, if not in crisis: being green in all careers is now a common sense thing to do.

As you embark on a green career, continue to learn, create a niche for yourself, and know that there are communities of people who share your concerns and your struggle. Each of us can help weave a strand in the web that sustains us all.

Career Profiles

Society needs people in all careers who recognize the value of environmental integrity and can work along many different routes to create solutions to environmental problems. The career profiles in this section provide examples of the enormous variety of abilities, perspectives, and approaches that are possible.

These narratives take green careers out of the realm of theory and into the experiences of people who have achieved them. Use them as models to help you make your own way, as a departure for your own ideas. Learn from them so that you can create for yourself the position you desire. In a quickly changing world without clear signs, the power of story conveys information we can use to guide our choices through people's experiences, inspiration, insight, ideas, and anecdotes.

Banking & Finance

Jonathan Berman *is a market analyst at Molten Metal Technology, Inc., an environmental recycling company, where he assesses potential markets; quantifies the value added by MMT's proprietary technology, Catalytic Extraction Processing (CEP); and works to keep the company abreast of regulatory and community issues that can affect strategic business development. He has an M.B.A. from New York University and a B.A. from Bristol University in England.*

HOW DID YOU BECOME INTERESTED IN ENVIRONMENTAL EMPLOYMENT?

While I was at business school I had time to think about the type of career that would give me job satisfaction—a career in which making money was important but not my motivation to go to work every morning. A career in the environmental sector appeared to offer me both while accomplishing something good on a bigger scale. But I still got very lucky when I ended up at MMT.

WHAT PAST WORK EXPERIENCE DID YOU HAVE?

I worked as a consultant in Salomon Brothers' Environmental Affairs Department in business school and for over a year afterward until I joined MMT. Before business school, I worked for two years in the wine business, where I developed a fondness for natural products.

HOW DID YOU GET THIS JOB?

I was in the right place at the right time, which I did not realize until they called me back one and a half years later! In October of 1991 I heard about the company from another student at Stern (NYU) and went up to Boston for an informational interview. I was still in school, and MMT had only twenty employees at the time, so there was not really an opportunity for me there. Still, I kept in contact afterward with people I had met there. MMT grew very fast, and when a position arose there in the summer of 1993, I was remembered as an eager inquirer and called for an interview.

ANY SUGGESTIONS, WISDOM GLEANED FROM YOUR JOB HUNT?

It's hard, but take risks and try to think creatively—especially if you want to be in the high-technology side of the environmental sector. Also, remember that this sector attracts some of the best people from more traditional industries, so don't feel you will be giving up much in the way of business experience once you get into it.

HOW CAN OTHERS ENTER THE ENVIRONMENTAL SERVICES FIELD?

My advice to people who want to work in the "environment" is to figure out what your business skills are, what type of business culture you want to be a part of, and how much money you want to make. Then start looking for companies that will satisfy those conditions.

WHAT ARE THE CHALLENGES OF WORKING IN AN ENVIRONMENTAL CAPACITY AT MMT?

MMT is a three-and-a-half-year-old company with about 150 employees and great market potential. The first challenge is to make sure the company realizes its potential. The second challenge, for all its employees, is to accomplish our goals according to our stated company values: "We are committed to be creative and innovate, proactive and dedicated, kind and considerate, open and honest, good listeners and team players." At every review we have to explain how we've contributed to these values.

WHAT ARE THE TRENDS YOU SEE AFFECTING YOUR INDUSTRY?

The trends in U.S. industry, in our society, and in other societies around the world are toward recycling and waste minimization. These trends are driven by public opinion and by the realization of companies and governments that natural resources are finite and have to be preserved. In addition, it is becoming apparent that recycling and waste-minimization practices can enhance rather than disrupt business practices.

WHERE DO YOU SEE THE JOBS IN THE NEXT FIVE TO TEN YEARS?

I don't really know. What I will say is that I have discovered that there is life outside the typical business school career track, and that M.B.A.s do not have to jump directly into corporate America to live happy lives with successful careers. I work with many people who have opted out of typical career paths. By any measurement of career success—job satisfaction, money, visibility—the people I work with are as successful as the people I "left behind" but generally seem to have much more job satisfaction. Maybe that's because our corporate culture is dynamic and results oriented. Maybe it's because we don't have a dress code, and "having fun" is written into our mission statement.

WHAT SKILLS DO YOU RECOMMEND FOR PEOPLE WHO ARE INTERESTED IN YOUR FIELD?

Since I work in marketing, I'd have to say marketing skills. If you asked one of the ex-investment bankers in our financial group, he would probably say finance skills. Ask one of our engineers, engineering skills. Like any company, MMT is trying to attract bright, eager employees with a wide range of skills.

Christina Kunek Halpern *is a credit analyst for the Overseas Private Investment Corporation (OPIC). She worked in law placement for two years and held internships at two internationally concerned institutions in Washington, D.C., the International Trade Commission and the Council of* *the Americas. She has a B.A. in Latin American studies from George Washington University and an M.B.A. in finance and international business from New York University.*

WHAT DOES OPIC DO, AND WHY DID YOU CHOOSE THIS FINANCIAL INSTITUTION?

OPIC provides capital and risk insurance to American companies in countries where other commercial banks and insurance agents fear to tread. This is what differentiates OPIC from the other market institutions. The corporation is in the forefront of encouraging American participation in Russia, the Newly Independent States, South Africa, and the West Bank and Gaza Strip, while still maintaining support for Latin America, less developed Asia, and sub-Saharan Africa. In a world whose political and economic circumstances change so dramatically, it is typical to find that political uncertainty creates a slowdown in an institution's work flow. Not so here. OPIC's raison d'être is such political and economic uncertainty. Stable, prosperous nations don't require OPIC's involvement. There are 140 nations around the world where we are open for business.

OPIC is clearly on the leading edge in its assessment of what effects the projects it supports have on both the host country and our country. We are unique in providing insurance, financing, and other investor services only to projects that have no negative economic impact on the United States in terms of balance of payments and employment. Not a single U.S. job will be lost in the process of promoting development in other regions. On the contrary, foreign U.S. investment generates U.S. exports, which in turn creates U.S. jobs.

OPIC's interest in the environment reaches further than meeting a set of internationally recognized requirements. It doesn't just follow the letter of the law, it embraces its spirit. The agency is now involved in establishing a set of forestry standards for Russia. Russia has opened previously inaccessible natural resources to foreign investment in order to gain access to hard currency. OPIC is seeking to minimize the potential for destruction of such valuable resources as the nation embarks on development.

Finally, OPIC's commitment to the environment and innovation in its activities is seen in its support of a privately owned and managed direct investment fund known as the Global Environment Emerging Markets Fund. The fund was set up in early 1994 to promote venture capital to environmental technology companies that are too small or undercapitalized to jump into the global environmental goods and services market. The $50 million that OPIC is guaranteeing could generate $500 million in American environmental projects worldwide.

WHAT DOES YOUR WORKDAY INVOLVE?

The Credit Analysis Group analyzes the credit issues of proposed financing projects in less developed countries. A memo outlining credit strengths and weaknesses is prepared for upper management. Discussions take place with the project team and upper management on how to improve the credit quality of the project. OPIC operates on a quarterly basis, and, as in any other corporation, the work flow revolves around the quarterly board of directors meetings, where projects over $30 million need approval.

My duties revolve around monitoring and maintaining statistics on new projects and on the existing portfolio of finance projects. This requires regular interaction with officers in the Finance and Treasury departments.

WHY DID YOU CHOOSE THIS JOB?

The term "development" means different things to different people. Some envision dams and electricity generation funded by the World Bank; others consider the educational and agricultural work of Peace Corps volunteers in small villages. For me, development meant an opportunity to work with a multitude of such issues as the environment, health conditions, and employment opportunities.

I knew that I wanted to work for the Overseas Private Investment Corporation after learning of it in college. Here is an American government agency created for the purpose of fostering development around the world. Yet I saw that this agency balanced the need to create jobs and foster economic growth against the environmental impact that projects may have on the host country. I was impressed that projects requesting financing or political risk insurance from OPIC that were financially viable were regularly rejected on the basis of environmental concerns.

ANY ADVICE TO PEOPLE INTERESTED IN YOUR FIELD?

Persistence in networking with people in the international and environmental sectors. Do not be discouraged if you speak with a string of people whose current experience is not 100 percent in line with yours, because everyone has something to contribute to your knowledge base and network.

Also, keep in mind that very often a stepping stone is needed between the place where you currently are and the place you want to be. It is just as important to focus on the skills you still need to acquire or improve as it is to maintain the skills you already possess. Get relevant work experience through part-time internships or volunteer positions. Travel to developing countries and get involved with environmental entities on both the local and international levels. The most difficult thing to accept is that finding the "perfect" job requires being at the right place at the right time as much as it does having the right experience: so be thorough, organized, and don't give up!

Evan C. Henry *is vice president and manager of environmental services at Bank of America. He has a B.S. in geology from Tufts University and an M.S. in natural resources from the University of New Hampshire. He previously held positions as a hydrogeologist.*

WHAT ARE YOUR JOB RESPONSIBILITIES?

I am responsible for the technical assessment of environmental conditions that would affect the lending and trust activities of the bank. Put simply, borrowers that have environmental costs and liabilities can be a higher lending risk. To assess that risk, the bank needs people who understand and can evaluate the nature and extent of technical issues. I manage a group of environmental professionals who understand those issues and can translate them into a banking context so that the bank can factor environmental risks into evaluation of overall credit risk. In addition to my internal company responsibilities, I frequently speak at professional events about environmental issues facing the lending community.

The job is primarily office oriented. I spend considerable time in meetings and on the telephone. Due to the nature and size of Bank of America's business activities, I travel occasionally.

HOW DID YOU COME TO YOUR PRESENT POSITION?

After working for almost ten years as an environmental consultant, I wanted to be involved in environmental issues on a much broader scale than the specific project-focused view that is necessary for and typical of environmental consulting. In the year or so before I joined Bank of America, I prepared myself to expand beyond the consulting profession by attending seminars and local university courses. I focused on property assessment and liability, and recognizing property transfer investigations as a potential market in real estate development.

WHAT IS THE STATUS OF BANK OF AMERICA'S ENVIRONMENTAL SERVICES UNIT?

In the five and a half years the Environmental Services Unit has existed, it has grown from a one-person position to a fifteen-person unit. It now employs eleven environmental professionals with backgrounds primarily in environmental consulting.

WHAT ARE IMPORTANT QUALIFICATIONS FOR ENTRY INTO AN ENVIRONMENTAL PROFESSION?

People who work in this type of function should recognize the value of the technical side of their jobs and should gear education and experiences accordingly. I am a firm believer in professionals who have worked in a technical field, even if they ultimately apply that knowledge in business or other areas. They have to have paid their dues to have a true depth of understanding and credibility to operate in other realms. However, I do not believe that it is necessary to be scientifically or technically trained to have a major impact in the environmental arena. The bottom line is to have an appreciation of the environment and to work in one's personal life and in one's professional life to understand and act in accordance with environmentally sound principles.

WHERE DO YOU SEE FUTURE OPPORTUNITIES IN THIS FIELD?

There will be a continued modest growth in the number of available technical jobs at larger corporations that deal with real estate, such as insurers, lenders, developers, and real estate management companies. The number of real estate investment trusts being developed will also create a demand for consultants with legal and technical environmental expertise. These professionals will be needed to provide support to lending and property transfers. There will also be many opportunities for people who do not have technical training or education to develop technical knowledge. There are opportunities in virtually every part of the country to study environmental issues through extension courses at local universities and community colleges. This enables the nontechnical environmental professional to become considerably skilled and do very good work, at least in the majority of cases, with respect to environmental compliance and risk assessment.

By far the largest potential market for the environmental industry is international. The market for transfer of environmental technology and pollution prevention and conservation concepts and programs will be readily exportable and, in general, low cost. Many of the environmental needs of developing nations are more basic, revolving around clean water and appropriate domestic and industrial waste treatment and disposal. The environmental risks of industries like mining and natural resource issues that stem from them are much more difficult to deal with and will need a depth of scientific understanding to ultimately rationalize the preservation of natural resources.

ANY FINAL THOUGHTS?

The most successful individuals in this field will believe that their profession is both a vocation and an avocation. I try to keep current on technical and legal issues related to the lending industry through an "airplane reading file" that accompanies me on my out-of-town trips. This includes a variety of different trade journals, magazines, and rag sheets sent by legal counsel, and other information that may come across my desk. In addition, I will periodically read environmental books such as those published by World Watch, and I have been known from time to time to pull excerpts from Al Gore's *Earth in the Balance*. I am also a member of the Nature Conservancy. The information available from that organization is a good counterpoint to many of the more business-related environmental issues that I deal with day to day. In addition, I am very active in a local environmental organization working to preserve and restore a valuable wetland in Southern California. The issues associated with that type of endeavor provide a different environmental framework than those I encounter when dealing with hazardous waste and liability issues.

I am fortunate to work for an organization that respects the many aspects of environmental issues, be it preservation, business risk, human health, sustainability, or other imaginable definitions of environmental concerns. In my experience at Bank of America in the last five and a half years, the bank has provided me a forum to both learn and grow with an expanding definition of the environment as well as express some of my own views in a way that can be heard.

***H. Stephen Jones** is senior vice president and manager of NationsBank's Environmental Services Department (ESD). Mr. Jones is a registered ar-*

chitect in Texas and Colorado and is certified in all fifty states by the National Council of Architectural Registration Boards. He is a national registered environmental professional, a registered environmental assessor in California, and an accredited asbestos inspector and management planner. He has a B.A. in environmental design and an M.A. in architecture from Texas A&M University.

WHAT DOES YOUR DEPARTMENT DO?

ESD is a corporate-wide department that safeguards the bank from avoidable environmental liabilities and losses associated with the ownership of real estate property.

This is partially accomplished by performing Environmental Site Assessments (ESAs) on real estate property to identify and evaluate environmental risks associated with that property before the bank takes ownership of it or accepts it as loan collateral.

A major portion of ESD's role is cost and quality-control management of independent environmental consulting services. The environmental consulting industry currently is not governed by federal or state regulations to establish standard terminology, minimum scopes of work, or acceptable standards of performance. There are no minimum education or training requirements and no standard professional credentials required of the individuals performing ESA services.

WHO WORKS IN YOUR DEPARTMENT? WHAT DO YOU LOOK FOR WHEN HIRING A STAFF MEMBER?

ESD has a staff of twenty-one employees with diverse backgrounds who were hired to expand the capabilities of our department as a team to address virtually any environmental issue we would encounter. ESD has an administrative group that handles contracts, invoices, and project tracking, and a group of environmental analysts (EAs) who manage environmental projects and provide technical reviews of the processes and results. When staffing an EA position, I look for candidates with college degrees and continuing education backgrounds in chemistry, petroleum engineering, geology, hydrology, forestry, environmental science, biology, industrial hygiene, and hazardous waste management. Each EA must have a minimum of three years' working experience with environmental regulations, environmental site assessments, compliance audits, sampling and analytical testing, contamination assessments, and corrective clean-up actions.

TELL US ABOUT YOUR CAREER HISTORY.

Prior to NationsBank, I was the director of architecture and construction for HAWCO, a Canadian development company; project architect for TGI Fridays; a draftsman and specifications writer for Bank Building Corporation; and a designer/planner for Grogran and Scoggins Architects. I taught evening industrial art classes on architectural-scale model building at North Texas University for four semesters in the early 1980s. I have been an instructor for Texas A&M University's Engineering Extension Center's Environmental Safety Training Division since 1990. I've also been an instructor for the American Institute of Bankers, Executive Enterprises Inc., and the Lincoln Graduate Institute.

HOW DID YOU BECOME INTERESTED IN THIS FIELD?

I am the third generation in my family to enter the construction industry and the only one in the environmental industry. My career was greatly influenced by my dad, an architect, and my grandfather, a general contractor, under whom I gained hands-on experience in more than a dozen construction trades. In 1970, the year I started college, both the EPA and the Occupational Safety and Health Administration (OSHA) were formed, and that also influenced my college education objective. As a result, I have education and work experience in both the construction and environmental industries.

WHAT IS YOUR ADVICE FOR PEOPLE WANTING TO WORK IN AN ENVIRONMENTAL POSITION?

Folks contemplating a career in the environmental industry should seek a broad and diverse knowledge base. The environmental industry is young, growing, and destined to change substantially over the next decade. A key to success is being resourceful and open to change while continually networking to stay on the cutting edge of pertinent environmental information, regulations, and technology. Education is a process rather than an accomplishment, and we're all on the learning curve.

WHAT RESOURCES DO YOU RECOMMEND?

Trade journals, books, magazines, and newsletters are essential to stay on top of laws, regulations, and technology in the environmental industry. The following resource materials are found in my office: Buraff publications, EPA Journals, the Federal Register, Lewis

Environmental Science publications, *West Environmental Law and Statutes*, *Environmental Testing and Analysis* magazine, *TNEJ National Environmental Journal*, and newsletters from environmental consultants, attorneys, and environmental organizations.

ANY FINAL THOUGHTS?

Everyone can do something that will make a difference.

During Earth Day (April 22) week for the last five years, I have taught an Environmental Awareness and Safety course in elementary and middle-school science classes. The youngest generations need our help and knowledge now about the effect of hazardous substances and wastes on life, health, and the natural environment in order to make a difference in the future when their generation is running our country and taking care of us old folks.

Also, as an Earth Day '94 project, my department formed a community service program called Friends for Life. We and more than one hundred volunteers planted sixty trees at four locations in Dallas County. This fall Friends for Life plans to build a baseball diamond with a backstop and trees at an undeveloped park in a lower-income section of Dallas. I know from firsthand experience, we can make a difference if we join together with one common goal: to help each other protect and preserve our planet and its natural resources.

Richard Morrison *is senior vice president of Bank of America, where he directs the bank's Environmental Policies & Programs unit. He has a B.A. and an M.A. in international relations from Stanford University.*

WHAT DO YOU DO ON THE JOB?

I coordinate a twenty-seven-person environmental team of senior officers. The team has representatives from all major functional and geographic divisions of the bank.

The team coordinates all aspects of the corporation's environmental program. My activities include organizing the team's annual objectives; encouraging, monitoring, and assisting the various team members in meeting their objectives; taking on certain objectives for myself; and reporting progress to the company and the public once a year. Work is about evenly divided between internal and external contacts. A fundamental objective is to use the bank's position and influence to help bridge the gap between environmentalists and the business community. I spend much of each day developing relationships in both communities and working on projects (alone or with team members) that will result in "wins" for each.

WAS THERE A KEY TO GETTING THIS POSITION?

I was in the right place at the right time. I was rolling out of my previous position and exhibited a great deal of enthusiasm about a small, environmentally related project I was asked to do. This got people thinking, since at that time the bank's environmental principles were being finalized. Senior management was wondering whether to just adopt the principles and let nature take its course, or to have someone oversee their implementation. Luckily for me, they opted for the latter. Aside from blind luck on timing, the keys to getting the job were probably the credibility I had built up within the bank over a twenty-five-year career with Bank of America and the fact that I wasn't shy about showing my enthusiasm for the environment.

Additionally, I was finding my enthusiasm for typical bank management jobs not as high as it once was. Continuing to climb the corporate ladder was not my highest priority. I wanted to shift directions, but at the age of fifty-two I felt I could not financially afford a radical career change, especially just three years from qualifying for retirement benefits. When I was offered the environmental job, I did not hesitate before accepting.

HOW CAN OTHERS ENTER THIS FIELD?

There is very little opportunity for people to do what I do. Most corporations maintain an environmental compliance function, but few look beyond compliance and operate a fully integrated "good environmental citizen" program such as the one Bank of America has. Many people send résumés to us looking for employment or leads to other corporations, but, for the most part, the jobs just are not there.

My suggestion is that people interested in helping the environment develop skills in some aspect of business, succeed within their discipline, and, while doing so, introduce an environmental aspect to their job. The difference is not going to be made by staff groups. If business is going to become environmentally responsible, it will be because engineers, plant managers, investment analysts, packaging designers, and everyone else engaged in the nuts and bolts of designing, manufacturing, and marketing products understands the environmental implications of what they are doing and tries their best to minimize the adverse impacts.

WHAT ARE THE TRENDS AFFECTING YOUR INDUSTRY?

Some major pieces of federal environmental legislation have placed huge burdens on business without commensurate benefit to the environment—they are not well balanced. Over the next several years there will undoubtedly be efforts to rationalize the laws. Environmentalists will feel threatened by this, and big fights may result. On the other hand, if constructive dialogue can take place, the necessary revisions could be accomplished without sacrificing environmental protection, achieving saner and less costly compliance at the same time.

Another trend is the development of environmental practices standards by the International Standards Organization (ISO). Once implemented, these standards could significantly affect international trade and such specifics as life-cycle analysis and labeling.

WHAT ARE THE MOST PRESSING CHALLENGES FACING BUSINESS GROWTH AND ENVIRONMENTAL MANAGEMENT?

The biggest challenge is to find ways for both the environment and the economy to "win." This entails getting people on both sides to understand that it is in their long-term interest to have both healthy. More specific challenges are (1) land-use planning, i.e., developing ways to create jobs and housing without allowing urban sprawl to gradually overtake all our open space, and (2) protection of endangered and threatened species without relying on a species-by-species approach.

WHAT OTHER CHALLENGES DO BUSINESSES FACE?

The biggest challenge is getting everyone who inputs to corporate decisions to understand that there are environmental implications to every decision and that those implications must be taken into account. There are still too many people who focus solely on the short-term profit opportunities and ignore the adverse cumulative effect many business decisions can have on the environment.

On the other hand, businesses compete fiercely for markets and capital, and, if they are joint-stock companies, management has a fiduciary obligation to shareholders. Management is understandably reluctant to make decisions that are environmentally responsible if those decisions will raise long-term costs without some bottom-line benefit. The challenge is to find ways for companies to be environmentally responsible without putting them at a competitive disadvantage.

WHAT QUALIFICATIONS ARE VALUABLE FOR SOMEONE WHO WANTS TO WORK IN A POSITION LIKE YOURS?

In my job, the most important qualification has been my knowledge of the bank. In spite of my enthusiasm for the environment, I really did not know many details of the major issues. I did, however, know a great deal about banking in general and Bank of America in particular. That gave me credibility. Someone who knew lots more about the environment and nothing about the bank would have had an extremely difficult time. I can imagine this would be true to one degree or another in all large companies. My advice is learn the business, and then make it environmental.

DO YOU HAVE ANY OTHER ADVICE FOR PEOPLE WHO ARE INTERESTED IN ENVIRONMENTAL CAREERS?

Most of all, become educated and develop a set of unique skills *in anything!* Virtually any field will lend itself to improving the environment. Once a person is established and has earned credentials, focusing on the environmental aspects of that field should be relatively easy. At that point in a career the person brings value. They understand and can talk the language of the field and, therefore, are more likely to have a receptive audience. We have too many well-intentioned but not very well-informed outsiders trying to make seasoned veterans in a field change their ways. What we need are people working from within respective fields to move their special fields toward becoming more environmentally responsible.

WHAT PUBLICATIONS DO YOU READ?

Our unit receives vast amounts of reading material, and we maintain an extensive library. There is too much to read as it comes in, so most of it gets filed and then read when there is a need to know more about a specific subject. We do read *Garbage* and *In-Business* magazines, and we have found that the early issues of *Corporate Environmental Strategy* have been good. The research publications of the World Resources Institute and Resources for the Future are excellent. Newsletters I read include *The Green Business Letter*, *Environmental Business Journal*, and *Science News*.

Jonathan Sandberg Naimon *is the manager of Corporate Environmental Programs at the Investor Responsibility Research Center (IRRC). He has an M.S. in public health from the Environmental Management Program at the University of North Carolina at Chapel Hill.*

WHAT ARE YOUR JOB RESPONSIBILITIES?

I'm responsible for designing surveys of corporate environmental practices, managing analysis of relevant government-supplied environmental data, and explaining environmental laws to an audience that generally wants all issues summarized on one page. I write articles for a variety of periodicals to inform potential subscribers about our service. I speak at conferences that address environmental investment, environmental programs, and, increasingly, environmental reports.

At IRRC I've developed a system for analyzing corporate environmental performance relative to other companies operating in similar business areas. The program is designed to provide investors, foundations, universities, and companies with a means of systematically analyzing the environmental risks of more than five hundred corporations that form the backbone of most institutional investor equity portfolios. More recently, I've been involved in financial performance research, corporate reporting of environmental matters, and benchmarking.

WHAT DID YOU DO PRIOR TO YOUR CURRENT POSITION?

Prior to joining IRRC, I worked as an environmental consultant for Asea Brown Boveri (ABB), a Swiss-Swedish conglomerate in the power-generation, transportation, and environmental industries, and for ICF-Kaiser, an environmental economics and engineering firm. At both companies I assessed benefits and costs of proposed environmental programs. At ABB I was also involved in identifying applications and markets for environmental technologies that the company licensed or developed.

How did you find your current position?

I have been keenly interested in the question of whether environmental management programs cost money or save money for society and for individual companies since I worked for the U.S. Congress between my sophomore and junior years in college. That interest, coupled with friends from that experience, led to my current position.

How does IRRC hire people?

IRRC primarily hires people with undergraduate degrees from private liberal arts schools. An ability to write clearly, knowledge of computer software packages, and attention to detail are important, as are traits such as flexibility.

How could others find a job like yours?

I'd recommend working for Congress or the EPA. I would focus on creatively dealing with research challenges involving heterogeneous data sets and would practice communicating technical matters to nontechnical audiences. Since the job opportunity appeared out of the blue, I'd recommend that anyone interested in the environmental field consider any option that comes along, rather than limit themselves to one use of their skills. I feel that virtually every job offers some opportunities for advancing one's environmental goals.

One key to getting a job in environmental management is graduate school, which enabled me to get offers from firms that spurned me only a few years earlier. If you are not an engineer, a graduate degree is almost like a union card; it gets you into the interview.

What are the trends you see in your field?

A striking trend is the Securities and Exchange Commission's emphasis on clearly reporting various types of environmental liabilities, such as Superfund expenditures, in securities filings like 10-K statements and annual reports. This will place pressure on companies to conduct audits and more accurately identify incentives and assess environmental risks associated with their institutional portfolios.

Another important trend is the change in standards of care required to avoid criminal liability. In the past, not intending to do wrong was sufficient. In the future, the prevention of ecological harm may be the standard. EPA has already prosecuted managers who had the capacity to improve a situation but did not. That may mean that it is incumbent on all of us to work toward environmental solutions whenever environmental problems are identified.

WHAT DO YOU THINK IS THE GREATEST ENVIRONMENTAL CHALLENGE FACING SOCIETY TODAY?

Perhaps the greatest environmental management challenge facing the United States is the justification of environmental programs that do not have compelling economic benefits. There is a trend toward painting economic benefits onto virtually any environmental program. Instead, people should acknowledge that certain things should be done simply for their environmental benefits.

The second greatest challenge is to take virtually meaningless terms such as "sustainable development" and translate whatever you think those terms mean into something that can be acted on or understood.

One tool to help us define and quantify those terms may be the notion of full-cost accounting. In a sense, IRRC's research into the relationship between financial performance and environmental performance constitutes one step toward integration of environmental considerations into financial analysis.

The simplest way to achieve full-cost accounting is for the government to put a price on natural resources such as air and water that are currently free, or to increase the price of commodities such as fossil fuels or nuclear fuel. When prices change, corporations react swiftly, as the oil price rise in the 1970s and the resulting improvement in corporate energy efficiency show.

WHAT ADVICE WOULD YOU GIVE PEOPLE INTERESTED IN ENVIRONMENTAL CAREERS?

Build on an existing skill, such as computer programming or languages, and consider volunteering part time at an organization you respect. The individuals you'll meet, along with your friends, are among the best resources for finding out about jobs and getting the low-down on various types of organizations.

***Dena Siegel** is an assistant vice president for National Westminster Bancorp, Inc. (NatWest). She graduated from Brandeis with a B.A. in 1988 and in 1992 earned an M.B.A. from NYU Stern School of Business.*

HOW DID YOU FIND YOUR JOB?

I sent my résumé to NatWest for a position I saw posted in my business school's placement office after I graduated. When the bank saw my environmental experience, they interviewed me for a position in

Corporate Planning. That position included responsibilities as an environmental coordinator.

WHAT ARE YOUR JOB RESPONSIBILITIES?

Environmental responsibilities are approximately 50 percent of my job. As the environmental coordinator and main liaison with the Environmental Management Unit (EMU) of our parent company, National Westminster Bank in London, I contribute to both internal and external publications produced by EMU: I provide information about U.S. environmental law for the bank's involvement in the creation of United Kingdom and European Economic Community environmental law, and I respond to requests as they arise.

Within Bancorp itself, I am responsible for ensuring that we properly respond to environmental risks and comply with legislation (e.g., Clean Air Act). I also handle any other matters related to the environment.

WHY IS NATWEST INVOLVED IN ENVIRONMENTAL ISSUES?

The primary reason for NatWest's interest in environmental issues is to ensure that related risk issues are properly addressed. These issues include lender liability, fiduciary risk, reputational risk, and risks related to our internal practices.

HOW DID YOU BECOME INTERESTED IN ENVIRONMENTAL EMPLOYMENT?

During the summer between my first and second years of business school, I worked for J. Ottman Consulting, an environmental marketing and consulting firm. When I first started in that position, my primary goal was to gain marketing experience; however, I quickly found myself more interested in the environmental aspects of the work. During my second year in business school, I took a course in environmental issues and participated in extracurricular activities related to environmental issues.

WHAT ARE THE TRENDS YOU SEE AFFECTING BANKING WITH REGARD TO ENVIRONMENTAL ISSUES?

Our approach to dealing with environmental issues must be a practical one, where we focus on the areas that have the greatest impact.

Instead of doing a little bit in a lot of areas, we would be better off doing a lot in fewer areas.

The biggest issue is lender and fiduciary liability. We are closely monitoring legislative and judiciary activities, which are often contradictory and have not yet offered banks protection from being held liable for their customers' activities.

In dealing with environmental issues with a business-oriented focus, the biggest problem is how we are going about responding to these issues. Under current U.S. laws, cleanup of contaminated sites is done arbitrarily. Without a priority system that focuses first on those sites that are clearly causing the most damage to the environment, there will be no improvement.

WHAT SKILLS DO YOU RECOMMEND PEOPLE ACQUIRE?

No specific skills other than knowledge of the issues.

Peter Stein *is a managing partner at the Lyme Timber Company in Lyme, New Hampshire. He has a B.S. in environmental planning from the University of California, Santa Cruz, and a Certificate in Advanced Environmental Studies from the Harvard Graduate School of Design. Prior to his current position, Mr. Stein worked for fifteen years at the Trust for Public Land. He currently sits on the boards of the Appalachian Mountain Club, the Land Trust Alliance, and Island Press.*

WHAT DOES THE LYME TIMBER COMPANY DO?

The Lyme Timber Company (LTC) is a closely held timberland and real estate investment partnership that specializes in the acquisition of property with conservation value.

WHAT IS A TYPICAL DAY LIKE FOR YOU?

We look at and analyze forty or fifty investment prospects for their possibility of a good economic and environmental outcome. I spend time analyzing the potential project and running the numbers and evaluating possibilities for project acquisition.

WHAT KIND OF SKILLS ARE NEEDED IN YOUR FIELD?

The ability to perform economic analyses of real estate properties.

The ability to communicate and to get political groups to support public funding for conservation dispositions and conservation easements by public agencies.

WHY DOES YOUR COMPANY COMBINE ECONOMIC DEVELOPMENT WITH A CONSERVATION ETHIC?

We think it is good business. We own timberland. We do not want to turn this land into subdivisions. It might be economically advantageous, but, philosophically, it is not in our interest. We work with public agencies and nonprofits to sell development rights to public agencies in those states in which we have land holdings. We get money that way. We consider it a conservative approach—to not put money at risk to the cycle of the real estate market. We get capital back early on and generate higher returns from timber harvesting. We cooperate with conservation groups with a limited development track. We portion out the conservation easements from the development, and we joint venture with the nonprofit organization or the state to do the development part.

HOW DO YOU PUT TOGETHER YOUR TEAM?

We are an investor and a developer. We put together a team that consists of engineers, landscape architects, and planners. The financial risk is borne by LTC.

HOW DID YOUR COMPANY CHOOSE TO FOCUS ON THIS ASPECT OF DEVELOPMENT?

We decided that our niche in the investment development field would have a strong environmental concern, which differentiates us from other developers. Our projects are viewed by other developers as difficult. We work with major wetland systems and endangered habitat. What would discourage many conventional real estate development firms we see as an attribute.

WHAT DISTINGUISHES YOU FROM OTHER DEVELOPERS?

What distinguishes us from other developers is our ability to consult with conservation groups and interact and engage at an intensive level. We take scattered land and make a business out of it. For instance, we have a project on Mount Desert Island. The Maine Coast Heritage Trust was seeking protection of a property adjacent to Acadia National Park. The trust could not afford to buy the land, so

LTC bought it. We created a subdivision in an environmentally sensitive manner, on a small portion of the site, and put in conservation easements as well. A percentage of the sale of each property in the subdivision goes to the trust to monitor the easement.

WHO WORKS AT LTC?

There are four full-time general partners, one partner with business background, one with law, one with expertise in the paper and forest industry, and me, with my background in environmental sciences and planning. In the next five to ten years we see having one or two more partners and developing another level of staffing with project managers.

WHY IS IT BENEFICIAL TO CREATE PARTNERSHIPS WITH NONPROFITS WHEN DEVELOPERS AND ENVIRONMENTALISTS ARE KNOWN TO BE AT ODDS WITH ONE ANOTHER?

Working with nonprofits can ease and make more efficient the regulatory approval process. Environmental groups become advocates for environmentally based development, and it saves time in what can be a lengthy approval process. This can be a valuable benefit to developers. Also, nonprofits have good ideas regarding site planning. For instance, in the Acadia project, the National Park Service identified a recreation trail that goes through the development property. The Park Service generated this idea, which ultimately benefits the property subdivision in connecting the development to the park at large.

WHAT IS THE GREATEST CHALLENGE FACING REAL ESTATE AND THE BUILT ENVIRONMENT?

Unplanned development. A lack of planning and of a land-use ethic in America that puts state and local populations at risk of losing control of their open space and development options. We need a better sense of management of land use. We also need a better sense of how the pitfalls of urban sprawl can be avoided if people are educated to understand the value-planned communities that are designed with a sense of place and connection to landscape.

HOW CAN DESIGNERS HELP TO MEET THAT CHALLENGE?

Designers need to be better acquainted with the true environmental costs of design suggestions. Designers need to be able to use the natural contours of property to deal more effectively with water systems and storm-water management. Many designers look to difficult infrastructure solutions instead of letting the assets of the natural landscape assist in environmental and aesthetic development. Designers can use natural systems; for example, they can use wetlands as a natural storm-water management system rather than building an ugly engineered catch basin.

WHAT SKILLS ARE IMPORTANT FOR DESIGNERS?

A basic grounding in ecosystems and ecology and whole-systems thinking are valuable. Design is not just the facade on buildings. Designers need a holistic understanding of how to integrate systems into designs, whether for single-family dwellings or skyscrapers. There are benefits from incorporating natural features and systems into design. The result is a more cost-effective design, less impact on the environment, and ultimately a project with increased market appeal.

WHAT PUBLICATIONS DO YOU RECOMMEND?

Design with Nature by Ian McHarg provides an excellent grounding of the range of systems and issues that affect landscape. I also recommend journals from the Conservation Fund, including *Common Ground* and *The Land Letter; Environment and Development* from the American Planning Association; and *Back 40*, a legal-technical journal on land conservation law from the Hastings Law School in San Francisco.

Communications

Gordon Dancy *earned a B.A. in economics from the University of Connecticut in 1962. During the next fifteen years he worked in the paper-packaging field for both Continental Can Corporation and Hoerner Waldorf Corporation. He now runs Phoenix Recycling, a plastic recycling company on Paley's Island, South Carolina. He is also the host of a radio show that is educating the public about the solid-waste crisis and about the need for reducing, reusing, and recycling.*

HOW DID YOU GET INTERESTED IN RECYCLING AND STARTING PHOENIX RECYCLING?

In 1979 I developed a plastic grocery sack and sold the idea to Sunoco

Products Company. They then asked me to work for them for a year to get the product launched, and one year turned into eleven years. I retired as a corporate vice president of Sonoco Products Company in September 1990. Since that time I have spent many hours defending plastic as being more environmentally friendly than paper and finding alternative uses for plastic sacks.

In my capacity as corporate vice president at Sonoco, I traveled extensively all over the world. Visits to over forty-five countries challenged my thought process concerning different approaches to the disposal of plastic and solid waste. Witnessing the aggressive strategies many other countries adopted toward solid waste helped me to realize the magnitude of the problem and gave me the inspiration to play a small role in finding the solution.

DO YOU CONSIDER YOURSELF AN ENTREPRENEUR AT HEART?

I have always been considered an entrepreneur and have owned and started several businesses, the plastic sacks being the most successful. In retirement I wanted to rest, play golf, write a book about the solid-waste solution, and do some consulting. I have written the book. I feel it presents a plausible solid-waste solution that is both interesting and entertaining; however, it is poorly written and is not yet published. I have started a small recycling company called Phoenix Recycling, which recycles plastic grocery sacks through schools across the country and turns them into garbage bags. Phoenix has good possibilities of success. I play a little golf.

I spend much of my free time as Dr. Garbage. Hosting a weekly radio talk show called "Let's Talk Trash," writing a newspaper column, and involving myself on a local level with recycling, waste disposal, and other complicated environmental problems.

HOW DID YOU CREATE YOUR IDENTITY AS DR. GARBAGE?

The personality Dr. Garbage started out as a paid radio advertising campaign for Phoenix Recycling and evolved over the past year into a regular Saturday morning talk show with a strong local following. Recently, Dr. Garbage started producing a series of two-minute environmental messages. They are heard by two million listeners on over thirty stations from South Carolina to Rhode Island every weekday. The messages are simple and encourage consumers to "buy recycled." Radio is an excellent medium to educate Americans about ways that they can play an active roll in improving the environmental situation.

HOW CAN PEOPLE GET INVOLVED IN ENVIRONMENTAL WORK?

Volunteer—Keep America Beautiful—read my book—pick what interests you the most and become an expert ... that's what Dr. Garbage did!

***Susan Garman** is an account supervisor at Burson-Marsteller in Washington, D.C., where she is responsible for the day-to-day oversight of several accounts in the Washington Environmental Issues Management Group. This includes counseling, strategic planning, and other activities ranging from making media calls to attending conferences, monitoring hearings, producing press releases, writing opinion pieces and letters to the editor, creating video scripts, directing shoots, and handling billing. She has a B.A. in communications from the American University. Prior to joining Burson-Marsteller she worked for the Chemical Specialties Manufacturers Association (CSMA) as their newsletter manager.*

WHAT IS A TYPICAL DAY LIKE FOR YOU?

Since joining Burson, I have been involved in issues ranging from asbestos in buildings to pesticides in food to product liability and litigation communications to electromagnetic fields. There is no typical day at Burson-Marsteller. Daily activity depends on client need and is often driven by external forces such as public perceptions, media coverage, legislation, regulatory or legal action, and emergence of new science or crisis.

HOW DID YOU GET THIS JOB?

I got my present job by sending an unsolicited letter to the co-chair of Burson-Marsteller's Worldwide Environmental Practice Group, who later became my boss. Beyond a certain element of luck, the key to getting this job was a firm grasp of environmental issues as they affect corporate America, and strong writing skills.

HOW DID YOU BECOME INTERESTED IN THE ENVIRONMENTAL FIELD?

My past work experience played a pivotal role both in my decision to pursue a career with an environmental dimension and in obtaining my present position.

Prior to joining Burson-Marsteller I worked for the Chemical

Specialties Manufacturers Association as their newsletter manager. I started with CSMA right out of college, thinking I would gain some writing experience and move on. I had a background in journalism not science, and no real interest in the chemical industry. In tracking the regulatory, legislative, and scientific issues affecting the consumer products industry, I realized that environmental issues are not black and white and that environmental decision making is an intricate process that considers risks, benefits, costs, and feasibility as well as public sentiment. Because most people tend to think in terms of black and white and good and bad, I find that communicating with the public and policymakers on environmental issues—particularly from the perspective of industry—is challenging.

WHAT IS THE MOST PRESSING CHALLENGE IN YOUR WORK?

The greatest challenge I face in the field of environmental public affairs is communicating to the layperson about the technical, scientific, or legal aspects of environmental issues—particularly when he or she often has preconceived opinions about these issues and how they should be handled. Since nearly everything we do in our work revolves around getting people to, at a minimum, listen to a different side of the story, getting over this communications hurdle is critical to our effectiveness and ultimate success.

WHAT TRENDS DO YOU SEE IN ENVIRONMENTAL COMMUNICATIONS?

Environmental communications is a continually evolving field affected by regulatory climate, media focus, and public sentiment. For instance, while the environmental labeling trend of the late eighties and early nineties has subsided, America's rush to "go green" has had a definite effect both on public expectations and on the way companies do business. Those consumers concerned about environmental issues are more wary of environmental claims today. Also, many companies stung by consumer and regulatory backlash against unsubstantiated environmental claims have taken a step back to reassess their environmental communications.

As a result, environmental issues are less likely to be dealt with superficially or separate from other corporate communications programs. For many companies, new regulatory realities and a more environmentally savvy public have brought environmental considerations into the realm of everyday business. Total quality management and product stewardship programs now include an environmental dimension.

WHAT SKILLS ARE NEEDED FOR A JOB IN ENVIRONMENTAL PUBLIC AFFAIRS?

The ability to write and communicate well is essential. Relevant experience is important. The ideal candidate has both and is a quick study and adaptable to all situations.

Recent college graduates often feel as though they are caught between a rock and a hard place because they can't get a job without experience and they can't get experience without a job. Internships and part-time jobs count if you've done professional entry-level work—particularly if you have something to show for it (newspaper clips, reports, press releases, or any materials that you played a significant role in developing).

WHAT RECOMMENDATIONS DO YOU HAVE FOR THOSE INTERESTED IN ENVIRONMENTAL CAREERS?

Stay abreast of environmental trends by reading newspapers (particularly for legislative and regulatory news), magazines (for issues with a public health and safety angle—women's magazines cover a lot of environmental issues), and books. Call or become a member of environmental groups to find out what the most pressing issues on their agendas are (most put out newsletters or magazines for members). Research the companies or organizations you might want to work for—*know what their approach to environmental issues is before you approach them* (an inaccurate assumption about a group's position on an issue is a sure way to get your résumé tossed in the trash).

***Jeanine Jensen** is managing editor for environmental publications at Baxter International, Inc., the world's leading manufacturer of health care products and services, where she is responsible for producing many of Baxter's corporate environmental publications, including the* Baxter Environmental Update, Environmental Highlights, Waste Minimization *and* Pollution Prevention Abstracts, *and the external edition of Baxter's annual environmental performance report. Ms. Jensen also manages the corporate environmental media relations, community relations, investor relations, and employee relations efforts. She has a B.A. in communications with a minor* *in journalism from Northern Illinois University and is currently in the executive M.B.A. program at the Lake Forest Graduate School of Management.*

HOW DID YOU BECOME INTERESTED IN ENVIRONMENTAL EMPLOYMENT?

Prior to working at Baxter, I was production editor, then managing editor of *PIMA* magazine. PIMA is the Paper Industry Management Association. I helped write, edit, design, and produce each issue. While at PIMA, I wrote articles about environmental issues such as recycling, de-inking paper, and dioxin. In addition, I helped staff people coordinate other association activities, including two yearly conferences.

My experiences working at a small association affiliated with the paper industry made me aware of environmental issues. The more I learned, the more I realized these issues affect everyone. Working at Baxter confirmed this. Baxter also taught me that good environmental programs make good business sense. Now I am very interested in environmental employment. I don't think I could work for a company that did not act responsibly toward the environment.

WHAT ARE THE CHALLENGES OF WORKING IN AN ENVIRONMENTAL CAPACITY AT BAXTER?

Baxter has made a profound environmental commitment. The fact that I am employed as a managing editor of environmental publications is a testament to the depth of the company's commitment. Part of the price Baxter pays for being a pioneer in environmental leadership is constant evolution. As a company Baxter has pledged to become state-of-the-art environmentally worldwide by 1996. Progress is measured annually. As environmental management evolves, the standard for establishing state-of-the-art practices changes. The bar continually gets higher. Recognizing this and working to maintain that level of excellence creates innumerable challenges.

For myself, challenges arise constantly because environmental communications is not a well-defined, fully developed field. In part, I am creating the wheel. This is certainly true at Baxter. No one else I know of in this company of more than 60,000 employees has my title or job responsibilities. Making my job what I envision it to be is the source of my greatest frustration as well as my greatest satisfaction.

WHAT ARE THE TRENDS YOU SEE AFFECTING YOUR INDUSTRY WITH REGARD TO THE ENVIRONMENT?

Business today is global, and learning to operate in a world where the environment is truly valued will be a continuing challenge. More attention will be paid to industrial ecology, including life-cycle analysis and closed-loop systems. In communications, reporters and editors will need to broaden their understanding of environmental issues because these issues will play an increasingly important role in politics and industry. Also, once polarized groups such as corporations and nonprofits will work to increase cooperation to affect positive change.

WHAT SKILLS DO YOU RECOMMEND FOR PEOPLE WHO ARE INTERESTED IN YOUR FIELD?

Before one can specialize in environmental communications, one must first acquire a firm background in communications. There is no substitute for solid journalism skills such as writing and editing. In addition, one must develop an awareness of environmental issues and regulations, of how they are written and how they are approved. Learn the alphabet soup of acronyms associated with environmental issues (CERCLA, SARA, RCRA, etc.) as well as an understanding of the requirements involved in complying with each. The industry is inundated with information; therefore, time- and project-management skills are essential, as is an ability to stay organized in the heat of chaos.

WHAT BOOKS, TRADE JOURNALS, ETC., DO YOU READ TO KEEP ABREAST OF ENVIRONMENTAL ISSUES?

Many resources are routed throughout the department. Individual department members look for different things. In my groups are environmental lawyers, managers, engineers, assistants, and myself. Our ongoing reading lists include *Baxter's Environmental Manual*, *Bureau of National Affairs*, *Environmental Reporter*, *International Environmental Reporter*, *California Environmental Reporter*, *Environment Today*, *Environment Watch*, *The ENDS Report*, and *The Earth Times*. In addition, we regularly receive a number of newsletters and brochures from many environmental organizations, including Arthur D. Little, E. Bruce Harrison, and Executive Enterprises. Many professional associations distribute material as well, including the Chemical Manufacturers Association, the Health Industry Manufacturers Association, and the Business Round Table, among others.

ANY SUGGESTIONS GLEANED FROM YOUR JOB HUNT?

Never underestimate the power you possess to affect positive change. Network wherever possible and do not compromise your principles or beliefs for the sake of monetary profits. Complete your education. Consider starting your career with a small company. Small firms provide invaluable opportunities to get involved in diverse projects. It's easier to be a big fish in a small pond than a minnow swimming in the ocean.

Remember to enjoy your work. Have the courage of your convictions to honestly assess potential job opportunities and ensure that the firm's philosophy and practices align with your own, especially in regard to the environment.

***Jeanne Meyer** is vice president and general manager at Dan Klores Associates, a public relations firm in New York City. Her previous jobs include working as manager of environmental affairs at Lever Brothers Company, where she managed the company's Environmental Task Force, conducted cause-related marketing and community relations, handled media relations, wrote and gave speeches, and created and managed an environmental ad campaign aimed at their retail customers. She has a B.A. in journalism with an advertising emphasis and in political science from the University of Missouri.*

WHAT IS THE KEY TO GETTING A JOB IN ENVIRONMENTAL MANAGEMENT?

Environmentalism has become mainstream in the corporate world—while there may not be tons of specific "environmental" job titles, you'll find opportunities to embrace environmentally related work in many existing jobs. And, because many companies are downsizing, reengineering, and restructuring, more and more workers must be "utility" players, who can wear a lot of hats. That means if you're in sales, you have to have a better understanding of how the purchasing people work, how the financial and legal people work. The walls that once relegated workers to one department are crumbling now.

Environmental stewardship is not a concept that corporations have written off as a trend, however. Every business must factor in environmentalism today to survive, to become more efficient, and for public accountability, and that means there's a need for employees to make that happen. One other way to get your foot in the door in my field is to volunteer for a nonprofit, cause, or political campaign; all are areas that beg for good event planners, good writers, good communicators, and creative thinkers. Volunteering builds you a portfolio of work to show others and sometimes leads to full-time jobs.

Even in an existing job you can creatively broaden your job description to include stuff. For example, I wanted to expand my work on marketing to include environmentally oriented business in my former agency, so I "volunteered" to help out another account team on an environmental policy project to prove that I could do it. On the next go-around, I was instantly pulled in as an official part of the team. It meant late nights and weekends, but it was a good time investment.

HOW DID YOU BECOME INTERESTED IN ENVIRONMENTAL ISSUES?

Quite by accident! I created cause-related marketing programs designed to launch two very different consumer products: a beer and a laundry detergent. Both programs involved enlisting the support of volunteers to come out to a local park or school to pick up trash, hand out recycling literature, etc. I saw a real need to communicate the need for individual responsibility to help improve the environment, and made it a career.

WHAT ARE THE MOST PRESSING CHALLENGES FACING OUR COUNTRY WITH REGARD TO ENVIRONMENTAL MANAGEMENT AND SUSTAINABLE DEVELOPMENT?

The biggest task: making sure people—from environmental activists to industry people to government—have the facts.

Making sure these groups are listening to each other and constantly engaged in healthy dialogue is also key. That means we have to start listening to the scientists, to the economists, to the local governments, who are often stuck with the bills for environmental cleanups.

Often environmental issues are based on emotion—and emotional debates are favorites of the news media. The news media like to portray environmental debates as "Big Bad Polluting vs. The Crunchy Granola Hippy Activists." It's not that simple. These issues have lots of factors, and they're never black and white. Rights and wrongs are not always evident.

WHAT IS THE BIGGEST FUTURE CHALLENGE FOR INDUSTRY, THE TRENDS TO WATCH?

The "It's the economy, stupid" principle will increasingly become a factor when environmental policy is being formed. Here's an example. This country has a garbage problem, and recycling is now seen as a major silver bullet that will cure all our environmental evils. Recycling is a good step—as of 1994, more than six thousand communities had recycling programs. And as with the antismoking campaign, children learned about recycling at school and became a major influence on their parents. But with all this emphasis on recycling, the other recommendations to handle waste were getting ignored, including the best way: source reduction, or eliminating waste before it happens. Only one in four people understand source reduction! Making people think about this when they go shopping is a big challenge for business. Convincing lawmakers that source reduction (something that's hard to measure) should be considered in addition to recycling (which is not always an economically feasible step) will be an even bigger challenge.

WHAT READING DO YOU RECOMMEND?

If you are a communicator, you have to be a real media junkie—read everything you can get your hands on. I read five newspapers every morning, digest trade magazines along with my lunch, and save business and news weeklies to read on the stairmaster. Check out environmental marketing trades like *The Green Business Letter*, consumer magazines like *Garbage* magazine and *Audubon*, or trade magazines like *Biocycle*.

A good environmental business book (in addition to *Green at Work*) is Joel Makower's *The E Factor*. Two other books I recommend for deeply probing into the challenges business face in working to make the globe more sustainable include *Changing Courses*, edited by Stephen Schmidheiny, and *Costing the Earth* by Frances Cairncross. And finally, *The Lorax* by Dr. Seuss—it's the ultimate environmental morality tale.

WHAT ARE YOUR RECOMMENDATIONS FOR SOMEONE WHO WANTS TO WORK IN THE ENVIRONMENTAL FIELD?

First, to work within the environmental field, you'll have to be prepared to drop preformed opinions and begin listening to other points of view. Even advocates who are not particularly interested in changing their minds have to listen to the "other side" to understand their position. Remember to keep an open mind.

You'll also have to be like the guy on *The Ed Sullivan Show* who could spin fifty million plates without dropping them. You have to get rid of the notion that you'll be working nine to five. You have to love millions of challenges and the excitement and rush that comes with walking through a proverbial mine field. You also have to make sure you can justify everything you do on a bottom-line basis. Simply telling the boss or the client that you're saving the world does not cut it on the financials.

WHERE DO YOU SEE ACTION OR GROWTH?
Everywhere! but especially in financial analysis, package design (design for recyclability, less packaging, or reduced environmental impact), communications.

WHAT IS YOUR FAVORITE QUOTE?
"Communication is not reaction, it is an essential part of the action"—Sir Isaac Newton—I try to weave it into every speech I write or make.

WHAT SKILLS ARE NEEDED TO DO WHAT YOU DO?
A never-ending thirst for knowledge and strong writing and verbal communication skills (a prospective employer hates to hear "Hire me because I'm a people person"). The ability to listen to and communicate with people from all walks of life is key.

Belle Nolan *is the executive director of the* Environmental Action Report (EAR), *an environmental radio show based in Santa Rosa, California. She is currently enrolled at Sonoma State University.*

WHAT DO YOU DO ON THE JOB ON A TYPICAL DAY?
There is no typical day working for the *Environmental Action Report*, and that's the way I planned it. Weekly, certain tasks have to be done in order to make sure that our network of stations receives their features in a timely fashion. For example, one week we may be soliciting underwriting from businesses for a program that airs in two months but produces in three weeks. That same week, we might be following up on tapes that were sent out to people already featured in the reports to get feedback and to network. Also, during that time we could be lining up interviews for another week of programs. I write the features, review them, and then eventually, usually at week's end, find myself in a studio at the crack of 5 A.M. to produce the new programs.

There are always phone calls to be made, paperwork to shuffle, and desks to clean.

HOW DID YOU FIND OR CREATE THIS JOB?

I created this job out of my love for nature and the environment and my background in radio. People interested in doing this work have to have a burning desire to want to do this. Hopefully in the future there will be more opportunities in all media as well as other industries.

Creating this job required everything I have ever done in my life in all facets of my career in radio. As a former music, production, and promotion director, assistant program director, on-air person, and producer of a specialty show, all roads led to this juncture. I had to be able to deal with radio stations, understand their needs and requirements, and be able to talk their language to get them to be receptive to the idea of broadcasting a program like EAR. I had to have the wherewithal to know how to research the information I needed to obtain the material to write the features. Phone and research skills were absolutely mandatory. I had to have the radio background to know how to write the reports in a way that would be welcomed by program directors. Knowing how to deal with intense pressure and ongoing deadlines was also critical in maintaining schedule commitments. Discipline and management experience have been crucial in keeping things afloat and organized.

WHAT IS YOUR PAST WORK HISTORY?

Radio, radio, radio. I started in 1975 in a podunk station in Apache Junction, Arizona (home of the Superstition Mountains, graduated to the big-time rock world of Phoenix, Arizona, and left in 1978 to go to the Bay Area that had "called" to me since my youth. After a three-year stint at one of the coolest radio stations in the world, KTIM, San Rafael, California (one of the last bastions of free-form FM), I landed in the thriving metropolis of San Francisco at KRQR in 1982. I remained in the market at various stations until June of 1990 when I left radio to devote myself full time to my project.

WHAT IS THE KEY TO GETTING A JOB WITH AN ENVIRONMENTAL DIMENSION (IN YOUR CASE AS REPORTER FOR A RADIO SHOW)?

I'm thinking of the adage, "Find a need and fill it." But many radio stations don't yet realize they need this information. It's an educational process of getting stations up to speed on understanding the breadth of these issues.

WHO IS PART OF YOUR ENVIRONMENTAL TEAM AND STAFF?

We are a nonprofit organization working under Earth Options Institute. We have a board of trustees and an advisory committee made up of people from every part of the community, including business, agriculture, education, and media. Working full time with me is Denise Torres, our marketing director. Denise is responsible for soliciting underwriting and for developing and increasing our station base of subscribers. Working part time is Morry Strauss, a godsend to this organization, who has continually jumped into the trenches whenever there has been a project to complete, paperwork to handle, or any other task needing his special touch.

WHAT ARE YOUR WORK PRIORITIES WITH REGARD TO ENVIRONMENTAL ISSUES?

Our organization focuses on consumer-oriented information. As consumers, we wield incredible power with our purchasing decisions, so this is what we address in our reports. Helping people become informed shoppers is what we emphasize. Reports explain the manufacturing process of making clothes, underscore what coffee or art has to do with the environment, or show how to promote biodiversity in supermarkets. This information enables consumers to become more aware and empowered in the decisions they make, decisions that shape our economic and environmental well-being.

WHERE DO YOU SEE YOURSELF IN FIVE TO TEN YEARS?

I see the *Environmental Action Report* as the leading radio program on environmental education. I anticipate a nationwide syndication of our program on commercial and public stations everywhere. We also have plans for a global distribution. I would like our organization to be recognized as one of the definitive sources for environmental consumer information. Our hope is that by using EAR as a marketing tool, companies will take a new approach to advertising, supporting efforts like ours that seek to educate rather than deluge the public with messages that foist products on them they may not need.

WHERE DO YOU SEE JOB GROWTH IN AREAS OF ENVIRONMENTAL COMMUNICATIONS?

In the future, stations will have to have an environmental expert on staff to deal with environmental information. I envision a time when stations will have a typical business report and then will offer an environmental interpretation. An example might be a report on housing starts followed by a report on what increased housing starts mean: how much habitat is lost or displaced, how much wood is being used, the amount of energy expended in gas, electricity, etc., the cost increases to the community. Our current growth calculations don't take these other factors into consideration. At some point, they will have to. It will be too costly not to.

WHAT SKILLS ARE NEEDED TO ENTER THIS FIELD?

It never hurts to have the technical background, education, and training to work in any field, and the environmental field is no different. Many colleges are offering exceptional programs in environmental studies and natural resource management. Environmental communications is also offered in some universities. It's important to be well rounded and grounded in the field, whether it's technical or academic. Having the educational background as a basis for becoming a good reporter is important. Where it comes from doesn't matter. There are many places to go to gather information. Volunteering for different environmental groups or interning at local radio stations to learn the ins and outs of the broadcasting business is helpful too.

WHAT DO YOU READ AND RECOMMEND FOR PEOPLE TO KEEP ABREAST OF TRENDS AND TO STAY COMPETITIVE IN THIS FIELD?

Organic Gardening, *E Magazine*, *Garbage*, *Eco Traveler*, *Waste Age*, *Environment Today*, *Natural Health*, and *Green Alternatives*. There is a wealth of newsletters available that will help in keeping current on trends and alternatives. A few are: *The Wary Canary*, *The Green Business Letter*, *Interior Concerns*, and *EMA* (Environmental Media Association). There is a plethora of catalogs available that are chock full of helpful information (as well as products and tools for healthy living). Some examples are: Seventh Generation, Real Goods, and Earth Care Products.

My favorite magazine is *Organic Gardening*. Editor in chief and EAR advisory member Mike McGrath has transformed the magazine from a traditional gardening manual to an entertaining digest for proactive, organic advocates of the nineties.

WHAT IS THE MOST PRESSING PROBLEM YOU SEE WITH REGARD TO THE ENVIRONMENT?

I think part of the problem with our environmental crisis is that the issues are seen as separate from us. Our voracious consumer appetites, our addictive society that feeds us goods and products we don't need all contribute to (pardon the cliché) a dysfunctional society that is hungry all the time. It is my belief, and the belief of others, that this hunger stems from a disassociation with who we really are. We are disconnected from natural processes. And we keep trying to fill ourselves up with stuff ... all temporary, all illusive. Bringing the issues home, up close and personal, in a way that fosters change is our biggest challenge right now. Education is the key that will unlock the door.

Evan Pilchik *is an environmental specialist at* Good Housekeeping *magazine, where he evaluates for truthfulness, accuracy, and relevance any environmental claims made in advertisements of products. He received a B.A. in biology from the University of Delaware in 1988 and an M.S. in biology from Fairleigh Dickinson University in 1992.*

HOW DID YOU GET THIS JOB?

I got this job through my graduate school mentor. He was contacted by the director of chemistry at the Good Housekeeping Institute when she was looking to fill the environmental specialist job opening. My mentor asked me if I would be interested, since he knew I was looking to change jobs.

Prior to joining the Good Housekeeping Institute, I was analytical manager of an independent environmental testing laboratory.

WHAT ARE YOUR FAVORITE ACTIVITIES ON THE JOB?

One of the best things about my job is that there aren't any typical days. The products that I evaluate encompass a wide range—from laundry detergents to home air filters, to batteries to plastic trash can liners. Product evaluations account for about half my time. The other half is spent on various committees and task forces about environmental issues, technical editing of the "Green Watch" section of *Good Housekeeping*, writing articles, doing research, representing *Good Housekeeping* to both the environmental community and to advertisers, etc.

I have always been interested in the impact of humans on the environment, especially in manufacturing, using, and disposing of products. Thus, it was natural to connect my interest to a consumer-product-based magazine. This job offered me a chance to be in a lab but also to be out in the world. The opportunities are tremendous.

WHAT BOOKS AND MAGAZINES DO YOU RECOMMEND?

Magazines: *E*, *Environmental Science & Technology*, *Garbage*, *Green Consumer Letter.* Books: *Biologic* by David Wann, *The Diversity of Life* by Edward O. Wilson, *Rubbish!* by William Rathje and Cullen Murphy.

WHAT IS YOUR ADVICE TO PEOPLE WANTING TO ENTER THE ENVIRONMENTAL FIELD?

I recommend that they broaden their education and experience to include biology, chemistry, economics, industrial design, law, and political science. The environment is as complex as life itself; everything is interconnected.

Lorna Sass *is the author of several cookbooks, including* Recipes from an Ecological Kitchen, Cooking Under Pressure, *and* To the Kings Taste. *She is a food and travel writer as well as a lecturer on the history of gastronomy. She has a B.A. in English from the University of Massachusetts at Amherst, an M.A. in English from City College, and a Ph.D. in medieval history from Columbia University. During the seventies Ms. Sass pursued two careers, one teaching English on the college level and one writing and lecturing on the history of cooking. She is now a full-time journalist, researcher, and cookbook author, and resides in New York City.*

HOW DID YOU GET INVOLVED IN WRITING COOKBOOKS?

At Columbia, while working on my Ph.D., I discovered a published collection of fourteenth-century manuscript recipes and started cooking these ancient dishes. In 1975, I wrote my first cookbook, *To the Kings Taste*, which included recipes adapted from a manuscript dated approximately 1390 and associated with King Richard of England. My dissertation focused on this manuscript, on the culinary vocabulary of medieval England. I've been writing cookbooks and articles on all aspects of food since that time. My most recent book, *Recipes from an Ecological Kitchen*, describes the way I cook and eat today. My diet—which concentrates on grains, vegetables, and fruits—is based on my belief that what is good for my health is also good for the health of the planet. My interest in the relationship between food and ecology was inspired by John Robbins' *Diet for a New America* and Frances Moore Lappé's earlier *Diet for a Small Planet.*

WHY DID YOU DECIDE TO WRITE ABOUT FOOD, HEALTH, AND THE ENVIRONMENT?

After recognizing the devastating effects that chemical agriculture and large-scale cattle rearing have on the ecosystem, I wanted to offer some quick and delicious options to people who had similar concerns and were interested in shifting more toward a vegetarian diet. I wanted to point out that by following some of the simple guidelines of ecological cooking, anyone could eat more healthfully while participating in the healing of the earth. These guidelines include focusing on grains and vegetables, buying organic food whenever possible, favoring regional and seasonal produce, and reducing garbage by opting for minimally packaged, unprocessed goods. My aim in *Recipes from an Ecological Kitchen* is to defy the conventional notion that vegetarian dishes take a long time to prepare and are brown, bland, and heavy. Many people still associate vegetarian food with the soybean loaves of the countercultural sixties, and they haven't had the opportunity to taste really well-prepared, sophisticated vegetarian fare. I use the pressure cooker and the wok to turn out fresh and vibrant, nutritious food in record time.

HOW DO YOU INTEGRATE YOUR CONCERN FOR THE ENVIRONMENT WITH YOUR CAREER?

Spirituality is a big part of my career. I feel peaceful about what I eat, and I like to give thanks to Mother Earth for providing the bounty that I get to enjoy. It's important for people to get in touch with the miracle of the plant world and to bring a sense of the sacred back into everyday life. This can be done by treating food with respect and approaching the function of eating as a sacred act. There are many ways to express what really matters to you. Consider your body as well as our earth and think of food as something that passes through you, becomes you, and then gets released back into the soil and the universe to be recycled. Make it as free of poison as possible.

WHAT TIPS WOULD YOU GIVE TO PEOPLE INTERESTED IN YOUR WORK?

My advice to those interested in careers involved in food and nutrition and in writing is that you must be open to create a career out of that which interests you. Follow your heart and get whatever training, education, background, and experience is appropriate for you along the way. I believe that we make our own luck. I happened to see a book on fourteenth-century cooking and started cooking from it. Something happens. Wait patiently with your eyes wide open and keep developing your skills. Keep the faith. Follow your inclination, even if it doesn't make logical sense. If you are drawn to it, things will come together, and you will create something for yourself.

Also, especially for aspiring writers, remember that only 5 percent of people make their living as writers. This is a reality to keep in mind. Before you go freelance, have money in reserve and, as Toni Morrison says, think about doing it on the "edge of day." It is hard to be creative when you are worrying about how to pay your next month's rent. Have an operating base, preferably in a related field. In the food area, the good news is that there is burgeoning interest in health food and opportunities for creative health-oriented cooks in restaurants as well as catering. If you are interested in cooking and catering careers, take courses in ecology and nutrition and carve out a career that makes sense for you. Like the old adage "Go hire yourself an employer," figure out your angle and go with it.

Ellen H. Schaplowsky *is the executive vice president and founder of marketing for the Environmental Group at Ruder Finn, Inc., a public relations firm with headquarters in New York City. She has a B.A. in speech and drama from Catholic University of America in Washington, D.C.*

WHAT IS A TYPICAL DAY LIKE?

My typical day tends to be long. Clients often call to ask me to think about an issue or respond with a strategic plan about how to approach a given issue. I spend time talking with clients about programming and about communications tools that they currently need or will need; work with staff on moving client programs forward; respond to calls, sometimes from new business referrals, sometimes from individuals with innovative ideas and proposals. Because environmental issues are dynamic and eclectic, it's important to have networks to tap into for both formal and informal information gathering—so some time is spent discussing broad issues with colleagues.

HOW DID YOU GET OR CREATE THIS JOB?

In 1990, we formalized our long-time environmental expertise into a new division, Marketing for the Environment. We developed an important strategic premise for this division: to help foster the dialogue between various parties so that practical solutions could be found. From the beginning, our aim has been to help clients move away from or avoid the adversarial approach that traditionally influenced the business-environmental group relationships and help all parties understand commonalities of goals rather than focusing on the divisiveness of their issues. Marketing for the Environment has also been selective in its client base—taking on cutting-edge programs with nontraditional partnerships, as well as helping to launch many new consumer-targeted initiatives. One of our latest programs is the creation of a series of private "Dialogues for the Environment," the first guest being Maurice Strong, chairman of Ontario Hydro and secretary-general of the 1992 Earth Summit.

WHAT IS YOUR PAST WORK HISTORY?

My first job was a receptionist for a small New York PR agency. However, the fledgling agency just happened to handle the consumer products of Union Carbide Corporation including Glad, Prestone, Simonize, Eveready, and subsequently STP. Its biggest news was the introduction of the polyethylene bag—Glad—along with the ubiquitous Man from Glad. So, since the very beginning of my career, I've been involved with an environmental product. One of my first projects as a junior account executive was on the "New York City Experiment," a landmark project with the New York City Sanitation Department that tested and proved that plastic trash bags for curbside pickup were quieter, were safer for workers, and created less vermin. It was only a matter of time before our agency was developing programs to educate municipal solid-waste managers in other major cities about changing curbside pickup regulations to include plastic bags.

WHAT ARE THE MOST PRESSING CHALLENGES FACING YOU IN YOUR WORK?

Developing staff so they can understand the core issues underlying client needs, identifying those who can determine the nexus of problems and unravel the complexity of the issues and persuade clients to look at things from a different perspective when possible and appropriate. Getting staff to think strategically is also a challenge. One of the other pressing challenges is analyzing the vast amounts of information produced on environmental issues for the intelligence necessary to do an outstanding job for clients.

WHAT DO YOU SEE AS THE MAJOR TRENDS IN ENVIRONMENTAL COMMUNICATIONS, PR, AND MANAGEMENT WITHIN YOUR INDUSTRY?

With the mind-boggling growth in new media, especially the Internet and CD-ROM, and the ability of people to communicate rapidly and frequently outside of traditional venues, it is especially important for communications professionals to comprehend the virtual explosion of data and details that can fuel environmental issues. I believe there will be more sophistication on the part of grassroots constituencies in organizing themselves around key issues—especially through the use of new media. I see the acceptance of environmental responsibility as a corporate necessity, with better integration and cross-functional implementation. An awareness that environmental responsibility can help make a company more competitive will continue to grow. Overall, if communications professionals are smart, they will become indispensable to the leaders of corporations and organizations. They will become the voice for win-win solutions and recognize, respect, and foster multi-stakeholder dialogues to help ensure lasting solutions.

WHERE DO YOU SEE JOB GROWTH IN THESE AREAS?

Possibly at PR agencies, as they help various parts of corporations and organizations think through very complicated and complex environmental issues. As senior managers are charged with making their processes and products environmentally responsible they will need smart communications partners to evaluate how various actions impact their image and business—globally, nationally, and locally. Hopefully, the environmental communications function will move internally closer to the top than ever before—not just in the safety, health, and engineering box.

WHERE DO YOU SEE YOURSELF IN FIVE TO TEN YEARS?

Expanding Marketing for the Environment's business more deeply into consulting on environmental issues as well as the fields of sustainable development and social responsibility. We're also developing innovative global trade programs that bring low-cost environmental technology to developing nations—we know the planet cannot afford to have countries like India and China go through an industrial revolution. Part of our economic growth will depend on developing and exporting green technologies.

WHAT SKILLS ARE NEEDED TO ENTER THIS FIELD?

Volunteering, real-life experience in the trenches, is quite valuable. Good research skills, good mind for facts, and skill at looking for the "story behind the story," understanding of communication tools like CD-ROM and interactive media, a fundamental understanding of grassroots marketing—an ability to help stakeholders think globally, act locally.

HOW CAN SOMEONE GET YOUR JOB?

We are in a service business. It's important to grasp what that really means. It means being proactive, anticipating clients' needs; it means helping them do what they have to do better, faster, and smarter. Learn to understand the clients' goals and help the clients think more creatively about their issues. Bring them outside perspectives about their business so that decisions—large and small—are grounded in a "big picture" context. And always remember that God is in the details.

WHAT ARE YOUR FAVORITE ENVIRONMENTAL AND TRADE BOOKS AND MAGAZINES?

My favorite books are those that cut across many disciplines and attempt to provide a unique holistic view of the massive changes the planet and its population are undergoing. Some are: *Seat of the Soul* by Gary Zukhav, *Politics of the Solar Age* by Hazel Henderson, anything by Dr. Deepak Chopra. The magazines I like are *Psychology Today, Discover, Harvard Business Review*, and science journals, which help many people understand the deep intelligence of the body and consequently the environment in which the body moves.

ANY PEARLS OF WISDOM?

Everyone has something valuable to say . . . if only you can hear it.

Mike Silverstein *is president of Environmental Economics, a think tank based in Philadelphia. Mr. Silverstein is author of many books including* The Environmental Factor, *and* The Environmental Economic Revolution *and is a features writer for* In Business *magazine. He is an adjunct professor at New York University.*

WHAT IS A TYPICAL DAY LIKE FOR YOU?

Whatever is necessary. There always seems to be an interesting and (at least to me) important something hovering that has to be taken care of. So after I do what's needed to meet the rent and get the health insurance premiums paid, I do it.

HOW DID YOU GET YOUR PRESENT JOB?

I invented it.

WHAT'S THE KEY TO GETTING AN ENVIRONMENTAL JOB?

The entire world is falling apart. There are therefore an infinite number of things to be done. Wake up, and the work automatically presents itself.

WHAT SKILLS ARE NEEDED TO ENTER THE ENVIRONMENTAL FIELD?

All skills have a function here.

WHAT MEDIA HELP TO STAY ABREAST OF DEVELOPMENTS IN THIS FIELD?

Al Gore called "the environment" the central organizing principle of the next century. It is actually the central disorganizing principle. And the next century has already begun. Environmental decline is the underlying force shaping virtually every human institution in virtually every part of the planet on virtually a second-by-second basis. If you can't tap into this reality in virtually any medium always, you are already dead and there is no point seeking job counseling.

AS A WRITER OF ENVIRONMENTAL ECONOMICS, WHAT DO YOU SEE AS A MAJOR PROBLEM FACING OUR COUNTRY?

One major problem facing people today is how to select and make use of information. Information is, in and of itself, pretty useless. There has been a tremendous increase of information available to people but no increase in visionary intelligence. It is analogous to an ocean with no direction to its waves. We need to give a better direction to the nebulous and voluminous body of facts. That is where I see myself. A conceptual artist whose work is to help give some direction to the field of environmental economics.

WHAT IS ENVIRONMENTAL ECONOMICS?

My view is that environmental and economic goals are not antagonistic. They are synergistic today. Environmental economics is just good economics. It is a better way for the marketplace to operate. It is more efficient and less wasteful, meets consumer tastes better, reduces future liabilities, and allows a greater competitive advantage. It also provides an opportunity for the creation and use of the newest technologies and, in turn, job creation and an expanded export base.

The green economy is simply the most advanced type of economy. Just as on the way from a charming childhood to a useful adulthood, people must inevitably pass through a grotesque adolescence, economics must pass through a pollution-based adolescence to go from underdevelopment to being environmentally sensitive.

WHAT DO YOU WANT TO ACHIEVE WITH YOUR WORK?

The environment is a precondition for life. There are certain physical and chemical balances that must be maintained in order for all the glories and all the horrors that constitute human civilization to continue. Thus, when I think of the environment, I find it dull. To me it is picking up the garbage better than we used to pick it up. My writing merely seeks to educate people about the new environmental economics so "real" human life remains a possibility.

I work from an individual rather than an institutional base. I am not the president of DuPont or a professor at Harvard or a reporter for the *New York Times*, I created a letterhead and built my activities from a letterhead and a vision. I believe individuals do not have to be helpless. Vision provides power—if you can conceptualize what is happening and what needs to happen in the future.

WHAT IS YOUR ADVICE TO PEOPLE INTERESTED IN WRITING AND ENVIRONMENTAL ECONOMICS?

In order to have vision, it is important to keep a sense of humor—about other people and, most important, about yourself. You can't be a security nut and achieve anything in this world. It is just plain impossible. You can't expect people to love you. If you do something new, people won't give you money, won't show you respect. It is like the old Nike saying, "Just do it!" Empowerment is knowing what you want, attaching yourself to a vision, and going along for the ride despite the ups and downs you meet along the way.

***Denise Steinberg** is principal of DMS, a graphic design firm located in Bloomingdale, Illinois, which specializes in strategy and planning for corporate communications programs. Services also include editorial development, graphic design, and project management. Ms. Steinberg has a B.A. in studio art and art history and an M.A. in art history from Northern Illinois University.*

HOW DID YOU CREATE THIS BUSINESS?

I started my business with only a t-square and the desire to express my creativity, to learn, and to use my talents and abilities. I've always been good at juggling multiple responsibilities. I gained confidence as a professional in my first position with Merrill Chase Galleries, where I combined my talents in design and art history. My position encompassed designing and managing production of marketing and materials, public relations, writing about artists, planning special programs, giving gallery talks, and establishing and maintaining graphics in nine galleries.

HOW DID YOU BECOME INTERESTED IN ENVIRONMENTAL ISSUES AS THEY RELATE TO YOUR WORK HISTORY AND EDUCATION?

When I started my business, becoming an expert on paper products was among my top priorities. I wanted to learn more about the market, to be able to offer clients the most appropriate options available. I contacted all the major paper manufacturers and distributors and got on their mailing lists. As more and more information pertaining to the environment and recycling began to cross my desk, my interest began to grow.

Environmental concerns have become crucial to paper manufacturers over the past several years. In the beginning, recycled papers were an anomaly, rough in appearance, not very appealing, and difficult to come by. It has been interesting to watch quality increase and availability become virtually no problem at all, as a result of the demand for recycled paper products. Quality and availability are major concerns when specifying papers for projects with tight deadlines—which most of them are. Now, recycled papers have become the papers of choice for most graphic designers.

I believe what is key to getting a graphic design job with an environmental dimension is understanding the needs of business. In my case, knowing about recycled papers, specializing in the health-care industry for a number of years, and being familiar with TQM (Total

Quality Management) concepts all contributed to opening up opportunities for me in the area of environmental communications.

WHAT DO YOU SEE AS MAJOR TRENDS IN ENVIRONMENTAL COMMUNICATIONS?
As more companies become involved with TQM principles, design opportunities for environmental communications are a natural outgrowth. Opportunities for graphic/industrial designers in environmental package design are on the rise.

New and better recycled and environmentally sensitive papers will continue to revolutionize the printing industry, as will soy-based inks. Many firms will request only recycled papers.

WHAT ARE YOUR FAVORITE ENVIRONMENTAL AND TRADE BOOKS AND MAGAZINES?
The Sense of Wonder, Rachel Carson; *Trade U&LC (Upper & Lower Case)* published by the International Typeface Corporation; *Recycled Papers: The Essential Guide* by Claudia Thompson. General design publications include *Communication Arts, Step by Step Graphics, Print, How Magazine, International Design,* and AIGA and ACD publications.

WHERE DO YOU SEE JOB GROWTH IN THE AREA OF ENVIRONMENTAL COMMUNICATIONS?
In graphic design, the best bets are probably in the area of package design (which I am not involved in), exhibit design, publication design, and interactive media. Many companies that do not specialize in environmental communications have invested in desktop publishing equipment, so in-house staff positions are also a place to look.

WHAT SKILLS ARE NEEDED TO ENTER THIS FIELD?
Designers must be computer literate. Experience on QuarkXPress and Adobe Illustrator are extremely important. These are the programs of choice for most graphic design firms. Print production knowledge is a plus, too. Learn as much as possible about art, culture, and type, and teach yourself about design and art history. You need good presentation and project management skills, and critical thinking and writing skills are also essential.

WHAT IS THE MOST PRESSING PROBLEM YOU SEE WITH REGARD TO THE ENVIRONMENT?
Our own spiritual poverty is the most pressing problem we face. We

are sorely lacking in spiritual connectedness to ourselves and nature. We consume too much, we discard too much, we take advantage too much.

WHAT ARE YOUR RECOMMENDATIONS FOR PEOPLE WHO ARE INTERESTED IN ENVIRONMENTAL CAREERS?

Meet and talk with professionals who are doing what you think you'd like to be doing. Get a sense, a picture of what your ideal job would be like. Acquire the skills necessary to attract the kind of companies you're interested in working for. Join an organization related to your field, stay focused on your goal, learn as much as you can from whatever situation you find yourself in.

WISDOM GLEANED FROM YOUR EXPERIENCE?

If you get what you want and it turns out not to be what you wanted after all, have the courage to switch gears. If you go after what you want and you don't get it, let it go. Know that your worth is not related in any way to what you accomplish. Develop your intuition and spend time listening to it. It will tell you when you are going down the wrong path. Realize that relationships are what is most important, not personal glory, benefits packages, awards, possessions, or whatever. Remember, counselors involved in death and dying tell us that no one on his deathbed has ever said, "I wish I had worked more."

Community Environmental Affairs & Public Policy

***Peter N. Britton** is the director of community environmental affairs at Johnson & Johnson's corporate headquarters. He has worked at Johnson & Johnson since 1961 as a research director, director of regulatory affairs, and director of exploratory research. Prior to his positions at Johnson & Johnson, Mr. Britton worked as a research chemist for American Cyanamid. He has a B.A. in natural science from Rutgers University, an M.S. in physical chemistry from Seton Hall University, and a Ph.D. in physical chemistry from Stevens Institute of Technology.*

HOW IS MOST OF YOUR TIME SPENT ON THE JOB?

Much time is spent meeting with executives both domestically and internationally, discussing environmental issues and developing plans to resolve their specific issues. This requires a good deal of travel since my environmental responsibilities are worldwide. Additionally, this function provides training to top management in environmental responsibility—which includes training in environmental awareness, corporate objectives, crisis management, partnerships with community, government, NGOs, etc.

WHO IS PART OF YOUR ENVIRONMENTAL TEAM OR STAFF?
Two members, both technical (one M.S., one Ph.D.), one focusing on technical/regulation impact, and the other focusing on technical communications.

WHAT ARE THE MOST PRESSING CHALLENGES FACING OUR COUNTRY WITH REGARD TO ENVIRONMENTAL MANAGEMENT AND SUSTAINABLE DEVELOPMENT?
The most pressing challenge facing our country and industry as well is to find the delicate balance between economic growth and reduced environmental impact of our products, processes, and services.

WHAT CIRCUMSTANCES OR EXPERIENCES INFLUENCED YOUR DECISION TO WORK ON THIS?
Johnson & Johnson has a firm commitment to responsible environmental management as set forth in our credo, the document that dictates how we manage our business. My decision to work in this area is a result of that commitment and my interest in the general area of environment.

HOW CAN OTHERS ENTER THIS FIELD?
Be committed to environmental responsibility and go for it. Expect challenges, disappointments, and rewards.

WHAT KINDS OF CHALLENGES DO BUSINESSES FACE WITH REGARD TO ENVIRONMENTAL RISKS AND LIFE-CYCLE ASSESSMENTS?
The major challenges relate to defining and understanding risks and their real impact on the environment and then translating this to impact on human health. *Sound science* must be applied in defining and analyzing such risks.

WHAT TRENDS DO YOU SEE AFFECTING INDUSTRY WITH REGARD TO ENVIRONMENTAL LIABILITIES (E.G., SUPERFUND), ENVIRONMENTAL AUDITS, THE CLEAN AIR ACT, AND OTHER LEGISLATION?
The major trends that I see will relate to public reporting of environ-

mental performance by corporations. Some companies are already preparing public environmental reports. Such reports are being requested by stockholders, investment houses, etc., and are being made part of environmental management systems on a global basis such as is taking place under the purview of ISO 14000 (standard for responsible environmental management developed by International Standards Organization). If a company follows legislation and abides by regulations and plans strategically, I don't see liabilities as a major factor.

WHERE DO YOU SEE THE ROLE OF ENVIRONMENTAL COMMUNITY DEVELOPMENT AND AFFAIRS IN THE COMING YEARS?

Environmental community development will be a major focus of corporate management systems. There is an ever-increasing awareness in corporations that they must demonstrate that they are community residents and hence must show such responsibility. They will become more involved in community partnerships even to the level of leadership in many of these areas such as education, open-door policies, disclosures, emergency management, etc.

WHERE DO YOU SEE JOB GROWTH IN THE ENVIRONMENTAL AFFAIRS AREA?

I see future job growth in the environmental area in understanding and applying life-cycle assessments, developing total environmental management systems, and generally including environmental responsibility as a component of corporate management.

WHAT SKILLS ARE NEEDED TO ENTER THIS FIELD?

The major skills needed are technical background, some selling skills, and public relations skills.

WHAT DO YOU READ AND RECOMMEND FOR PEOPLE TO KEEP ABREAST OF TRENDS AND TO STAY COMPETITIVE IN THIS FIELD?

I read everything that has the word "environment" in the title.

WHERE DO YOU GO FOR INSPIRATION?

To meetings of national and international environmental NGOs such as World Industry Council for the Environment (WICE) and Health and Environmental Sciences Institute (HESI). I also get inspiration by talking with others in this field and discussing environmental issues.

HOW CAN SOMEONE GET A JOB LIKE YOURS?

If you are an undergraduate student, find a graduate school that has incorporated environmental responsibility into the various curricula. There are not too many universities doing this, but Tufts University is one of them. If you are a graduate in the sciences, look for a company that has taken environmental responsibility seriously. Look at annual reports and environmental reports to get a sense of what companies are doing and where you see yourself fitting into their overall corporate culture and mission.

Matthew Brown *is senior energy policy specialist for the National Conference of State Legislatures in Denver, Colorado. He formerly served as project director for New York City's Telecommunications and Energy Department. He has a B.A. in history from Brown University and an M.B.A. from New York University.*

WHAT YOU DO ON THE JOB?

In my capacity as a senior energy policy specialist, I advise state legislatures on a wide variety of energy issues, including energy efficiency, renewable energy, and alternative fuels. I spend part of my time doing research and writing reports on energy and environmental issues and part of my time developing policies and programs based on that research. I concentrate on renewable energy and alternative transportation fuels.

For example, I recently completed work on financing renewable energy projects like wind farms, hydro, and biomass power plants to identify specific barriers to financing renewable energy projects, so that energy policymakers can design policy to address those barriers. I spent several months doing research; interviewing representatives from investment banks, commercial banks, and institutional investors and lenders; and then wrote a report on my findings that will be distributed to most organizations involved in energy policy in New York State.

I also have worked with local utilities to write legislation requiring that the city government buy a certain number of alternative-fuel vehicles. I then developed, in concert with local utilities, a financing package to support the program.

I try hard to integrate my understanding and knowledge of finance with my interest in the environment. I am a practical environmentalist. I try to see, from a governmental perspective, the best way to make environmental products attractive to the business community. I spend a lot of my time writing, developing programs, and talking on the telephone.

HOW DID YOU GET THIS JOB?

I got this job through a circuitous route. I was interested in environmental issues both before and during college. After college, I worked for Peat Marwick and Co. while getting my M.B.A. That job did not deal with environmental issues but taught me about finance and the business world. I then worked briefly with an environmental consulting firm, which ran into financial problems shortly after I joined it. Finally, I saw an advertisement in the newspaper for the job I now hold. I applied and got the job.

WHAT IS KEY TO GETTING A CITY JOB?

All government jobs are "posted" for a certain period of time and are often, by regulation, made available to people who already work for other agencies or departments in the government. It is possible for employers to navigate around requirements to hire from within the existing government workforce. So the key is to network, to get to know people in the field, by going to conferences, getting people's names, and calling them.

WHAT ARE THE CHALLENGES OF WORKING IN AN ENVIRONMENTAL CAPACITY?

Environmental work is by its nature political. Many times, it involves convincing people to spend money now to save on pollution for years to come. The trick is to produce arguments to spend that money in a convincing way.

Environmental work involves working with many different constituencies, from business to government to environmental groups to the general public. One of the biggest challenges is to develop programs or policies that satisfy, or placate, each constituency.

WHAT ARE THE TRENDS YOU SEE AFFECTING ENERGY?

The energy field divides in two parts: transportation energy and electric power, or gas heat utilities. Most cities now recognize that automobiles contribute more than any single source to air pollution. As a result, there may be tremendous growth in the transportation field over the next few years as interest mounts in alternative-fuel vehicles and more fuel-efficient automobiles.

I also expect a continuing push for utilities to use more renewable energy. The utility industry is in a time of dramatic changes, however, and is reluctant to make large monetary commitments to new technologies at the moment.

HOW CAN OTHERS ENTER THIS FIELD?

A variety of paths are available to enter the energy and environment field: government (offices at local, state, and federal levels); utilities; nonutility power producers such as wind power companies; and environmental groups.

WHAT SKILLS ARE NEEDED TO ENTER YOUR FIELD?

To be successful, one must write well, be able to present ideas and speak persuasively, be able to manage well many people and constituencies with conflicting ideas, and be patient with the pace of change. A thorough understanding of finance is a valuable and unusual skill that is increasingly in demand.

WHAT DO YOU READ AND RECOMMEND?

Public Utilities Fortnightly and *Independent Energy* offer overviews of what is happening in the utility/renewable energy field. Several newsletters exist that deal with alternative fuels, but magazines are rare. The Electric Transportation Coalition in Washington, D.C., is a good clearinghouse for information about electric vehicles; and the Natural Gas Vehicle Coalition, also in Washington, D.C., is a good clearinghouse for information about natural gas vehicles.

Environmental groups like the Natural Resources Defense Council and the Environmental Defense Fund (both based in New York) and the Union of Concerned Scientists (based in Washington, D.C.) have useful publications. As for a favorite book, *Steering a New Course* by Deborah Gordon (published by the Union of Concerned Scientists and Island Press) provides an excellent discussion of alternative transportation fuels.

WHAT IS THE MOST PRESSING PROBLEM YOU SEE IN THE ENVIRONMENTAL INDUSTRY?

The recent recession made industry and the general public more concerned about money issues. Environmental fixes generally cost money. The difficulty will be to continue to keep people interested in the environment despite the additional costs of preserving the environment.

ANY ADVICE ON GETTING AN ENVIRONMENTAL JOB?

Talk to people again and again about what they do. Figure out where the needs and gaps are in the field and pursue jobs in those areas.

John Currie *is a speech language teacher in New York City, where he incorportes environmental education into his core curriculum. Prior to his work as a language teacher, he held positions as assistant to a veterinarian and as a bartender while pursuing his undergraduate degree. He has a B.S. from New York University.*

WHAT IS THE GREATEST CHALLENGE IN BRINGING EDUCATION INTO A POSITION OF IMPORTANCE IN ADDRESSING ENVIRONMENTAL AND SOCIAL CONCERNS FACING OUR COUNTRY?

The great difficulty in environmental education is overcoming the selective distance we, as humans, have put between ourselves and nature. As Westerners, we are pitting ourselves against the great forces of nature, placing ourselves outside of it simply because we have the ability to name the animals.

TELL US ABOUT SOME OF YOUR PROJECTS.

With funds from Chase Manhattan Bank and the help of the Fund for New York City Public Education, our students, my colleagues, and I were able to publish a Spanish/English newsletter, which involved the use of computer technology. Students wrote articles that often included urban environmental issues such as pregnancy, homelessness, economic success and failure, drugs, and violence. They also wrote fictional stories and short poems about and around these issues.

Also, two years ago I began planting flowers and vegetables with my junior high students. The school had had a murder toward the close of winter, and I was desperate to do something life affirming. I started with a few students who seemed interested, and I kept it very simple. Soon I began to notice that those students who had shown no interest in planting started to act out verbally against the growth of their friends' plants. Or they would become fascinated while their friends worked with the plants.

I don't know how much I taught these students about plants. I do know that when we did it again, more than two-thirds of the students participated, planting and monitoring plant growth. Some students began to use rulers effectively; others became fascinated with the origins of flower names. Our garden became a focal point for our part of the school and had many visitors, something I never expected. Students were able to witness a natural reality, the basic processes of life and death, and interdependence. I had many discussions with them about how, in all of nature, things grow according to varying schedules.

I have also taken students to the Pocono Environmental Education Center. This allowed me to see them in a different environment, completely foreign to some of them. There are not nearly enough programs like this. If we are not careful, we will see how impossible it is to teach anything "environmental" without direct exposure to what the words we teach refer to.

WHAT DO YOU SEE AS THE MOST PRESSING ENVIRONMENTAL CONCERN HAVING TO DO WITH HOW OUR CITIES FUNCTION?

The difficulty of teaching inner-city children about the environment is teaching students to appreciate and incorporate that which may appear irrelevant to their lives. Many of our students fail. This is in part, I believe, because they see most of what is offered them as either undesirable or unattainable. Nature is as far away a concern as university is to a fifteen-year-old functional nonreader.

CAN YOU SUGGEST WAYS FOR PEOPLE TO GET INVOLVED IN AN ENVIRONMENTAL ISSUE AS AN EDUCATOR?

To create meaningful environmental education, the concept of the family becomes the starting point as an environmental concern—in its importance in the web of life and in the mutuality and interdependence of that web. I hope that greater links are formed between the home environment and the school environment. It is often the internal breakdowns within these "ecosystems" that further the social ills getting so much play in the media: the breakdown of families, the "fear" of children who we now know are more often the victims of crimes than its perpetrators.

WHAT SKILLS AND PRINCIPLES ARE IMPORTANT FOR APPROACHING ENVIRONMENTAL PROBLEMS?

Thoroughness, completeness, reflection upon one's life and the lives of others, and interdependency are some of the more important factors in the process of a balanced education. The implied skills necessary for a constructive exploitation of one's environment in an urban setting require that literacy take a primary role. Specifically, literacy that is lexographic, visual, empathic, or technologic becomes primary in an area where the "real" object of study—say, the food chain—is abstracted by geography.

HOW CAN EDUCATORS BE MORE ENVIRONMENTALLY AND SOCIALLY RESPONSIBLE IN THE WORK THEY DO?

By fostering a concept of inclusive language. It is "we" and "our" in education, not "my," or "yours," or "theirs." There is no "those" people, no "these" people. That perspective, like any claims of separateness from environment, is fiction.

Michael Greene *is a database administrator in the Information Systems Area of Brooklyn Union Gas. He has a B.S. in environmental studies from Empire State College.*

HOW DID YOU BECOME INTERESTED IN THE ENVIRONMENT?

In 1975, I began studying high-yield labor-intensive gardening practices through an environmental organization that was training people to teach these techniques in Latin America. I was less interested in going abroad than in trying to apply this approach in some of the poorer neighborhoods here in the United States. For the next few years, I worked to help develop community gardens in various places ranging from Santa Barbara to the South Bronx.

In 1979 I began working with a group called the New Alchemy Institute researching aquaculture and solar energy technologies. I also continued to be active in community-related environmental issues such as community gardens and energy co-ops.

In 1982, I returned to New York City to find a new direction and a more mainstream career. I began working for Brooklyn Union Gas in 1986 as a computer programmer.

HOW DID YOU CREATE AN ENVIRONMENTAL POSITION FOR YOURSELF AT BROOKLYN UNION?

For most of the time I have been employed at Brooklyn Union, I was not actively involved with environmental issues. In 1991, our company began to move its main offices. Our preparations included purging massive amounts of old printouts and records that had been laying around in various files and drawers throughout the building. As one might imagine, a significant amount of potentially useful material, such as old loose-leaf binders, was being thrown out.

While the company was making an attempt to recycle these materials, it was nowhere near the scope that was required. I couldn't stand to see these resources wasted, knowing that there were kids and teachers throughout the city who could really use this stuff. I posted signs all over the building and made drop-off points where people could save any usable binders. During lunch hours and after work, I ran up and down the building, collecting the binders and getting teachers, custodians, and parents to pick them up. The employees really appreciated the effort, and we were able to donate thousands of these used loose-leaf binders to local schools.

I really enjoyed this project, and it rekindled my interest in community-environmental activism. Shortly thereafter, I organized a recycling system for used laser-printer toner cartridges. Lanier Worldwide, a firm that remanufactures these cartridges, donates $5 for every cartridge we send them; Brooklyn Union's Urban Affairs Department matches this amount; and the money is used to support environmental programs in local schools. We've received tremendous support from our fellow employees and have directed thousands of dollars toward these efforts.

WHAT OTHER PROGRAMS HAVE YOU DEVELOPED?

Since developing this program I've had the good fortune to link up with a number of employees within the company who are deeply interested in environmental issues. Our environmental focus has been on four major points:

- continually improving Brooklyn Union's internal recycling procedures and increasing its purchase of goods made from recycled materials;
- attracting new environmental businesses to New York and retaining existing industry by helping it become less polluting;
- promoting neighborhood preservation and beautification efforts; and
- supporting environmental education.

In addition to initiating or supporting various environmental activities, I've been appointed to chair Brooklyn Union's Environmental

Task Force. This group acts as a forum within the company to discuss a wide range of environmental issues. Our publication, *Brooklyn Union's Environmental News*, describes the varied environmental efforts of the company and also shows the positive impact a utility can make in supporting community-based environmental programs.

WHAT ARE THE ENVIRONMENTAL CHALLENGES FACING YOUR INDUSTRY?

Brooklyn Union has actively been researching and promoting environmentally superior technologies such as natural gas vehicles, gas cooling, cogeneration, etc. The challenge for our industry is to gain a wider acceptance in the marketplace for these technologies.

As a utility in an urban setting, our company also faces the challenge of a shrinking industrial base. Here in New York we hear stories all the time of businesses leaving the city to open up in more rural locations rather than expand into adjacent abandoned sites. The reason is often either that they are unwilling to take on potential environmental liabilities associated with these properties or that banks are afraid to lend them money because of these potential liabilities.

Our society has created unreasonable environmental standards for industrial properties. We should encourage the use of our existing infrastructure to create new jobs in urban settings where they really are needed, instead of making the laws so onerous that businesses find it easier to build a new plant on a virgin site.

Samara Swanston *is chief of the Eastern Field Unit of the Department of Environmental Conservation's Division of Environmental Enforcement, which works with Superfund sites in southern New York. As an adjunct professor at Pace Law School she also teaches a course in environmental justice as well as an environmental law course. Prior to this position Ms. Swanston worked for three years as an attorney for the EPA in Region II. She has a B.A. in English from York College and a J.D. degree from St. John's University.*

WHAT IS A TYPICAL DAY LIKE FOR YOU?

A typical day would include a conference call with my managers in Albany to discuss policies concerning landfills and remedial programs. I also would typically receive a phone call from people who seek voluntary assistance from our division to study their site and project cleanup costs. I manage my staff and speak with the technical division about decisions they make with regard to contaminated sites. The engineers are our clients. Our job is to make sure that the liability issues are thought through. Corporations come to us all during the year, and our goal is to help them resolve the liability issues and facilitate the cleanup process.

I also work as a mentor to the interns in our department. I review their work and provide them with guidance. I spend time preparing for talks I present on topics as varied as water issues, redevelopment of waste sites, and lender liability on contaminated sites. Additionally, I manage the externship program with Pace Law School. Law students get four credits for working at the DEC. I help develop materials for the classroom part of the externship. I also receive phone calls from pro bono groups, nonprofits, and the press and respond to any questions they may have about a site.

WHAT GOT YOU INTERESTED IN PURSUING AN ENVIRONMENTAL CAREER?

I was an English teacher, and I was also a person who likes nature. I used to take my kids walking in wetlands when they were young. I didn't see myself as an environmentalist. A person of color may not see themselves as an environmentalist but can be very interested in nature and recreation. When I did a clerkship in the Court of Appeals I saw some environmental cases. They made immediate sense to me, and I knew I would enjoy working on them. I requested these cases involving natural resources protection, and I felt satisfied at the end of the day. I was able to protect resources not only for myself but for people all over the state. Because of my work a power plant wasn't built, and a dwarf pine forest, one of three dwarf pine forests in the world, was preserved on Long Island. I gravitated to environmental law because I saw a need to protect natural resources, and I got immediate satisfaction from working in this area of law. When I tell people I protect natural resources, children think it is wonderful. I don't care what reputation lawyers have, environmental lawyers are treated with respect. You can do good work in helping companies comply with government laws and assisting in cleaning up sites. Once I got into environmental law I knew I could do it for the rest of my life. As a lawyer I can make my mark. I never lose sight of the fact that I can make a difference in helping to protect natural resources and human health.

WHAT IS ENVIRONMENTAL JUSTICE?

Environmental *in*justice is environmental decision-making that creates disadvantages for poor people and people of color while creating advantages for others. Environmental justice looks to equitable management of environmental land-use law and policy that does not unfairly burden poor people and people of color. Disposal is not the only issue. It has to do with proper and adequate sewage, housing, and fair and equitable transportation, which are crucial to environmental quality and health. Social justice is also environmental—such as removing lead in housing. Education is an important part of the environmental justice movement.

The Clinton administration executed an executive order in February 1994 to review practices and make recommendations on environmental justice issues as they relate to federal agencies such as Housing and Urban Development, the Occupational Safety and Health Administration, and the Department of Health and Human Services. It mandated that working groups be formed to design an environmental justice strategy and put it forward in the federal agencies.

HOW DID YOU GET INVOLVED IN ENVIRONMENTAL JUSTICE?

I got involved in environmental justice when I first started teaching at City University of New York. I was asked to give a talk to the State Bar of New York about the lack of minorities in the environmental law field. The notion is that minorities are busy dealing with crime, drugs, and unwed pregnancies, and because of these concerns, there was no time to be involved in environmental law. There were no representatives in the Sierra Club, Wilderness Society, etc. The traditional environmental groups did not see minorities as part of the movement. They were wrong, though. The United Church of Christ has been doing environmentally oriented work. The law students weren't aware of how they could involve themselves or of the relationship between race and environmental issues. Professors and lawyers had not informed them. The law professionals had not done their job. Minorities have always been interested in public interest law. We had not apprised them of the opportunities. Now there are internships for black, Hispanic, and Asian people. I am now involved with a group working with the Department of Environmental Conservation and the EPA Federal Facilities group.

WHAT ARE SOME OF THE GOALS OF ENVIRONMENTAL JUSTICE?

The goal of environmental justice is to set standards to protect health. That means setting standards to protect the most vulnerable individual. There is low-level exposure causing problems. We need to protect the health and the environment, not corporate bank accounts. With regard to Superfund, environmental justice looks at placing the burden on foreseeable conduct that causes harm. It was legal in the past to excuse these acts, but since it was foreseeable that it would cause harm, these companies need to clean up sites that they contaminated.

Environmental justice looks to create justice in those communities where there have been a disproportionate number of dump sites that affect the health of those living there. It looks to create ways to have an equitable distribution of risk in all communities, not just poor and disadvantaged neighborhoods. If there was equitable distribution, there would undoubtedly be higher standards to protect the health of the most vulnerable individuals in our society.

HOW CAN PEOPLE GET INVOLVED?

People who want to do work in environmental justice need to realize that there is plenty of work. Businesspeople can ask questions such as what companies are doing with regard to pollution prevention, existing systems, leaking valves. Businesses need to ask themselves how they are handling their disposal practices, identify where waste is going, and make sure that it is going to a properly run facility. Community groups can start surveying community resources and working with planning agencies. There is opportunity to take ISTEA (Intermodal Surface Transportation Efficiency Act) money and work to lessen automobile traffic. Minority and poor communities suffer from air pollution; 86 to 90 percent of the people of color live in urban areas. Community grassroots organizations, local environmental community groups, law students can all work toward improved environmental quality.

The worst environmental ills are found in poor and people of color neighborhoods. By improving the quality of life, there will be ramifications for people of color and the poor. Economic development projects need to be carefully analyzed to make sure that communities benefit. If they designate a community for a hazardous waste site, contractors need to provide adequate training and clothing materials. Programs need to be carried out with safeguards such as showers for rinsing potentially toxic materials off clothing. Environmental justice is a broadened view of environmentalism—it isn't just looking at a sewage treatment plant. It is looking at the placement of bus depots, homes, buildings that are suitable for inclusion on historic registers. People need to be aware of line items for environmental community projects—such as open space for parks. People need to look at every issue: industrial land, emission loads, thoroughfare to other places, spill-off from highways, transportation analysis to see how quickly one can get to a hospital. There are a broad range of community issues that are part of the environmental justice movement. It includes economic development activities and making sure that people from communities are participants in the decision-making concerning economic development. This ensures that projects aren't imposed on the community but are chosen through a more participatory democratic process.

Consulting

James W. Armstrong, *Certified Safety Personnel, is President of JWA and Associates, an environmental and safety consulting firm based in Racine, Wisconsin. Over the years, he has worked with multinational corporations in more than fifteen countries.*

COULD YOU GIVE US SOME INSIGHT INTO YOUR SAFETY AND ENVIRONMENTAL EXPERIENCE?

I started in safety and fire protection as a management trainee for Republic Steel Corporation in Cleveland, Ohio, in the early 1960s. I was there when the Cuyahoga River caught on fire. Pollution in the 1960s and 1970s was everywhere, including the Great Lakes. This was before the U.S. Congress decided to create the environmental protection and occupational safety agencies as independent units of government as we know them today.

ARE THERE DIFFERENCES IN ENVIRONMENTAL AND SAFETY CONCERNS INTERNATIONALLY?

The differences are usually related to local culture and economy. In developing countries—Nigeria, Ghana, and China, for example—people have a high concern for both safety and their environment, but they have limited resources and may not be as advanced in applying technology as other, more developed countries. South America and even some areas of Europe are struggling with the concept of sustainable development.

WHAT TRENDS DO YOU SEE IN EUROPE?

Chernobyl, Sandoz, and pollution of the Rhine and North Sea have not gone unnoticed by the population. There is a strong undertone of family concern for safe food supplies and green products. Watch regulation for recycling of products.

After thirty years of little coordination among environmental policies in Europe, a wide-ranging reform effort is taking shape. The European court has ruled that environmental protection can take priority over trade under common market treaties.

Watch the European environmental agency anchor its policy in the EC governing charter. There will be more political and business economic incentives to protect national environmental interests. How long will it take before all products are recyclable? How long will it take before European and U.S. environmental requirements converge?

DO YOU EXPECT THIS TREND WILL CONTINUE?

Yes, I see the 1990s as a period in which social interests will influence investments in companies and products that minimize environmental impact. Companies that demonstrate their commitment to environmentally safe practices will benefit from the economics of the environmental movement.

WHAT IS THE MOST PRESSING PROBLEM YOU SEE WITH REGARD TO THE ENVIRONMENT?

Most environmental professionals would answer air quality, water contamination, solid and hazardous waste, or discuss technical issues with end-of-pipe control. Some would talk about ozone depletion, Superfund, the Clean Air Act or some other regulation, or global warming.

I see all of the above, but in the context of world population and business expansion in a global economy. I have heard predictions that world population will grow from five billion today to between eight and fourteen billion by the mid-twenty-first century. At the same time, predictions of a tenfold increase in the size of the overall world economy are going to stretch natural resources and expand waste generation. The most pressing issue from this perspective is the need to develop new technology that will eliminate the words "waste" and "pollution" from our vocabulary. Perhaps TQM will eliminate all inefficiencies, or perhaps scientific breakthroughs are needed to eliminate waste and achieve global sustainable development.

WHAT EXPERIENCES GOT YOU INTERESTED IN THE ENVIRONMENT?

I spent the first years of my youth on a farm in northern Ohio. Raising animals and working fields puts one close to Mother Nature. Today I run a small Christmas tree farm as a hobby. Following my formal education, I started my business life in the steel mills. Fire, dust, noise, vats of steaming hot sulfuric acid with fumes attacking the building roofs, complaints from the neighbors of paint damage to their cars, odors in their backyards got my attention. My science and medical education focused my interest on health and environment impact of both employees and the community.

WHAT DO YOU RECOMMEND FOR PEOPLE TO KEEP ABREAST OF TRENDS AND STAY COMPETITIVE IN THEIR FIELD?

This is a three-part answer. Courses, reading, and professional groups.

Courses—there are hundreds offered each year, but the one or two I have found most valuable are those sponsored by the Conference Board (New York) or Arthur D. Little (Cambridge, Massachusetts). They present leading-edge information and allow contact with one's peers in progressive companies.

As to reading, the *Federal Register* is a bore but a must to stay abreast of the moving targets called regulation. The *Environmental Forum* and the *Environmental Law Reporter*, both from the Environmental Law Institute provide analysis of the law and how to interpret it.

For both reading and peer contact, many of the business trade groups provide environmental/safety forums. The Organizational Resources Counselors in Washington, D.C., and the National Association of Manufacturers are but two of several groups. *Prism*, published quarterly by A.D. Little, highlights environmental and management trends.

IN YOUR CAREER, WHAT DO YOU FEEL HAVE BEEN YOUR GREATEST ACCOMPLISHMENTS?

There are two actually. In the late 1960s, the CEO of my company received a call from Washington with a request for a company volunteer to work on a safety task force made up of government, industry, and private sector representatives *and* the American National Standards Institute. For over nine months, I attended meetings working on production and process safety standards, and then the working groups were disbanded. About a year later, Congress created OSHA, and OSHA adopted many of the standards our group had developed.

The second has been the ability to work with, and personally know, many of the environmental and safety leaders of the 1990s. None of us, as individuals, may have a significant influence in this profession; in networks and groups, there are great accomplishments, and seeing one's ideas adopted or implemented provides personal satisfaction.

WHAT INDUSTRY EXPERIENCE HAVE YOU HAD, AND WHAT HAVE YOU ENJOYED THE MOST?

Aerospace, aircraft, automotive, electronic communications, industrial tools, forest products, consumer products, commercial wall and furniture coverings, munitions, resort property, and sporting goods (tents, fishing lures, trolling motors, backpacking gear, bicycles, tennis balls, etc.).

The sporting goods and resort property industry are fun, as one can play with the products or services at the same time environmental safety issues of concern to manufacturing or the consumer are being addressed. That is not to say aerospace is not fun, but I do not know of many in the industry who have actually rode in their products.

HOW DO YOU SEE YOUR OWN ROLE WORKING WITH AN ORGANIZATION?

The answer is somewhat complex. It is my job to stimulate, assemble, and promote company-wide critical thinking on safety and environmental management; to assist in improving the safety and environmental performance of business through example and leadership; to promote a company-wide business ethic for safety and environmental management, doing what is right for the corporation; to help forge partnerships and relationships with other companies, government agencies, trade groups, and the communities in which the business is conducted.

Many times my role is to help management focus on a single issue that may be as simple as, "How does a company prevent accidents?," or it can be working with groups as they integrate environmental and safety issues with an overall business strategic plan.

Norma Dulin *is the manager of marketing and communications for Energy Simulation Specialists, Inc. (EES), where she pursues new projects and clients and serves as communications advisor to a technical staff of approximately eighteen engineers and architects. She received a B.A. degree with a dual major in biology and political science from Scripps College in 1984.*

WHAT IS ESS?

ESS is a consulting company that works on creating energy-efficient buildings and energy conservation programs. We perform computer modeling for building design and retrofit, assist utilities in developing and evaluating conservation programs, and design building automation systems that control and schedule energy consumption. Our projects range from Sony buildings in California to Motorola manufacturing facilities in Phoenix.

WHAT ARE THE ESSENTIAL SKILLS NEEDED FOR A POSITION IN MARKETING AND COMMUNICATIONS?

Learn to write in a variety of styles on a variety of subjects, not just promotional pieces. Learn about specific techniques from direct mail, advertising, and brochures. Learn to write a press release. Learn how to use a library and how to ask directed questions. Although your trade is marketing, you're only as good as your information and your interpretation of it. Learn something about graphic design and at least one word processing software package. Learn database software as well, so that you can create targeted lists. Marketing involves promotion, determining which products or services a company offers, how they are distributed in the market, and how they are priced. These types of decisions require an understanding of business operations, capitalization, and profitability. Classes in accounting and economics are highly useful. You also need to be comfortable with technical information. For instance, in my writing and communications projects, I write about concepts such as demand-side management, load-shape management, and end-use monitoring.

Everything I've done in marketing and communications requires three basic skills: information gathering, writing, and analytical thought. My writing projects include technical proposals, company background materials, staff qualifications, press releases, advertisements, sales-oriented letters, and direct-mail pieces. They all require the ability to "read" an audience, to research and anticipate the motivation and needs of the audience, and to effectively address those needs. In turn, that requires understanding of the industry and the forces shaping it at the time.

ANY OTHER THOUGHTS?

I am an enormous advocate of humanities-based undergraduate education. It is this broad view and understanding that is so critical in solving environmental problems. Those problems incorporate science, economics, philosophy, politics, international law and government, and a host of other disciplines. If we are to solve environmental problems, we must gather information from a variety of sources and find innovative, forward-looking answers. Those answers will not come from those who think from one perspective and perform their work according to steps carefully outlined by someone else.

John Ganzi *is president of Environment and Finance Research Enterprise, which consults to private industry and nongovernmental organizations on all aspects of how the environmental field and the financial service industry interrelate. Prior to creating this business, Mr. Ganzi worked for eleven years at Citibank. He has a B.S./B.A. in business management and economics from Georgetown University, an M.B.A. from the University of Michigan, and an M.A. in environmental studies from New York University. He resides in Durham, North Carolina.*

WHAT PROMPTED YOU TO START YOUR OWN BUSINESS?

I realized I wanted to do something that made a difference. What I was doing in traditional banking was not important to society or the world overall. A waking moment for me occurred during a heated discussion I was having for close to an hour with a client, another intelligent person, a person earning over a million dollars a year, about whether a credit card customer of ours should have a $750 or $600 credit limit. We compromised at a $650 credit limit, and I thought, "There has got to be something more meaningful I can do with my life and my skills."

HOW DID YOU GO ABOUT IT?

The next logical step was to figure out where my proper niche was. I looked at all the skills I had acquired in my eleven years of banking and asked myself and others in the environmental world how I could apply them. I founded Environmental Management Services and started to divide my time between multiple clients. My two main clients for over four years have been the Environmental Defense Fund (EDF), the large nonprofit, and Salomon, Inc., the parent to Salomon Brothers, the investment bank. At EDF I focus on banking relationship questions, while always looking for possible new services that EDF could offer to its members that would provide an added benefit to the member, and while helping to raise money for EDF's program areas. At Salomon Inc., I work with the environmental affairs vice president on a variety of environmental issues. In 1991 and 1992 we created an in-house directory of the best firms in the environmental services industry for use by all Salomon staff worldwide in their hiring of consultants, lawyers, and other environmentally focused professionals. Over the last two years I have focused primarily on the banking and deal support side of the equation, working heavily with Salomon Brothers line staff in making sure that all environmental aspects are reviewed on a transaction and that they are able to negotiate the best price and terms given the condition of the property or business involved.

WHAT ARE SOME OF YOUR CURRENT PROJECTS?

I am working with the United Nations Environment Programme to survey the top two hundred financial services companies worldwide about their environmental practices and policies. Besides my long-term relationships with EDF and Salomon, I also teach a course at New York Universities Management Institute. The course focuses on the environmental challenges and opportunities facing the financial services industry. At the National Audubon Society, I have just completed a two-year project that focused on estimating how they respond to the tens of thousands of public inquiries they receive each year.

WHAT DO YOU SEE AS THE MAJOR ENVIRONMENTAL PROBLEM FACING OUR WORLD?

The biggest issue facing humankind is our ability or inability to quantify the value of traditionally "free natural things." Right now a dolphin is not worth anything, nor is a mango tree. We don't even see clean water or air as having any value. We don't put a price on it, but everything in our society is economics based. Full-cost accounting is a step in the right direction. Another environmental challenge is who will provide the leadership needed for change. Nonprofits have traditionally been run by lawyers and scientists, not managers, and they do not have the power, which in our society is driven by economics. You need business to lead the change for two reasons: money, and management skills for full-scale change.

HOW CAN ONE FIND WORK IN THE ENVIRONMENTAL FIELD?

There are two ways you can enter the environmental field—through networking or volunteering. Networking is simply being tenacious. It's making one or two contacts, getting to meet those people, and then asking them for the names of other people you can talk to. Leave each networking session with two or three names. Continue to build on networking opportunities. Given the need for good people, it is just a function of time before you are networking with someone who needs your skills. Once you've established good relationships, maintain them! They will remember to call on you. Networking and continuing to follow up are critical. That is how all my jobs came about. The other way to get in, especially in the nonprofit sector, is to volunteer. This means that if you are a lawyer, offer to do pro bono legal research; if you are in public relations, work in the media department; if you work in sales, volunteer in fund-raising and development; if you're a controller or accountant, offer to work in the financial control area.

There will be a multitude of environmental jobs in the future in the private, public, and nonprofit sectors. Many opportunities will be available in the fast-growing environmental manufacturing and service sectors. Many of these organizations lack experienced management and could make good use of a person with management, financial control, or marketing expertise. Make sure you educate yourself first, have that knowledge base, and then network like crazy.

Gail Miller *is a senior associate at Coopers & Lybrand, an accounting firm, where she works on various environmental projects. She received a B.A. in legal studies from the University of California at Berkeley in 1984 and an*

M.B.A. in marketing and international management from the University of Pennsylvania in 1991.

WHAT DO YOU DO ON THE JOB IN A TYPICAL DAY?

A combination of client project work and business development (writing proposals, attending conferences, following up on client contacts).

HOW DID YOU GET THIS JOB?

Believe it or not, my résumé did all the work. My background is a blend of litigation experience and environmental work, and our environmental team is part of our litigation group. My skills are applicable to both.

WHAT IS THE KEY TO GETTING A JOB IN ENVIRONMENTAL CONSULTING AND ACCOUNTING PROJECTS?

The skills that are in constant need are knowledge of environmental litigation and risk-management issues, cost-accounting skills, some knowledge of process and/or manufacturing, pollution prevention principles, management systems and internal control techniques, and total quality management.

HOW DID YOU BECOME INTERESTED IN ENVIRONMENTAL ISSUES AS THEY RELATE TO A BIG-SIX ACCOUNTING FIRM?

As the big-six firms diversify into areas beyond traditional audit services, they are gaining expertise in systems areas such as information systems, risk management, litigation, activity-based management, mergers and acquisitions, etc. This diversity of service offerings allows us to offer a multidisciplinary approach to environmental issues. In addition, I think the independent, quantitative ethic of accounting firms is a positive benefit to clients.

WHAT CIRCUMSTANCES OR EXPERIENCES INFLUENCED YOUR DECISION?

I chose Coopers & Lybrand for several reasons: (1) transfer or exchange opportunities are possible, given the size of the company; (2) the work is diverse; and (3) the quality of the people here is top-notch.

HOW CAN OTHERS ENTER THIS FIELD?

Do things in your spare time: take environmental courses, ask to be put on environmental task forces at work.

WHAT KINDS OF CHALLENGES DO BUSINESSES FACE WITH REGARD TO ENVIRONMENTAL RISK?

With CERCLA being reauthorized this year, some liability issues are up in the air. However, more proactive companies are leaving the regulatory requirements behind and designing environmental systems that define their notions of risk and manage to minimize those risks, sometimes beyond regulatory requirements.

HOW DO YOU SEE THE NOTION OF FULL-COST ACCOUNTING COMING INTO THE MAINSTREAM OF CORPORATE AMERICA?

Some corporations are beginning to implement environmental-cost accounting systems now, but none are beyond the initial stages of analyzing internal costs. Until these systems are up and running, it will be difficult to extend them to include external costs, required under a total cost-assessment approach.

WHAT TRENDS DO YOU SEE AFFECTING THE BIG-SIX BUSINESS OPPORTUNITIES WITH REGARD TO ENVIRONMENTAL LIABILITIES, ENVIRONMENTAL AUDITS, DISCLOSURES?

Environmental disclosures are a hot topic right now. The SEC rules have fully come into effect, and everyone is struggling with the positive and negative trade-offs of environmental disclosures. A related issue is environmental annual reports, which are becoming refined as a result of published standards, such as those being promulgated by GEMI. Adding more quantitative teeth to these reports, as well as coordinating financial and environmental reports for consistency, is an emerging issue.

WHERE DO YOU SEE JOB GROWTH IN AREAS OF ENVIRONMENTAL ACCOUNTING AND CONSULTING?

Environmental accounting and information systems, environmental management systems, third-party reviews of environmental systems and reports, and integration of international environmental standards for multinationals.

WHAT SKILLS ARE NEEDED TO ENTER THIS FIELD?

Excellent writing, quantitative and presentation skills, organization skills, and the ability to see connections between seemingly unrelated concepts.

WHAT ARE YOUR FAVORITE ENVIRONMENTAL BOOKS OR MAGAZINES?

BNA Environmental Reporter (weekly) and *Access EPA*, a guide to EPA departments, as well as publicly available databases, libraries, information lines, etc.

WHERE DO YOU GO FOR INSPIRATION?

I have a really terrific manager who is always coming up with new ideas, views, perspectives, etc. His ability to see different sides of environmental issues inspires me to think creatively. Also, my husband and family are very supportive and help me to deal with the stress that is inevitable in consulting.

WHAT IS THE MOST PRESSING PROBLEM YOU SEE WITH REGARD TO THE ENVIRONMENTAL INDUSTRY?

Inability to quantify environmental costs and benefits so that management decisions are based on measurable, objective data rather than assumptions and gut feelings.

WHAT DO YOU RECOMMEND PEOPLE TO DO WHO ARE INTERESTED IN ENVIRONMENTAL CAREERS?

Environmental issues are too varied, complex, and far-reaching to be learned all at once. Pick a topic that interests you and concentrate on that. Strangely enough, I've found that most environmental issues are related in some way, and you will learn about other issues as they relate to your core topic.

ANY SUGGESTIONS, WISDOM GLEANED FROM EXPERIENCE?

Assess the skills, training, education, and experience you have gained in the past and evaluate how those attributes would fit with an environmental career. Fill in the gaps you identify and keep learning. Keep trying!

Maria Moyer-Angus *is an independent consultant for the Gap. She has a B.A. in East Asian studies and Chinese language from UCLA. She designed and developed the first official recycling program at UCLA in 1988 and since 1990 has been employed by Brown, Vence and Associates (BVA), a waste management and energy consulting firm in San Francisco. She has public and private sector consulting experience and draws on her broad academic*

and professional consulting background with her work at the Gap and other projects in solid waste and recycling. She volunteers at the Earth Island Institute and the Sierra Club and is a board member of Brush Dance, Inc., a recycled-product gift company in the Bay area.

HOW DID YOU GET YOUR JOB AT THE GAP?

A good friend of mine is vice president of an LA-based consulting firm called E2, which is contracted by the Gap to do green building and energy-efficiency work. In early 1993, she and her partner introduced me to the Gap's CFO, Bob Fisher, who leads the Gap's environmental practice. I shared with him some of the ideas that I had developed on managing this growing environmental effort at the Gap. Soon thereafter, we began working together.

After years of consulting with BVA, I've developed an ability to manage complex projects that require my technical knowledge and an ability to facilitate processes that involve many parties with varying degrees of responsibility. This is valuable experience that I use in working at the Gap, where most of the people in the Gap's Environmental Organization (GEO) are volunteers with primary responsibility in other areas.

WHAT IS A TYPICAL WORK DAY LIKE FOR YOU?

I work with members of GEO, which is comprised of employees from every department, to facilitate decisions (which include environmental criteria) on issues such as clothing manufacture, store design and construction, purchasing, shipping and transportation, and recycling. I work with GEO members to develop achievable work plans, and I help them to make progress on the tasks they set out to achieve.

The most pressing challenges GEO faces are those associated with manufacturing clothes, building stores, and developing effective educational tools and communication venues to ensure that every employee—all 40,000 of them—has access to information that will aid them in making environmentally educated decisions. The Gap does not own its own mills or factories but is sharing responsibility for the environmental impacts of clothing manufacture with facility owners. The Gap educates contractors about alternatives to conventional laundering and dying practices and is making significant efforts toward incorporating into clothing organic and naturally colored cotton, recycled cotton fabrications, low-impact dyes, and alternatives to stonewashing, and electroplated fasteners. The Gap's architects, store designers, and building planners use recycled, low-toxic building materials and energy-efficient lighting and mechanical systems to create sensible retail and office spaces.

Since I have been at the Gap, I have been consistently impressed by the environmental ethic of the Gap's CFO and the Gap's ability to embrace this challenge with the high level of creativity and energy you see in their stores. GEO has been at work since 1990, but the Gap hasn't talked much about these efforts publicly. That is because GEO's been too busy trying to figure out what an effective, company-wide environmental practice looks like.

WHAT IS YOUR ADVICE TO OTHERS?

Read everything! Books on environmental management abound. My favorite journals are *Environmental Action* and *Earth Island Journal.* Volunteer. There is no substitute for experience, and volunteering is one way to receive as much experience as you have the energy and time to give.

WHAT DO YOU SEE AS THE MOST PRESSING ENVIRONMENTAL PROBLEMS?

Biodiversity loss and species extinction. Drinking-water aquifer contamination.

WHERE DO YOU SEE YOURSELF IN FIVE TO TEN YEARS?

Although I have done some endangered species preservation work in Asia, I hope to use my East Asian studies background and Chinese language skills in addressing the ecological issues in Asia that are shared by all developing countries. I am currently exchanging ideas with contacts in Asia-related government departments and global financial entities. Though preliminary, there seems to be a mutual interest in working together.

***Nina Orville** is an independent environmental consultant based in New York City, where she works for a range of companies and nonprofit organizations. Her services include identifying sources of raw materials, handcrafts, and manufactured goods with strong international market potential that provide social and environmental benefits to the producers, and developing* *marketing strategies for such products. She earned a B.A. from Oberlin College in 1985 with majors in government and history and is now enrolled in the M.B.A. program at Columbia.*

WHAT IS YOUR EMPLOYMENT HISTORY?

After graduation from college, I sought employment opportunities in Latin America. This led to two years working in orphanages in Mexico and Central America. During this time, I became aware of the appalling lack of choices available to the rural poor. I began to explore the concept of assisting marginalized people to strengthen their position by harnessing the power of international markets. This interest led to a small Latin American crafts-importing venture and ultimately to Cultural Survival.

DESCRIBE YOUR WORK AT CULTURAL SURVIVAL.

Cultural Survival, a nonprofit human rights organization assisting indigenous people, established an innovative division, Cultural Survival Enterprises (CSE), in 1989. CSE provided technical assistance and marketing services to indigenous peoples and other forest residents producing goods for the international market. Our goal was to assist forest peoples living on undisturbed lands to be involved in sustainable forms of agroforestry, or reforesting degraded lands.

As trade manager, I was responsible for managing the purchase of goods (such as nuts, oils, and crafts) from producers in four continents and the sale of those goods to manufacturers such as Ben and Jerry's and The Body Shop. In addition, I evaluated new sources and assisted in the development of marketing strategies and PR.

HOW DID YOU BECOME INTERESTED IN ENVIRONMENTAL ISSUES?

I became interested in environmental issues primarily through my commitment to promoting human rights and economic development. Land rights and natural resource management are often the primary challenges facing native peoples and rural poor.

WHAT TRENDS CAN YOU IDENTIFY IN YOUR FIELD?

I have noted a broader recognition of the links between conservation, economic development, and human rights. Environmental conservation organizations are now more likely to consider the needs of local peoples in the elaboration of conservation plans. Likewise, development organizations and agencies are more likely to consider the ecological implications of economic development initiatives. This trend toward a more holistic vision is encouraging.

WHERE DO YOU SEE JOBS FOR PEOPLE IN THE ENVIRONMENTAL FIELD?

I am enthusiastic about ventures that are economically self-sustaining. Though the rain forest wave (ridden and, in part, created by Cultural Survival) has peaked, corporate and consumer interest in environmentally sound products in general continues to deepen. I also feel that opportunities for collaboration between nonprofit organizations and for-profit companies will continue to burgeon. Dovetailing of interests between these types of entities is common and they often have expertise and resources that are complementary.

WHAT CAN PEOPLE DO TO GET INVOLVED IN THE DIALOGUE ABOUT SUSTAINABLE DEVELOPMENT AND MAKE A DIFFERENCE IN THEIR OWN LIVES?

The first step, of course, is to educate ourselves. There is a wealth of information available now through publications and conferences about the overlapping issues of conservation, population, and development.

WHERE DO YOU GO FOR INSPIRATION?

I have found that the more deeply involved I become with the field of environmentally sound development, the more charged I become with my travels. During a visit to Indonesia as a U.S.-Asia Environmental Partnership Fellow, I witnessed development pressures and resultant human rights violations and environmental destruction remarkably similar to that found in parts of Latin America. The challenges are similar around the world, and it is very useful to be able to recognize these universal patterns.

ANY SUGGESTIONS GLEANED FROM YOUR EXPERIENCE?

Identify your strengths and be strategic in choosing a field or a position that allows you to build on them. Stay alert for opportunities to collaborate with other entities and individuals with similar goals and complementary methods or resources.

Jacquelyn A. Ottman *is founder and president of J. Ottman Consulting Inc., advisors to industry on how to develop and promote environmentally* *sound consumer products. Her firm's clients include Colgate-Palmolive, Kraft General Foods, DuPont, General Electric, and Eastman-Kodak. She is the author of* Green Marketing: Challenges and Opportunities for the New Marketing Age *(NTC Business Books, 1993). She is also a co-author of* Environmental Consumerism: What Every Marketer Needs to Know *(Alert Publishing, 1991), and she edited the* Green Marketing Anthology *(1994), a compendium of her speeches and writings. Ms. Ottman also edits* The Ottman Report, *a quarterly newsletter on environmental marketing and green product development. She is a featured columnist for* American Marketplace.

HOW DID YOU COME TO START J. OTTMAN CONSULTING?

I founded J. Ottman Consulting to satisfy some long-held desires to become an entrepreneur and consultant, and to work in the areas of trend watching and analysis, new product concept development, and information services.

As a consultant to an advertising agency I began researching environmental issues for new business. We figured that "the environment" (air and water pollution, solid waste, ozone layer depletion, food contamination) was going to be a hot issue for marketers of packaged goods in the 1990s.

It was through this project that I became aware of the seriousness of environmental issues (and started to change my habits); realized that my colleagues in the business had no clue as to what was happening; realized that there was very little information publicly available on the implications of environmental issues for marketing and new product development; discovered I had a knack for extrapolating the implications of environmental issues for marketing as well as for creating exciting concepts for new, more environmentally sound products and packages; and concluded that there was a niche for a marketing and new-product development consultant who could help marketers of packaged goods understand and act positively on the issues.

In 1989, I founded J. Ottman Consulting "to help corporate America develop the next generation of products designed with the environment in mind."

WHAT IS THE AREA THAT YOU ARE MOST INTERESTED IN RIGHT NOW?

Helping my clients use ecological processes, materials, and designs as inspiration in creating concepts for new green products.

For the past two years I have spent practically all of my free time researching how nature works and integrating my learning with creativity and innovation techniques I learned while in the advertising business. In fact, nature's processes are at the heart of the Getting to Zero® process I created. The process involves teaching client teams about how nature works and then using that learning to generate new products—products that, for example, "think in circles" (are reusable, recyclable, refillable), as opposed to being linear (destined to make a one-way trip from manufacturing plant to landfill).

I am very excited about the potential for educating corporate America about ecological principles. I believe if we all started to appreciate and internalize how nature works, then we all would have much simpler, more productive, meaningful personal and work lives.

***James A. Rogers** is president of Rogers Environmental Management, Inc. (REM), a New Jersey–based compliance management firm with three major business markets: comprehensive environmental, occupational, health, and safety compliance management for operating manufacturers; litigation support for federal and state cases; and the usual remedial investigatory and management consulting. Mr. Rogers is also partner and vice president with Green Village Technology, a company which designs, packages, and sells environmental control, monitoring, and measurement technologies to domestic and international markets. He previously served as director of Continental Waste Industries, Inc., a publicly traded solid-waste collection and disposal company headquartered in Clark, New Jersey, with major operations and landfills in the Midwest. In spring 1994, Mr. Rogers visited the People's Republic of China as a member of a trade delegation inspecting petrochemical and petroleum refineries for health, safety, and environmental problems through the sponsorship of the Citizens Ambassador Program.*

WHAT IS ROGERS ENVIRONMENTAL MANAGEMENT, INC.?

REM occupies a unique niche within the environmental industry due to our history and perception of fundamental changes in the international economy. Our response to the market concurs with the international view that environment has permeated business. As a prime assumption, REM contends that the apparent conflict between economic productivity and environmental quality can be more accurately and ecologically described as symbiotic mutualism. Through its work for clients, REM advocates an integration of these two seemingly disparate objectives. During the late 1980s, REM welcomed and then marketed the change from inspection of individual pollution sources of effluent and emissions to facility-wide pollution prevention programs. For sophisticated clients, REM has assisted with the transition from doing business as usual to pollution prevention planning and total (environmental) quality management (TEQM). REM has itself progressed from simply remediating past problems to preventing future incidents, through what we call comprehensive compliance management. What this means for the client is an intense professional focus on facility-wide aspects of liabilities derived from environmental and occupational health regulations.

As a corollary, REM believes that competitiveness is achieved through compliance. It begins with our intense review of process from the perspective of management. That is, if a product is made using less energy and with fewer raw materials and its manufacture generates less waste and fewer emissions, then it will be made more efficiently and, in turn, more competitively. Thus, compliance with regulations becomes integrated with quality performance.

WHAT IS YOUR WORK HISTORY?

Except for a summer internship with the Council on Environmental Quality in 1974, I have been working as a consultant to industry with a disciplinary foundation in chemistry. I have found an understanding of broad chemical principles to be most helpful, even in policy debates. Without a basis in science, the practice of politics and the implementation of policy occur in a vacuum. While working with two firms in Washington, D.C., New York City, Denver, and Newark, I realized early on that lack of equity meant little control over one's destiny. In resolving to become an owner, I have been involved with three start-ups, two of which I served as sole principal, growing two firms and selling one. Since 1974, I have worked within every environmental regulatory program at the federal level, from RCRA to FWPCA to CAAA to SDWA to SMCRA to ToSCA to OSHA and pesticides and radiation. On the state level, the New Jersey consultancy covered not only the above regs but also ECRA/ISRA, BUST, TCPA, PEOSHA, RTK and risk-based cleanup standards. Clients have included manufacturers of chemicals, rubber, pharmaceuticals, electronics, aircraft/automotive parts, machine and metal products, cosmetics, flavors, fragrances, plastics, and vitamins; also, developers, investors, professionals, BOMA members, contractors, solid and hazardous and c&d waste haulers, disposers, collectors, and recyclers.

EXPLAIN YOUR VIEW OF JOBS VS. THE ENVIRONMENT.

This conflict is a red herring, a creation of demagogues attempting to mislead, based on outdated concepts. First of all, factories close for reasons of technology, market, capital, skills of available labor, and mismanagement, not environmental regulations. Second, more jobs are created by environmental regulation than are lost to restrictions for purposes of preserving a species or quality of groundwater.

WHAT ABOUT INTERNATIONAL MARKETS FOR JOB GROWTH?

The demand for U.S. development of environmental technologies and services overseas cannot be underestimated. There is a potential for hundreds of billions of dollars of sales of high value-added capital goods to developing economies. The Rio Conference on the Environment, and the Cairo Conference on Population have developed marvelous concepts and language that shape the conceptual framework for "green manufacturing." However, there is a vacuum of leadership at the national level and a similarly sized market to be filled by small U.S. businesses. The United States has nearly twenty-five years' experience with environmental regulation; the states have adapted national mandates to specific situations (and sometimes extremes) in implementing their own versions of environmental statutes. Working across state lines prepares one for differences in cultural and sociological uses of natural resources. For example, why does China have very little waste? Why were Germany and Japan able in the 1970s and 1980s to make products using half the energy and one-quarter the materials as U.S. factories? There are cultural and sociological reasons, but we have the technologies. Despite the cultural gap, the demand for American expertise and technology will grow dramatically as the U.S. economy leads the world in productivity over the next few years and in environmental solutions over the next decades. The fact that China uses a billion tons of coal annually suggests several alternative strategies for limiting pollution: conservation, alternative fuels, alternative sources (solar), alternative technologies.

WHAT ENVIRONMENTAL TRENDS AND CHALLENGES DO YOU FORESEE IN THE NEXT THIRTY YEARS?

REM and its affiliates will operate offices in other countries in the next five years. Manufacturing within environmental guidelines will continue to evolve. Recently, leading international manufacturers have increased the green component in their products, parts of which can be recycled or reclaimed at the end of their useful life.

Additionally, when used as intended, these products generate fewer emissions and less waste. Over the next decade, all corporations will improve manufacturing by becoming more efficient in the use of energy and materials, or they will cease to be competitive. Thus, environmental quality becomes just one more incentive for economic productivity.

WHAT PUBLICATIONS AND ENVIRONMENTAL RESOURCES DO YOU SUGGEST?

There's too much to read; here's a suggested list: *Scientific American, Science, Technology Review, Environmental Science & Technology, Chemical Week, Waste Tech News, The New York Times* Science Section, *Journal of the Air & Waste Management Association.* Also trade publications such as *Hydrocarbon Processing, Metal Finishing, Plating & Surface Finishing;* economic periodicals such as *The China Daily Business Weekly, The Far Eastern Economic Review, The Economist.* Local sources include *Northern New Jersey Business* and the *New Jersey Industrial News* and the many environmental law letters and newsletters from environmental groups. That's a lot of reading, but it's essential to the professional practice.

John Sherwin *is president of J.L. Sherwin & Associates, Inc., an environmental consulting firm that is helping companies to improve profits, enhance their public image, and prepare for "rates and dates" legislation through packaging reduction, reuse, and recycling. His approach is to provide companies with an analysis of environmental information about their packaging so they can effectively plan, monitor, and report efforts to improve packaging and increase overall company value. He has a B.S. in finance and economics from Lehigh University and an M.B.A. in marketing and international business from New York University.*

WHAT DO YOU DO ON THE JOB?

J.L. Sherwin & Associates was started to help firms increase the reduction, reuse, and recycled content of their packaging. Much of our work centers around the use of a computer model called Smart Pak® that maintains and processes environmental information about our clients' packaging. This form of information management is the key to having a well-managed packaging source-reduction program. On a daily basis, we talk with prospective clients to educate them about the benefits of managing packaging reduction using our strategic process. In addition, we work with several associations to further the goals of source reduction and enhance the benefits for companies who participate in this activity.

PLEASE TELL US ABOUT YOUR CAREER BACKGROUND.

I started my career at Nabisco Foods Company, initially in finance and culminating in brand marketing. After receiving an M.B.A. from NYU I decided I would apply my consumer product marketing and business management skills to some sector of environmental business. I looked at environmental consulting, not-for-profit, the government, and environmental product management. After many informational interviews and phone conversations, I was able to directly transfer my consumer product marketing experience into an environmental marketing position.

Happenstance led me to a division of Warner-Lambert called Novon Products that was marketing a new biodegradable material that could be made into packaging and products that could then be organically recycled into the soil after use. For the next year and a half I became Novon's manager of product positioning, responsible for educating consumers about new biodegradable materials and nature's age-old recycling method called composting.

WHAT PROCESS DID YOU GO THROUGH TO CREATE THIS COMPANY?

While at Novon, I worked with a Canadian consultant who had developed an information management approach to help firms in Canada satisfy government packaging regulations. After analyzing what companies were doing in Canada, I realized that the approach they were taking would also be appropriate for companies in the United States who are driven by an interest in cost savings, state legislative compliance, and positive consumer relations. So I started J.L. Sherwin & Associates to help companies gain these competitive advantages through environmental packaging efforts.

WHAT DO YOU SEE AS THE MAJOR TRENDS WITHIN YOUR INDUSTRY?

The major trend in this industry is the specialization and finding of very specific niches that environmental consultants can use to create value for their clients.

WHAT ARE YOUR WORK PRIORITIES WITH REGARD TO ENVIRONMENTAL ISSUES AND PROJECTS?

One of my main goals is to get source reduction and reuse as waste-reduction activities to take their rightful place above, or at least next to, recycling. It seems that in this country we have embraced recycling and forgotten about the other alternatives for solid-waste management. In a larger sense, I believe that packaging as it contributes to our solid-waste management problems is a subset of a more major issue, natural resource conservation. Overpopulation and poverty are also serious environmental issues.

WHERE DO YOU SEE JOB GROWTH IN YOUR FIELD?

When you consider the environmental job market, consider also the development of environmental issues over time. Consumers and environmentalists seized solid-waste management as the issue of the day and packaging waste became a rallying cry because of its visibility. Even the perception of an environmental problem creates job opportunities. I see plenty of other opportunities in the environmental market, including new product development and marketing, compliance of all types, government opportunities—at local levels as more community programs are developed and at the state and national levels as more regulation is proposed—and in environmental consulting as opportunities present themselves in all of these areas.

WHAT SKILLS ARE NEEDED TO ENTER THIS FIELD?

The skills needed to start your own business are the same for any industry, including the environment. Technical expertise is necessary in varying degrees depending on the type of business you start. I can't overemphasize interpersonal skills, and if your business goes international, cultural awareness is a must. As with most consultants, the ability to market yourself and to position your service as needed is paramount.

WHAT DO YOU READ AND RECOMMEND FOR PEOPLE TO KEEP ABREAST OF TRENDS AND TO STAY COMPETITIVE IN THIS FIELD?

As an environmental business consultant focusing on packaging issues, I stay on top of the packaging trade journals *(Packaging, Packaging Digest)* and the solid-waste and recycling journals *(Waste Age, Waste World, BioCycle, Environment Today)*. But even more important than all of these combined is the need to read the newspaper (if not more than one) on a daily basis. I try to read the *New York Times* every day to stay current. I also try to read a futuristic magazine to keep my mind open to future trends and possibilities. I am a member of the World Future Organization, and their magazine satisfies this need.

However, reading is less than half of the battle. Finding other experts in many different forums related to your particular field of endeavor is the best way to become an expert yourself. For example, based on my need to become an expert in packaging as it relates to the environment, source reduction, reuse, recycling, and recycled content, I became a member of several organizations including the Institute of Packaging Professionals (IoPP), the Coalition of Northeastern Governors (CONEG), and the National Recycling Coalition (NRC), as well as Businesses for Social Responsibility (BSR). Through my leadership, participation, and meeting of other experts in these organizations, I hope to learn enough to become an expert myself one day. The basic requirements for most of your efforts in this arena are energy and desire.

Rena Shulsky *is founder and chair of GreenAudit, Inc., a consulting firm based in New York City, which provides companies with an independent assessment of their environmental performance. She is also the founder and chair emeritus of Green Seal, a national environmental seal-of-approval program that rewards products that are environmentally superior. Ms. Shulsky is also a founding member of the Social Venture Network, a member of the executive board of the Harvard Journal of World Affairs, a board member of the Center for Sustainable Development and Alternative World Futures, and a member of the advisory board of Ecotech. She has a B.A. in political science from Boston University.*

WHAT ARE THE GOALS OF YOUR COMPANY?

Helping every organization and corporation achieve a meaningful standard of environmental excellence. Fostering both the planetary shift toward valuing environmental excellence as much as maximizing profits, and the realization that the two goals are not mutually exclusive.

WHAT DO YOU DO ON THE JOB?

Oversee all aspects of the mission of the company, including monitoring our testing services; delivering assessment and audit services to clients; establishing procedures and processes specific to each client; recruitment of personnel; a host of administrative tasks; and ensuring that the delivery of our services is most effective in serving the needs of the client and the planet. A typical day involves extensive discussion with the acting CEO and other key personnel regarding our clients and services.

WHAT DO YOU SEE AS THE MAJOR TRENDS IN ENVIRONMENTAL AUDITING?

The European Union's initiatives toward environmental regulation; the changing ISO standards; the burgeoning recognition that began with socially responsible businesses but is seeping quickly into the mainstream of the need to go beyond regulatory compliance and become proactive environmentally; the emerging realization of the compatibility of environmental consciousness with profitability.

HOW DID YOU GO ABOUT CREATING YOUR COMPANY?

I perceived a need for a proactive environmental auditing and assessment company that would help companies and organizations go beyond regulatory compliance and achieve environmental excellence. I then recruited appropriate staff and let people know of the existence of our new company. Our debut was at Ecotech.

WHAT ARE YOUR WORK PRIORITIES WITH REGARD TO ENVIRONMENTAL ISSUES?

To keep abreast of global developments and regulations and know where the cutting edge is; maintaining up-to-date contact with the scientific community to ensure that GreenAudit's procedures and processes always remain cutting edge.

WHAT SKILLS ARE NEEDED TO ENTER YOUR FIELD?

A strong commitment to do the right thing without compromise, a knowledge of business, a broad awareness of the environmental issues, and a large Rolodex.

WHAT PUBLICATIONS DO YOU RECOMMEND?

Embracing Earth: New Views of Our Changing Planet by Payson

Stevens; all books by Hazel Henderson, especially *Paradigms in Progress,* the *Environment Newsletter,* the *Green Business Letter, E Magazine; The Ecology of Commerce* by Paul Hawken; *Green is Black* by Ted Saunders.

WHAT EXPERIENCES GOT YOU INTERESTED IN THE ENVIRONMENT AS PART OF YOUR LIFE WORK?
Love Canal, Three Mile Island, Chernobyl, and having a number of friends get sick with illnesses directly traceable to toxics in the environment.

WHAT IS THE MOST PRESSING PROBLEM YOU SEE WITH REGARD TO THE ENVIRONMENT?
Because the problems are so insidious, and for the most part invisible, the public can ignore the problems until it's very late.

WHAT ARE THE MOST PRESSING CHALLENGES FACING YOU IN YOUR WORK?
Needing more hours in the day.

WHAT DO YOU RECOMMEND TO PEOPLE WHO ARE INTERESTED IN ENVIRONMENTAL CAREERS?
Become familiar with the broad gamut of issues and choose the one that's most interesting for you. Examine areas that aren't covered and think of new solutions. Then market your ideas and yourself to the relevant organizations or businesses.

ANY SUGGESTIONS, WISDOM GLEANED FROM YOUR EXPERIENCE?
Don't accept the conventional wisdom. Never take no, or it can't be done, for an answer. The world is full of naysayers; ignore them and do what you believe in. Do what you love. On a spiritual level, I believe that the planet will ultimately help you if you are sincerely and with integrity trying to help it.

***Nina Simons** is a marketing and public relations consultant to Seeds of Change and coproducer of the Bioneers Conference, a nonprofit project of the Gila International Center of Diversity (GICD), soon to be called the Common Heritage Institute (CHI). She has a B.A. in theatre management from Cornell University.*

Tell us about your career history and how you got involved with Seeds of Change.

Idealism led me toward a career in theatre, which I felt was a powerful medium to affect people's awareness and lead them to consider new ideas and points of view. After several years of working in professional theatre management, I met my partner, Kenny Ausebel, who was then completing a documentary feature film about alternative cancer therapies and the politics of medicine. I joined him to promote and market the film. I then went on to become the director of special projects for the Santa Fe Chamber Music Festival, becoming involved in grant writing, fund-raising, and event production. In 1989 Kenny cofounded Seeds of Change, the nation's first all-organic seed company, one committed to maintaining biodiversity. I became increasingly interested in the issues the company addressed. Not being a gardener, the notion of working to promote an organic seed company was somewhat alien to me. The more I learned about issues related to health, the environment, and the need for people to reconnect with nature and respect the fabric of diversity, the more I felt called to lend my voice to the vision of the company. Companies like Seeds of Change, whose very product is environmentally restorative, demonstrate that economics and the environment are not mutually exclusive.

I worked with Seeds of Change for about three and a half years, during which time I was variously director of sales, director of public relations and marketing, and the company's president. My current position, consulting with the company on public relations and marketing, evolved through a realization that my passion lay more in communications than in business management. As a communicator, I am sparked by the process of sharing complex and important ideas in a mainstream way.

What is your goal in "mainstreaming" environmental issues in your work?

All of the work I do involves mainstreaming environmental issues to the public: making the issues accessible and real and empowering people to feel that they can make a difference by engaging in the struggle to restore or preserve our environment. My strongest commitment is to move people to experience a connection with nature and the miraculous complexity of life that is around us. One of the most serious environmental ills is a crisis of spirit; people have lost their sense of relationship with the whole and have become detached, often in denial, about the severity of our planetary condition.

WHAT ARE THE CHALLENGES IN YOUR FIELD?

One of my primary interests is in coalition-building toward positive action. Too often, small interest groups focus on their particular interests, and miss opportunities to collaborate with others to form a stronger, more effective whole. What is most needed in the environmental work-world is people whose primary intent is to bridge the gaps, to create unity among disparate ecological agendas, and to lobby and conduct research within the system to affect change.

ANY ADVICE FOR OTHERS?

The most effective way to build an environmental career is to follow your passion, to find the area that most sparks your interest and embark on a long-term learning curve to educate yourself about the issues and about who else is out there doing related work. Whenever possible, I suggest connecting with an organization that is aligned with what you want to do. Starting new enterprises and getting them funded is an extremely difficult and long-term task. I am also a great believer in developing many skills, so that it is possible to respond to the various needs of an organization or movement without being pigeon-holed into one position.

George Vera *is a partner of Arthur Andersen, where he directs the Western Environmental Services practice. Prior to coming to California in 1990, he worked with Arthur Andersen in Boston for fourteen years, in Houston for four years, and in Vancouver for four years as an auditor and consultant serving large and small businesses. He received his undergraduate degree in chemistry in 1965 from Harvard University and his M.B.A. in finance from Harvard Business School in 1968.*

WHAT IS A TYPICAL DAY LIKE FOR YOU?

Since the Western Environmental Services practice for Arthur Andersen is a new practice, I spend my day interviewing and hiring people, developing marketing materials, calling on potential clients, and selling our new service line internally. The most challenging part of the job is preparing presentations that successfully present our qualifications to potential clients.

HOW DID YOU GET THIS JOB?

My firm saw the opportunity to assist companies to cost-effectively manage environmental functions and chose me to lead that activity in the California offices.

WHERE DO YOU SEE YOURSELF IN FIVE OR TEN YEARS?

Leading a rapidly growing management consultancy in the western United States that helps organizations (companies, regulatory agencies, and citizens groups) responsibly deal with environmental issues from a position of strength because they have solid information on environmental issues rather than simply speculating about environmental costs and achieving only minimal compliance.

WHAT STRENGTHS ARE IMPORTANT TO ENVIRONMENTAL CONSULTING AND ACCOUNTING PROJECTS?

You need to be comfortable with the role of consultant. You need to be able to sell yourself. An analytical approach to problem solving is crucial, as well as the ability to manage projects to a budget. A high energy level is needed, as is the ability to educate oneself on environmental issues.

HOW DID YOU BECOME INTERESTED IN ENVIRONMENTAL ISSUES AS THEY RELATE TO A BIG-SIX ACCOUNTING FIRM?

I saw many companies getting hit with large liabilities in connection with Superfund and other sites. I thought there was a way these companies could improve their internal procedures and approaches to reduce liabilities and keep compliance costs under control.

DO YOU SEE THE NOTION OF FULL-COST ACCOUNTING ENTERING MAINSTREAM CORPORATE AMERICA?

The Securities and Exchange Commission continually has been increasing the requirements for more comprehensive disclosures, both in audited financial statements and elsewhere in the annual reports of major companies. Environmental costs will have to be computed on a full-cost basis. There is really a long way to go, however, since many companies have limited ability to get the information to determine what these costs are. Our firm has just developed a new product called Eco-Accounting, which addresses this issue.

WHAT TRENDS DO YOU SEE AFFECTING ACCOUNTING FIRMS' BUSINESS OPPORTUNITIES WITH REGARD TO ENVIRONMENTAL LIABILITIES, ENVIRONMENTAL AUDITS, DISCLOSURES, ETC?

As the field matures from polarization and disputes to environmental groups and corporations working together, the need for reliable, timely information will grow exponentially. Some businesses now don't want to know their liabilities because ignorance is a good defense. As the business climate changes, accounting systems will need a major overhaul to identify, analyze, and present environmental costs properly. The environmental management field will grow like the computer field.

WHERE DO YOU SEE THE JOB GROWTH IN AREAS OF ENVIRONMENTAL ACCOUNTING AND CONSULTING?

I think that, by the year 2000, each of the big-six firms will have significant environmental consulting practices. They will be looked to as leaders in environmental management as it will then be defined. Most people today believe that environmental management involves managing compliance activities. It will become much broader than that in the future.

HOW CAN OTHERS ENTER YOUR FIELD?

The best way is to have an engineering or technical degree. Experience in an engineering firm is very helpful. Also getting an M.B.A. is crucial to understanding business issues, together with some work experience.

WHAT DO YOU READ AND RECOMMEND FOR PEOPLE TO STAY COMPETITIVE IN THIS FIELD?

The types of books most relevant at this point are reengineering and change management books such as *Reengineering the Corporation* by Michael Hammer and James Champy, and *Process Innovation* by Thomas Davenport.

WHAT IS THE MOST PRESSING PROBLEM YOU SEE WITH REGARD TO THE ENVIRONMENTAL INDUSTRY?

The industry needs to mature to the point where management skills are brought to bear on environmental problems and cost/benefit considerations. The lack of adequate information has hampered development in this area in the past. Now that better cost information is becoming available, this hoped-for maturing of the industry can become a reality.

Design & the Arts

Jean Blackburn *is an artist who lives in Williamsburg, New York. She received a B.F.A. from Rhode Island School of Design (RISD) with a major in painting and an M.F.A. from Yale Art School. She is currently a member of the adjunct faculty at RISD. When she isn't teaching, she is making art.*

HOW DID YOU GET INTERESTED IN ART AND THE ENVIRONMENT?

The three things I remember being fascinated by as a child were art, archeology, and the ocean. I grew up on the water, in Massachusetts and Rhode Island. The ability of the water to change from a placid, shimmering mirror into a raging storm-whipped froth has always held my interest. It has been a symbol for me of change, mystery, and boundlessness. In the first grade, I took drawing classes. I decided early on that art was what I really wanted to do. I also had an interest in archeology. Archeology made me aware of transitions in history and of how objects represent ideas, which create stories that are then woven into what we call history. People's experience of the present is shaped by the way they define the past. We have the power to investigate our past. Both artist and archeologist are curious; both dig—one into the earth and one into the subconscious—and unearth powerful artifacts, signs, or clues from which they build something that creates meaning.

I believe that the study of nature helps students see the diversity of strategies available to them for designing. Not only do my students become more observant of their surroundings, they become more aware of the links and similarities between the natural and creative process. If they can take these strategies back into the studio, they have a well of endless possibilities available to them.

WHAT DO YOU WANT TO TEACH YOUR STUDENTS ABOUT ART AND THE ENVIRONMENT?

My goal is to build awareness among students of how nature acts as a warehouse of possible configurations and forms. Students observe the sculptural forms that occur in nature, from spirals to geometric shapes to the actual architectural forms that shape our surroundings. An example of a form occurring in nature is the three-pronged equi-sided triangle (think of the Mercedes Benz triangle). It is the strongest of any structure—one finds it in insect wings, the way mud cracks to relieve tension, patterns in tree bark, and sea horses. The 120-degree angle between each two bars of the triangle acts as a building block, which you can also see in bubbles when they connect to each other.

After observing forms in nature, students then examine structural patterns found in architecture such as buildings and bridges. I then have my students look at theoretical issues such as time, history, and people's ideas about themselves. Students realize how myriad the possibilities are for people to see the same thing and structure it in a variety of ways. Students come away from the class being able to better observe and question how we set up structures to know the world, whether they be scientific or philosophical, and better understand the variety of possibilities before them.

HOW DOES YOUR ART RELATE TO NATURE?

My artwork speaks to the notion of things in flux, of things changing. I got cancer a few years ago, and as a result of my sickness, my life turned around. On the surface I looked fine, but my body had contracted cancer. Although I have recuperated, this experience changed my life. I now look at the appearances of things and question their inherent reality. Whether it's one's body that looks beautiful on the surface, or oceans that are calm and inviting, or air that appears clean to the eye and smells refreshing to the nose, we never really know what is going on under the surface. There can be cancer and disease ravaging a body, and air and oceans filled with pollution or toxins. I now question and try to uncover clues to what I see. My work reflects this process.

My recent work has transparent photographs of water incorporated into glass cubes. The cube symbolizes logic. I use glass because its properties are ephemeral and fragile like us. The box in my sculpture is a metaphor for the head/mind as a container. It represents how the mind in dialogue with the senses gives rise to our understanding of the world. The photographic images of water are from the outside natural world. When we look at them, we stand outside the box looking in. Our normal viewpoint looking out at nature is reversed. Nature is bounded and limited. Our view of nature is defined by our own mental constructs. I'd like people to question their relationship to the physical world that is both around them and part of them. Ironically, we are nature and yet we also define it. My art expresses this tension.

Water images are found in many of my sculptures and installations. Water becomes the metaphor for constant flux in my life. It is the place I retreat for solitude, the place that calms me as well as provides me with a place to question. It humbles me as the source from which we evolved and in its ability to destroy and overpower. Water holds vast mysteries. Seven-eights of our planet is water and all evolved from there. It is a common currency of life that flows and circulates. It links all things. Because everything is linked, I want people to question what they see. I make the connection to the wonders of nature and the human-made warning signals that could simultaneously be at work around them.

WHAT ADVICE WOULD YOU LIKE TO GIVE TO ARTISTS?

Be true to yourself and your artistic process. Trust that things occur for us to be in touch with what we are here to learn. There are no accidents!

Wendy Brawer *is principal of Modern World Design (MWD), a consulting firm that promotes public participation in the environment. She has designed a unique series of Green Apple Maps® that chart New York City's urban ecology. Ms. Brawer has written articles, given talks, and created a database of ecological designers. She was the 1993–94 chair of the Industrial Designers Society of America's Committee on Environmental Concerns.*

HOW DID YOU GET INTERESTED IN ENVIRONMENTAL DESIGN?

In 1989 I started to concentrate on watch design and joined the Industrial Designers Society of America. Then my big turning point came. I attended a watch show in Hong Kong in the fall of 1989, where I was overwhelmed and disgusted by the thousands of watches on display. I left Hong Kong for a visit to Bali. This was a pivotal trip for me in that I found a beautiful place, rich in culture and craft, that would most likely, over the course of my life, lose its pristine beauty and diverse cultural art forms. Seeing the destruction of natural ecosystems due to burgeoning tourism and accompanying development interests also influenced my direction toward sustainable design practices. It was the combination of these two experiences that had me take a hard look at what I was doing. I realized that I wanted to do something to help preserve and sustain the world. I wanted to understand how I could help lessen product pollution and started to study environmental issues as they related to my work as a designer. Once I was on this path of learning, many projects unfolded that expressed my design concerns and vision for new product development and education.

WHAT KIND OF PROJECTS HAVE YOU WORKED ON THAT ARE ECO-DESIGN ORIENTED?

As a designer I take part in public policy and local development initiatives. For instance, I am a member of the Manhattan Citizen's Solid Waste Advisory Board. This affords me the opportunity not only to provide creative solutions to solid-waste issues in NYC but also to learn about the logistical, political, and technical considerations in prioritizing citywide waste prevention strategies.

I also involve myself with consulting projects that vary from writing and lecturing on design for the environment to working with clients and their development teams on specific projects. As an owner of my own business, I find that I am interested in the long-term effects of my work. My vision is to offer my clients an environmentally elegant response to their complex problems. MWD takes on small projects, which allows me to develop my abilities and to grow my business with care. Being a designer means I get involved with all kinds of exciting projects and work in nonconventional ways. As my own boss, I have the freedom to set my own priorities and hours, which happen to be long. While I am not making a lot of money, I believe I am making a lot of positive things happen that will help ensure our common future.

My products have included a Stamp Out Junk Mail kit, which provided information on how to lessen the amount of direct mail that comes to your mailbox. The Green Apple Map® is an accessible, affordable reference guide that helps people in New York City develop their interest in local environmental stewardship, build networks, and become actively involved. It also promotes eco-tourism at home. I am now working on a Green Mapping System® that will guide local producers in the creation of our Green Maps®. These can be marketed through a central outlet, so they will be very accessible for travelers. I also won a recycling-bin design competition for King County, Washington. The bins are designed to convey the tangible value of the collected materials by using symbolic architectural detailing based on a neoclassical savings institution. I've also produced Deposit Banks®, self-emptying recycling bins for redeemable bottles and cans for Times Square in New York City.

WHAT TRENDS DO YOU SEE FOR THE DESIGN INDUSTRY WITH AN ENVIRONMENTAL FOCUS?

I foresee a big future in preventing waste with new systems of delivery, packaging, and product design, and in remanufacturing. There is also an opportunity for a great awakening of ideas that integrate environmental concerns into areas including indoor air pollution and other health-related assessments and remediation, urban planning and transportation, and research and education at all levels.

On a personal level I look forward to continually tackling great challenges and working toward more effective solutions to our environmental problems. The problems are so serious. We all must seek to balance our egos, share ideas and skills, and use our creative power responsibly to avert widespread disaster. Since we design the future, we must transform obsolete traditions in favor of more sustainable ones.

John Danzer *is president of Munder Skiles, Inc., a garden design and furniture manufacturing company based in New York City. His company has an environmental philosophy, which influences his use of materials and company vision. Before he started his company, in early 1991, Mr. Danzer worked in strategic planning for McGraw-Hill; he has had more than a decade of work experience in the information services industry at IBM, Dun and Bradstreet, and McGraw-Hill. He majored in art history, graduating from Skidmore College in 1975.*

WHAT IS YOUR BUSINESS?

My business idea is to design a line of furniture that allows people to enjoy the garden. My inspiration comes from the past, from old processes that were used in printing, construction, painting, and finishing. I have spent the last year researching these areas and how history and industrial inventions have changed the quality and design of garden furniture. What I have come to realize is that everything that is new has its roots in the past. I study history and ecology to examine the old techniques that have endured the test of time. I have a love for the distressed look caused by weather. I equate it to appreciating the aging process, and it is something I wish to capture in my furniture line.

HOW IS YOUR LINE ENVIRONMENTAL?

My line is meant to last, not be bought for a few years and then thrown away for a new set of furniture. What is long lasting and can be passed on for generations is environmental. It is wise use of materials, not designed for obsolescence. I also am looking into initiatives in recycled plastic. It is a great material with which to produce a line of garden seats, possibly even designs from the American Museum Houses. How about a Thomas Jefferson bench in recycled plastic? My stationery is printed with soy-based inks on handmade recycled paper using the old process of metal plates and press type. This gives my customers a sense not only of a historical process of printing but also of the handmade beauty and quality reflected in my products.

WHY DID YOU LEAVE THE CORPORATE WORLD AND START YOUR BUSINESS?

I left the corporate world because I developed a problem with authority. I had become disillusioned and confused by working with information technology and computers. I felt lost and really didn't know anything well. I wanted to focus my life on two things that gave me pleasure—gardens and furniture. When I got laid off in 1989, I realized that the only authority I actually responded to was Mother Nature. What I experienced in the corporate world was a major problem in management. Today in America, people are not managed but bribed with insurance policies, salaries, bonuses, and sales plans. So few people are inspired by their work. I believe the greatest work comes from teams and partnerships in which various viewpoints and skills are respected. In my business, I learn as much from my builders as I do from the archivists in the library.

WHAT IS YOUR ADVICE TO PEOPLE WANTING TO START A BUSINESS?

Consider your personal financial position. It takes at least three years to get a positive cash flow going. You'll need to do extensive research if you are going to be successful. All my jobs in the past have helped me in organizing my present business plan. I learned how to speak to people and ask questions. I know how to access information databases on my computer from all the years in the information services industry. You need to be able to assess the skills you have, develop them, and put them to good use. Networking is essential.

Get out and visit any and all related businesses. Imitate what works, but in your own unique way. You also need to know your limits and how to get the expertise to move your company along. I have advisors who help me with an array of business tasks from organizational, legal, and technical questions that may have to do with licensing agreements, to accounting systems, to manufacturing prototypes or maintaining product inventory.

As in any business, what you need is patience, perseverance, and a long-term view. I believe the environment will continue to be a growing concern, and that a new business that considers the environment will fill a need for those who welcome a return to high-quality products and services.

***Lynda Grose** is the director of research and development for Esprit Ecollection. She received a first-class honors degree in fashion design from Kingston University in London.*

WHAT IS A TYPICAL DAY LIKE?

A typical day is quite interesting and varied. It may include talking to a spinner about the availability of organic wool fiber in the United States, a natural dye specialist about how best to utilize the character of natural dyes in the final garment, or a recycling specialist about how to handle the logistics of shipping our production cutting scraps to be shredded and spun into new fiber. By now, we have a team of R&D people focusing on fabrics and yarn development, trims, and wet processing and finishing. We work on fabrics from fiber to finished product always with environmental concerns being paramount. It's a challenge and very exciting.

HOW DID YOU GO ABOUT CREATING AN ECOLINE?

It's essential that environmental ramifications of the whole process of garment manufacture be understood at the very conception of the line. The normal considerations in designing an Esprit line are aesthetics, style, fabric, color, trims, price, quality, and timing. All these elements come together through design, and hopefully the final garment looks unique, marketable, and is a good value for the money.

Add to this the element of environmental impact, and the whole process changes. Design has to be aware of everything—how the fiber is grown, harvested, spun, woven, dyed, finished, what happens to production scraps when garments are cut, etc.

Designing into and around environmental issues as carefully as we consider price and style gives rise to a whole new aesthetic for clothing—natural colors designed to fade beautifully, recycled yarns that deliberately exhibit recycled qualities, and so on.

HOW DID YOU GET INVOLVED IN ECOLLECTION?

In the late 1980s at Esprit, employees were encouraged to consider and implement ways we could reduce impact on the environment in our day-to-day office activities. We were also exposed to high-caliber environmentalists through our company "Be Informed" lecture series. The whole company was buzzing with awareness and ideas. Guided by our Eco-desk managers, we set a company-wide, employee-driven audit in motion. This included in my area, design, looking at the impact garment manufacture had on the environment. Before long, I was asked by the owner, Susie Tompkins, to design a line that later became known as Ecollection.

WHO IS A PART OF YOUR STAFF?

Besides our R&D team, we have a two-member production team that attends to the quality make of our garments, pricing, and delivery. We now have a two-member sales team that handles U.S. wholesale accounts for Ecollection and services our European retail stores. We also have graphics and communication support from our corporate office, for brochures, press kits, and in-store display items. Not to forget our business manager, who constantly has to employ "creative accounting" to ensure that a more expensive line is a commercial success. Everyone is extremely enthusiastic about the concept and excited to contribute to the program.

WHAT ARE THE MOST PRESSING ENVIRONMENTAL CHALLENGES FACING YOU?

The most pressing challenges are shifting the company perceptions and systems to accommodate an environmentally and socially responsible clothing line. The core values of this line are contrary to conventional business thinking, and it takes constant education and re-education to keep environmental and social aspects in the forefront of everyone's mind. Communication skills, business knowledge, patience, and sheer doggedness are a prerequisite, besides design skills and environmental awareness.

WHAT DO YOU SEE AS THE MAJOR TRENDS IN FASHION?

With Ecollection, it's important to stay abreast of the fashion market trends, just as it is important to be informed about past sales figures and costs of our business. However, these elements are part of our peripheral vision. We focus on our design objectives and mission and constantly try to improve on our process and concept. If an "eco trend" comes and goes in the fashion industry, we would continue, "business as normal." Ecollection isn't a trend. In time, we hope to shift our whole company to be "Ecollection."

HOW DID ECOLLECTION CHANGE YOUR DESIGN SENSIBILITY?

By now, the environmental ramifications are well integrated into my thinking and that of the R&D team. That I can only have aesthetically what our environmental standards and objectives allow rather than demanding exactly what I imagine or create—you start to let the process and guidelines come to rest on a solution. It's very liberating. You have to be very open-minded to the restrictions and the possibilities that come out of them.

Color sensibility is the first to shift. When using unbleached cotton, the colors that harmonize are necessarily more subtle in cast and shade. Brilliant neon colors and bright turquoises stand out as harsh and synthetic. Bleached white also looks "synthetic," when once we would have considered it to be "pure."

WHAT DO YOU WANT TO SEE IN FASHION?

My desire is for all designers to take this approach seriously, and it is already happening at Esprit Europe. We have a very creative design department, and there are many ideas and applications of the Ecollection concept happening on our main lines. This will be proof to the industry that the Ecollection concept is commercially viable.

So my new desire would be for this concept to be accepted as an ongoing process. Environmentally responsible design/clothing is just a stepping stone to the next level of awareness—reducing the number of manufactured goods while maintaining a business I think will be the next area of focus . . . although I don't quite know how to get there yet!

WHAT TIPS WOULD YOU GIVE TO PEOPLE WANTING TO ENTER YOUR FIELD?

Develop your own guidelines according to environmental and social considerations. *Never* compromise your guidelines. This will force creative thinking and solutions and will result in unique products. *Always* trust your concept and don't rely on market analysis and trends too much (but remain informed). Build on your concept, learn from it, improve and refine it constantly. The results will speak for themselves.

***Doug Kelbaugh**, Fellowship American Institute of Architects, is a professor of architecture and urban design at the University of Washington and a principal in Kelbaugh, Calthorpe and Associates in Seattle. He is presently writing a book,* The Seattle Charrettes: Regionalism in Theory, Design, and Practice.

AS AN ARCHITECT-PLANNER, WHAT INFLUENCED YOU TO INTEGRATE ENVIRONMENTAL AND SOCIAL CONCERNS INTO YOUR WORK?

I was first influenced by the social and environmental ethic prevalent when I was a VISTA volunteer and graduate student in the late 1960s and early 1970s. This ethic was student-initiated rather than something we learned from our teachers, although I did study under Victor Olgyay, a solar pioneer at Princeton University.

TELL US ABOUT SOME OF YOUR PROJECTS.

Between undergraduate and graduate study, five of us founded a community design center in the inner city of Trenton, New Jersey. We designed and built a Black Arts Cultural Center and several other buildings and playgrounds. We were driven by idealism, but also by a sense of collective guilt and a desire to avoid being drafted to serve in Vietnam. After the oil embargo in 1972, I designed and built a passive-solar house in Princeton—the first to use a Trombe wall in America. At the time, I was working for the Trenton Department of Planning and Development, where we did several housing, institutional, and urban design projects in the same neighborhood I worked as a VISTA. Unexpectedly, this turned out to be my professional internship. I never worked in an architectural office per se, although we tried to turn this city department into something akin to a design office. For about three years, I was doing social architecture during the day and moonlighting on solar architecture at home. By 1978, I had enough outside work to leave my city job and start a design practice, first out of my residence, and soon at small offices around the corner. This practice focused on passive-solar architecture and included some pioneering work. For seven years, my partner, Sang Lee, and two to six employees did dozens of projects around the region and occasionally nationally. We won about fifteen design awards, often for energy conservation, and successfully competed in several national design competitions. The moral and economic climate in the country was such that we could base an architecture practice on energy-conscious design. Indeed, I was invited all over the country to consult and to lecture on our work. A group of us organized several local and national solar conferences. As energy prices softened in the mid-1980s, some of us switched to full-time positions in the academic world, where we had formerly had design studios and lecture courses on a part-time basis.

I moved to Seattle in 1985 to assume the chairmanship of the University of Washington Department of Architecture. I enjoyed switching gears to a more theoretical agenda, writing more and more. Specifically, I espoused critical regionalism, which expanded on the site-specificity of passive-solar design, perhaps the movement's greatest contribution to architecture, to include regional building practices, materials, history, ethnicity, and mythology. In short, it was a more culturally and less technically based approach to design. Since then, I've organized ten design charrettes, in which faculty, students, and visiting design professionals address local environmental and civic problems and opportunities. I have not been able as a full-time academic to pursue much private practice. However, my small firm, a loose association with Peter Calthorpe of San Francisco, has designed and built several projects, including a National Forest facility with photovoltaic power, passive sun-tempering, and composting toilets. This project required Kelbaugh, Calthorpe and Associates and its consultants to provide close to $100,000 in pro bono services. Presently, I'm involved in several buildings and planning projects.

The planning projects address many of the social, economic, and environmental problems of sprawl.

WHAT DO YOU SEE AS THE MOST PRESSING ENVIRONMENTAL CONCERN HAVING TO DO WITH HOW OUR BUILT ENVIRONMENT AFFECTS US?

In America, the most pressing problem to do with the built environment is suburban sprawl. This placeless, mindless pattern of development is today's primary mode of development and the characteristic dwelling pattern of our time. It also ensures the continued dependence on the automobile, which is even more environmentally and economically expensive than it appears. Disinvestment in our cities also has long-lasting social consequences. Our generation can do better.

HOW CAN DESIGNERS HELP SOLVE ENVIRONMENTAL PROBLEMS?

The built environment accounts for over one-third of the energy pie of this nation, which, in turn, consumes that much of the world energy supply. We are by far the most gluttonous country in the world. We need to build more energy-efficient, nontoxic, and recyclable buildings. But even more important is what designers and planners need to do for transportation, which eats up more like two-thirds of the energy pie in a typical suburban community. Our cars and trucks consume considerably more energy than our houses, offices, stores, and other buildings. More compact, walkable neighborhoods with public transit are essential to sustainability. We have more cars per capita than ever and drive them farther every year—at least ten average trips per household per day in suburbia. If you consider that the number and length of trips is a measure of dysfunction, i.e., people not being where they need or want to be, it's a damning statistic. Practically no trips in suburbia are done by foot and very few by transit. The average car produces its weight in carbon dioxide each year. Each car costs its owner about $500 per month, plus societal costs like roads, police, oil spills, and pollution cleanup—not to mention defense expenditures and wars to secure stable sources of oil. Some households spend more on cars than on shelter.

We need new models for suburbia. Designers, who can conjure up and illustrate scenarios of development better than anyone, are needed to inform policy, which is usually drafted by lawyers, bureaucrats, and elected officials dealing with words and abstract ideas. Design has been conspicuously absent from political debate. Urbanism should be one of government's priorities—right up there with other critical issues such as health care, education, crime, homelessness. In fact, a place-centered approach to society's panoply of problems and opportunities would be superior to a problem-centered one, the modus operandi of most government programs and initiatives. It would be more effective to concentrate government funds on neighborhoods and regions, rather than municipalities, which are increasingly meaningless as economic and political entities.

WHAT IS THE NEW URBANISM? HOW CAN PEOPLE READ AND LEARN MORE ABOUT IT?

The new urbanism is a reaction to modernist design and planning, which tended to be hyperrational, sterile, universalist, and anti-street, antiurban, and antienvironmental. The East Coast version, started by Andres Duany and Elizabeth Plater-Zyberk, is called traditional neighborhood design (TND) or neotraditionalism. The West Coast version, started by Peter Calthorpe and others, is called transit-oriented development (TOD) or Pedestrian Pockets. They represent a remarkably similar convergence of traditional urban form and environmentalism, both applied to the suburbs. They are about mixed-use, transit-oriented, walkable, human-scaled development in finite, bounded places with a legible hierarchy of streets and civic spaces. Peter Katz's *The New Urbanism* is a good place to read about it, as is Peter Calthorpe's *The Next American Metropolis* and *The Pedestrian Pocket Book*, which I edited.

WHAT VALUES ARE CRUCIAL IN APPROACHING YOUR WORK?

Imagination, perspective, perseverance, and willingness to not always leave your personal signature. The last of these traits is a very difficult lesson for me and most architects, who often feel they are ordained to leave their heroic mark on the world.

CAN YOU SUGGEST WAYS FOR PEOPLE TO GET INVOLVED IN AN ENVIRONMENTAL ISSUE AS A DESIGNER-PLANNER?

Take on zoning and property rights in your hometown or metropolitan area. Zoning laws have more or less codified and sanctified suburban sprawl. It's against the law in most places to build an old-fashioned neighborhood or town.

WHAT SKILLS AND PRINCIPLES ARE IMPORTANT TO APPROACHING ENVIRONMENTAL PROBLEMS?

A good knowledge base and honesty will get you further than sensational facts and chest beating. At times honesty may get you into trouble, but if you don't lose faith, it will usually get you out of it. The most important skill is the ability to clearly articulate your ideas in drawings and words.

HOW WOULD YOU DEFINE THE TERM "ENVIRONMENT"?

The environment to us is what water is to fish—the sum total of our natural and built world, including cultural, aesthetic, and spiritual as well as physical dimensions and experiences. It is taken in with our senses as well as our mind. "Sustainability" is a harder word to define. The best definition I've heard is "doing what screws the world up least for future generations."

WHAT PUBLICATION, BOOKS, MAGAZINES DO YOU READ?

National Geographic, *Progressive Architecture*, *Architecture*, the *Seattle Times*, *The Weekly*, *The New Yorker*, *Sports Illustrated*, *The Urban Ecologist*, *On the Ground*, *The Journal of Architectural Education*, *University Week*, *The Gridlock Gazette*, *Arcade*, and *Bicycling* are the periodicals that I presently read. The best books that I've read recently are Jane Jacob's *Systems of Survival*, Paul Hawken's *The Ecology of Commerce*, John Steinbeck's *Grapes of Wrath*, and the *Columbia History of the World*. I wish I had more time to read novels by writers like Wallace Stegner.

WHAT ROLE CAN DESIGNERS PLAY IN BEING SOCIAL ACTIVISTS WITH THE SKILLS THEY HAVE?

With charrettes and workshops, generate illustrative designs for new policies and for needy communities and institutions.

HOW CAN YOU CONVINCE BUSINESSPEOPLE AND DEVELOPERS ABOUT THE VALUE OF YOUR KIND OF DESIGN?

Logic, humor, rhetoric, persuasion, and good color slides. Good drawings and taking them on site visits help.

HOW CAN DESIGNERS AND ARCHITECTS BE MORE ENVIRONMENTALLY AND SOCIALLY RESPONSIBLE IN THE WORK THEY DO?

Placemaking is the highest, most important act designers and architects are involved in. They should read the literature, visit the environmentally and socially responsible places and people, brood over it all, and act. But designers should never give up on good design and aesthetics in their zeal to improve the world.

Beth Nelson *is owner and director of Printed Matter Ltd., a graphic design company in London, England. She received a B.F.A. and an M.F.A. from the University of California, Santa Barbara.*

WHAT IS A TYPICAL DAY LIKE FOR YOU?

A day at Printed Matter usually involves a staff meeting first, as this is a very hands-on business and requires a lot of organizing and detail. The studio is extremely important to me, and I hope I have created a workplace that feels wonderful to be in. We are a cottage industry, and therefore it is important that all the staff get on, as it is a small intimate environment. Everything we sell is made by hand, in the studio, and packed and shipped here. The handmadeness of our products is one of the most important issues for me. During the day the staff are making products, while I might be doing anything from selling, to designing, to paperwork.

Having a small business requires a dedication and faith far beyond any other kind of work. One must be prepared to live with a certain amount of uncertainty. Every day is an act of faith.

WHAT PROMPTED YOU TO DO THIS?

I had wanted to return to my printmaking background and began by making some small handmade stationery goods to sell in a shop venture that I was involved with at the time. I wanted people to see that paper, and the art of writing, could be environmentally sound without looking like paper towels. I wanted to travel again and resume my interest with words and images. I wanted to start something that was handmade, beautiful, and encouraged the opposite impulses that the technology age was inspiring. I wanted my love of paper and love of craft to manifest in something that was contributing to the environment, not taking away from it, and I wanted to be a dreamer again, which is what making art is partially about for me.

WHY DID YOU CREATE AN ENVIRONMENTAL GRAPHIC DESIGN BUSINESS?

I think I have always been interested in the environment because of the way I was brought up and by my years living in Santa Barbara. I grew up on a farm, with an Amish grandmother, who instilled in me a love of nature and appreciation for all things of the earth. I was also taught to work from an early age, because the Amish say, "The greatest things are done with the help of the small ones." It is only now that I am forty that I begin to see what an influence all of this has had toward how I have organized Printed Matter.

I also spent seven years in Santa Barbara, California, which then was very much more a village and had an immense sense of it being a special place on the earth. Traditionally, it had been a healing place for thousands of years, and I believe my time spent living there left a profound impression on me. Living in the European world these twelve years, I find myself being attracted to the Mediterranean places much like Santa Barbara. So again—full circle.

WHAT ARE THE PRESSING CHALLENGES OF PRINTED MATTER?

The challenge of running a small business in a large business world is the number one issue. Many people believe it to be impossible. Making something by hand is very difficult in a machine age. Technology is getting faster, while what I do remains at the same pace. One of the things we find difficult to get people to understand is that ordering more from Printed Matter does not make the price cheaper. Handmade things exist within certain boundaries.

Being a small business in Britain was easier for me than being a small business in America, because Britain truly is "a nation of shopkeepers." There is also a very big appreciation for things handmade, and for artists and craftspeople. Finding suppliers who will support small business is another dilemma. It is difficult to buy small quantities of many of the raw materials required to make my product.

WHAT ARE THE TRENDS IN GRAPHIC DESIGN AND THE PAPER INDUSTRY?

You have a strange dichotomy at the moment—the computer age with the environmental. I would like to see the two mix; some say they are incompatible. I think a higher value will be placed on the written word and the handmade the more popular mass communications become.

I very much dislike recycled being equated with more expensive. It achieves the opposite effect it should. We need the powers that be to accept the responsibility for damaging the environment and begin educating everyone toward new thinking about one's place in the world picture.

WHAT ARE YOUR WORK PRIORITIES WITH REGARD TO THE ENVIRONMENT?

I cannot imagine ever not working in both something I love and something that contributes to the the big picture. People could empower themselves so much more if they simply began somewhere at work. I was highly impressed by my mother's recycling efforts at home, which were started by local government, but also highly disappointed that the amount people were consuming was not an issue at all. Reeducate is the key. Traveling in other countries certainly makes you highly aware of the amount of excess and waste most of the industrialized world is participating in.

IS THERE JOB GROWTH IN THE PAPER AND STATIONERY INDUSTRY?

In the last five years there has been a huge leap forward in social stationery and recycled goods. I think this will continue. It has to start filtering down now through the advertising industry, the book industry, publishing, graphics, etc.

WHAT SKILLS ARE NEEDED TO START YOUR OWN BUSINESS?

Tenacity if you want your own business. And you must really believe in what you are doing. Background might be in anything from art, to package design, to graphics. Working for someone's small business is the best way to see if you could actually manage the stress and if you have the commitment.

WHERE DO YOU GET YOUR INFORMATION ON PAPER AND GRAPHIC IDEAS?

A lot of my knowledge comes from working with my manufacturers. Going to the factory and seeing everything often inspires a new idea. Also, traveling and seeing the natural progression of recycling that exists in a lot of cultures is one of the best teachers. Often I will simply see a material that I like, and it all starts from there.

Michael Payatok *is founder of Payatok and Associates, an architectual consulting firm in Oakland, California. His projects are exclusively sponsored by nonprofit housing and economic development corporations serving lower-income communities. Mr. Payatok also teaches courses on architecture at the University of Washington, Seattle. He has a degree in architecture from Harvard University.*

WHAT INFLUENCED YOU TO INTEGRATE ENVIRONMENTAL AND SOCIAL CONCERNS INTO YOUR WORK?

I graduated from Harvard's Graduate School of Design in 1967 at the peak of the civil rights campaign, the anti-Vietnam war protests, and the growing environmental movement. As an intern in architectural offices in New York City, I would leave work during my lunch breaks to join the nearest protests in the streets and my weekends I spent traveling to Washington to protest in front of the Pentagon. The contrast between what was happening in the professional offices and what was happening in the world around me led me to abandon the professional world after one year and take a position in academia for the next ten years so I could link architecture students with low-income communities in "community design" programs.

After ten years of full-time academia I recognized that I could not serve the interests of the underclass as an architect from within the cocoon of the academy alone, or even through community outreach programs. I moved to Oakland, California, whose cultural and racial diversity most closely mimicked Brooklyn, and settled there to continue my work. I taught part time to subsidize my ideology and worked in offices that had been designing facilities in lower-income communities sponsored by various government programs still limping along in the late 1970's and early 1980's. In 1984, after 17 years of incubation, I felt I was sufficiently experienced to open my own office. I wanted to create a practice that facilitated community self-development and create an architecture that was as much a product of the dreams and aspirations of the lower-income communities I was serving as a product of my own hand. I ignored the architectural press, and establishing my place in the profession by simply concentrating my attention on developing participatory design methods, living in the communities I was serving, and taking up their battles with them.

WHAT DO YOU SEE AS THE MOST PRESSING PROBLEMS WITH THE BUILT ENVIRONMENT?

The most pressing problems for lower-income households of the inner city today are finding and creating decent-paying jobs. The lack of quality housing, education, recreation, healthy environments, and other essentials in life can simply be traced to the abandonment of America by its corporate industrial base for cheaper labor elsewhere. The underclass lost their economic ladder up to more comfortable living conditions as this job source systematically evaporated in the last three decades. Creation of quality jobs is the key to quality environments for America's underclass. All other programs—experiments in housing, community gardens and parks, drug rehab centers—are spitting into the wind without dignified, meaningful work that helps build people, their families, their communities, and their country. Slapping burgers and hotel bed making may supplement family incomes but cannot sustain them on their own.

WHAT DO YOU SEE AS THE MOST PRESSING PROBLEM FACING OUR COUNTRY?

The most pressing problem is the unjust distribution of resources, whether it be food, health care, education, or housing. My particular concern is the cost of housing for the bottom third of the U.S. population. In the inner city, for low-income renters, it can be as much as 50 to 70 percent of their income, so that every other essential in their lives is seriously short-changed. "Decent and affordable housing" means not just adequate shelter but the aggregate quality. Housing can be rather modest, even inferior, and be tolerable if all of the other dimensions of "location" or neighborhood are superior: good and cheap mass transit, retail services within walking distance, good schools nearby. But the most critical factor is the availability of good-paying jobs for those with lesser education. The U.S. industrial and manufacturing infrastructure used to supply the working classes with good-paying jobs with which to raise a family. Those jobs are gone at the same time that education budgets are shrinking, preventing lower economic classes from gaining access to jobs of the information and higher-tech industries.

HOW CAN WE TACKLE THESE PROBLEMS?

To achieve affordable housing for all Americans means that there must be a major intervention into the market system in the production and ownership of housing. The private market, with its profit incentive, is not interested in building housing for the bottom third of the nation and cannot be expected to be. There is simply no profit there. Those programs at the federal, state, and local levels that created additional incentives in the past need to be revitalized, but in new forms. These subsidies should not discourage the mixing of ages, incomes, or land uses as they have done in the past. Housing subsidies should permit seniors and families to coexist, mix different incomes so that low-income or high-income ghettos are less likely to occur, mix businesses and retail—particularly home-based businesses—into government-assisted housing to make retail and job opportunities conveniently available and to stimulate entrepreneurship.

Higher-density housing not only helps combat sprawl, but decreases costs and increases the critical mass needed to support mass transit, local retail, and small, local businesses, all of which are critical to lowering living costs for lower-income households. Higher-density housing can be designed to be secure and intimate if small clusters of families, no more than thirty or so, share courtyards, garages, parking lots, or front entries. All others are physically kept out except as guests of a resident. In this manner, families can know each other, look out for each other's children, and keep track of who should be walking within their development and who is an outsider. This type of tight cluster planning was not true of most government-assisted housing in the past. Aside from the social benefits, the environmental benefits of higher-density housing mean less consumption of agricultural land at the cities' fringes, less consumption of materials and energy for construction, and less consumption of energy in operation.

What is the new urbanism?

This is a peculiar term that has been recently coined to describe nothing other than all of the old characteristics of sensible town planning and city block planning that existed prior to the post-WWII decades of explosive suburban growth. I sometimes think the term was invented by people of my generation who grew up in the suburbs, hated it, and did not discover the real virtues of urban living until they were adults and practicing professionals. So to them this form of urbanism is "new." To those of us who grew up in neighborhoods of the older inner cities, these principles of town planning are things we thought to be natural laws. The best way to learn about the "new urbanism" is to move back into an old inner-city neighborhood, or any small town that was mostly built before WWII.

What skills are crucial for an architect to work this way?

Before discussing skills, the critical question is: "What ought to be the attitude of designers and architects necessary to tackle social and environmental problems?" First, they must believe that there are some profound problems in the way that humans are relating to the planet; they must be passionately upset about those problems; and they must recognize that environmental design, when it functions as an extension of the fashion industry's preoccupation with "style," is one of the main sources of those problems. Second, they must see that there is inevitably a "class" dimension to those problems: (a) those who own and control resources and their transformation in production are largely responsible for shaping consumption patterns; (b) how resources are transformed to look after being "designed" is also controlled by those with wealth; (c) the culture of the wealthy also dominates the intellectual content of those institutions that shape the attitudes of designers.

A design originating from such intellectual roots has nothing to do with the biosystems of the region that is to receive it or with the region's social ecology and the changes taking place in both. I try to insert myself into a community in such a way as to get to know it from its point of view. I must use my experiences gleaned from many neighborhoods, world travel, and designing other places as a mirror that shows people how what they do and want compares to what other people are doing and wanting. Both the place and its people on the one hand, and myself on the other, should expect to be changed by this effort to design something for them, whatever it is. Frequently for me that task is designing higher-density housing for lower-income households.

I have developed three-dimensional "modeling" kits (no computers) over the years, which help people invent and simulate designs within their communities. These permit them to learn firsthand what kinds of trade-offs are necessary when making changes to their environment. Working in teams of ten or less, fifty residents in five groups can simultaneously develop many alternative designs for discussion and debate, revealing their opinions and creating a stage that can also test ideas inserted by the designers.

This work requires: (a) an insatiable thirst for other people's opinions; (b) a skill at visualizing in three dimensions; (c) a facility for inventing and interpreting form and space configurations without computer assistance; (d) and a highly developed innate ability to draw and to use drawing as a means to invent. These are the traditional skills of the architect and will always be essential to design.

WHAT ROLE DOES COMMUNITY PARTICIPATION PLAY IN YOUR WORK?

Participatory approaches to design, employed at the earliest stages in the process, is the sine qua non of twenty-first-century planning. Any development entity that believes there must be a change—the addition of more housing, the incorporation of nonresidential uses, a change in traffic—should approach the community first, before any professionals are hired. The community must participate in the hiring of the design professionals, in the definition of the project, in the analysis of its physical and financial feasibility. Otherwise, the victims are not just the immediate players but the development process in general, which requires more than ever a sensible, rational, deliberate approach to inserting ourselves in the environment in a way that saves rapidly depleting resources.

In addition, I would argue that when serving the interests of lower-income communities, because the system is stacked against them, the professional must often conspire with them on how to manipulate the system to overcome its inherent biases. Those cultural and economic biases of the economically more powerful are often codified in planning and zoning ordinances, design review guidelines, real estate appraisal methods, lending practices, etc. To achieve a more participatory approach requires an equalizing of leverage, which means lower-income community groups cannot always be totally open about their strategies and tactics with the circumscribing institutions.

HOW WOULD YOU DEFINE DESIGN LITERACY AND HOW CAN ONE MAKE DESIGN'S IMPORTANCE MORE APPARENT TO LAY PEOPLE?

There is a level of delight, charm, pleasure, and even mystery that designers must bring to people. The real design problem is that they must learn to do this with less "stuff," less material, and less energy, even if recycled. This requires more inventiveness, more dependence on the simple manipulation of shape, spatial order, and sequence, the play of light and color on shape and detail. It requires more human labor to work the surfaces that surround us, to bring that level of delight to walls, ceilings, floors, plazas, streetscapes, or what is under our rumps, etc.

When I design housing for low-income people, aside from using highly participatory methods to ensure cultural compatibility, I personally see to it that there is a level of detail that will bring a smile to even the most seemingly insensitive philistines. The best compliment I ever received was from an older, crusty gentleman who was a property manager. He had recently become the manager of a fifty-unit family project I had designed. In his words, "you know I've been managing projects all my life, but this is the first time I look forward at night to come out there in the courtyard, when all the kids are gone, with my chair and just sit and enjoy these buildings and the landscape in the night light and moonlight. You know, there really is something to this aesthetics thing."

WHAT DO YOU READ AND RECOMMEND FOR THOSE WHO WANT TO GET IN TO YOUR FIELD?

I have little to recommend about what to read about architecture with one exception: *Progressive Architecture* magazine. Two books that I think are important for designers to read are by Robert Bellah and his colleagues: *The Good Society* and *Habits of the Heart.* Both examine the soul of America at these crossroads and give good guidance to professionals, young and old, about what ought to be the big issues addressed with their careers.

Robert Phipps *has a B.F.A. from Harvard University in art history and an M.A. from Boston University in painting and drawing. He has taught painting and drawing at various colleges and universities including Harvard, University of New Hampshire, and College of the Atlantic. He lives in Bar Harbor, Maine, and shows his work at the John Ames Gallery in Belfast, Maine, and through his New York City agent.*

AS AN ARTIST, WHAT INFLUENCED YOU TO INTEGRATE ENVIRONMENTAL CONCERNS INTO YOUR WORK?

I was born in 1933 in Harrisburg, Pennsylvania, one mile from Three Mile Island, when the Susquehanna River still roamed wide and free. I grew up amid great rolling farms bordered by inviting woods. In my youth I saw the woods cut down and the farms cut up into house lots. I saw a way of life vanish forever. As a young man I traveled to Japan. When the ship entered Yokohama Harbor, the air was so thick with pollution that I choked. In the years there I experienced the schizophrenia of my species in relation to the natural world. Most of the Japanese I met revered the natural world on the one hand and on the other allowed themselves and others to pollute or destroy it indiscriminately. When I returned to the states, I rode by Greyhound through the strip mining in Ohio and western Pennsylvania. I was so disturbed by the implications of what I saw happening that I went to the Pennsylvania Bureau of Mines. As I came alone, representing only myself, the politicians there scoffed at my concern.

The nineteenth-century impressionists could take delight in the natural world. In the 1990s I create metaphors and images that will revolutionize, delight, and disturb myself and possibly others about our human connection with and dependence upon the entire diversity and complexity of life on the planet.

In the spring of 1986 I traveled with a friend to the island of Samos, Greece. We stayed in the village of Ambelos high up in the mountains. The Mediterranean danced far below us, and the hillside bloomed with wild poppies. The village and the farms all interwove into one ancient living garden of grapevines, olive trees, donkeys, and humans. It was Greek Easter, and the Greek Orthodox priests sang plain chant over the loudspeakers. We went to a party on the Friday before Easter. Everyone was silent. A villager told us that the accident at Chernobyl had happened. No one knew whether the radioactive cloud was heading toward Greece or not. In the years since, Chernobyl Easter in Greece has become a point of departure for a series of paintings and prints that I continue to work on as the tragedy unfolds.

HOW CAN ARTISTS AND DESIGNERS HELP SOLVE ENVIRONMENTAL PROBLEMS?

I hesitate to speak for other artists and designers. Instead I will describe my contribution to the struggle to save the Penobscot River, Bucksport, and the Penobscot Bay of Maine from a huge coal-fired plant proposed by Applied Energy Services (AES). For four years I attended hearings in Bucksport, Maine, in which AES tried to win support for its outdated technology or defend itself legally for its various questionable maneuvers in the town of Bucksport. For four years I wrote letters to the editor about the hearings and the implications such a massive power utility at the mouth of the Penobscot River would have for Maine. I became an impresario briefly to stage a benefit for STOP (State Taxpayers Opposed to Pollution) at the College of the Atlantic in Bar Harbor. An art exhibition, a poetry reading, and a concert involved many artists in the cause and brought the issue before the press and the public. I contributed paintings and prints to an auction to raise money for STOP. In the moment of our victory I was one of several Mainers who helped to create the Coalition for Sensible Energy, a nonprofit offshoot of STOP.

CAN YOU SUGGEST WAYS FOR PEOPLE TO GET INVOLVED IN ENVIRONMENTAL ISSUES AS DESIGNERS AND ARTISTS?

Landscape architecture has changed profoundly as a discipline. It is no longer a decorative process for the creators of built environments but stands on its own as a way to integrate city and country, humans, and all the other living things. The numerous environmental organizations need the help of artists and designers.

WHAT ROLE DO ART AND DESIGN/ENVIRONMENT PLAY IN DAILY LIFE?

Art and design have the ability to drive away despair, illuminate thought, and give new purpose to the day. The music of Mozart always does that for me. On the dark side, art and design have the ability to mesmerize and condition me into thinking and feeling that everything is fine. Much of television is like that for me. On the bright side, art and design have the ability to revolutionize my everyday thought and make me aware in new ways. The two hundred drawings and the painting by Picasso of Guernica have engraved on my memory forever the terror of German fascism and remain a catalyst for action in this time when ecofascism surfaces all around the globe. I also find that I need to be surrounded by living things, trees, ocean, eagles, flowers, people to find meaning for my life.

WHAT GOT YOU INTERESTED IN LOOKING AT RELATIONSHIPS BETWEEN ART AND NATURE?

As a small child one of the first books I saw was the *Birds of America* by the naturalist and artist John James Audubon. The inextricable balance of scientific study and artistic invention in his work stayed with me all my life.

WHAT HAVE YOU LEARNED ABOUT NATURE AND ENVIRONMENTAL PROBLEMS THAT MOTIVATED YOU TO CONTINUE TO WORK AS AN ARTIST ON THESE ISSUES?

With the end of the Cold War the ecofascism of the multinational corporations compels me to continue to work as an artist on these issues. Hydro Quebec's proposed annihilation of James Bay in Canada and the adjacent lands of the Cree Indians for electric power compels me to speak out, to write, to visualize the implications of this ecocide. The huge scale of this proposed hydroelectric project, the Valdez disaster, and Chernobyl express the exponential increase in the destructive effect of humans on the planet. It is in this context that I continue to work as an artist. If I can make myself laugh and cry about the beauty of the New World and the rate at which it is being destroyed, then maybe I can do that for others.

Clare Smith *has served as president of Farmington, Connecticut's Aid to Artisans for the past eight years. Prior to this position she was the owner and manager of Primitive Artisan, a New York–based import firm specializing in handcrafts of developing nations, from 1968 until 1982. She has traveled extensively in South and Central America, Asia, and Europe. She has a B.A. in history from Smith College.*

WHAT DOES AID TO ARTISANS DO?

I have to emphasize that Aid to Artisans is not a business. We try to get the artisans into business, we train them, and we try to link them with responsible buyers—and then our job is done, and we move on.

To do this we need money, and that's how I spend most of my time, funding projects that are worth doing, finding the funds to do them. Aid to Artisans is a "do good" organization, and all the consultants and staff people who work with us are experienced in design and in business—we know what's needed, and we do it.

We are especially gratified when we find for-profit companies, large ones like the Nature Company and Esprit, and smaller importers like Mesa International, Samii, Sandor, Colbert, and Bamboula, that want to work with us.

WHAT'S A TYPICAL DAY?

I reply to inquiries from all over the world, artisan groups needing help and buyers wanting to find products that are original but traditional, environmentally benign, and also bright and beautiful. We get pictures, samples, pleas from the producers, phone calls and faxes from the buyers. We try to put different people together when we think they can create a partnership. The hard part is that it usually won't work without a lot of adjustments and time-consuming negotiations between our organization and the two groups we try to bring together.

WHO STARTED THIS ORGANIZATION?

It was started by Jim and Mary Plaut in 1976 on Jim's retirement as secretary general of the World Craft Council. The Plauts felt that crafts and craftspeople were "endangered" much as rare birds and plants are, and they felt that better markets were the solution.

I have been on the board from the beginning but became president in 1986. I did not at the time think this would be my life's work, but I had already been an importer of crafts for fifteen years, owner of Primitive Artisan, a well-known import and distribution company, and I knew that the gap between the work of a rural craftsperson and a New York store was huge. And I knew from my own profit-and-loss statement that there is not enough surplus in craft importing to do the kind of product development and marketing training that is essential. It would have to be by a nonprofit or agency.

HOW DID YOU GET INTERESTED IN THE ENVIRONMENT?

My father was a Vermont conservationist, and wise use of natural resources has always been a moral imperative to me; handcrafts with all their lore and appeal are usually well suited to that ethic.

Mierle Laderman Ukeles *is the "official, unsalaried" artist-in-residence for the New York City Department of Sanitation and a member of its Executive Committee. She is represented by Ronald Feldman Fine Arts in New York City and has exhibited widely in the United States, Europe, and Asia in "non-art" public spaces as well as galleries, museums, and international expositions, creating permanent as well as temporary sculpture, installation, and performance art. An utterly public artist, she has been able to continue her work because she has received many grants, public art commissions, and fellowships from the Guggenheim Memorial Foundation, the Andy Warhol Foundation, the National Endowment for the Arts, and the New York State Council on the Arts, among others. Recent lectures include Harvard, Weber State University in Utah, Yale, Virginia Polytechnic University, and the Tate Gallery in London. She has a B.A. in international relations from Barnard College and an M.A. in interrelated studio arts from New York University.*

HOW DID YOU BECOME INTERESTED IN ECOLOGICAL ART?

What got me interested in ecological art was the disconnection between spending my time creating art and spending my time raising children, and something shifted as I was forced to take care of something other than myself. When I became a mother, people would ask me, "Do you do anything?" There was no cultural or social value attached to my role as a mother, as a maintenance worker. People didn't see me. I was furious, but it opened a door. My work has progressed from being responsible for my baby's survival as a profound kind of maintenance work to looking at the larger systems of maintenance in our society, such as sanitation.

Many people spend their time working at jobs that consist of maintenance activities. The notion of "taking care of"—whether taking care of a city function, a river system, or our planet—includes the maintenance of systems that are integral to our health and well-being. Creation takes place in an instant, but the maintenance function takes the rest of life.

WHAT IS THE DIFFERENCE BETWEEN THE ARTISTIC PROCESS AND THE MAINTENANCE PROCESS?

As an artist I am free, free to create. We are free beings. Along with this reality is the reality of the finite natural resources on which we depend. My work collides the infinite nature of artistic expression into the reality that we have finite resources with which to create the material world and to sustain the population. It comes out of the question of what to do with limited resources, what to do that is meaningful. I use garbage as my medium to push the issue of our power to transform garbage into something that connects people to the earth.

The sanitation labor force is a classical maintenance system. They work twenty-four hours a day, keeping the city going. Most people do not understand this. Sanitation workers feel invisible, and there is a stigma connected to garbage. The sanitation workers will ask, "Why call me a garbage man or woman? I'm a san-worker! It's not my garbage, it's the people's."

The biggest maintenance system in New York City is the Sanitation Department. Sanitation is one of the most essential services in any city. But the population as a whole has an "out of sight, out of mind" mentality. People think sanitation is outside of culture. The challenge is to get the public to understand that waste is an extension of ourselves and how we inhabit the earth. There is a relationship between the role of mother, one who attends to the basics of life, and the role of the maintenance worker, who tends to the vital needs of our cities. We are dependent on these relationships for our survival.

TELL US ABOUT THE SANITATION SYSTEM AS A MEDIUM FOR ART. WHAT KIND OF PROJECTS HAVE YOU DONE THAT INCORPORATE ART AND GARBAGE?

One of my performance pieces involved shaking hands with all of New York City's 8,500 sanitation workers. I shook hands with each worker, and said the truth, "Thank you for keeping New York City alive." I went along thousands of curb miles with thousands of workers, literally walking out the city, making a human map that constituted a portrait of New York City's living underbelly. It took five years.

Since 1983, I have been working on Flow City at the 59th Street Marine Transfer Station, on the Hudson River. It was the first municipal infrastructure disposal system designed as a public art physical and video environment built right into daily operations. I know it was a groundbreaker as a concept, because we had to get new zoning for it. It had simply been against the law before that for the public to have a permanent place in a sanitation facility.

This work is inching along. My design is built into the facility's structure. It still needs about $750,000 to open up. Since the rest of the waterfront in this area, both to the Riverside South (to its north) and the Hudson River Park (to its south) are beginning to be developed, I have hope for it.

I am also beginning work on a Percent for Art Commission I received to be the Artist of New York City's Fresh Kills Landfill, the world's largest "man-made" structure. I will work as a member of the design team to plan and then implement the closure, end use, restoration, and transformation of this site. Hopefully, eventually, it too can become a public site. I think it can be a great Free University of Transformation and Ecology, a social sculpture we have all made in common.

My work has been as varied as a permanent commission with thousands of "agitated" recyclables for a museum in Taejon, Korea, to performance art involving the choreography of twenty-seven trucks and three barges carrying one hundred tons of crushed cobalt-blue recyclable glass on the Rhone River in France.

WHAT IS THE BIGGEST CHALLENGE FACING EARTH ARTISTS?

There are few opportunities to do research and development, which is vital. There need to be opportunities for artists to experiment, invent, and innovate to make ecological concepts understandable through art. Now we have scientists and engineers do infrastructure work, and it is out of the public eye. Much of the infrastructure is under the jurisdiction of government, which is in the public domain. Artists can replace the aesthetic of out-of-sight, out-of-mind with one in which people take an interest in how our cities function and how they affect us.

WHY IS IT IMPORTANT TO CREATE PUBLIC SPACES OUT OF LANDFILL SITES?

Our garbage sites are sites of transformation and renewal. I believe that landfill and Superfund sites can have the same transformative power as churches. In churches, one can come into contact with one's sins and failures in a sanctuary and be transformed. The sites of landfills and garbage can be transformative as well: the place of decay becomes the place of renewal, the place of decomposition becomes the place of transformation.

I have been working on a project with the Mountain Lake Workshop in Virginia, with its director, Ray Kass, and the world-renowned methanogeneticist, Dr. James Ferry. I want to make the "other world" transparent: the world of "anaerobes"—single-cell microscopic microbes that decompose organic material. They're the real workers at the landfill, and inside our intestines as well. They are our partners in the carbon cycle. They represent a quarter of all life on the planet. They make our survival possible. I want to create images of the whole living world—including these creatures. We cannot actually face ourselves and understand ourselves—who we are, what we can do—without understanding whole systems into which we fit, including methanogens.

WHAT IS THE FUTURE OF PUBLIC WORKS ART?

If we allow government regulators, engineers, and lawyers to design the remediation of degraded and abused places—the new infrastructure—of which there are thousands and thousands of sites available each year, we will fill up the American landscape with meatloaf-shaped anonymous humps. Is that us? Is that the landscape we shall leave behind? A double ugly legacy plopped on top of polluted air, earth, and water? There are many, many creators, artists, architects, landscape architects, who want to join other professionals and officials and citizens at the table and be responsible for designing everything about the public sphere. Everything. Re-creating our public infrastructure can be the great design challenge of our time.

WHAT OTHER CHALLENGES FACE OUR COUNTRY WITH REGARD TO MAKING CONNECTIONS BETWEEN ART, ECOLOGY, AND THE URBAN ENVIRONMENT?

Our educational system has stripped people of their senses. People are dreadfully impoverished. The way to change this is to learn about natural processes and systems and to make engineering and the science of nature public rather than private languages. We need to restore people's confidence in their ability to perceive the world around them through their senses.

Artists can bring a personal resonating voice to the public sphere. My dream is that this voice can retain its unique individuality even at great public scale, even in the middle of the most necessary everyday public workplace. I believe that this creating voice isn't drowned out in the swirl of everyday. It is precisely this individual voice that each member of the public body can respond to, voice to voice, feeling to feeling. Artists can help to make unique places out of "anywheres" where people from everywhere can feel enlivened, like a singer whose song comes back to connect you with the deepest recesses of your being.

Anneke Van Waesberghe *is president of East Meets West (EMW), an international nonprofit organization involved in design-for-the-environment (DFE) issues based in New York City and the Netherlands. She has been involved with environmental projects for the last ten years and is interested in looking at the aesthetic issues related to design and the environment.*

WHAT DOES EAST MEETS WEST DO?

East Meets West is a design-oriented organization that works as a liaison with nonprofit organizations, designers, government, and corporations to assist them in greening their product lines. Products range from furniture to textiles to proposals for new products made from renewable resources such as bamboo, jute, kenaf, seaweed, coconut, and banana leaves.

HOW DOES EAST MEETS WEST DIFFER FROM OTHER ORGANIZATIONS INVOLVED IN DFE ISSUES?

What distinguishes EMW from other organizations is that I look at the aesthetic side of environmental design. I am interested in integrating principles of sustainable development with the aesthetics of design so consumers don't have to compromise when making decisions about the products they want to buy. I want DFE to influence products to be competitive, attractive, and environmentally sensitive. What also distinguishes EMW from other organizations is my interest in the use of alternative materials for new product development.

WHAT IS A TYPICAL DAY LIKE FOR YOU?

I spend a lot of time bringing people from different walks of life together so they can understand what an important role designers can play in environmental issues. My daily activities may include being on the computer, sending faxes, hosting international colleagues, presenting lectures, taking phone calls, facilitating design competitions, and meeting with the president of Russia. What makes my work so interesting is being able to do all these things and appreciating the value of each of them.

WHAT ARE THE MAJOR PROBLEMS FACING US?

Overpopulation and poverty.

WHERE DO YOU GO FOR INSPIRATION?

I love looking at textiles and contemporary art.

WHAT ARE YOUR FAVORITE BOOKS OR MAGAZINES?

Tao, Teilhard, and Western Thinking by Allerd Stikker and *Business and the Environment* by Cutter Communications.

HOW DID YOU BECOME INTERESTED IN ENVIRONMENTAL ISSUES?

Through the Global Forum for Spiritual and Parliamentary Leaders, which brings together people from all over the world with different religious, spiritual, scientific, and arts backgrounds to talk about how to construct a sustainable future.

ANY ADVICE TO PEOPLE WANTING TO ENTER THE ENVIRONMENTAL FIELD?

Fund-raising is something that most nonprofits spend 80 percent of their time doing. It is a drain on all the good work you can do. So try to make a business out of your work.

PEARLS OF WISDOM?

Relax and do it.

Entrepreneurs & Small Business

Jason Grant *is cofounder of EcoTimber International, Inc., a business involved in harvesting, manufacturing, and distribution of ecological forest products. He has a B.A. from Reed College. Prior to his involvement in EcoTimber, Mr. Grant was a teacher and environmental activist.*

WHAT MOTIVATED YOU TO CREATE ECOTIMBER INTERNATIONAL?

While visiting a friend in England in the summer of 1991, I met the founders of an enterprise called the Ecological Trading Company (ETC)—to my knowledge, the first business in the world to attempt to create a market for tropical hardwoods stemming from community-oriented sustainable forestry. It was the career equivalent of love at first sight. I knew then with certainty that my future lay in what I would later call the "good wood" business.

Then the work began. I returned to the United States with a short list of contacts and began networking. Within six months, I had established myself in San Francisco and identified the individuals with whom I was to cofound EcoTimber International. Another year was devoted to researching and writing our first business plan. After our incorporation in October of 1992, we begged and borrowed seed money largely from family and friends to launch the enterprise. By early 1993 we had taken the plunge: rented a warehouse, ordered our first shipment of hardwoods from small-scale "ecoforestry" operations in Papua New Guinea, and initiated the colossal task of building markets for sustainable forest products.

WHAT WAS THE KEY TO CREATING YOUR BUSINESS?

I think one of the basics of entrepreneuring lies in recognizing that, whatever the nature of your business, a large part of your eventual success will ride on your ability to identify and win the support of the key individuals or stakeholders who can best further your cause. Potential stakeholders can include customers, vendors, investors, advisors, friends, interns, employees, and anyone else who might have a stake in helping you to succeed.

WHAT ARE THE MOST PRESSING CHALLENGES?

Our challenges lie in explaining the complex issues that underlie deforestation and providing a rationale for sustainable forestry in an upbeat and compelling marketing message, managing supply irregularities and customer expectations in an emergent industry that is still struggling to meet the standards of the mainstream timber trade, and stimulating demand for sustainable forest products without overburdening the production capacity of currently existing ecological forestry operations.

WHAT ARE THE MAJOR TRENDS IN ECOENTREPRENEURSHIP, SPECIALLY WITH REGARD TO WOOD USE?

There is a worldwide movement to define standards and procedures for monitoring and certifying sustainable forestry that is rapidly gaining momentum. Forestry certification is similar in many respects to certification for organic agriculture. Both types of certifiers send teams of professionals to assess a given operation's on-the-ground practices according to a preexisting set of environmental and—in the case of forestry certification—social criteria. If the criteria are met, the certifier then provides a "stamp" that can differentiate the ecological product in the marketplace. Whether it's for forestry or agriculture, the rationale is to empower consumers to cast a dollar vote for more sustainable practices.

Although environmental certification for forestry and forest products is still in an early stage, a number of credible certifiers have already arisen, including the Smart Wood program of the Rainforest Alliance (New York) and the Green Cross program of Scientific Certification Systems (Oakland,), both of which have already certified several well-managed forestry operations in the United States and abroad.

Critical to the institutional future of forestry certification is the international nongovernmental organization the Forest Stewardship Council (FSC). Officially founded in 1993, the FSC is currently elaborating broad yet comprehensive guidelines for ecological forestry in temperate, tropical, and boreal forests. The FSC has also been charged with accrediting certification organizations that adhere to FSC guidelines—in effect, certifying the certified. In providing baseline standards and acting as an independent watchdog over certification organizations, the FSC's main task is to reduce confusion for industry and consumers alike.

Certification has provided the basis for a number of large companies in the United States and Europe and even some governments to begin promoting a market transition toward sustainable forestry. The more far-sighted companies recognize that public awareness of the many negative environmental and socioeconomic impacts of global deforestation and demand for sustainable forest products will grow concomitantly.

BOOKS, TRADE JOURNALS, OR MAGAZINES THAT YOU READ OR RECOMMEND?

Printed resources for staying abreast of developments in the good wood movement are presently limited due to the newness of the field. Two of the most useful publications are *Understory*, published by the Woodworkers Alliance for Rainforest Protection (WARP), and back issues of *Initiatives*, published by the Forest Partnership. The Forest Stewardship Council has been generating regular newsletters, and Island Press offers a useful book called *Defining Sustainable Forestry*.

ANY ADVICE FOR THOSE INTERESTED IN STARTING THEIR OWN COMPANY?

Anyone either planning an environmentally aware career or thinking of starting an ecological enterprise will have to confront the contradictions inherent in doing business and behaving ecologically. We tend to consume far more energy and resources and produce far more waste than necessary. We need to ask ourselves how to produce products and minimize environmental risk. We must not lose sight of the fact that the goal of ecological entrepreneuring is to manifest a steady-state economy and provide a practical basis for sustainable business practices. If we do, we risk becoming party to a process of greenwashing (advertising environmental benefits that do not reflect the larger operating practices of a business) despite our best intentions.

***Paula Healy** is a product manager at Tom's of Maine in Kennebunk, Maine. She received a B.A. in English from Boston College in 1983.*

WHAT IS A TYPICAL DAY LIKE FOR YOU?

As part of the marketing brand team at Tom's, I am involved in many aspects of developing and growing our brand of natural personal-care products. My focus is on helping Tom's understand the market and our customers so we can best plan for future growth. It includes analyzing potential market and product opportunities. A typical day's agenda may include revising a sales forecast; working on new packaging for a product launch; researching market trends and competitors; doing a profit-loss analysis for entering a new market; reviewing new legislation on packaging labels; attending a new-product development team meeting; and meeting with our sales or production people to discuss the status of a project.

HOW DID YOU GET YOUR CURRENT POSITION?

I was promoted recently to product manager from assistant product manager (of oral care). My new role was created to help us better plan for the future and understand the issues that affect us. My promotion was part of a restructuring of the brand team, from strictly a product line focus to one that now includes products and new initiatives. It allows us to be more intentional and proactive in responding to trends and issues, including those relating to the environment.

WHAT IS YOUR PAST WORK HISTORY?

Prior to Tom's I worked at a sail and power boat company, Sabre Yachts, as promotions manager for four years. It was smaller than Tom's but had a similar corporate culture or "conscience" and entrepreneurial spirit that I enjoyed.

Other positions since college have had a marketing focus and include advertising salesperson for a local newspaper, assistant marketing communications manager for a biotech firm, and registrar at a computer training center.

WHAT IS THE KEY TO GETTING A JOB WITH AN ENVIRONMENTAL DIMENSION OR STRATEGY?

In my experience at Tom's, if you are competent, creative, and skillful at what you do and you're someone with a caring attitude—about those around you and the environment—then you have a great start.

WHO IS PART OF YOUR ENVIRONMENTAL TEAM OR STAFF?

To a certain degree everyone at Tom's is part of our "environmental" team. We each have a responsibility to do what our environmental mission directs us to do.

WHAT ARE THE MOST PRESSING CHALLENGES IN YOUR WORK?

Doing my part at Tom's, in the balancing act of being financially, socially, and environmentally responsible, includes among other things having a full understanding of the regulatory environment and keeping abreast of all the trends in packaging. What's considered good for the environment today may not be tomorrow as new technology and new regulations move us forward. Staying on top of it all—that's a challenge in itself.

WHAT ARE YOUR WORK PRIORITIES AS THEY RELATE TO ENVIRONMENTAL ISSUES AND PROJECTS?

Get a better handle on state legislation about recyclability claims so I can anticipate where we will need to be in two to five years. Continue to promote recycling. Continue to be innovative in introducing products that are not "wasteful" in any way but that make sense, are effective, and make use of our natural resources in a *sustainable* way. Do an in-depth life-cycle analysis (cradle to grave) of the packaging materials we use. Work with vendors to find packaging solutions we can all benefit from (for example, a recyclable plastic tube). Share our expertise with others and learn from a meaningful dialogue with them. This means being educational and informative in our communications with consumers and everyone else we deal with in our business.

WHERE DO YOU SEE JOB GROWTH IN AREAS OF ENVIRONMENTAL MANAGEMENT?

Everywhere. I think the environment is *the* number one issue for business. It has to be, or there will be no environment for our children and their children.

WHAT BOOKS OR TRADE JOURNALS DO YOU RECOMMEND?

Newsletters are among the most helpful sources for us: the *Green Business Letter* published by Tilden Press, Inc. (Washington, D.C.); and the *Public Pulse* (the Roper Organization, New York) are all good. We get a host of personal-care newsletters and magazines, which are important reading: *FDC Reports for Toiletries, Fragrances and Skin Care (The Rose Sheet)*, *Household and Personal Care Products Industry*, and *Soap, Cosmetics, Chemical Specialties*. *Packaging* magazine is very helpful when working with purchasing to source green packaging materials and get industry information. Also, there are the publications that specifically deal with the channels of distribution in which we do business, like *Natural Food Merchandiser, Chain Drug Review, Progressive Grocer, Supermarket News*. Consumer magazines are helpful for green ideas and trends: *E Magazine, The Environmental Magazine*, *Outside*,

Natural Health, *New Age Journal*, *Mother Earth News*, and *Garbage* are some I read on a regular basis.

WHAT IS YOUR FAVORITE ENVIRONMENTAL BOOK OR MAGAZINE?

I don't really have a favorite, but as an aspiring gardener and a Tom's of Maine employee, I recently enjoyed a beautifully written little book of observations on "backyard nature" called *Saving Graces* by Roger B. Swain. It gave me some interesting insights on witch hazel, an ingredient in our mouthwash!

ANY ADVICE FOR PEOPLE INTERESTED IN GREENING THEIR CAREERS?

You can be an environmentalist at any level and in any organization you work for. You don't have to look for ways to come to you. You create them. You bring your inspiration and knowledge about the environment to your work.

Nancy Hirshberg *is the environmental coordinator of Stonyfield Farm Yogurt in Londonderry, New Hampshire. She received a B.A. from Hampshire College in 1985 with a concentration in agriculture and education.*

HOW WOULD YOU DESCRIBE A TYPICAL DAY?

Chaos. Priorities change frequently, but presently my primary responsibility is setting up an environmental management system at Stonyfield. We have many sound environmental practices in place already, and my task is to institutionalize them so that as Stonyfield continues to grow; a strong environmental ethic and responsible practices permeate all aspects of the company. I also oversee and help coordinate the institution of new environmentally responsible practices within the company. I am studying everything from our waste water and chemical use to product packaging, indoor air quality, and solid-waste minimization.

HOW DID YOU GET YOUR JOB?

Because of my education and agriculture background, I was contracted by the company to help open a visitors' center. I had planned on leaving after the center opened. At that time, however, Stonyfield was experiencing rapid growth that was requiring much of the president's (Gary Hirshberg's) time. Gary had primary responsibility for overseeing the company's adherence to its environmental mission. I was hired to relieve him of those responsibilities. I report directly to Gary, and we have weekly debriefing meetings.

How did you become interested in the environment?

When I began my college education, I believed that if people only knew the extent of the earth's environmental problems, they'd change their behavior. I saw education as a path for effecting change, whether the vehicle was teaching, making movies, writing, or whatever. As time went on, I began to see that in addition to education, we must have positive models that demonstrate the kinds of changes we must make to sustain the earth's resources. Business has an enormous impact on the use of natural resources, and it's essential that we develop models that demonstrate how businesses can minimize their impact on the environment. Stonyfield Farm is striving for maximum ecological efficiency with a minimum of negative environmental impact.

What skills are needed to do your job?

An extensive, holistic understanding and awareness of environmental issues and directions are needed to reverse the current trends. An understanding of how to effect change. Education. Writing, communication skills, the ability to make highly technical information comprehensive to people and in a form that they can *act* on. Technical background: engineering, agriculture, soils, ecology, writing, writing, writing.

What is the greatest challenge in your job?

First, to empower all employees to take personal responsibility for seeing that the company adheres to our environmental mission. If my coworkers think that the environmental impact of our operations is "the environmental coordinator's job," then I have failed. Second, to develop new solutions to old problems. To seek innovative solutions to minimize our impact on the environment and use resources wisely.

Where do you see yourself in five to ten years?

I imagine that this position will develop into an operating team–level position (the top management). We will likely have facilities in locations throughout the world with environmental staffing at each site.

WHERE DO YOU SEE JOB GROWTH IN YOUR FIELD?

I get calls almost weekly from companies interested in starting a position such as the one I hold. Corporations are beginning to see that ecological efficiency increases a company's overall efficiency, reduces costs, improves employee morale, and improves the bottom line. As long as the environmental coordinator can demonstrate these results, there will be increased opportunities.

WHAT TRENDS DO YOU SEE?

Traditionally, environmental affairs people are either regulatory compliance, health and safety, marketing, communications, or "fire fighters." I think the trend will move toward more proactive environmental initiatives.

WHAT BOOKS OR MAGAZINES DO YOU READ OR RECOMMEND?

State of the World and *World Watch Publications*, *Rocky Mt. Institute Newsletter* and publications, *Utne Reader*, *New Farm* magazine, *Plastics News*, *Dairy Foods* magazine, *BSR Newsletter*, and I attend lots of great conferences.

WHERE DO YOU GO FOR INSPIRATION?

Conferences . . . to see other people and companies doing it! Especially Businesses for Social Responsibility.

WHAT EXPERIENCE GOT YOU INTERESTED IN THE ENVIORNMENT?

The proposal of a nuclear power plant in Seabrook, New Hampshire, when I was in eighth grade. Through my work in opposition to the power plant, I developed an awareness about energy and waste and the world's limited resources.

Victoria Johnson-Parratt *is president and founder of One Song Enterprises, a catalog of environmentally friendly products. Each product is evaluated for its environmental merits for inclusion in the catalog. Ms. Parrat resides in Willoughby, Ohio.*

WHAT IS YOUR BACKGROUND?

My childhood was spent on stage. In my teens I studied and taught dance, sang in church, with a female trio spent a summer touring in a theatre troupe, and won awards for acting at state levels. After graduation, I taught ballroom dance professionally till, nearly bankrupt and unwilling to live on the street, I married and took a string of "regular" jobs leading to seven-year employment at a large, loud, and filthy factory. The pay and benefits were top-notch and allowed me to teach on a limited level and contract out as a professional choreographer for local theatre groups and schools without worrying about my next meal.

I then moved from the front range of the Rockies to Cleveland, Ohio, in August of 1988 and shocked my body into total toxicity. I saw a doctor who told me I was allergic to Ohio. I had to get out of Ohio or get creative by becoming a food detective, learning more than the average citizen ever wants to know about colors, additives, preservatives, packaging, and industry growing practices. About the same time the press was starting to release stories about the twentieth anniversary of Earth Day, providing leads to new knowledge about issues that in some way or another affected me. All this led to the uneasy realization that I had to take responsibility for the effect of what happens around me.

I called my local city hall to volunteer for Earth Day. I started by passing out recycling bins on my street. I used the same sleuthing skills I had acquired to learn to live without the four major food groups to find out everything I could about recycling. The more I learned, the more I asked. Friends started asking me about other products and issues being discussed in the media. The more I looked, the more incredible things I found, but my frustration levels grew in proportion to the hassle it was to first learn about new products and then to find them available for sale. Somewhere on the way to calling over one thousand companies and organizations that I found listed in books, magazines, lists compiled by animal rights and environmental groups, business referrals, addresses I pulled off products, magazine ads, and anywhere else I found a connection, I realized that this much work, although fun and informative, is a job that somebody should do *as* a job. Someone had to find these neat products, learn as much as possible about them, and offer them for sale so I could buy them and use them. The logical choice seemed to be me. With that simple realization, One Song was born.

HOW DID YOU GO ABOUT CREATING ONE SONG?

There were no degrees in this particular career and few examples of others trying to do or doing projects similar to mine. That gave me the freedom to follow a few simple business rules, then make the rest up exactly the way I thought it should be done.

I wanted to create something to support my family while doing the most good for the planet they will inherit. I want a comfortable and safe workplace with creativity and social consciousness a requirement. I went forward determined to learn everything I could about what I needed to know before I offered anything for sale. I've done this backwards. I have no business degree—I've never even taken typing—but I have tutored two people through bookkeeping and accounting courses at high school and college levels. I had an idea, an answer to a question that came in so clear and crystalline as to be termed a vision. I had defined my wishes, and the angels heard.

I spent the first two years learning the key threads to the web of planetary concerns, defining the issues I wanted to deal with and the parameters I would set. I spent many hours in my local library and took advantage of every service they offered. Friends and family helped test products, and eventually we had six test families for personal care and cleaners, half with allergies and sensitivities and half not affected by generally available products. I tracked down answers to fun questions like: Do sponges have nervous systems? (Not really, but they do react to stimuli.) What is carmine, and is it really cruelty free? (It's a little red bug from the high desert, and no, it's not technically cruelty free.) What are ingredients really made of and can they pose a threat to people and the planet we live on? It took six months to weed through the six hundred companies that made it through the first round of tests and study to arrange the thirty that made it into the first catalog, published in the spring of 1992. We printed without gloss and wasted space with soybean ink on 100 percent postconsumer paper, listing the 382 products we felt best fit our standards of being environmentally friendly, cruelty free, recycled, organically grown, and socially conscious.

WHAT DO YOU WANT YOUR CUSTOMERS TO COME AWAY WITH?

I firmly believe that as simple consumers, consuming being something we naturally do with every breath, we can direct the use of the majority of our planet's resources every year simply by paying attention to what we buy. By sheer numbers, we can control the demand side of business. American industry has to take the brunt of the blame for the general trashing of the American environment, and undoubtedly, the

American consumer has to take the brunt of the blame for allowing it to continue. By educating ourselves and asking questions beyond the thirty-second sound bite, we can determine what we really want and what we're willing to do for it.

In a policy deemed insane and self-destructive by mainstream business advisers, One Song never goes where we're not invited, allowing potential customers and media to discover us and share us with their friends. Without ever buying, renting, trading, or sharing a mailing list, the first one thousand catalogs quietly wandered into every state in the union and fifteen foreign countries.

HOW DO YOU STAY INFORMED?

I recommend and refer to the writings and works of Deborah Dadd-Redalia, Joel Makower, Annie Berthod-Bond, John Robbins, Al Gore, Jr., Adam Rogers, Rachel Carson, Adolf Steiner, David Brower, David and Nikki Goldbeck, and Jimmy Carter. I read *E Magazine*, *Garbage*, *Earth News*, and *Green Alternatives* magazines, Co-op America's *Green Pages* and *Boycott Action News* and *Utne Reader* voraciously. I use the *Clinical Toxicology of Commercial Products* by Gosselin and Smith to find out how most things are made; I use GAO (General Accounting Office) reports to keep informed on what's happening in Washington, D.C.; and I ask a lot of questions of people who make it their responsibility to have answers. I also recommend the use and support of public libraries for a world of information.

PEARLS OF WISDOM?

To anyone brave or crazy enough to commit to following a dream, my advice to you is define your questions, study everything you possibly can, never be afraid to ask what seem to be dumb questions of anyone willing to patiently explain things to you, be nice, and don't quit. Margaret Mead once said, "When the people lead, the leaders will follow." We have to admit that we are the people and we make the change.

Julie M. Lewis *is founder and vice president of research for Deja Shoe, a company that manufactures shoes out of recycled material. Prior to starting Deja Shoe, she was a teacher and nutrition educator. She received a B.S. in biology in 1977 and an M.S. in nutrition and biochemistry in 1981 from Southern Oregon State College.*

HOW DID YOU DECIDE TO START YOUR COMPANY?

I was motivated to start Deja Shoe because markets for recycled materials hadn't kept up with the improved collection programs. It was obvious to me that a product needed to be developed that not only created a market for recyclables but also was useful and durable and by its very presence educated people about the uses for recyclables.

I went to a conference in 1989 on creating markets for recycled materials. It was there that I learned how even exporters in the field of solid waste were lamenting the fact that there were limited markets for recyclables. After researching materials for products, I learned of a grant program that Metro, a regional government agency that owns our landfills and runs our zoo, was offering to promote markets for recyclables. Luckily, I fit all the criteria necessary to apply for the grant, so I went through the lengthy application and proposal writing process. In the meantime, I acquired a shoe component source book and started calling vendors to ask if they'd consider using recycled material in their processes. I eventually got companies that cooperated with me. I got a local shoe manufacturer to produce a prototype for me. Prototype in hand, I made a presentation as a finalist on Metro's "grant hopefuls" list.

A month later I was awarded $110,000 in seed money to manufacture the first five thousand pairs of Deja Shoes. They rolled off the production line in the summer of 1990. After that I was going crazy shipping the shoes out of my basement at home.

Later, a friend who is a business lawyer suggested I form a management team and make it a real business. He hooked me up with the former CEO of Avia Footwear, Dean Croft. Dean and I met and had numerous conversations about the direction of my company. He recommended two other former employees of Avia: Bruce MacGregor, former vice president of marketing and development, and Scott Taylor, former chief financial officer. The four of us moved into offices and worked for nothing for six months. Dean, Scott, and Bruce put up their own money to keep us going until we could land some venture capital money. In March 1992, after doing fifteen presentations to venture capital groups, we landed our initial venture funding of $2.5 million. We also became incorporated as Deja, Inc.

WHAT IS A TYPICAL DAY FOR YOU?

A typical day of work for me includes meetings to discuss a variety of issues at Deja Shoe, such as information sharing among employees, strategy, marketing, and finance, and following up on new material leads. It may include a presentation at a local school on recycling issues and/or green business or entrepreneurial subjects. I often travel to conferences to make presentations, as well. Sometimes I spend a couple of hours looking through books for ideas either for a material to use in the shoe or for something to stimulate my thinking for a new idea.

WHAT IS THE KEY TO CREATING AN ENVIRONMENTAL BUSINESS?

Be sure to "walk your talk." In other words, your credibility suffers if one product you produce follows some "environmental" ethic (becoming a token product that you think defines who you are) while nothing else you make follows those codes. The same is true for the way your business is run. If you make claims about your product being somehow safe for the environment, yet you don't buy recycled office paper, you're just playing a marketing game.

An environmental business also has to maintain its credibility in the business world. Many times well-meaning environmentalists think their product will sell on its virtues alone. The best combination to make an environmental business work is respect for the environment and understanding of the ways of corporate America. The two must come together if we are to really make a difference. We must stop thinking that the two are at odds. We must learn to listen to each other.

WHAT IS THE MOST PRESSING CHALLENGE YOUR COMPANY FACES?

The most pressing challenges we face include educating the consumer about the importance of supporting businesses concerned with sustainable development; getting continued cooperation from vendors and associates as we go through start-up growing pains; handling our materials (because we have such specific requirements that we can only get our component supplies from certain vendors); and convincing vendors to use recycled content in cases where it's less expensive to use virgin content.

DO YOU HAVE ANY ADVICE FOR PEOPLE WHO WANT TO START A BUSINESS?

Think about how you can do good for the environment and make a real business as well. This might mean that your product has to perform as well or look as good as a comparable virgin product. It may mean having to change preconceived notions about environmental products being of lower quality by making a product that performs even better than its virgin counterpart. Be sure the price is also competitive. Even though studies show consumers are willing to pay more for an environmentally "good" product, we have found that when it comes right down to it, most won't.

ANY FINAL THOUGHTS OR RECOMMENDATIONS?

The environmental industry is wide open. There is lots of room for innovation in recycling technology, waste reduction strategies, life-cycle analysis for determining a product's true impact on the environment, methods for analyzing the true cost to the environment of doing business (placing monetary value on the use of our resources), and education in the "how to" of creating a business based on environmental and economic sustainability. I don't believe there are any formal education programs that can teach you these things—aha! another opportunity! But a basic education could aid any creative person to dig in and find out what they need to do to get these types of programs going.

RECOMMENDED BOOKS, JOURNALS, MAGAZINES?

Publications I recommend are magazines such as *In Business* magazine, and *Garbage* magazine. Books include *The Ecology of Commerce* and *Growing a Business*, both by Paul Hawken, and *Environmental by Design* by Kim Leclair and David Rousseau. I recommend the newsletter *Business and the Environment.*

***Jeff Lindenthal, Melissa Smedley, and Jodi Lindenthal** are the founders of Found Stuff Paperworks. Jeff Lindenthal has a B.A. from Alfred University and an M.S. in public policy from the University of Massachusetts, Boston. Melissa Smedley has a B.A. in fine arts from Brown University and an M.F.A. from the University of California, San Diego. Jodi Lindenthal has a B.A. in human ecology from the College of the Atlantic. (The questions that follow are answered by Melissa.)*

HOW DID YOU START YOUR COMPANY?

Jeff started making paper in 1990 for our wedding invitations. His interest in learning the craft of paper making in combination with his career at the time as a recycling consultant gave rise to the idea of making paper from junk mail (which was arriving in unforeseen proportions at his door). So, after the wedding we continued to make paper in our backyard using equipment Jeff had built. We tried selling it for the first time as postcards on Earth Day 1990 and sold everything we had made in a few hours. From there we gradually refined our methods and began producing notecards and envelopes. By sending out samples and prices to a few selected stores, our 100 percent Junk Mail stationery was soon for sale at establishments such as Smith & Hawken and the Whitney Museum of American Art gift store.

Paper can be made from virtually any plant material, and we started to consider the many other materials we could use that were destined for a landfill. We have focused on the use of textile scraps from various manufacturers of environmentally friendly clothing such as organic cottons, hemp, and linen. Not only does this help us, as a new company, to be provided with low-cost or free materials, but it also helps those proactive manufacturers who are interested in finding a way to produce goods that generate very little waste or negative environmental impact.

WHERE DO YOU SEE THE COMPANY IN THE FUTURE?

We see ourselves studying the whole phenomenon of paper. We plan to continue to make technical innovations with our paper-making procedures so that we can invent more kinds of unique paper-based products, all of which are created from "found stuff."

Challenges are for us to continue to grow at a pace we can manage and to generate additional capital. Also, our challenge is to make a specialty product here in the United States using hand labor, and to face the consequences of our papers being a little more expensive because of this. Another constant effort is to devoting a portion of our work to educating customers as we sell things. We can't just sit back and think that we're doing something good for the environment and therefore it should succeed. There is still a need for consciousness raising done in such a way that people buying the products recognize that they can be participants in something positive—that their choices matter.

WHAT IS KEY TO CREATING AN ENVIRONMENTAL BUSINESS?

The key to creating an environmental business is to learn what it means to conduct business in an environmentally sound manner and to completely integrate those principles into your way of going about living. The word "environmental" can't be like a hat you put on. Its got to be your whole head and body. This way starting a business, growing a garden, running a household all take place with a natural conscientiousness toward the environment.

Growing a garden is an analogy we like for running a business because it implies a cyclical process. You have to do things like composting and applying compost to build up your soil to produce the crops you grow for market. All the while, you don't introduce anything to your garden that would compromise its ability to produce. Business can likewise be conducted in such a holistic and sustainable manner.

WHAT SKILLS ARE IMPORTANT IN YOUR FIELD?

More than specific skills, it seems that what is necessary is a matter of attitude, an understanding of human participation in nurturing our own ecology, in both our personal lives and our local communities. As a "field," environmentalism needs to disperse itself into every kind of workplace. It needs to become the only way of doing business, rather than a specialty.

WHAT PUBLICATIONS DO YOU READ?

We read *In Business* magazine and *Buzzworm's Earth Journal*, trade journals, and library books. We also recommend reading the business section of any major newspaper. It is vital to keep abreast of what's going on.

We've found the writings of Paul Hawken to be inspirational, *Growing a Business* and *The Ecology of Commerce* in particular. It has been helpful to attend conferences and trade shows such as Ecotech and Eco Expo. Those opportunities for networking, sharing stories, and building a community of colleagues have been very important.

ANY FINAL THOUGHTS?

It seems that we are still in the midst of a culture where consumption, convenience, and disposability are too prevalent. So many things could be designed more intelligently with regard to the environment, but a sort of spiritual or moral imperative doesn't seem to be enough to put the really significant changes into motion. The necessary structural and societal progress will take a lot of time. Working for the environment can feel as though you're swimming against the tide. We recommend finding community wherever possible that connects your individual efforts to those of others, thereby adding to the momentum and creative energy that it requires for us all to keep forging ahead.

John Rothman *is co-owner of Tewsbury Gardens, a company that creates figurines out of cow manure for gardens. Mr. Rothman calls himself an entremanure. He has grown his business out of his basement in Lebanon, New Jersey. He has a Ph.D. in pharmacology from Tulane Medical School.*

WHAT MOTIVATED YOU TO START THIS COMPANY?

I was motivated to create a company that would allow me to work at home. I used to be the director of Clinical Drug Development for Hoffman LaRouche pharmaceuticals. Although I had built a ten-year career in the pharmaceutical industry, I wanted to do something else. I now have a very small company that makes shit figures.

WHAT DO YOU DO ON THE JOB?

I do everything on the job. I don't have a secretary. I lick every stamp, I address every envelope, I pay every bill. My partner, John Flaherty, and I take care of all of the administration. Not having a secretary means that you get interrupted about every thirty seconds with phone calls. The company has grown. In the year and a half we've been in business we're now selling in all fifty states as well as through two Canadian distributors and in the UK. So it's very lively, it's very busy. And there is no end to the detail. In fact, being detail oriented is the secret to our success.

HOW DID YOU CREATE THIS BUSINESS?

I created the business because I had an idea that making cow manure figurines might be commercially viable since cow manure is probably nature's finest fertilizer. It has been used since time immemorial as a structural building material. Humankind was building homes out of dung bricks before we could cut wood. So I figured if you could make a cow manure turtle or a cow manure frog that would last in the garden and withstand the elements and leach fertilizer into the soil as it sat there, you might have an advantage over, for example, a concrete turtle or a soapstone figure. It would be utilitarian as well as aesthetically pleasing.

In refining the concept, I took it out to Amish country, because I was looking for a handmolded craft work, and the Amish have a tradition of handcraft work as well as a high work ethic, and they are a dairy culture, so they are not put off by cow manure and the molding or shaping of it. Further refinements included the concept of making these things all natural and biodegradable. Actually, this was one of the pillars of the concept. So we began to use seeds for eyes. There is a whitewash on some figures made out of cottage cheese and lime. It's all natural. We package them in excelsior that is made out of poplar and aspen wood in recycled corrugated boxes. So basically the whole thing is very green in concept and execution. They are handmade, hand finished, completely 100 percent cow manure figures. I put together a network of Amish farmers who mold these on their farms. It's a cottage industry. There are probably fifty people doing it now. Our demand far outstrips our supply. We are shipping eight to ten thousand figures a week, and we're seven weeks backed up.

HOW DID YOU BECOME INTERESTED IN ENVIRONMENTAL ISSUES?

I have always been interested in environmental issues. I live out in the country; I'm a committeeman in an area that is trying to preserve its rural character. It's an old dairy farming area in New Jersey, halfway between New York and Philadelphia. We are striving against an incredible amount of developmental pressure to retain our character. We have no street lights, we have no sewers, and that's the way we like it, and that's the way we are going to keep it.

WHAT TIPS WOULD YOU PROVIDE FOR PEOPLE WHO ARE INTERESTED IN STARTING THEIR OWN GREEN BUSINESSES?

Clear the decks and be prepared to work sixteen to eighteen hours a day. Don't underestimate it. There is a high burnout factor. I'm fairly singed around the edges. Right now, I'd love to take some time off, but it's not possible. We will probably be doing a million and a half dollars this year. I've put every penny of that back into the business. I'm not pulling out any more money a year and a half after I started than I was the day I started. And I'm working every bit as hard as I've ever worked in my life.

WHERE DO YOU SEE YOUR BUSINESS IN FIVE TO TEN YEARS?

Lots of new product lines. Bigger fixed facility, a bigger workforce. Lots of ideas for products. I've yet to bring this company under control. It's still growing like a weed. We've got lots and lots of developmental problems, suffering from real growth pains. I have ideas for a number of products that would cost a fair bit to initiate in terms of up-front capitalization. This business is not yet capable of sustaining that capitalization. I'm fairly debt averse. I don't like to assume debt, although I may have to pretty soon. I would like to be able to pay my own way and not owe anything to anyone, but I don't know if that's possible in this day and age.

WHAT SKILLS ARE NEEDED IN THE FIELD?

Perseverance. You need to be able to keep on keeping on. It's nice if you are bright, it's nice if you are talented, it's nice if you are insightful, but all of that doesn't matter unless you persevere. That's the single most important attribute you need.

WHAT DO YOU RECOMMEND TO PEOPLE WHO ARE INTERESTED IN ENVIRONMENTAL CAREERS?

Just do it. Talk is cheap. You are gauged by your actions—not your thoughts or your talk, but your deeds. Do it.

ANY SUGGESTIONS OR WISDOM GLEANED FROM YOUR EXPERIENCE?

The one thing I would say is work hard, work often, work long. And if you put in a couple of years full of fifteen-hour days, you'll get lucky. Keep at it. Do it.

Helen Sizemore *is an executive assistant to the president of Real Goods, a company that provides energy-efficient products and educational materials for environmentally efficient living. Ms. Sizemore is responsible for human resource management as well as assisting the president. She received a B.A. in philosophy with a minor in art history from Ohio University in 1970.*

WHAT IS A TYPICAL DAY LIKE FOR YOU?

My day holds much variety—as executive assistant, I handle all of the mail that goes to the president, screen his calls, and schedule his calendar. I also work on special projects like contacting billboard sign painters for our new building site and consulting our lawyer on the wording of documents for our employees. I compiled the invitation list for the recent Small Business Awards reception and coordinated the event locally.

TELL ME ABOUT YOUR WORK HISTORY.

My work history includes grassroots political campaign work and community organizing. More recently, I worked for the state of California as a field representative and office manager for our local assemblyman. I developed an ability to research issues and compose letters in response to questions and/or constituents. I also honed my skills with regard to community needs and found I could see both sides of an issues if I listened to both sides. Most of my work has involved managing people and directing their energy to the task at hand.

HOW DID YOU COME TO BE WORKING WITH HUMAN RESOURCES?

My interest in human resources manifested itself when I realized that Real Goods would be significantly expanding its workforce in a relatively short time. I review our files, maintain the paper flow for new and terminated employees, revise the personnel handbook, and investigate alternative health insurance options. I also interview and hire for the administration department and forward the appropriate applications to managers who have spots to fill.

WHAT KIND OF QUALIFICATIONS DO YOU LOOK FOR IN A CANDIDATE?

We have a large pool of very qualified people in our area, many of whom moved here after completing college. Some of our positions are filled by recommendation and an application and interview process. We also receive inquiries from people from all over the country who are interested in working for us because they like our mission statement and purpose.

The environmental career training that we respect most is practicing a lifestyle that has the least impact on the planet. Our technical sales staff use the energy systems they discuss with customers, and many of our employees ride bicycles to work or carpool. Since we are a mail-order catalog company, marketing and sales training are also important.

WHAT IS THE MOST PRESSING ENVIRONMENTAL CHALLENGE FACING YOUR INDUSTRY?

It really bothers me to see new construction, especially in California, that does not take advantage of solar energy. Structures built without regard for the possibilities of passive-solar heating and without provision for outdoor views for refreshment of the mind and spirit seem antiquated.

WHAT TRENDS DO YOU SEE IN THE AREA OF INDEPENDENT, ENERGY-EFFICIENT LIVING?

It seems that more people are interested in building alternative-energy homes, evidenced by the growth of our Institute for Independent Living. These are seminars that meet for a weekend or a week and offer hands-on education in all aspects of alternative energy systems.

WHAT READING DO YOU RECOMMEND?

I read lots of environmental essays in magazines such as *Natural Health*, *Vegetarian Times*, and *Mother Jones*. I also read selections from *Money*, *Business Ethics*, and *Atlantic Monthly*, as well as daily newspapers and local weeklies.

Joshua Taylor *is president and founder of Cloud Nine, Inc., a company in New Jersey that offers a line of all-natural gourmet chocolate bars in non-traditional flavors. Before starting his own business, Mr. Taylor served for ten years as creative director for Caswell-Massey, a family perfumerie founded in 1752. He received a B.A. in journalism cum laude from the University of Texas after attending Boston University for two years and taking time off from college to follow the Grateful Dead and to serve as an apprentice to a master perfumer in France. He also worked as a professional jazz guitarist for three years after his college graduation.*

WHAT GOT YOU INTERESTED IN STARTING YOUR COMPANY, CLOUD NINE?

After Caswell-Massey was sold in 1989, I was trying to figure out where I was going. Having been a member of Greenpeace and the Sierra Club in college—and after following the Grateful Dead, who have a very strong environmental message—I decided to try to work for an environmental organization. So I began interviewing and spent many months hoping that one of those organizations would have a unique position for my intuitive marketing style. I didn't find that kind of position, so I decided to bring my consumer product marketing skills and my environmental concerns all together and create my own company. Cloud Nine affords me the opportunity to be the ultimate decision-maker combined with an environmental commitment, which makes the work worthwhile.

WHAT DID YOU HAVE TO DO TO GET STARTED IN THE CHOCOLATE BUSINESS?

When I decided to start my own business, I began to research with focus groups assembled in my home. I held taste tests of types of chocolate from Germany, Belgium, Switzerland, Brazil, and the United States. When I began to have an idea of what type of chocolate we were looking for, I began to research where to have the bars molded. It took eight to nine months of research to find a qualified plant that shared our environmental concerns. When it boiled down to the exact product we wanted to make, very few plants met our qualifications. Our flavors presented tremendous production problems because no one had ever made them before, so we had to run test lines of different flavors to get the bars right. Every time we introduce a new flavor, we're confronted with another technical difficulty because our machinery is so specific.

HOW DID YOU GO ABOUT GREENING YOUR PRODUCTS?

In order to get information to make a company environmentally friendly, it's valuable to consult with anthropologists, scientists, and researchers who know about this stuff. Through attending events such as the Eco Expo and contacting organizations with a strong environmental mission such as Cultural Survival, I found that there is a real network of environmental professionals for people to tap into. People love to talk about what they know. Hundreds of people offered me help and advice.

Our philosophy, as shared by all environmentalists, is to give back to the environment as much as we take from it. In our manufacturing process, we make every effort to conserve energy and natural resources by reprocessing heat, water, and electricity. Our packaging is made from recycled paper and printed with soy ink. We recognize that our environmental efforts from a manufacturing perspective are not enough. There is a need to support organizations such as the Rainforest Alliance in their effort to educate people on the biodiversity of the rain forest gene pool, because cocoa beans grow within ten degrees of the equator. Thus we contribute 10 percent of our profits toward these efforts.

WHAT ADVICE CAN YOU GIVE TO PEOPLE INTERESTED IN ENVIRONMENTAL ENTREPRENEURSHIP?

The concept of giving when you are in the business to make money is an oddity, but it speaks loudly of an entrepreneur's sincerity in his environmental efforts. Many people tried to dissuade me from giving money to environmental programs, but probably 50 percent of our sales have been a direct result of giving money away. Our success lies not only in the quality and uniqueness of our chocolates, but also in our interest in social responsibility.

In creating your own business, it's important to be prepared to live with risk and to be able to tolerate the pain of uncertainty, because it exists for years. What's also important is your capacity to hire. That's your number one decision. Know what you are good at—and don't kid yourself—and hire people with the qualities you need. I make sure I am surrounded by great people.

Also, for me, variety is not the spice of life; risk is the spice of life. Life begins on the other side of risk. I'm not talking about silly risks. Take the right risk, the appropriate risk, and there's a real benefit from arriving at the other side. It's a long process. Shoot high, start small, and be cautious in between.

Environmental Management

Leslie Carothers *is vice president of Environment, Health and Safety at United Technologies Corporation in Hartford, Connecticut, where she directs department activities worldwide. Prior to this position, she served as a commisioner for the department of environmental protection for Connecticut's programs for pollution control and management of state parks, forests, and fish and wildlife resources. She received a B.A. in government from Smith College, a law degree from Harvard University, and an L.L.M. from George Washington University.*

HOW LONG HAVE YOU BEEN INTERESTED IN THE ENVIRONMENTAL FIELD?

I entered the environmental field about twenty-five years ago when I went to work for an environmentalist congressman and, after that, to EPA. The field is intellectually demanding, and the goal of restoring and protecting the natural environment is one that I care about. It has been endlessly interesting for twenty-five years.

WOULD YOU DESCRIBE YOUR STAFF?

My staff of about forty includes environment, health, and safety people with technical and legal training. As a corporate staff office, we develop goals, standards, and training programs for the company, audit and report on performance to top management, and also manage the environmental cleanup of plant or disposal sites owned or used by discontinued operations of UTC.

This staffing level will decrease somewhat over time as we complete the site remediation work and as the standards development work reaches a maintenance level.

WHAT IS THE GREATEST CHALLENGE FACING YOUR COMPANY?

The biggest challenge to our company is integrating environment, health, and safety (EHS) awareness and accountability into all functions and operations of United Technologies worldwide. The time is past when you could manage the EHS effort as strictly a staff function.

Another challenge is to develop policies for international operations that promote sustainable development and properly manage future liabilities. This is an important task for our company as it is for other multinational businesses.

WHAT ARE SOME OF THE TRENDS IN YOUR INDUSTRY?

There is a trend toward fuller public disclosure of environmental performance, including measurements of performance against corporate goals. We need better measurements of environmental results at both the company and the country levels to know whether we are succeeding in improving the environment.

Financial tools like full-cost accounting can be a powerful means of highlighting real environmental costs and integrating consideration of them in decision-making.

ANY THOUGHTS ABOUT HOW PEOPLE CAN OBTAIN AN ENVIRONMENTAL POSITION?

Many disciplines can prepare people for environmental careers. There are plenty of scientific, technical, and legal problems to be solved, as well as managerial, marketing, and communications activities involving the environment. There is also challenging work to be done in business, government, education, and the nonprofit sector. People interested in environmental careers should think about what problems interest them and what sector they would like to be in and acquire some relevant academic training. Once you get your first job in the field and do well, other opportunities tend to open up for you.

WHAT PUBLICATIONS DO YOU READ?

I read publications from the Environmental Law Institute such as the *Environmental Forum* and the various reports as well as newsletters from organizations like the Nature Conservancy. I think books about the environment tend to be somewhat dry, and I don't have many favorites. Vice President Gore's book, *Earth in the Balance*, was thought provoking. Frances Cairncross' *Costing the Earth* is also worth reading.

WHAT DO YOU SEE AS THE MOST SERIOUS ENVIRONMENTAL PROBLEMS?

I think the most serious environmental problems internationally are the pressures of poverty and population growth. Here in the United States, the biggest environmental problems are wasteful and haphazard land development and the impacts of dependence on automobile transportation. In both U.S. and international arenas, the business community has the opportunity and the obligation to conduct its operations in a way that leaves the lightest footprint on the environment. Minimizing industrial pollution is necessary, but it is not, in my opinion, nearly enough to address the larger social and economic problems that are degrading the environment.

Rick Carr *is the Continuum® program manager for Crane and Company, Inc., in Dalton, Massachusetts. He received a B.S. in psychology at the University of Santa Clara in 1982 and an M.B.A. from Pepperdine University in 1992.*

WHAT ARE THE RESPONSIBILITIES OF YOUR JOB?

My primary responsibility is the establishment of a new business for Crane and Company. The Continuum program seeks to apply papermaking expertise as a waste-stream solution. We seek out situations where we can divert a waste stream and use our processes to add value to it, with the ultimate goal of returning it to the manufacturer (or a third party) for a second- (or third-) generation use. Our second project is making paper from shredded, worn U.S. currency that is normally landfilled after being deemed unfit for circulation. Each year 13.5 million pounds of currency shred is landfilled. We hope that the prospect of turning this material into a useful, second-generation paper product will motivate both government and private industry users to find uses for Old Money®.

HOW DID YOU GET THIS JOB?

A rather circuitous route. I made my connection with Crane through friends met while doing a year's work with the Jesuit Volunteer Corps (JVC) on an Indian reservation in Montana. The future wife of one of my roommates worked for Crane and Company. When I finished my volunteer service, she alerted me to a sales position with Crane in Philadelphia. I spent the next eight years in different sales positions throughout the United States.

After completing my M.B.A. in 1992, I was looking for a way to apply what I'd learned both in school and in eight years of day-to-day customer contact. Tim Crane, a seventh-generation papermaker, had recognized the opportunity to apply our paper-making expertise to waste stream diversion and closed-loop recycling. He asked me to pursue the idea and find out if it was worthwhile. After a year's work, the concept shows great promise. On our own and through partnerships and associations, we are making paper products from the waste of various textile and apparel manufacturers, as well as totally diverting the waste stream from the Federal Reserve Bank of Cleveland into the production of Old Money.

WHAT IS KEY TO GETTING A JOB IN POLLUTION PREVENTION OR CLOSED-LOOP RECYCLING?

Being able to see the entire picture (understand the concept of life-cycle analysis) and to be an evangelist for your ideas, programs, and products.

HOW DID YOU BECOME INTERESTED IN AN ENVIRONMENTAL CAREER?

Some early experiences in 4-H, raising farm animals (sheep) and becoming acutely aware of the effects a polluted environment can impose on living creatures. Growing up in California in the 1970s certainly imprinted me with a heightened environmental awareness. My tour with JVC and my exposure to its core philosophies of simple lifestyle and social justice, as well as the nature-integrated spirituality of the northern Cheyenne people, helped me see the benefits of society becoming less wasteful and more environmentally aware. Reading *Small Is Beautiful* and *Silent Spring* in college helped set the stage.

WHO ELSE WORKS ON YOUR PROGRAM?

Everyone at Crane and Company. Each of our business unit managers have extended extensive support and encouragement for this effort, as have the managers of our subsidiary firms. The people that work in every unit have matched the managers in dedication and thoughtful support of the Continuum program.

WHAT ARE THE MOST PRESSING CHALLENGES IN YOUR JOB?

Standardizing the practice of life-cycle analysis, which will allow the benefits of environmentally positive expenditures to be recognized throughout the life cycle of a given process or product.

WHAT INFLUENCED YOUR DECISION TO WORK ON THIS?

Not enough people were doing it, and it has to be done.

HOW CAN OTHERS ENTER THIS FIELD?

Look for enlightened businesses or proactive government agencies interested in tackling these issues. Try and become an expert in some aspect of recycling, energy management, or government environmental compliance.

WHAT PUBLICATIONS DO YOU READ TO STAY ABREAST OF TRENDS?

Waste Management News, *Advertising Age*, *Communications Arts*, *Women's Wear Daily*, *How Magazine*. My favorite book is *Encounters with the Archdruid* by John McPhee.

***Jane Hutterly** is vice president of Environmental & Safety Actions Worldwide for S.C. Johnson and Son, Inc., in Racine, Wisconsin. She received a B.S. in business from Centenary College of Louisiana in 1974 and an M.B.A. from Cornell University in 1976 with a concentration in general management and marketing. She worked at S.C. Johnson for almost thirteen years in classical product management, new business development, mergers and acquisitions, and service, sales, and marketing before being offered her current position in April 1990.*

HOW DID YOU GET THIS POSITION?

In 1989, our chairman, CEO, and members of the management committee of senior executives made a strategic decision to increase efforts in environmental management at S.C. Johnson, and as a step, they created this department. Management thought through the balance of experience and skills needed to direct the office—someone with a scientific or legal background versus a person with general business management—and decided on the latter. Because the department is a policy- and strategy-setting office, there would be significant interface with senior-level management. Consequently, they looked for someone with business experience first, with demonstrated ability to grasp and manage the regulatory and scientific issues.

WHAT ARE YOUR JOB RESPONSIBILITIES?

My primary responsibilities are setting worldwide environmental policies; establishment of long-term environmental goals and strategies and coordination of key global action plans; communication, both internally and externally; and proactive government relations. Under my office's leadership, we have put procedures in place to track our emissions around the world in forty-eight countries in which we do business. My office is a central point for information. We synthesize data so it is understandable and applicable for operations and senior-level management.

Historically, S.C. Johnson has largely built awareness of its brands rather than awareness of the company itself. A different balance is needed in today's world. The public now expects to understand the company that stands behind the brands. The product is not of sole importance. To date, the response with regard to our past environmental record and future initiative has been very positive. Care for the environment is one of the leading concerns and key trends in the United States. Importantly, there is a growing segment of industry that is beginning to appreciate the real bottom-line value of ecoefficiency.

WHAT ARE THE SKILLS NEEDED FOR YOUR JOB?

The business orientation is critical to the effectiveness of this position, as is the ability to communicate well in representing the company both internally and externally with business, government, and the media. The essential requisites for this position are good business judgment, solid business decision-making skills, the ability to evaluate risks and initiate ideas, and effective negotiating skills, coupled with the ability to coordinate and facilitate diverse groups within the organization, and a networking capacity both internally and externally. My general business background is crucial, along with an ability to understand the strategic environmental aspects of good management. I am self-taught with regard to the environment.

The environment in general, and the work of the department specifically, are high priority at S.C. Johnson and provide the Environmental & Safety staff with the opportunity to have a significant impact on and for the company. For me personally, it has been a great broadening experience. Typical work weeks can include overseas travel to review our operational progress against goals, strategy sessions with senior-level executives, and meetings with federal or state policymakers and national environmental leaders. This broad exposure to the environmental arena helps me better identify the environmental issues facing our company and allows me to more effectively monitor our environmental progress relative to progress overall.

ANY FINAL THOUGHTS?

I count myself among those lucky in the environmental management area to work for a company as committed to the environment as S.C. Johnson. Never before in my career have I been so rewarded on both a professional and a personal level—professionally, for the contribution that responsible environmental management makes to the company, and personally, for knowing that my work today contributes to a better world tomorrow.

Stephanie Madoff *is the environmental affairs coordinator for Fingerhut Companies, Inc., located in Minnetonka, Minnesota. She has a B.A. in cultural anthropology from the University of Colorado, Boulder.*

WHAT DO YOU DO ON THE JOB?

Each day consists of a variety of activities both at the office and outside. Responsibilities include setting, maintaining, and expanding recycling programs at each of the fourteen Fingerhut locations and advising employees on ways to expand the current programs for reducing, reusing, and recycling solid waste; communicating environmental programs and policies to Fingerhut's suppliers and vendors regarding packaging and packing materials and advising them on alternatives to their current packaging; working with local communities to help develop catalog, magazine, and mixed-mail recycling programs and to develop educational and promotional materials; staying abreast of proposed environmental legislation on local, national, and international levels; and working with Fingerhut's governmental affairs department to communicate information and issues to employees and legislative leaders.

HOW DID YOU GET THIS JOB?

In 1990 Ted Deikel, Fingerhut's CEO sent a memo to officers stating that Fingerhut should assume leadership to present solutions and/or identify positive steps that industry could take to address the key elements of the catalog and package-material recycling issues. As a result of direction from the top, two intern positions were created to evaluate Fingerhut's environmental programs, conduct an internal study, and report recommended actions to the senior vice president of consumer, corporate, and environmental affairs. After six months of internal study, Fingerhut created an Environmental Affairs Department with two full-time positions for environmental affairs coordinators.

WHAT IS YOUR PAST WORK HISTORY?

I had two summer jobs prior to graduating from college that directly increased my interest in environmental issues and working with people. In the summer of 1986 I worked as a canvasser on Cape Cod for MassPIRG, working to gain support for a clean water bill. In 1989, I worked at Windfall Farm, an organic farm in Campbell Hall, New York. After college I began my internship with Fingerhut Corporation.

WHAT IS KEY TO GETTING A JOB WITH AN ENVIRONMENTAL DIMENSION?

General awareness of issues, plus specific knowledge about basic environmental topics facing communities and organizations. Being open-minded to different views and personalities. While it is easy to work with like-minded individuals, I have found it to be educational and rewarding to work with different groups of people with varying interests and concerns.

WHAT SKILLS ARE NEEDED TO ENTER THIS FIELD?

Work as an intern if you have the opportunity. You never know where an internship might lead, and you will gain valuable experience along the way. Attend conferences, seminars, and workshops related to your field and interests. It is important to interact with different people and learn what their positions and interests are with regard to environmental issues, business, and consumers. Other skills include reading, researching, and communicating what's been learned to varied audiences. Learn to facilitate meetings and discussions on environmental topics.

In addition, gain knowledge of what is in the waste stream, develop research skills, and be willing to "get your hands dirty" as part of the learning process.

WHAT TRADE JOURNALS AND MAGAZINES DO YOU RECOMMEND FOR PEOPLE TO KEEP ABREAST OF TRENDS IN THIS FIELD?

Magazines I enjoy are *In Business, Business Ethics, E Magazine, ECO, Business and the Environment, Recycled Paper News, Resource Recycling, Buzzworm's Earth Journal* (no longer in print), and *National Geographic.* I recommend you read everything you can get your hands on and ask friends, coworkers, and family members to be your personal clipping service.

Dennis R. Minano *is vice president of the General Motors Environmental and Energy Staff, where he is responsible for developing and executing GM's environmental direction. In 1993, Minano was appointed by EPA Administrator Carol Browner to the National Advisory Council for Environmental Policy and Technology (NACEPT) Superfund Evaluation Committee and served on President Clinton's federal Fleet Conversion Task Force. In 1994 GM signed the Coalition for Environmentally Responsible Economies (CERES). He is also a member of the Corporate Conservation Council of the National Wildlife Federation. Mr. Minano has a B.A. in history from the University of Dayton and a J.D. from the University of Detroit.*

WHAT IS A TYPICAL DAY ON THE JOB?

Fast paced, never dull. I work on new challenges every day and try to find solutions. I am in constant communication both internally and externally about the environmental direction of the company.

HOW DID YOU GET THIS JOB?

There was a convergence of needs: overall environmental direction, regulatory requirements, and perhaps a new set of eyes. I had been in the environmental legal area. I also understood some of the engineering technical challenges and had hands-on experience in working with the government and working on broad corporate strategic issues.

HOW DOES ONE GET A JOB IN ENVIRONMENTAL AFFAIRS?

It really comes down to four things: work hard, understand the issues, be a problem solver, and like working with people. You have to have all four. All you are doing is working with stakeholders—inside and outside the company. You also must be able to see the forest for the trees, in terms of looking at the big picture, long term.

HOW DID YOU BECOME INTERESTED IN ENVIRONMENTAL ISSUES?

I've had it as an assignment since 1976. It was uncharted waters. I could see that it was uncharted, and I like being involved in those areas.

WHAT ARE THE GREATEST CHALLENGES IN YOUR JOB?

Areas GM wants to improve include developing a comprehensive system of environmental management worldwide; continuing to make strides in fuel economy and automotive emissions; working collaboratively with industry, government, and environmental organizations to develop the technology to make additional strides achievable; working collaboratively to ensure that future environmental regulations benefit the environment and are technically and economically feasible by using sound science; continuing our efforts on pollution prevention through our Waste Elimination and Cost Awareness Reward Everyone (WE CARE) program and on vehicle recycling through our Design for the Environment program; and ensuring that the environment becomes part of everyone's job within GM, just like quality.

WHAT ENVIRONMENTAL TRENDS DO YOU SEE IN THE INDUSTRY?

The trends are going to be significant regulations on air toxics and more stringent limits on water discharges by nonpoint sources of pollution. There will be a trend toward increased cooperation between corporations (particularly supplier companies) and government agencies on solving environmental issues. That will have to happen if the challenges are to be met. In addition, there will be more emphasis on upstream in the process controls, with a focus on prevention. Sustainable development will be actionable rather than conceptual, as it generally is today.

WHAT BOOKS, MAGAZINES, AND JOURNALS DO YOU READ?

Bureau of National Affairs weekly publications, environmental news publications—have to keep up with those. *Green Work* is on the list, *Automotive News*, the *Ecology Quarterly*, the *Wall Street Journal*. It's important to understand business needs.

WHERE DO YOU GO FOR INSPIRATION?

I walk around and talk to my staff. That's really where I get my inspiration.

WHAT DO YOU SEE AS THE MOST PRESSING ENVIRONMENTAL PROBLEM?

The need for communication and cooperation, to bring science, economics, and opposing environmental strategies together. That's paramount.

SUGGESTIONS, WISDOM FOR THOSE INTERESTED IN ENTERING THE FIELD?

Listen. Environmentalists, regulators, and industry: we all need better listening skills. If you listen, you can start to figure out what is needed to move forward. Then you can work on the solutions.

HOW CAN SOMEONE GET YOUR JOB?

Know your area. Work hard and be fair. Be comfortable with constant change, uncertainty, and making risk decisions, fast decisions. You must have a sense of humor.

***Ann C. Pizzorusso** is director of environmental affairs for Philips Electronics North America Corporation in New York City. Previously, she was a field geologist, hydrologist, and environmental manager. She has a B.S. in geology from Northern Arizona University and an M.B.A. in finance from the University of Southern California. She also received a Certificate in Environmental Studies at the University of California at Long Beach.*

WHAT DO YOU DO ON THE JOB?

Plan and implement cleanup projects. Keep track of new regulations, communicate environmental information throughout the corporation. Develop new ideas for environmental programs, reduce the amount of hazardous material we use.

WHO IS PART OF YOUR ENVIRONMENTAL TEAM?

Other scientists, lawyers, and consultants.

WHAT ARE THE MOST PRESSING CHALLENGES FACING OUR COUNTRY WITH REGARD TO THE ENVIRONMENT?

The economy. Without money, environmental projects cannot be funded.

WHAT KINDS OF CHALLENGES DO BUSINESSES FACE WITH REGARD TO ENVIRONMENTAL RISK, LIFE-CYCLE ASSESSMENTS, AND ENVIRONMENTAL MANAGEMENT?

The cost of environmental cleanup is astronomical. Unless businesses are healthy, they don't have the money to pay for this.

WHAT TRENDS DO YOU SEE AFFECTING INDUSTRY WITH REGARD TO ENVIRONMENTAL LIABILITIES, ETC.?

Superfund is being reauthorized. It will be slightly more fair but not as effective and cost efficient as it should be. There is a tremendous amount of money that is not being used for cleanup associated with Superfund.

WHAT IS KEY TO GETTING A JOB IN ENVIRONMENTAL AFFAIRS?

Intelligence and versatility. It is a profession that requires you to know a lot about many things, so being a generalist is good. You might want to take courses, subscribe to magazines, or volunteer.

WHERE DO YOU SEE THE ROLE OF ENVIRONMENTAL ACTIONS GROWING IN THE COMING YEARS?

There will be more awareness from an operating standpoint. Also, new buildings will be built with environmental safeguards and equipment in place, and they will not be built on contaminated property.

WHERE DO YOU SEE JOB GROWTH?

Clean Air Act scientists, hydrologists, pollution cleanup technology, worldwide environmental management, environmental products.

WHAT BOOKS, TRADE JOURNALS, MAGAZINES, OR COURSES DO YOU RECOMMEND?

There are so many, you could never truly keep up, but various monthly or weekly newsletters are a good start. *Hazwaste Management* magazine is my favorite.

WHERE DO YOU GO FOR INSPIRATION?

Several of my friends are renowned scientists working on state-of-the-art solutions for environmental pollution problems. They give me a lot of hope, and they energize me.

WHAT DO YOU RECOMMEND PEOPLE TO DO THAT ARE INTERESTED IN ENVIRONMENTAL CAREERS?

Read, take classes, then see if your company has an environmental department. Get to know the people in it. If you're changing jobs, use your skills and apply them to the environment.

ANY SUGGESTIONS, WISDOM GLEANED FROM YOUR EXPERIENCE?
This is not a glamorous job, nor one filled with instant gratification. You must be prepared for a lot of frustration, bad news, and wasted money. The little progress you make is worth it.

HOW CAN SOMEONE GET YOUR JOB?
It takes a lot of experience. Nothing can replace all the experience you've gained along the way. But, if you want it, get a breadth of experience and work hard.

***Nicholas A. Shufro** is the manager of public regulatory affairs at United Technologies Corporation. Prior to holding this position, he worked at GE Capital in its Transportation and Industrial Funding Group and at Global Environment Fund, as an environmental project finance associate. He received a B.A. in history from the University of Michigan in 1984, an M.B.A. in finance and international business from New York University, Stern School of Business, in 1987, and an M.S. in industrial environmental management from the Yale School of Forestry and Environmental Studies in 1994.*

WHAT GOT YOU INTERESTED IN THE ENVIRONMENT?
I have always been interested in the environment and the great outdoors, beginning with my Boy Scout days when I earned camping and environmental merit badges, to sea kayaking trips in southeastern Alaska, family horseback-riding pack trips in Wyoming, and a solo transcontinental bicycle ride. I did not pursue my environmental interests initially in my career but followed more traditional scholastic and career tracks: a liberal arts undergraduate education, followed by an internship in the corporate offices of a publicly traded company, and then an M.B.A. in finance and international business. With these credentials, I began my career in the Capital Markets department of a major investment bank, arriving on October 19, 1987, the date of the big crash of 1987. I then worked as an investment analyst for the next three years.

After a period of time reevaluating my career goals, I joined a start-up venture called Global Environment Fund, L.P. (GEF). GEF is a small private partnership that invests in profitable proenvironmental companies and technologies. My major responsibility at GEF was to evaluate business plans of small privately held companies seeking to launch environmental technologies or products.

WHAT DID YOU LEARN FROM WORKING AT AN ENVIRONMENTAL FUND?

The major lessons I learned at GEF were that the environmental umbrella can be broad and include a number of industries and endeavors, ranging from air pollution control equipment to developing markets for taiga buttons sustainably harvested from tropical rain forests. Conversely, people use the environmental umbrella to promote a variety of interests, some with true proenvironmental benefits, and others designed primarily to enrich the entrepreneurs. Just because a company claims to be proenvironmental, that doesn't mean it is so. To make an investment in a company, that investment should be good for the environment, a good financial investment, and make sense economically. I also learned that I needed to supplement my liberal arts and financial education with some environmental training. Hence, my decision to enroll in Yale's School of Forestry and Environmental Studies.

WHAT DID YOU STUDY AT YALE?

I chose the industrial environmental management concentration, a catchall track that allowed me to take a variety of courses in a variety of disciplines, environmentally important courses like hydrology, natural resource and environmental management, and quantitative methods for environmental decision-making; toxicology at the School of Public Health; public policy evaluation, competitive strategies, and environmental economics at the School of Management; domestic and international management at the Law School; and water and wastewater treatment at the Engineering School.

WHY DID YOU CHOOSE YOUR CURRENT POSITION?

In my current position at United Technologies, I hope to make the transition from environmental finance to environmental management. Practical experience dealing with environmental issues, problems, and opportunities will be challenging and will allow my career to take off in any of many directions.

ANY SUGGESTIONS FOR PEOPLE SEEKING EMPLOYMENT IN ENVIRONMENTAL FINANCE AND MANAGEMENT?

- Attend environmental conferences whenever possible. Always get the attendee and presenter contact lists. Review them periodically. It's a small universe, and names pop up frequently. Network!
- Keep a clipping file as you read the *New York Times*, *World Watch*, and *Science*. New environmental issues arise frequently. Although you don't have to keep current on all issues at all times, having a file with several articles is often enough to understand the crux of a problem.
- Take adult education courses and attend seminars whenever possible.
- When considering a position, don't allow yourself to be pigeonholed too narrowly. Don't become a microspecialist in one environmental area too quickly.

Bryan Thomlison *is the director of environmental affairs at Church & Dwight, which markets Arm & Hammer brand products. He is responsible for their Corporate Environmental Improvement Process and Corporate Environmental Marketing Programs. He received his B.S. from University of Alberta and his M.B.A. from York University in Toronto. He started his career in sales at Proctor & Gamble, and was later employed in marketing by Carnation and Lever Brothers, Inc.*

WHAT IS KEY TO GETTING A JOB IN ENVIRONMENTAL AFFAIRS?

It depends on the type of environmental affairs job one is seeking. In most companies, environmental affairs encompasses all environmental, health, and safety responsibilities. At Church & Dwight, we believe the approach to such issues as environmental responsibility should be guided by a professional communicator. This communicator should be someone skilled in empowering all internal and external stakeholders through information exchange and the creation of win-win programs that focus on creating solutions not managing problems.

HOW DID YOU BECOME INTERESTED IN ENVIRONMENTAL ISSUES AS RELATED TO THE JOB?

I was the marketing director of our Canadian subsidiary when I developed a "stakeholder relations" model that allowed me to demonstrate that we could increase our profits by developing internal and external environmental education programs. Our internal programs were designed to empower all employees to work to minimize our environmental impacts; our external programs were designed to reach out to all stakeholders to form partnerships for environmental education in a way that all parties could benefit. The benefit to the Arm & Hammer brand was enhanced reputation, resulting in increased sales. Sales grew so dramatically that I was brought to the United States to create an environmental management and public affairs department here. After four years, our department can show that for every dollar spent for stakeholder outreach, we get ten dollar's worth of benefits.

WHO IS PART OF YOUR ENVIRONMENTAL TEAM?

The public affairs manager, Jean Reince, and I are responsible for all corporate beyond-compliance environmental programs, corporate public affairs and public relations, government affairs, community relations, employee communications (newsletters, etc.), and corporate philanthropy. We are able to excel in this role with limited resources because we draw on our stakeholders to help us out. For example, more than forty people from our offices around the world have volunteered to help us put together our bimonthly employee newsletter; a team of internal and external environmental enthusiasts help us with our pollution prevention programs; and more than 1,800 people in our database are involved in one way or another with our overall efforts. With this kind of effective staffing, it is easy to see why our company has sales per employee of almost three times the Fortune 500 average.

WHAT DO YOU LIKE ABOUT YOUR JOB?

The chairman and CEO and the two divisional presidents that I report to are very supportive. They give me almost complete autonomy to manage different responsibilities as Jean and I (and our internal and external stakeholders) see fit. Management at Church & Dwight is concerned about results not about command and control. I have been offered as much as twice my salary by other corporations but would not consider leaving.

WHAT ARE THE MOST PRESSING CHALLENGES?

The most pressing challenge is the group of influential die-hards who deny that we can create a robust economy while addressing environmental concerns. The environment is a mess, and it's time to stop arguing to maintain the status quo. The real issue is, how long can we afford to neglect environmental issues?

WHERE DO YOU SEE THE ROLE OF ENVIRONMENTAL ACTIONS GROWING IN THE COMING YEARS?

The next generation of business leaders will, as a matter of simple reflex, consider the environmental ramifications of all their decisions. Within the next decade or two, environmentally laggard companies will have a competitive disadvantage. The standards for environmentally responsible companies will be continually elevated to a point where Paul Hawken's dream of a "restorative economy" will actually draw near.

WHERE DO YOU SEE YOURSELF IN FIVE TO TEN YEARS?

We have irrefutable data that supports the hypothesis that "a company can do well by doing good." I hope to be in my current position, continually refining our model and creating awareness among public-policy influencers that multistakeholder partnerships are the only way to cost-effectively address social issues. American businesses spend $140 billion advertising and promoting their products yet provide only $6 billion in philanthropy. Imagine the positive impact on society if corporations expended more effort creating win-win outreach programs, realizing the same leverage factor of 10:1 as we do.

WHAT BOOKS, TRADE JOURNALS, MAGAZINES DO YOU RECOMMEND TO KEEP ABREAST?

I subscribe to almost every major environmental publication. I find *Environment Today* to be most helpful. Quite frankly, I am overwhelmed by the amount of information that comes across my desk, so I rely on my network of stakeholder allies to send me clips of articles that are germane to our mutual efforts. Most of my reading is research oriented these days, focused on the issue of corporate social responsibility.

WHERE DO YOU GO FOR INSPIRATION?

Every night I go home for dinner to my wife, Carolyn, and my sons, David (nine) and Greg (twelve). This is most important to me, and, in order to maintain that ritual despite our lean staffing, I generally get to the office between 4:00 and 5:00 A.M. In the winter I coach two hockey teams (one for each son), and in the spring I am assistant coach for my sons' baseball teams.

***Sandra K. Woods** is vice president of Environmental, Health & Safety Systems at Coors Brewing Company in Golden, Colorado, where she is responsible for internal coordination, external communication, and legislative affairs for EHS. Her past work history includes housing and urban development and economic development at the federal government level and work in real estate and water resources for Coors before her current assignment.*

HOW DID YOU GET THIS JOB?

Previously, I served as vice president of corporate real estate and environmental affairs. Environmental Affairs was split off and reorganized into Environmental, Health & Safety Systems with expanded responsibilities. I was selected from several internal candidates for the new position.

WHAT IS KEY TO GETTING AN ENVIRONMENTAL AFFAIRS JOB?

A combination of education and experience appropriate to the job made the difference for me. Communication skills and personal credibility are very important, as is the ability to establish teamwork. All of these skills enable me to integrate Environmental, Health & Safety Systems into operational business considerations. And, finally, a primary objective for this position is the establishment of policy direction and long-term strategy, for which I have demonstrated long-term success.

HOW DID YOU BECOME INTERESTED IN ENVIRONMENTAL ISSUES?

During my time with corporate real estate, I worked extensively with the company's water resources and other properties. Environmental management became a very important piece of our business, and I could clearly see the benefit of prevention over remediation.

WHAT OTHER PERSONNEL WORK WITH YOU?

Three EHS directors report to the vice president: External Advocacy and Outreach, Policy and Legislation, and EHS Systems (training, audits, etc.). Also on my staff are an environmental manager, office manager, and administrative assistant. Additionally, personnel in other involved departments have dotted-line and dual-accountability relationships to EHS. In all, about fifty people comprise the EHS day-to-day "team."

WHAT ARE THE MOST PRESSING CHALLENGES FACING THE COUNTRY?

I see four major challenges in the environmental arena: blending environmental with economic issues for win-win solutions; creating business and political incentives for voluntary solutions to problems; developing acceptable gauges to measure costs and benefits; and developing solid foundations of scientific data on environmental problems and solutions.

HOW CAN OTHERS ENTER THIS FIELD?

You can enter the environmental field in a variety of ways and with knowledge as varied as the sciences, lobbying or political processes, communications, engineering, and law.

WHAT IS THE GREATEST CHALLENGE FACED BY BUSINESS RE: ENVIRONMENTAL MANAGEMENT?

I believe that government and business and industry must work together to determine reasonable levels of risk that encourage R&D while providing certain standards of protection to human and ecosystem health.

WHAT ARE SOME OF THE TRENDS AFFECTING YOUR INDUSTRY?

Superfund reform is necessary; audits could become public information but with liability eliminated; legislation is likely to become more restrictive, but regulators may begin to relax required methods in favor of goal attainment. Coors supports voluntary audits and assessments that should not be used for enforcement.

WHAT IS THE ROLE OF ENVIRONMENTAL ACTIONS IN THE FUTURE?

In the future I see integrated, empowered employee teams solving problems as part of routine job performance; accountability built into job descriptions; more and more partnerships between business, government, and environmentalists; more demonstration projects at the local level.

WHERE DO YOU SEE YOURSELF IN FIVE TO TEN YEARS?

I see myself continuing and growing in the environmental management field, possibly extending into corporate policy and public affairs and incorporating other disciplines.

WHAT IS YOUR FAVORITE ENVIRONMENTAL BOOK OR MAGAZINE?
The Diversity of Life by Edward O.Wilson and *Bionomics* by Michael Rothschild.

WHAT IS YOUR ADVICE TO PEOPLE INTERESTED IN ENVIRONMENTAL CAREERS?
Continue to educate yourself about environmental issues, get work experience wherever you can, however modest, and build from there. Negotiation skills are crucial, as well as skills in human relations. Often you work with people from different backgrounds and skill sets, and you need to be able to communicate with people you manage and bring them on board to meet your goals.

PEARLS OF WISDOM?
All waste is lost profit! Find pollution, and you find something you paid for but cannot sell.

Environmental Nonprofit

Margi Briggs-Lofton *is director of special projects for the Natural Resources Defense Council (NRDC). Prior to holding her position at NRDC, she worked for ten years in fund-raising for the American Ballet Theatre (ABT). She has a B.A. in French and Russian from Lawrence University.*

WHAT ARE YOUR DAILY RESPONSIBILITIES AT NRDC?
As director of special projects, I work as part of the Development Department, which is responsible for raising the funds to keep NRDC going. My department is responsible for raising approximately $700,000 per year through projects such as benefit parties and concerts, marketing tie-ins, and NRDC credit cards. In addition to producing income-generating events, we organize donor cultivation and public education and outreach events.

Examples of some recent projects are a James Taylor benefit concert in San Francisco; the Los Angeles and New York premieres of *A Few Good Men;* a full-day NRDC member symposium in New York on population and the environment; and an environmental lecture series entitled "Writers and the Environment" in New York, San Francisco, and Los Angeles in conjunction with the Academy of American Poets. My position requires a great deal of planning and attention to detail, and the ability to manage several projects simultaneously.

WHAT DO YOU LIKE BEST ABOUT YOUR JOB?

One of the things I like best about the position is its variety. Even though the elements of producing a successful event remain constant, each project involves a different group of people and develops its own dynamic. The combination of collaborating on an ongoing basis with NRDC staff, donors, and volunteers and at the same time working with a changing group of outside contacts keeps the work fresh and makes it easier to deal with the pressures of fund-raising.

WHO IS PART OF YOUR TEAM?

I have a staff of five people working in my department, and I report to the deputy executive director of NRDC. I work very closely with the other unit heads in the Development Department—the directors of membership, major gifts, foundations, and planned giving—to develop cultivation strategies and activities and to ensure that our plans and activities are not in conflict. I also coordinate with the director of communications and his staff, since a great deal of our work has a strong public relations component. When working on an event or concert, I work closely with a volunteer committee to plan the event and develop a strategy to accomplish such objectives as selling tickets and finding sponsors. I am also often the key contact with outside organizations such as movie studios, public relations agencies, and the like when we are working on an event or project with them, and with designers, musicians, and other vendors involved in an event.

TELL US ABOUT YOUR CAREER HISTORY.

I have been working at NRDC for five years. Before that I worked as a translator and editor at a translation agency in Chicago for two years, and I spent ten years working in fund-raising, marketing, and public relations at American Ballet Theatre. When I left ABT, I was eager to remain in the nonprofit sector, because I like the idea of working for a cause I believe in and feel passionate about. Working in a nonprofit structure also often allows for flexibility and creativity that a more traditional corporate structure might not provide.

HOW DID YOU COME TO YOUR POSITION?

I heard about this position from a former colleague at ABT, who had become director of membership at NRDC. When I interviewed for the position, I was impressed by the quality and commitment of the staff and by the work and overall goals of the organization. It felt like this job would be a good fit, and I was fortunate enough to get it.

WHAT TRENDS AND OPPORTUNITIES FOR WORK DO YOU SEE IN THE NONPROFIT SECTOR?

"Special projects" is an area of fund-raising that holds great potential. As it becomes more difficult to raise ever-increasing amounts of money from traditional sources, more environmental groups will begin to explore cause-related marketing and other tie-ins. At NRDC, we are very cautious about becoming too closely involved with corporations and big business because of possible conflicts of interest. This limits our money-making options. Finding creative and effective ways to hook up with environmentally responsible companies and to collaborate with a wider variety of organizations to promote an environmental message remains a challenge, but I think it is a direction we need to move in to remain competitive.

WHAT ADVICE CAN YOU GIVE TO PEOPLE INTERESTED IN A CAREER IN THE NONPROFIT SECTOR?

To pursue a career in fund-raising, specifically in special projects, it is important to have good people skills, to be well organized, to be a good manager, and to be able to work well under pressure. Fund-raising staff are often an institution's first contact with donors or with key staff members of other organizations, and it is important that they be able to effectively describe the institution's work and its goals.

I became involved in fund-raising somewhat by accident, having started out as an administrative assistant in an organization I loved. I think a key to working successfully for a nonprofit is to have a real commitment to the work and the goals it pursues. When I worked at ABT, I was able to use my knowledge and love of dance to develop creative ways to reach ABT supporters.

It is sometimes possible to get jobs with organizations by doing volunteer work for them. This enables you to get to know the organization and the people working there, and it puts you in a good position to be considered for a full-time job if one opens up. At the least, you will have a connection to the environmental community and be in a better position to learn about job openings and new initiatives and projects.

***Ann M. Felber** is the senior associate for membership communications at World Wildlife Fund (WWF) in Washington, D.C. She has a B.A. in English literature from the University of Maryland, and has completed the basic continuing education curriculums of the American Booksellers' Association and of the Direct Marketing Association.*

WHAT DO YOU DO ON THE JOB IN A TYPICAL DAY?

I work to pull together information from hundreds of WWF field programs and policy activities to communicate with a broad-based audience. On a typical day, I meet with our newsletter editor to sketch out story ideas for future publications. Or with the heads of our public affairs, development, and membership departments to present concepts for advertising and direct-mail campaigns, or to inform them about what other conservation groups might be publicizing. I draft copy for direct-mail pieces, video scripts, catalogs, and other promotional material and edit the work of freelance copywriters. I sit on several task forces to present the "members' point of view," and I advance internal communications among editors, marketers, and fund-raisers within WWF.

What this job requires is strong interpersonal and communication skills; initiative, energy, and creativity; an institutional knowledge that goes wide and deep (some of the best marketing concepts are recycled ideas); an ability to read and process lots of information across varying levels of complexity; a thorough knowledge of direct marketing, advertising, and fund-raising concepts; and a love and appreciation for the ability of direct-mail copy to move people to act on their beliefs.

HOW DID YOU GET THIS JOB?

Ten years ago, I joined WWF as their direct-mail coordinator. As the organization grew, I became director of the membership department and then vice president for both the membership and marketing departments. The job I now hold at WWF as senior associate for membership communication is for me the result of a fortunate evolution in which I was able to return to the task I loved best: motivating people to get involved through direct-mail communications.

Getting to WWF in the first place was, as anyone with a liberal arts degree knows too well, the tricky part. My experience was clearly one of on-the-job training, in which work in related fields fused to produce a whole whose sum was greater than its parts. Part-time work in my college bookstore led to a job with McGraw-Hill in marketing. This gave me an edge when I landed a publications marketing job at the Conservation Foundation. My work at the Conservation Foundation—plus many direct-marketing workshops, luncheons, and seminars—made me eager to use my growing direct-mail skills in the kind of large-scale database marketing that WWF was pursuing in order to build a membership base.

WHAT DO YOU RECOMMEND FOR PEOPLE INTERESTED IN ENVIRONMENTAL CAREERS?

Informational interviews with people in the organization you've targeted for employment are an ideal way to better understand how a variety of professional skills apply to that group's particular situation. To find out which organization might be the best match for you, study their annual reports, subscribe to their newsletters, become a member, and read their direct mail. Learn as much as you can about what the organization sees as its most pressing needs for the next two, five, ten years, and then present your skills and interests in a context that addresses those needs.

WHAT SKILLS ARE NEEDED TO ENTER YOUR PARTICULAR FIELD?

Direct-response marketing requires basic training (database management, print production, market research, and quantitative analysis); project management aptitude (goal setting, budgeting, implementation, and reporting); strong interpersonal and communications skills (to ferret out information, build consensus, and marshal support for your ideas); and a real aptitude or healthy respect for direct-mail copywriting and design. A background in journalism, marketing, public relations, or advertising would be valuable in this field.

HOW DID YOU BECOME INTERESTED IN ENVIRONMENTAL ISSUES, AND HOW DOES THAT RELATE TO YOUR CURRENT POSITION?

I was lucky enough to grow up in a family that car-camped cross-country several times from Washington state to the Adirondacks during a time when you didn't need a reservation to stay at Yellowstone or Glacier National Park. Wilderness areas and nature have always been important to me. As a young adult, I became increasingly concerned about the rapid pace of development. And I learned that many people who had equally strong concerns about our environment wanted to help but weren't the kind of people to march in rallies, canvass door to door with petitions, or join the Peace Corps. I believed that direct-response marketing to a mass audience was one path to action. Direct-mail communications enable thousands of people to participate by supporting organizations that act on their beliefs.

WHAT TRADE BOOKS OR JOURNALS DO YOU READ TO STAY INFORMED?
I read *American Demographics, Chronicle of Philanthropy, Fundraising Management, Direct Marketing,* and many smaller newsletters like John Naisbitt's *Trend Letter.*

WHAT IS YOUR FAVORITE ENVIRONMENTAL BOOK OR MAGAZINE?
The environmental and naturalist books that have had the greatest influence on me are *Lives of a Cell: Notes of a Biology Watcher* by Lewis Thomas and *A Sand County Almanac* by Aldo Leopold.

WHAT DO YOU THINK ARE AMONG THE MOST PRESSING CHALLENGES FOR ENVIRONMENTAL ORGANIZATIONS TODAY?
Nonprofits are feeling the pressures of competing interests and demands. Many well-intentioned government and watchdog agency guidelines require nonprofits to add layers of administrative and reporting personnel. These incur costs that, in turn, increase administrative expenses, which, of course, are among the factors being so closely regulated.

Nonprofits today must be businesslike in their operations without becoming business ventures. Finding the proper balance between the communities they serve and the donor and regulatory communities on whose good will they depend is a tremendous challenge for environmental nonprofits today.

Susan Ives *is vice president and director of public affairs for the Trust for Public Land (TPL) in San Francisco, a nonprofit organization that "conserves land for people" through acquiring land for parks and open spaces to serve the recreation needs of our growing urban population. Prior to her current job, Ms. Ives worked in Massachusetts state government as special assistant to the secretary of environmental affairs and for Sierra Club as a pub-*

lic relations assistant. She has a B.A. in journalism from the University of Michigan and an M.A. in public administration from the John F. Kennedy School of Government at Harvard University.

WHAT IS A TYPICAL DAY ON THE JOB?

We have a very small public affairs department. We spend much time on media outreach and produce publications, including a magazine called *Land and People* and newsletters for seven regional offices. I help to plan meetings, talk to reporters, and do a lot of writing in the form of articles, press releases, plans, and descriptions of our projects and programs for internal and external audiences. As a senior officer, I also work on strategic planning.

HOW DID YOU COME TO BE IN YOUR POSITION?

I had just finished my masters studies at the Kennedy School and had come back to San Francisco to explore career opportunities. Before graduate school, I had had my own business in San Francisco doing public affairs consulting for a variety of nonprofit groups. Most of those groups were environmental organizations that needed public relations and communications services but didn't have the budget or the staff expertise to do it. So I built my public affairs firm largely serving that need in small and medium-sized nonprofit organizations. One of my clients, Huey Johnson, was a founder of the Trust for Public Land and a renowned and respected leader in the environmental movement. He suggested I speak with Martin Rosen, president of TPL, about how I might serve TPL's communications needs. It turned out that a position for a public affairs director had been budgeted for a couple of years, but they hadn't found the right person to fill it. It was a question of being in the right place at the right time. The TPL is an ideal place for me to work.

WHAT ARE THE CHALLENGES YOU FACE WORKING IN THE ENVIRONMENTAL NONPROFIT COMMUNITY?

The problems are really big, and they are connected to a whole lot of things that have to move in order to solve the problems. I think our country is overcoming the inertia that has affected us for a long time with regard to the environment, but it often seems we are taking three steps forward and two steps back. Part of the joy of working for TPL is that there are very tangible successes. We completed 135 land protection projects last year alone.

The environmental movement is grossly underfunded. Even though it is a primary concern of the majority of Americans, it just doesn't seem to translate into a political agenda that makes real progress possible. I think it's important to be an optimist when taking a job in the environmental movement and to take the long view. For the most part the results of our work may be something we'll never see.

DO YOU HAVE ANY ADVICE FOR PEOPLE WHO WANT TO FIND A JOB IN THE ENVIRONMENTAL MOVEMENT?

Volunteer and persevere. Most people involved in the environmental movement are really busy. I get a lot of calls from people who are interested in figuring out how they can break in, but unless they call me twice or three times, it's really unlikely that they are going to get to talk to me. As for the many people I've hired it's the ones who say, "I really want the experience, I really want to do this. I really want to learn, and I'm willing to put in some time as a volunteer to get my foot in the door." I've had several interns, all of whom, because of their hard work and dedication, we somehow found room for on the payroll, although in some cases it took half a year.

Nobody does this for the money. So if you can afford to volunteer, even just part time, it's a great way to meet people, make connections, and become part of the network. I think that's key to finding a job in any field.

WHERE DO YOU GET INSPIRATION?

My inspiration has been the writer Edward Abbey since I read *The Monkeywrench Gang* back in the 1970s. One of things he said is, "What we need now are heroes and heroines, about a million of them." He also said, "Sentiment without action is the ruin of the soul." Healing the earth is something I have always felt very deeply in my soul, and I knew too much not to do something about it. But being an environmentalist is not for sissies. It takes a healthy dose of outrage to make it a career. We all know there are plenty of reasons for that.

***Karin Kreider** is the director of finance and administration of the Rainforest Alliance in New York City. She has a B.A. in fine arts from New York University with a double major in film and television production, and history, and an M.B.A. from NYU's Stern School of Business.*

WHAT DO YOU DO ON THE JOB?

I manage the day-to-day operations of the organization and oversee the management of our growth. The Alliance was founded in 1987, and I was hired in mid-1987 as the second staff member. We have since grown to just over twenty staff members, with offices in New York City and Costa Rica. My position has grown and changed as the organization has grown.

On a daily basis, I have primary responsibility for the financial management of the organization. I supervise a full-time bookkeeper, write and monitor the Alliance's annual budget, and help project directors write and monitor their budgets. I also manage all of the personnel functions of the organization. That includes writing job descriptions, recruiting, interviewing, and hiring new staff, and making sure we're in compliance with government regulations. I also spend a lot of time helping other staff members, listening to them talk about their work, and helping to make decisions about how things should be done.

Managing the growth of the organization takes up a lot of my time. I have created all of its financial management systems and most of its management and administrative systems. Managing a growing organization is an exciting challenge—I need to constantly figure out how to most effectively use limited resources, both human and financial. I have worked on projects ranging from creating and implementing an annual planning system to deciding how much new office space we need and finding it.

HOW DID YOU GET YOUR JOB?

In the summer of 1987, I met one of the founders of the Rainforest Alliance. At that time the Alliance was a start-up group with one staff member and several active volunteers. They were planning an international conference on rain forests that October. I was working freelance in commercial film production and, through my film work, had developed experience in event production. I was looking for more socially, nonprofit oriented work, so when my friend asked if I wanted to help produce the conference, I accepted.

In addition to managing the conference I coordinated over fifty volunteers. Working with so many dedicated volunteers really made me feel terrific about my work. After the conference Dan Katz, the executive director of the Rainforest Alliance, said there might be a job for me if I was patient. Within a couple of months I was hired.

People have often commented that moving from film production to nonprofit management was an odd combination, but I learned a lot from film work that contributes to my management skills. In film, you have to make decisions quickly, be resourceful, and manage complex logistics. These skills all transferred to a nonprofit environment.

HOW DOES THE RAINFOREST ALLIANCE, AN ENVIRONMENTAL NONPROFIT, WORK WITH BUSINESSES?

The Rainforest Alliance develops and promotes economically viable alternatives to tropical forest destruction. Several of our programs work closely with businesses to find innovative ways to reduce their long-term environmental impact. Business-related projects at the Alliance range from an international network of organizations that certify well-managed timber sources to a database tracking pharmaceutical companies' policies toward biodiversity conservation and equitable economic returns of benefits to host countries.

WHAT ARE THE CHALLENGES OF WORKING IN AN ENVIRONMENTAL NONPROFIT?

There has been an increase in the number of environmental organizations over the last eight years. We have been part of that growth. This has increased competition for funds, from both private foundations and the general public. We're not the only organization raising money from the public to protect rain forests. Therefore, we have to more carefully define and communicate what we do and how we're different from all of the other organizations.

DO YOU SEE ANY EMPLOYMENT TRENDS FOR PEOPLE IN ENVIRONMENTAL NONPROFITS?

As environmental conservation and development issues become more closely intertwined, there is a need for people who can combine a knowledge of conservation and sustainable development with business skills such as planning and budgeting, product development, and international marketing. Joint degree programs, such as a masters in business administration and a masters in international affairs or environmental studies, offer a useful combination of educational backgrounds for these positions.

Environmental organizations have developed into sophisticated businesses with large budgets and a need for sophisticated managers. There is a trend toward viewing nonprofit management more seriously and toward hiring experienced managers to run organizations. As a result, there will be jobs for people with business experience and proven dedication to environmental issues.

WHAT IS KEY TO GETTING A JOB IN THE NONPROFIT SECTOR?

We usually don't hire anyone without nonprofit experience. Entry-level hires have usually had at least one internship with an environmental nonprofit. Volunteer experience is important. It is a way to meet potential employers, to gain some real understanding of how nonprofits work, and to prove to a potential nonprofit employer that you are seriously interested in its work. Taking classes or getting a degree in environmental studies or a related field is another way for career changers to show they are serious.

WHAT SKILLS ARE NEEDED TO ENTER THIS FIELD?

There are many general skills that are useful in a range of positions with environmental nonprofits. Good communications and writing skills are essential in almost any position. Knowledge of budgeting, long-range planning, and grant writing is used in most program and administrative positions. Advanced computer skills are helpful to manage the large amounts of data that programs track. For program-related work in an international environmental organization, international field experience and skill in a foreign language are essential.

WHAT PUBLICATIONS OR COURSES DO YOU RECOMMEND FOR PEOPLE TO STAY COMPETITIVE IN THIS FIELD?

For people interested in nonprofit management and fund-raising, the *Non-Profit Times* and *Chronicle of Philanthropy* are good industry publications. The Support Centers of America have offices in many major cities and offer day-long workshops on topics such as budgeting, grant writing, and board development for nonprofit employees. *The Economist* has frequent articles about international environment and development issues.

For people interested in learning about rain forest conservation issues, the best introduction is *The Primary Source* by Dr. Norman Myers.

WHAT WISDOM HAVE YOU GLEANED FROM YOUR EXPERIENCES?

People with liberal or fine arts degrees make great environmentalists because they have a well-balanced education. Don't let anyone try to convince you that a liberal arts education is a waste of time. As environmental issues grow and change, they cover a wide range of issues. Flexibility and a broad-based education will ensure your ability.

ANY FINAL ADVICE TO PEOPLE WHO ARE INTERESTED IN ENVIRONMENTAL CAREERS?

Get involved. Volunteer. Do an internship—or two. The people you meet volunteering will be important references when you start looking for a job. Learn as much as you can about the issues, and learn who is working on them. Figure out where you can best fit into the work that's being done. Join the organizations doing the work that you're interested in. Subscribe to publications advertising environmental jobs, so you can get a sense of what types of positions are available. You may need to be extremely persistent and patient, but if you really want to work for an environmental nonprofit, you can find a way.

***Jack Murray** is director of development for the Natural Resources Defense Council (NRDC) in New York City. He has a B.A. from Williams College and an M.A. and an M. Phils. in history from Columbia University.*

WHAT ARE YOUR JOB RESPONSIBILITIES?

As the person responsible for overseeing the fund-raising programs necessary to meet NRDC's annual operating and long-range capital needs, I spend a good amount of time working with the managers of the various individual fund-raising programs (Foundations, Major Gifts, Membership, and Planned Giving) to increase their effectiveness; formulating immediate and long-term strategies for increasing NRDC's funding base; setting up fund-raising strategies with and motivating NRDC's senior management, program staff, trustees, and volunteers to increase their fund-raising outreach; helping to develop and polish fund-raising proposals; and meeting with donors and donor representatives. I'm on the business and administrative side of NRDC, working to bring in the financial resources that will allow our scientists and attorneys to get on with their mission of protecting the environment. I derive satisfaction from bringing in the income so that the program staff can do their jobs. I market the vision, expertise, achievements, and experience of NRDC to donors.

HOW DID YOU MOVE INTO YOUR CURRENT JOB?

I had more than a decade of experience fund-raising for universities and hospitals and was well enough known by headhunting consultant firms to be contacted for senior-level jobs in the New York City region. A job-placement consultant called me and encouraged me to apply for the vacant position of director of development at NRDC. When I was offered the job after many interviews, I decided to work for NRDC because I cared about wilderness, natural resources, and pollution prevention. I realized I wanted to put my development skills to work for the protection of the environment, especially since the stresses on the planet will only intensify in the coming years.

HOW DID YOU ENTER YOUR FIELD?

I got into fund-raising in a serendipitous way. I was playing basketball in Riverside Park when I ran into an old friend who was then an alumni development officer for Columbia College. He was leaving to get an M.B.A. and told me about his job. I applied and, at age thirty, had my first job in development. I then went on to work in development in a variety of hospital and university settings before coming to NRDC in 1989. When I got involved in fund-raising, it was a fairly new profession. Now budgets for nonprofits have grown, and the fuel that these nonprofits need to run their programs is income.

DO YOU HAVE ANY ADVICE FOR PEOPLE SEEKING JOBS IN YOUR SECTOR?

People interested in securing a job with an environmental nonprofit organization should be well educated and care passionately about environmental issues. If your interest is in program work, you need to have the scientific, economic, or legal skills that will fit the needs of the organization with which you seek employment.

The same is true with securing a job on the administrative and management side of an organization. To be successful in development you need to be broadly educated. You are an institutional representative who meets with the individuals and entities that fund the institution. You need to know how to talk about what the program staff does in simple, direct, easy-to-understand ways. You need to be able to discuss the significance of their work. You need sales skills. In addition, you have to like the bottom-line nature of the job, because that is how your performance is measured. Can you pay the bills and meet the payroll? Can you launch new programs?

No matter how good your skills are, you also need to believe in the organization you work for. I feel much better using my financial, sales, and communication skills to protect the planet than I would using the same skills in a corporate setting.

WHAT ARE SOME OF THE TRENDS IN NONPROFIT ORGANIZATIONS?

Over the long term, the environment will be a jobs growth area. This will be true in both the not-for-profit and the for-profit arenas. There will be a need for skilled individuals who can raise money for these nonprofits. Environmental issues will become increasingly important in the decade ahead. Environmental organizations are not fly-by-night organizations. They have big budgets, and there is an increasing need for people with business skills to raise funds, run financial analyses, and do numbers crunching. The business side will be critical not just in fund-raising, but in accounting, human resources, and marketing. As budgets for environmental organizations grow larger, business skills will be in high demand.

***Robin Oanes** is a program assistant at the Center for Resource Management (CRM). She assists in the development of program concepts; facilitates activities of CRM coalitions consisting of representatives from governmental, academic, industrial, and environmental entities; writes grants and reports; researches foundations; travels to raise support among federal and other entities for CRM coalitions; and organizes conferences and meetings. She is most involved in CRM's Russian forest, renewable energy, alternative fuels, solid-waste management, environmental decision-making, and American Indian projects.*

WHAT IS YOUR EDUCATIONAL BACKGROUND?

My academic experience was different from most people's. I didn't start college until I'd been out of high school nine years. I'd done a lot of domestic and international traveling during those years and was finally drawn to college because I wanted to learn the Russian language.

I figured as long as I was taking one class, I might as well dabble in some others, anthropology in particular. It didn't take long for me to realize my real interest lay in anthropology, especially in the anthropological aspects of development. I changed my major to anthropology, but as I increasingly focused on development issues, I found a number of relevant classes outside that department. I was told I would have to petition the department to accept credits from other departments toward my degree. While I was contemplating that undertaking, I discovered that I could design my own interdepartmental major. It took some extra work, but I found so many development-related courses in the University of Minnesota curriculum that it wasn't difficult for me to design a cohesive major. I named it International Social Development and focused on the environmental impact of meeting basic human needs. I concentrated on population and health issues and the cultural considerations that surround them. While most of my course work focused on the less developed countries of the Southern Hemisphere, I also looked at development issues in the United States, particularly in American Indian country, as I'd supported and been involved in American Indian activism for well over a decade.

While I'd had a relatively easy time developing and gaining approval for my major, there were people who thought my academic choices—development, environment, American Indian studies, and Russian—were a bit of a stretch. One of my sponsoring professors urged me to study French or Spanish rather than Russian, but I was convinced that with all the momentous changes occurring in the then-Soviet Union the Russians were sure to become major players in the development and environmental arenas.

HOW DID YOU FIND OUT ABOUT YOUR CURRENT EMPLOYER?

As my senior year was about to begin, a conference called Greenhouse Glasnost was hosted by the Institute for Resource Management (IRM) and the Soviet Academy of Sciences. The conference seemed tailor-made to validate my eclectic studies. It received a great deal of media coverage and made me much more confident about the academic path I had chosen.

I began to research IRM. I found it to be a very small organization with what looked to me to be a meager budget. I fired off a letter and résumé anyway, figuring someone at the organization might know who would be interested in my education and experience. I received a reply from the president of IRM, telling me that while they weren't currently hiring, I should stop in to meet the staff if I were ever in Salt Lake City or Denver, where the IRM offices were located. When I graduated college, I did just that.

When I met with the IRM folks, they were undergoing a major reorganization. I was told to keep in touch, that maybe in a year or so things would be settled and they would be looking for someone with my background.

HOW DID YOU PURSUE OTHER JOB LEADS?

That afternoon, I went to the ACTION office and found a Volunteers In Service To America (VISTA) position that offered me an opportunity to work with Navajo and Ute communities in southeastern Utah for a year. I spent the next year running a workplace literacy project while the Institute for Resource Management settled into the Center for Resource Management. I kept in touch with the CRM folks during that year, calling with environmental questions and stopping in to visit when my work took me to Salt Lake and Denver.

At the same time they were keeping me in mind for positions that might open up within CRM, some of the staff I had gotten to know there offered valuable assistance in my broader search for a position in the environmental field after my VISTA service. As no position at CRM had presented itself when my year with VISTA was over, I took a temporary position as a consultant with the fledgling Nevada Indian Environmental Coalition.

When my Nevada gig was up, I headed back to Salt Lake City to look for a permanent job and stopped in again at CRM to offer to do some volunteer work. As it turned out, someone had recently given notice, and they were just starting to think about finding someone to replace her. I had an immediate "official" interview and was offered a position as a program assistant a few days later.

The president of the organization told me later that one of the main things that convinced him to hire me was my decision to spend a year working for VISTA. That position had given me not only additional experience with American Indian communities—with whom CRM often works—but also valuable grant writing and management experience. He also felt that my willingness to volunteer for a year rather than "settle" for something that paid a real salary demonstrated a commitment to the issues that are important to me.

ANY FINAL THOUGHTS, ADVICE FOR PEOPLE SEARCHING FOR A GREEN CAREER?

My reason for providing this long-winded explanation of my academic and job-landing experience is to support three suggestions I'd like to offer student readers:

(1) If the traditional academic programs at your university aren't meeting your needs, investigate what opportunities exist for you to

be creative within the system, particularly if your goal is a job in the environmental field. I participated in the Globescope Pacific Conference on Sustainable Development in 1989, and one of the recommendations that came out of the education breakout group was for universities to encourage interdisciplinary and interdepartmental programs for environmental studies. The issues have become so complex that there is a fear in some camps that many graduates are too focused, unable to grasp the big picture. Some may think that my experience was exceedingly unfocused, but I'm using my American Indian studies for our projects related to American Indian issues, my development background for our development-related projects, and my Russian background for our Russian forest work. True, I found an uncommonly good fit with CRM, but don't underestimate the value of an ability to appreciate the economic, environmental, social, and spiritual complexities of the sustainable development concept.

(2) When you find an organization you think fits your goals and ideals, don't hesitate to cultivate a relationship with that organization even if no positions are currently available. While there's a fine line between being assertive and being a pain in the neck when trying to sell yourself to an organization, if your interest in eventually working there is genuine, don't allow the staff to forget about you.

(3) A common complaint among job hunters is, "They want me to have experience, but they won't give me a job so I can get experience." Keep in mind the personal and professional rewards of the experience offered by VISTA, Peace Corps, and other programs of the sort. My experience, and that of my friends who have served with VISTA or in the Peace Corps, has shown that there is often considerable flexibility within assignments. You might very well find yourself gaining exactly the kind of experience your "goal" organization is looking for. Consider these options. You'll learn an immense amount, and you'll make lifelong friends.

Sally Parker *is the cofounder of Earth Spirit, a nonprofit environmental education organization. She "telecommutes" from Boulder, Colorado, where she builds CD-ROM products for Mammoth Micro Productions and also consults for entertainment companies and book publishers. Prior to cofounding Earth Spirit, she worked for CNN in Washington, D.C. She received a B.A. in 1992 from the University of Southern California in international relations and environmental politics.*

WHAT DOES YOUR ORGANIZATION DO?

Earth Spirit's mission is to inform, entertain, and involve kids and adults in overall environmental protection. Our work with schools consists of educational curriculum, live theatrical performances, and the establishment of electronically linked ecology clubs. Our on-line service, Earth Spirit Online, keeps kids informed by linking California schools (K–12) with environmental curricula, events, products, and services.

WHAT DO YOU SPEND MOST OF YOUR TIME DOING AT EARTH SPIRIT?

Just about everything! Public outreach, business planning, creative development, and fund-raising. I have spent a lot of my time developing a self-sustaining financial foundation for Earth Spirit. Even though we have received grants to implement our programs, it is obvious that there is increased competition for corporate and foundation dollars to keep nonprofit organizations running. Nonprofit organizations cannot rely on outside funding. They must learn to stand on their own. That is why Earth Spirit has conceived of Earth Spirit Online, which provides local, national, and international information from government agencies, nonprofits, universities, and the general public.

WHY DOES EARTH SPIRIT FOCUS ON EDUCATING CHILDREN?

Kids are our future—that is why I focus on childhood education. Being involved in environmental issues is not a novelty, it is a necessity. I hope to teach them good habits and respect at an early age.

WHY DID YOU TAKE ON YOUR CURRENT POSITION?

It is a challenge. With technology we are able to take environmental issues to the next level, using computers to attract kids' attention.

WHAT MOTIVATES YOU?

What has gotten me to where I am today is my passion and determination. That is what makes me happy every day. It makes me smile, gets me going, and is what I focus on. People need to think about what they want to do instead of what they should do. Listen to your heart. Wake up. Ask yourself what you want to do today, tomorrow. Success comes when you have passion. My passion is for Earth Spirit and for our children. They are our most powerful tool for change. Work hard for what you want. Nothing comes easy.

Almost everyone I know has gone back to graduate school. They looked outside the ivory towers and signed up for graduate school to return to the "real world" at a later time. Most people don't take initiative or look to pioneer something. It is easier to stick your head in the sand.

My cofounders, David Nichols, Christian Schrader, and Robert Greenhood, motivate me on the job. We all work well together—like puzzle pieces, we snap nicely into place.

WHERE DID YOUR INTEREST IN THE ENVIRONMENT ORIGINATE?

My interest in the environment comes from my parents. We are an outdoor-oriented family, and I learned at an early age that we must take pride in and protect the planet if we plan to survive. It's not about saving the "earth" as much as it is about saving the people *on* the *earth.*

The Blackfoot Indians have lived in north Montana for ten thousand years, and we can barely notice they were there. Western culture has been in North America for about two hundred years, and you can't escape our presence.

WHAT IS THE MOST PRESSING ENVIRONMENTAL ISSUE FACING US?

I think the most pressing problem facing us today is population control. We should be working toward achieving negative population growth.

WHAT ARE TRENDS IN YOUR AREA?

I believe electronic networking is the biggest trend. It is quick and provides easy access to up-to-date information.

Aaron Sachs *is a staff researcher at the Worldwatch Institute, where he is part of a staff that researches global issues of sustainability. Prior to his position at Worldwatch he spent a year working as a teacher at an environmental education center and several months working as an editor at an educational publishing company. He has an A.B. in history and literature from Harvard University.*

WHAT DO YOU DO IN YOUR JOB?

Worldwatch is a research organization that publishes its findings in two annual books *(State of the World* and *Vital Signs)*, in Worldwatch Papers, and in *World Watch* magazine. My job, as part of the research staff, is to contribute to the basic research and the writing for all of the institute's publications. Half of my job consists of doing my own projects—I publish an article in just about every issue of *World Watch*, and I write chapters for *Vital Signs*. The other half of my job consists of helping a senior researcher with a larger project—a Worldwatch Paper or a chapter in *State of the World* or (usually) both. Everyone who works as a researcher here is given lots of responsibility and substantive work and is expected to contribute finished documents for publication. Most of the job consists of research and writing. Research will involve a lot of phone calls, faxing, and other correspondence; some trips to the library; and huge amounts of reading. Compiling research will involve not only writing but also manipulation of data in tables and graphs. In addition, every researcher here acts as general support staff for the institute. All of us, for instance, spend a lot of time answering questions over the phone and responding to requests for information.

HOW DID YOU GET THIS JOB?

The hard way? The traditional way? The extremely lucky way? I sent in a résumé, cover letter, and writing sample and then prayed.

WHAT DISTINGUISHED YOU FROM OTHERS COMPETING FOR THIS JOB?

It was probably my writing samples. Since a big part of Worldwatch's mission has to do with communicating its analysis of global issues clearly and convincingly to the public, the organization looks for people with good writing skills. The people who hired me liked the fact that my writing showed an ability to think through issues deeply and carefully and to explain them clearly, but they also liked the fact that my writing has a lot of narrative influence and strives to tell an interesting, accessible story rather than simply present an analysis.

WHAT ARE THE CHALLENGES OF WORKING IN AN ENVIRONMENTAL NONPROFIT?

You have to be extremely self-motivated, because you're expected to do just about anything to help the cause. At Worldwatch especially, research can be extremely isolating work. People are working so hard that they don't have much time to build a community, and that just reinforces the solitary nature of reading and writing.

In the nonprofit world in general, everybody is under a lot of stress. Nonprofits are supposed to be alternatives to corporate culture, but don't expect too much of an alternative community. Every organization needs money to survive, so nonprofits are competing for funds as much as any private sector company and can be just as cutthroat. In other words, ideals about the way people should be treated sometimes do not affect the way nonprofit employees are actually treated. There is little security for anyone because everyone is pressed for money and time, so many people feel first and foremost the need to look out for themselves. You might be able to go to work wearing the kinds of clothes you'd wear on nights or weekends, but you might also be expected to work on nights and weekends. There is often an undercurrent of outright exploitation (especially of young people) covered up by rhetoric about paying dues, contributing to the cause, taking advantage of your opportunities, etc.

I should emphasize, though, that there will be internal politics wherever you go. These challenges do not prevent work in the environmental nonprofit sector from being fulfilling for just about everyone in the field. There are great opportunities for young people; it can be very satisfying to contribute to something you believe in deeply; and often it is possible to build an extraordinary community despite the factors that sometimes contribute to an every-man-or-woman-for-himself-or-herself mentality. Besides, there's a great nonprofit softball league in Washington.

WHAT ARE THE TRENDS YOU SEE AFFECTING ENVIRONMENTAL NONPROFITS?

The environment isn't going away. As a concept, it has worked its way into government structures and planning all around the world. Because people are finally beginning to realize that all of our economic activity depends on a healthy ecological habitat, they are also realizing that they cannot survive if they continue to degrade the environment. So, as we face the challenge of devising creative ways to build a sustainable economy—of getting the resources we need without using them all up—we'll need lots of creative thinkers and activists.

WHERE DO YOU SEE JOBS FOR PEOPLE IN ENVIRONMENTAL NONPROFITS?

It's a very interdisciplinary field—there will be jobs for people with backgrounds in writing, law, economics, biology, chemistry, health, business, etc.

WHAT IS KEY TO GETTING A JOB IN THE NONPROFIT SECTOR?

You have to be committed to the issues. People in the nonprofit world obviously have other things driving them besides money. They tend to be idealistic. They tend to respond favorably to people whose passion for the issues is apparent. It's also important to have an open, flexible mind, to enjoy thinking broadly and making connections between issues. If you enjoy the original concept behind liberal arts education, you'll make a good member of the environmental nonprofit community.

WHAT IS THE MOST PRESSING PROBLEM YOU SEE WITH REGARD TO THE ENVIRONMENT?
Poverty and inequity in the developing world combined with overconsumption by rich, industrialized countries.

WHERE DO YOU SEE YOURSELF IN FIVE TO TEN YEARS?
With luck, in a cabin in the mountains, writing about environmental history and sustainable development.

WHAT BOOKS, TRADE JOURNALS, MAGAZINES, OR COURSES DO YOU RECOMMEND FOR PEOPLE TO STAY COMPETITIVE IN THIS FIELD?
Whatever stirs you up. Again, think interdisciplinary: don't do all of your reading on the neurological effects of magnesium gasoline additives. A few books I've enjoyed: Aldo Leopold, *A Sand County Almanac;* Rachel Carson, *Silent Spring;* John McPhee, *Encounters with the Archdruid;* Roderick Nash, *Wilderness and the American Mind;* Lewis Mumford, *The Culture of Cities;* George Perkins Marsh, *Man and Nature;* E.O. Wilson, *The Diversity of Life;* William Cronon, *Nature's Metropolis.* Some of the more general magazines *(Harper's, The Atlantic, The Progressive, Utne Reader)* still have some of the most interesting articles. All the environmental magazines are worth reading: *The Amicus Journal, Orion, Audubon, E, Sierra, Environment, Buzzworm's Earth Journal.* People especially interested in environmental science will want to check out some of the most important science journals: *Nature, Science, Ambio, Scientific American, New Scientist, Science News.* People interested in sustainable development might check out *Development, World Development,* and *Population and Development Review.*

***Mike and Janice Whitacre** are codirectors of Ecotech, a conference planning and consulting firm in Steamboat Springs, Colorado. Janice received a B.S. in environmental, organismic, and population biology from the University of Colorado in 1982 and an M.A. in marketing and communications* *from the University of California at San Diego in 1985. Mike received a B.A. in history in 1983 and an M.A. in medieval history in 1986, both from the University of California at Santa Barbara.*

WHAT DOES YOUR ORGANIZATION DO?

The mission of Ecotech is to create forums for the business and environmental communities to discuss the integration of environmental initiatives into long-term business strategies and to consider the effects this will have on a sustainable future. Ongoing projects for Ecotech include organizing conferences and small workshops (or ECO-salons) for maximum exchange and discussion on environmental issues.

DESCRIBE A TYPICAL DAY.

A typical day is spent mostly corresponding either by phone, fax, or mail. Since Ecotech is located in Colorado and most of our conferences take place elsewhere, we are basically "telecommuters," and our lifeline is the phone line.

Our team for Ecotech consists of a vast network of friends and associates whom we're fortunate enough to be able to call on for advice and input. Otherwise, the two of us are the only ones in the office most of the time, with a part-time assistant helping out during the busy times.

HOW DID YOU COME TO CREATE YOUR ORGANIZATION?

Before we started Ecotech, we had our own marketing consulting business for about six years and had worked on several other related conferences. One of the projects we worked on was the Technology, Entertainment and Design (TED) conferences. Since the TED conference took place just before the twentieth anniversary of Earth Day in 1990, some of the attendees at that conference decided there was a need for a conference addressing the environment and its interrelationship with technology. We coined the name Ecotech and then started to put together our first conference. The first Ecotech conference took place in 1991. The key to developing Ecotech was using all of our resources, especially the people we knew and had worked with in the past.

HOW HAVE YOU BUILT ECOTECH SINCE YOU STARTED THE ORGANIZATION?

One of the most powerful forms of advertising is through word of mouth. This is the strategy we use when building our network of sponsors, advisors, volunteers, and participants. We try to put on a great event that people can't help but talk about. We also strive to get as much free publicity as possible through trade and association journals and environmental magazines and newspapers.

The advisory board, chosen by us, is an integral factor in the success of a conference. The members of the advisory board help to identify potential speakers and sponsors and to spread the word about the conference.

WHAT CHALLENGES DOES YOUR ORGANIZATION FACE?

As with most nonprofit organizations, the biggest challenge always seems to be raising the funds necessary to carry out the goals of the organization. It's a constant chore. Another challenge is convincing some corporations that it's imperative that they become part of the solution to the environmental crisis. Luckily, there are a growing number of corporations who see the positive bottom-line benefits to enacting environmental policies above and beyond government regulations.

WHAT TRENDS DO YOU SEE IN YOUR FIELD?

The environmental "industry" is just beginning to take off. I don't see it as a cyclic thing. Rather, it is a strong, fast-growing movement throughout the world. There is a definite growing environmental market. Businesses are quickly realizing how profitable it can be to fill this niche. Innovative green products and corporate environmental policy-making both contribute to a positive consumer image of a company.

DO YOU HAVE ANY ADVICE FOR PEOPLE WHO WANT TO FIND A POSITION LIKE YOURS?

The best way to get involved with environmental education and entrepreneurship is to make a plan and just do it! Don't worry too much about having everything in place. If you take it one day at a time and persevere, things will begin to gel. Trust yourself and have faith that others will believe in you in time. If you fully believe in your mission, it won't be long before others will believe too and join in your efforts.

WHAT SKILLS ARE IMPORTANT IN YOUR FIELD?

The skills needed to enter the environmental arena are not clearly defined. People from all different backgrounds are being drawn to the environment, since it is almost a crisis situation. We believe that to have the commitment and desire to promote environmental sustainability is more important than having a particular degree or education. You will learn by doing.

If you're interested in an environmental career, read as much as you can about your area of interest. Keep up to date on current issues by subscribing to a newsletter or journal. Speak with as many people in your field of interest as possible. Don't be afraid to call on people that you've read about or admire. I've found people dealing with the environment to be most willing to help in any way they can. Conferences are also an excellent way to stay on top of opportunities and the latest goings-on.

WHAT IS THE MOST IMPORTANT ENVIRONMENTAL CHALLENGE FACING US TODAY?

There isn't one specific pressing problem with regard to the environment. There are many, many problems that are all interrelated. It's important not to get overwhelmed but to take it one day at a time and contribute what you are able to.

WHAT PUBLICATIONS DO YOU READ?

Some good journals and publications are *Cutter's*, *Business and the Environment* newsletter, *The Whole Earth Review*, *Utne Reader*, *Business Ethics*, *Outdoor Magazine*, and the *Wall Street Journal*. For job seekers, *Environmental Opportunities* newsletter is valuable.

Some books I recommend: Paul Hawken's *The Ecology of Commerce*, Donella Meadows' *Beyond the Limits*, Marlo Morgan's *Mutant Message*.

Ludmilla Zhirina *is a coordinator for Viola, an NGO (nongovernmental organization) in the Bryansk Oblast, an area in southwest European Russia. She is a doctor of biological sciences and the rector of the Bryansk Pedagogical Institute. She wrote and published a pamphlet entitled* Self-Help Guide to Protecting Yourself Against Radiation. *She is a lifetime member of the Socio-Ecological Union, a network of over two hundred environmental groups located throughout the former Soviet Union.*

DESCRIBE THE WORK OF VIOLA.

Thirty percent of the territory of the Bryansk Oblast falls in a zone contaminated by Chernobyl. I have been networking with teachers in the more contaminated school districts of the region to educate both teachers and students on preventive measures for reducing radioactive exposures and supplying individual schools with Geiger counters to monitor their environment. I am working to integrate radioactive preventive education into course work for teachers. Also, in 1994 with funding from USAID, Viola convened an international conference for NGOs involved in environmental education related to radioactive pollution. This conference resulted in a resolution to set up an e-mail network for exchange of information.

HOW DID YOU THINK TO START THIS PROGRAM?

It grew out of a sense that we had to do something to help the young—to face the ecological crisis they live with daily. Once they understand the connection between pollution and health, they become actively involved in trying to do something about the problem. Children are the ones most affected by environmental problems. They suffer from allergies, asthma, and bronchial diseases; they are forbidden to drink unboiled water, walk in the forests, or swim in the rivers.

The people in the Bryansk Oblast have suffered the most from the Chernobyl disaster. Since Bryansk is an industrial center, it is very much affected by industrial pollution as well. I was concerned about these problems so I carried out studies demonstrating that industry contributes to problems of heavy metals and organic compounds in our river water and high levels of acid rain. I wanted to get the word out about the Chernobyl-related pollution, including polluted drinking water, contaminated food, increased numbers of illness and psychological depression among the population.

WHAT WAS THE PURPOSE OF YOUR BOOK?

To touch on issues of importance in a nontechnical way and to educate people in contaminated regions about how to minimize their risk through food preparation, exercise, and spiritual work. The book is used by teachers, parents, people who have their own gardens and courtyards, people dependent on stores and markets—my purpose was to answer questions.

ANY OTHER THOUGHTS?

One must live—hope and healing to you.

Environmental Services

***Shelley Levin Billik** is the manager of recycling and environmental resources for Warner Brothers in Burbank, California, where she is responsible for source reduction, recycling, energy conservation, and other environmental programs. She has a B.A. in psychology from the University of California at Berkeley.*

HOW DID YOU GET THIS JOB?

Getting this job was a fluke. I was working at an environmental consulting firm with a group of engineers. That was in late 1989, the time that California's AB 939 waste reduction laws came into effect, and we were hired by cities and counties to write their SRREs (Source Reduction and Recycling Elements), which are their plans for complying with AB 939. We submitted permit applications for recycling, processing, composting, and landfill facilities. We dealt with waste haulers and government agencies. Then one day, a colleague asked if I knew someone interested in being the recycling coordinator for a large private company—a movie studio. And yes, I did know someone—me. Getting the job was the easy part. *Creating* the job is the real task. And for most companies, this is a new position, a new department, and a new way of looking at how they do business. Education is at least 50 percent of the job, educating management as participants in the programs, and educating employees in improving company operations.

WHAT IS YOUR OFFICE LIKE, AND WHAT IS A TYPICAL DAY LIKE?

My department consists of myself, an assistant who helps me keep my sights on the big picture by managing many of my daily tasks, and a recycling crew of four people. I also have a boss who is committed to environmental preservation and who supports my programs even when they are controversial. She and a Recycling Committee formed before I was hired were instrumental in getting my position approved. This group of about ten people from different parts of the company and I meet every month to discuss new ideas. In top management, there is an Executive Environmental Committee to whom I give quarterly updates, and whose support has been paramount in creating company-wide policies. Warner Bros. has shown me that it cares not only about the immediate work environment, but that its commitment carries over to its employees and their homes and families.

I meet with representatives from other studios through the Alliance of Motion Picture and Television Producers, Public Affairs Coalition. We meet about once a month, gather statistics on our waste reduction programs, and share resources on any subject relating to environmental concerns.

WHAT ARE THE CHALLENGES OF YOUR JOB?

Designing a waste prevention, reuse/donation, and recycling program at a motion picture studio is definitely challenging. Unlike many other industries, the motion picture industry hasn't changed very much in decades. The industrial revolution taught us that everything is disposable, convenience is above conservation, and the future is now. Given this cultural roadblock for new progressive programs, the biggest and most exciting challenge is to learn the many crafts and processes of the studio, and then come up with different, more environmentally sound ways of doing things. I'm known around our backlot as "hug-a-tree" or "huggy"—and I like it because I know that these craft people respect me and respect what I do. They consider me part of the team, and they trust me. They are part of the solution and enjoy coming up with new ideas. What is changing is the cultural mindset.

The challenge is to bring the notions of resource degradation and the need for preservation closer to home—without disrupting the company's end goals. And, demonstrating that this can reduce economic waste, improve the company's bottom line as well as its public and corporate image. There is absolutely no downside to being environmentally proactive.

WHAT ARE THE TRENDS IN THIS FIELD?

We need to use new methods of accounting and new methods of analyzing and communicating the bottom line. Antiquated methods of accounting look only at the dollar cost of manufacturing a product and rarely include the true cost of natural resources and their depletion; the cost of energy required to produce the product; the cost of pollution in extraction, manufacturing, and transportation; the cost of pollution abatement now and in the future; and disposal. If the price of products reflected all these true costs, our choices at the supermarket, in construction, and in our lifestyles would be very different.

A subject that requires much more attention is that of designing and constructing buildings for energy efficiency and using nontoxic, more resource-efficient construction materials with postconsumer recycled content. These can create a tremendous market for collected recyclables, and at the same time reduce our dependence on fossil fuels, reduce pollution, and create comfortable, healthful, efficient buildings.

***Susan Glass** is the director of Materials for the Arts, a jointly funded program of the New York City Department of Sanitation and the Department of Cultural Affairs since 1984. She received a B.A. in art history from the University of Wisconsin in 1978. Prior to her position at Materials for the Arts, she worked as a gallery assistant in exhibition design at the Hirschorn Museum in Washington, D.C., and as an administrative assistant for Columbia University's graduate program in arts administration.*

TELL ME ABOUT YOUR CAREER HISTORY.

I have been very fortunate in that my jobs have come to me through friends, networking, and being available for work at the right time. I believe that timing and some luck is key to finding employment in these times. I have certainly been very lucky. My job as director of Materials for the Arts has been intensely rewarding. I'm never bored. I have the ability and freedom to create and do what I want. There are frustrations, of course, but I work with over one thousand arts and social service organizations. I feel I make a great difference in the operations of these organizations by supplying them with materials that range from art materials to computers, film and video equipment, fabric, props, mirrors for dance studios, and a host of other materials that come into our warehouse and are used for a myriad of purposes.

WHY DO YOU DO WHAT YOU DO?

What I enjoy most about this job is that as one who is committed to the arts I get to support the arts and the environment simultaneously. Our program is a waste reduction model through reuse of materials that are donated to us. The idea is simple. There is very little money for arts programs, and we create a second or third life for these materials by furnishing groups with supplies. We also keep from our landfill tons of materials each month. Everyone wins. For instance, a company wants to dispose of old office equipment, or a manufacturing company has products that are obsolete. Our organization picks up these materials at no cost to the company. They receive a tax write-off, and these materials are then reused by other organizations, including the Metropolitan Museum of Art, the Riverside Symphony, and hundreds of other organizations. Materials for the Arts touches the lives of everyone in New York City, whether they know it or not.

Also, as program director, I have the opportunity to shift the focus from purely an arts orientation to a waste prevention program. I see a whole new dimension to what I do. I now bill my program as a waste reduction model. As such we weigh everything to keep track of the tonnage of materials we are keeping from the waste stream. Over 450 tons of materials come through here, with a value of $2 million on the market. If they were purchased new, it would be about $3 million. This reuse of materials eliminates wasteful disposal to our dwindling landfills. That is why our organization is supported by both the Department of Cultural Affairs and the Department of Sanitation.

WHAT DO YOU RECOMMEND ARTISTS DO THAT ARE INTERESTED IN THE ENVIRONMENT?

I think people must realize that many positions in the arts are heavily oriented toward fund-raising activities. It was easier in the 1970s and 1980s, when there was more support for the arts. Now, one needs good management and needs to be aware of what can work in this day and age. You need to ask yourself: What will someone fund? Why is my project or work important? What is innovative?

My advice to those searching for a green career is to remember that the most important aspect of your job search is networking. It's also the most exciting and most productive way to get information from people. Keep abreast of what is going on in your interest area. I have found my interests in the arts and the environment work together in a way that is creative and fulfilling to me. Programs like Materials for the Arts are springing up across the country. If there isn't one in your home town or city, start one and learn from the models that are working. Reuse organizations nationwide are working together to share program ideas and enterprise models.

David J. Hurd *is the recycling operations specialist for R2B2 Plastics, Inc. He has been an active participant in the recycling industry since graduating from Cooper Union with a B.E. in chemical engineering in 1981.*

WHAT DO YOU DO ON THE JOB?

I am responsible for the marketing of up to fifty thousand tons per year of secondary materials at Bronx 2000's Trashbusters company, especially in the area of postconsumer plastics. I provide technical assistance and business planning services in new recycling enterprise and program development to Bronx 2000's clients across the country. I'm involved in research and development of new processing and recycling technologies. I have developed, obtained funding for, and managed a $250,000, two-year R&D effort and feasibility study aimed at recycling consumer dry-cell batteries, resulting in the development of a laboratory-scale recycling process for one domestically produced battery product and the book, *Getting a Charge Out of the Wastestream*, published by the Council of State Governments in 1992. Other responsibilities include grant writing, solid-waste policy analysis and development, and regulatory review and comment. More recently, I have been acting general manager of R2B2 Plastics, Inc., Bronx 2000's for-profit plastics recycling subsidiary, supervising a staff of seven and producing fifty to sixty thousand pounds per week of plastics regrind. I am responsible for all financial management, trafficking, inventory, production, general administration, staff management, and plant management.

WHAT ARE YOUR FAVORITE ACTIVITIES ON THE JOB?

My favorite activities on the job tend to span the traditional blue-collar to white-collar extremes. I love the operational, hands-on aspects of my job: troubleshooting equipment, driving forklifts, moving thousands of tons of recyclables around the country to end users with a few phone calls. It gives you a sense of the scope and detail of what it takes to actually achieve the recycling objective of using recovered materials from the waste stream to displace virgin manufacturing feedstocks. Most important, it gives you a full understanding of the recycling industry, which then makes you an invaluable policy resource.

That is the other area where I get the greatest satisfaction. I guess one of the reasons that I wanted to become an environmentalist was to really have a say in and take an active role in helping improve the quality of the environment, to participate in the politics of the environment. Having participated in solid-waste management policy activities at every level of government has made me feel that I have achieved the voice I was looking for. I think that is where the real satisfaction lies.

WHAT SKILLS ARE NEEDED FOR THIS PROFESSION?

An open mind and exceptional communication and writing skills. Many environmentalists are on the leading edge of nationally pressing policy issues and, as such, in the public eye. In trying to affect the habits and consciousness of the general public, you need to be able to express yourself clearly and in simple terms, without ever appearing too zealous lest you portray the stereotype of the environmental fanatic, which threatens a lot of people.

I find having a firm foundation in science is beneficial. Also important is a special kind of stamina; many of the environmental battles are uphill ones, as essentially what we are ultimately trying to achieve is a complete shift in the manufacturing infrastructures so that secondary commodities take precedence over limited virgin raw materials.

WHAT ARE SOME OF THE TRENDS FOR THE RECYCLING INDUSTRY?

The recycling industry is one of the few growth industries of the decade. There is no shortage of solid waste in the United States, just a shortage of environmentally sound options for its proper disposition. Recycling not only is here to stay but is continually growing.

Alexander Joseph Varas *is a consulting engineer for Hazen and Sawyer in New York City, with extensive experience in managing large wastewater and water treatment design projects for the cities of Detroit and New York. He received a B.C.E. from Manhattan College in 1970 and an M.S. in civil engineering from New York University in 1974.*

WHY DO YOU DO WHAT YOU DO?

The seed to become an engineer was planted in my mischievous youth. While I was growing up in the Bronx a sewer was constructed on the street where I lived. In the evening, after the work crews had departed, all the neighborhood children would descend into the open trenches and reenact battle scenes and fashion dirt balls to attack each other.

During one of these seek-and-destroy escapades I found myself in the cab of the steam shovel used to dig the trench. Under the driver's seat was a three-ring binder with neat, clear notes and diagrams describing the entire sewer project. I was fascinated by the details and formulas. I realized that a physical project, a sewer, could be described in words and drawings and then made real. I wanted to be able to accomplish the same.

WHAT IS YOUR FAVORITE ACTIVITY ON THE JOB?

Managing construction activities. During the construction of a project there will be coordination problems involving numerous building trades. These problems require immediate resolution, and the engineer, acting as the agent for the owner, is called upon to resolve them.

WHAT TRENDS DO YOU PERCEIVE IN YOUR INDUSTRY?

I see growth in the water and wastewater segments of the environmental industry, growth driven by regulatory edicts and regulations. In order to meet present and future regulations, new and more complex technologies have to be implemented at municipal and industrial facilities. Cost will always be a factor. Although the hard costs (material, equipment, and construction) remain constant, those firms that can reduce the soft costs (design and construction documents) will prosper.

WHAT SKILLS ARE NEEDED FOR YOUR PROFESSION?

Communication skills, speaking and writing, are paramount in being successful in this and almost any professional occupation. Base technical knowledge has to be continually improved upon through specialized and advanced education. A detailed understanding of your field as well as its financial and social impacts is a must.

WHAT TIPS DO YOU RECOMMEND FOR NEWCOMERS?

Become technically proficient, and you will be sought after for your knowledge and expertise. Be efficient in your work tasks and become an active participant in the computer information age; this includes PCs, modems, and electronic mail. Be focused and responsive. Seek guidance when required and regularly inform supervisors as to your progress. Join professional organizations, attend meetings, and participate.

WHAT BOOKS DO YOU RECOMMEND FOR PEOPLE INTERESTED IN ENGINEERING AND THE ENVIRONMENT?

The Power Broker, by Robert Moses, *The Fall of New York* by Robert A. Caro, and *The Gate, The True Story of the Design and Construction of the Golden Gate Bridge* by John Van der Zee.

WHAT DO YOU THINK IS YOUR MOST IMPORTANT RESPONSIBILITY?

To strive to impart to the next generation of engineers the proper sense of ethical and moral conduct required when you are charged with the responsibility for providing for the public good.

WHERE DO YOU GO FOR INSPIRATION?

I'm surrounded by inspiration: bridges, tunnels, buildings, roads, industrial and manufacturing complexes.

Henry Waxman *is founder and chief executive officer of Metropolitan Mining Company, the leading "Bottle Bill" recycler in the Metropolitan New York area. MetroMining Company employs 140 people and accounts for more than 40 percent of the greater metropolitan area's returnable-container deposit redemptions and recycling. Mr. Waxman received a B.A. in fine arts from Brooklyn College of the City University of New York in 1967. He worked at Aluminum Company of America (Alcoa) from 1968 until 1983, when he established MetroMining Company.*

WHAT IS THE KEY TO GETTING INTO THE RECYCLING BUSINESS?

Recycling work is not for the faint-hearted. It is a hard business with low margins. To succeed you need a niche—vision alone will not do. That's if you want to start your own enterprise. If someone is coming out of school and is interested in environmental areas, I would suggest staying away from the niche companies. Virtually all major corporations have environmental divisions now, and there is a plethora of government offices (federal, state, and local) that offer excellent opportunities for the motivated. I believe people in the early stages of their careers should choose options where their energy and enthusiasm can make a difference. If young people have problem-solving skills, they will shine. If they ultimately become frustrated with the structure and restrictions placed on them by their employers, they may become the niche entrepreneurs of the environmental future.

I am a tremendous supporter of the value of business background, as taught by our Fortune 500 citizens. Nowhere can you get as good an overview of the interaction between people, our governments, and our global neighbors.

WHAT ARE THE TRENDS YOU SEE AFFECTING THIS INDUSTRY?

Government regulation, taxation, and the bureaucracy's need for an easy fix. These will be combined with a growing awareness of our nation's environmental needs, and in the area of recycling I predict growth, especially among the large haulers and niche recyclers. Governments unfortunately are crisis managers. Recycling is not new. Sparing you the clichés, it has been going on in an industrial sense since the birth of the industrial revolution. The reuse of materials, when economically feasible, has been an integral part of the manufacturing process since the word "profit" has been in the dictionary.

The growth of nonrefillable packaging along with trends toward convenience shopping, packaging, and consumption created a throwaway society in America for the last twenty or thirty years. Many people, aware of waste, depletion of natural resources, and even pollution, have led a quiet revolution for over a generation.

But landfills closing . . . that's what really did it. When it became apparent that, within our own lifetimes, we would run out of places to put our garbage, recycling went from a good deed or good business to a national mandate. It became a crisis. Governments had to act, and businesses are becoming more and more aware of the necessity of doing their part. They are buying products that are made from recycled materials. Even at that, however, one must watch their definitions. Recycled does not necessarily mean postconsumer waste.

WHAT KIND OF JOBS ARE BEING CREATED THROUGH RECYCLING INITIATIVES IN BUSINESS?

Recycling is creating jobs from the very low skilled to those requiring an M.B.A. All businesses need managers, receptionists, clerks, secretaries, data processing personnel, accountants, and the like. These jobs are being created in neighborhoods, not on Madison Avenue . . . that's some of the good news. Mothers and fathers can work and be accessible to home and school. Small companies can be flexible in some ways that major corporations cannot. Recycling also provides great transitional labor. By that I mean it teaches basic business skills to a segment of society that has been and will continue to be overlooked. We also teach forklift operation, machine operations, light maintenance, machine repair, even simple arithmetic (bags of materials must be counted). New York City does not offer an unskilled job market, but it does have a large supply of unskilled labor. Recycling offers tremendous potential for unskilled workers to enter the workforce, reap some benefit from earning a living, and move on.

Company Directory

This directory includes over four hundred company listings that detail environmental programs, projects, management, policies, products, and services. Extensive as it is, this list is far from complete. Many companies not listed have significant environmental programs in place. Also, although some companies provided more information than others, the quantity of information listed does not indicate a company's level of commitment; some have better public relation departments and more environmental literature available than others.

The directory is intended to help you gather information, conduct informational interviews if appropriate, and network with professionals in your field of interest. It is organized alphabetically by company name and lists contact names (if given by the company), along with a short summary of a company's environmental programs. It is not a comprehensive analysis of environmental performance: there is no "green screen" or company rating. Many companies mention the amount of their environmental expenditures; this information should be evaluated in light of the size of the company and the percentage that amount is of its overall operating costs and revenues. You can use many of the publications and organizations listed in the "Resource Directory" (page 379) to gain a more comprehensive understanding of a company's environmental performance.

Important Note:

The company profiles and corporate contacts are to be used only to obtain additional information on a company's environmental programs and services. Company contacts in this directory have requested that résumés not be sent to them.

Company: ABET, Inc.
Industry: Consulting
Contact: Howard Lieberman, president
Address: P.O. Box 326, Whitehall, PA 18052-0326
Phone: (610) 770-1025
Fax: (610) 770-9280

What Company Does: Specializes in providing consulting services to small start-up or existing businesses, finding alternate sources for financing, providing transitional management to businesses too small to afford a chief financial officer.

Company: Abt Associates, Inc.
Industry: Consulting
Contact: Richard Wells, vice president
Address: 64 Wheeler Street, Cambridge, MA 02138-1168
Phone: (617) 492-7100
Fax: (617) 492-7100

What Company Does: Abt is a research-based consulting firm in Cambridge, Massachusetts, serving government and business clients.

Environmental Programs: Consults on environmental management projects for public and corporate clients. Examples of its projects include assisting companies in developing corporate environmental strategies, using total quality environmental management concepts, developing corporate measures of environmental success, and assisting government and industry in Mexico to address environmental issues. Abt employees have practical industry or government experience coupled with strong skills in business management, economics, environmental science, or pollution prevention.

Company: Adirondack Council
Industry: Nonprofit
Contact: Timothy Burke, executive director
Address: Church Street, P.O. Box D-2, Elizabethtown, NY 12932-0640
Phone: (518) 873-2240

What Company Does: Founded in 1975, the Adirondack Council works to protect and preserve the Adirondack Park through public education, influencing public policy, litigation, and mobilizing public opinion. The Adirondack Park is the largest of all parks in the contiguous United States and attracts over 9 million visitors annually. For internship possibilities, contact Donna Beal, administrator.

Company: Advent Advisors
Industry: Financial services
Contact: Farnum Brown, vice president
Address: 104 East Main Street, Durham, NC 27701
Phone: (919) 682-0308
Fax: (919) 682-4931

What Company Does: A fee-based money management firm specializing in social investing. Manages over $48 million, has a five-year track record, and draws on over twenty-five years of investment experience. Free brochure. Internships available.

Company: African Center for Technology Studies (ACTS)
Industry: Nonprofit, sustainable development
Contact: Calestous Juma, executive director
Address: P.O. Box 45917, Nairobi, Kenya, Africa
Phone: 254-2-565173
Fax: 254-2-565173 (night only)

What Company Does: ACTS conducts policy research, undertakes training, provides advisory services, and disseminates information on the policy aspects of the application of science and technology to sustainable development organizations.

Environmental Programs: Research programs are Environmental Governance and Technology Management. The former conducts policy research on environmental governance at the local, national, and international levels. It has an objective of contributing ideas relevant to the implementation of the Convention to Combat Desertification and the Framework Convention on Climate Change, especially on matters related to governance, land use, technology, biodiversity, and climate change. The Technology Management program conducts policy research on ways to facilitate implementation of the Convention on Biological Diversity, the Global Biodiversity Strategy, and the relevant chapters of Agenda 21.

Company: AgAccess
Industry: Agriculture
Contact: Jessica Brown, fulfillment manager
Address: 603 Fourth Street, Davis, CA 95616
Phone: (916) 756-7177
Fax: (916) 756-7188

What Company Does: An information company specializing in sustainable agriculture. AgAccess business divisions include publishing, custom research, and information services, and sales of all agriculture books in print via free mail-order catalogs and a bookstore.

Company: **Air Products and Chemicals, Inc.**
Industry: Chemicals
Contact: P. Brian Sullivan, manager, Marketing Communications
Address: Environment and Energy Systems, 7201 Hamilton Boulevard, Allentown, PA 18195-1501
Phone: (610) 481-4911
Fax: (610) 481-5084

What Company Does: Air Products is a major supplier of industrial gases and related equipment, chemicals, and environmental and energy systems, serving a variety of diverse markets. Its 1993 sales were $3.1 billion.

Environmental Programs: Air Products has made a solid commitment toward solving the country's environmental and energy needs by establishing three major businesses. These businesses address the challenges of solid-waste disposal, air pollution emission controls, and expanded clean energy sources.

Company: **Air & Water Technologies Corporation**
Industry: Environmental services
Contact: Richard B. Fulton, manager, Human Resources
Address: U.S. Highway 22 West and Station Road, Branchburg, NJ 08878
Phone: (908) 685-4600

What Company Does: Air & Water Technologies is a leader in air and water pollution control technologies and is involved in sludge and sewage treatment and plastics recycling. It operates under three business names: Metcalf and Eddy, Residuals Management, and Research-Cottrell.

Company: **Alexandra Avery**
Industry: Consumer products
Contact: Mary Anne Hartog, manager
Address: 4717 Southeast Belmont, Portland, OR 97215
Phone: (503) 236-5926

What Company Does: Alexandra Avery is a natural body care company that uses 100 percent natural ingredients. It offers a full line of facial and body products and four perfumes. Since 1976, Alexandra has been growing and wildcrafting herbs on her organic farm. The products are prepared from these gardens in small batches to ensure the freshest possible skin food.

Environmental Programs: Alexandra teaches classes on becoming an eco-sound consumer and has written a book about skin care with chapters on the importance of environmentally conscious and cruelty-free consumerism.

Company: **Allens Naturally**
Industry: Consumer products
Address: P.O. Box 339, Department SB, Farmington, MI 48332-0339
Phone: (313) 453-5410
Fax: (313) 453-8325

What Company Does: Allens Naturally is a producer of natural home care products that are environmentally safe and effective. These products are free of alcohol, dyes, and perfumes. They are concentrated and sold in HDPE containers that are recyclable.

Company: **Alliance for a Paving Moratorium / Fossil Fuels Policy Action Institute (APM)**
Industry: Nonprofit environmental organization
Contact: Jan Lundberg or Katie Scarborough
Address: 761 8th Street, Suite 3, Arcata, CA 95521
Phone: (707) 826-7775 or (707) 874-2052
Fax: (707) 822-7007

What Company Does: Calls for a stop to building new roads and parking lots and promotes alternatives to pavement and cars, including bike and foot paths, renewable-energy-powered rail transit, and "ecocity" building and re-structuring.

Environmental Programs: Depaving; auto-free city centers; closure of roads threatening endangered species; opposing NAFTA; warning against "clean cars"; wilderness protection. The mission of APM is to bring about "ecodemocracy" via a conservation revolution.

Company: **Alliance to Save Energy**
Industry: Nonprofit environmental organization
Address: 1725 K Street NW, Suite 509, Washington, DC 20006-1401
Phone: (202) 857-0666

What Company Does: Publishes guides, reports, and directories related to energy efficiency, including *Energy Efficiency Resource Directory: A Guide to Utility Programs*, a directory of energy-efficient and demand-side management programs across the country.

Company: **AlliedSignal Inc.**
Industry: Technology
Contact: Jonathan Plaut, director, Environment Quality, Corporate Health, Safety, and Environmental Policy
Address: P.O. Box 1057, Morristown, NJ 07962-1057
Phone: (201) 455-6570
Fax: (201) 455-4835

What Company Does: AlliedSignal is a worldwide advanced technology company whose primary businesses are aerospace, automotive products, and engineering materials. AlliedSignal businesses operate under such names as Bendix, Fram, Jurid, Garrett, King Radio, and UOP.

Environmental Programs: AlliedSignal has a formal worldwide health, safety, and environmental policy including safety and loss prevention, occupational health, product safety, hazard/needs assessment and crisis management, environmental audits, and comprehensive pollution control management and training.

Company: **Alternative Garden Supply, Inc.**
Industry: Gardening
Contact: David Ittel, owner
Address: 297 North Barrington Road, Streamwood, IL 60107
Phone: (800) 444-2837
Fax: (708) 885-8634

What Company Does: Specializes in pesticide-free gardening indoors and outdoors, including a complete line of organic fertilizers. Also offers an extensive selection of home beer brewing supplies. Call for free catalog.

Company: **Aluminum Company of America (Alcoa)**
Industry: Metals
Contact: Barbara Jeremiah, secretary and assistant general counsel
Address: 1501 Alcoa Building, Pittsburgh, PA 15219
Phone: (412) 553-4545
Fax: (412) 553-4498

What Company Does: Alcoa is the world's largest producer of aluminum and aluminum products used in the packaging, aerospace, automotive, transportation (railroad cars, truck bodies, truck wheels, rapid transit vehicles etc.), chemical, and building and construction industries.

Environmental Programs: Alcoa conducts a broad array of programs to address environmental issues. The company has recycled over sixty billion aluminum cans to produce new metal with only 5 percent of the energy required to produce metal from bauxite ore. The Pallets Plus program that allows Alcoa's customers to return pallets and packaging materials for recycling has reduced landfill material significantly. Alcoa's U.S. plants participate in the EPA's voluntary 33/50 program to reduce the amount of toxic chemicals released into the environment. Alcoa has achieved a 49 percent reduction in the amount of chemicals released and is far ahead of the reduction schedule specified in the 33/50 program. It is also a participant in the EPAs Green Lights program and a number of local waste-reduction programs.

Company: Amerada Hess Corporation
Industry: Energy
Contact: Robert Weiss, manager, Human Resource Development
Address: 1185 Avenue of the Americas, New York, NY 10036
Phone: (212) 536-8180

What Company Does: Amerada Hess is engaged in the exploration, production, purchase, gathering, transportation, and sale of crude oil and natural gas and the manufacture, purchase, transportation, and marketing of petroleum products.

Environmental Programs: Amerada Hess is a member of the Clean Gulf Association, which will respond to oil spills in the Gulf of Mexico. The corporation is also a member of a number of oil spill cooperatives in Canada. In 1990, Amerada Hess was one of twenty oil companies that created the Marine Preservation Association (MPA), an organization that will provide the financial resources necessary to respond in the event of a major coastal oil spill in the United States or the U.S. Virgin Islands.

Company: American Council for an Energy-Efficient Economy (ACEEE)
Industry: Energy
Contact: John Morrill, business manager
Address: 1001 Connecticut Avenue NW, Suite 801, Washington, DC 20036
Phone: (202) 429-8873
Fax: (202) 429-2248

What Company Does: ACEEE conducts in-depth technical and policy assessments, advises governments and utilities, works collaboratively with businesses and other organizations, publishes a wide variety of books, reports, and consumer guides, and organizes conferences. In all areas it explores the links between energy efficiency, economic prosperity, a cleaner environment, and other aspects of national and global concern.

Company: American Excelsior Company
Industry: Packaging and erosion control
Contact: Ken Starett, marketing director
Address: P.O. Box 5067, 850 Avenue H East, Arlington, TX 76011
Phone: (817) 640-1555
Fax: (817) 649-7816

What Company Does: American Excelsior is an employee-owned company with 650 people in twenty-eight sales, distribution, and manufacturing centers around the country. The company is a leader in innovative packaging materials that use natural materials from aspen wood, such as excelsior, animal bedding, erosion products, and evaporative coolers.

Environmental Programs: American Excelsior has developed ECO-FOAM®, a replacement for polystyrene peanuts that is 95 percent cornstarch. ECO-FOAM® begins to decompose once it is saturated with water, and no toxic residue is left behind. American Excelsior also converted its excelsior technology into an erosion control blanket that helps vegetation take root, then acts as a mulch while it degrades.

Company: American Express Travel Related Services Company, Inc.
Industry: Financial, travel, and information services
Contact: Martin Warfel, vice president
Address: American Express Tower, World Financial Center, 5th floor, New York, NY 10285
Phone: (212) 640-2000
Fax: (212) 619-9802

What Company Does: American Express Company, founded in 1850, is a world leader in charge cards, Travelers Cheques, travel financial planning, and international banking.

Environmental Programs: American Express Bank is working with the Nature Conservancy in arranging debt-for-nature swaps in Ecuador, Peru, Argentina, Costa Rica, and other countries in Central and Latin America, so as to provide long-term private financing for conservation. American Express provides grants to encourage environmentally friendly tourism. American Express is a signatory and charter partner of the EPA Green Lights program, which permits the company to install energy-efficient lighting technologies that cut energy consumption, and deter pollution. No jobs are devoted 100 percent to this function, but the company is working to raise the environmental awareness of all employees, shareholders, and customers as part of its corporate responsibility.

Company: American Farmland Trust
Industry: Nonprofit
Contact: Ralph E. Grossi, president
Address: 1920 N Street NW, Suite 400, Washington, DC 20036
Phone: (202) 659-5170

What Company Does: Works through conferences, education, and grassroots organizing to protect U.S. farmland through land acquisition. It is the only national, nonprofit, membership organization dedicated solely to protecting agricultural resources. Founded in 1980, AFT's mission is to stop the loss of productive farmland and promote farming practices that lead to a healthy environment.

Company: American Forests (formerly American Forestry Association)
Industry: Nonprofit
Contact: R. Neil Sampson, executive vice president
Address: 1516 P Street NW, Washington, DC 20005
Phone: (202) 667-3300
Fax: (202) 667-7751

What Company Does: Works through policy research and advocacy, education, and action programs to heighten public awareness, interest, and active involvement in care and management of trees and forests, from urban forests to wilderness areas.

Environmental Programs: Global ReLeaf is an international action program that plants and cares for trees to improve environments, curb fossil-energy demands, and reduce CO_2 emissions. Supports over seven hundred local nonprofit tree planting groups with information, financial sources, and training. Publishes *American Forests*, which focuses on forests, forestry, endangered species, public lands, pest management, and wildlife. Also publishes *Urban Forests*, which focuses on practical ways of furthering forestry and conservation in urban areas.

Company: American International Group, Inc. (AIG)
Industry: Financial
Contact: Ken Cornell and Jan Edlestein, vice president and special assistant, Commerce & Industry Insurance Company
Address: 70 Pine Street, New York, NY 10270
Phone: (212) 770-5810 or (202) 783-2440

What Company Does: AIG is the leading U.S.-based international insurance organization and the largest underwriter of commercial and industrial insurance in the United States. Its member companies write property, casualty, marine, life, and financial services insurance in approximately 130 countries and jurisdictions and are engaged in a range of financial service businesses.

Environmental Programs: AIG companies are leaders in developing and marketing property/casualty insurance and related services specifically tailored to meet the market's demands for pollution legal liability and environmental remediation insurance, as well as environmental engineering/loss control services. AIG has also proposed the establishment of a National Environmental Trust Fund (NETF). The NETF would be a special fund, like the National Highway Trust Fund, dedicated only to cleaning up old Superfund sites. It would be paid for by a broad range of companies without regard to liability.

Company: American Littoral Society
Industry: Nonprofit
Address: Sandy Hook, Highlands, NJ 07732-9989
Phone: (908) 291-0055
Fax: (908) 872-8041

What Company Does: A national nonprofit public interest membership organization of both professional and amateur naturalists who work to encourage a better understanding of the aquatic environment and the need to protect life along the shore. Offers extensive outdoor activities including hikes, dives, and explorations of the coastal areas. Publishes a quarterly magazine called *Underwater Naturalist*, as well as *The Coastal Reporter*, a national newsletter.

Company: American Nature Study Society (ANSS)
Industry: Nonprofit, education
Contact: John A. Gustafson, treasurer
Address: 5881 Cold Brook Road, Homer, NY 13077

What Company Does: ANSS is America's oldest environmental education organization and provides a link between its members and many other important environmental education organizations. ANSS publishes the journal *Nature Study*, which contains in-depth articles on environmental education and related issues and book reviews, and *The American Nature Study Society Newsletter*, which keeps members posted on society, members, and affiliate news.

Company: American Rivers
Industry: Conservation, nonprofit
Contact: Kevin Coyle, president
Address: 801 Pennsylvania Avenue SE, Suite 400, Washington, DC 20003
Phone: (202) 547-6900
Fax: (202) 543-6142

What Company Does: American Rivers is a national conservation organization, which since 1973 has been addressing river policy issues across the country. Its mission is to preserve and restore Americas river systems and to foster a river stewardship ethic. It works in six areas: nationally significant rivers, hydropower reform, urban rivers, clean water, endangered aquatic species, and Western water issues. Members receive the quarterly newsletter *American Rivers.*

Company: American Telephone & Telegraph (AT&T)
Industry: Telecommunications
Contact: Tricia Geoghegan, media relations manager, Environment and Safety
Address: 131 Morristown Road, Room B1338, Basking Ridge, NJ 07920
Phone: (908) 204-8264
Fax: (908) 204-8549

What Company Does: AT&T's primary business is moving and managing information: providing quality products, systems, and services in U.S. and international markets. Its Worldwide Intelligent Network carries voice, data, image, and facsimile messages around the world. AT&T telecommunications and computer products, which can be networked into integrated systems, provide global access to information. In addition, AT&T is in the general purpose credit card business and provides financial and leasing services for AT&T and other equipment.

Environmental Programs: AT&T's environment and safety goals are: (1) phase out CFC emissions from manufacturing operations, 50 percent by year-end 1991 and 100 percent by year-end 1994; (2) eliminate total toxic air emissions, 50 percent by year-end 1991, 95 percent by year-end 1995, and

100 percent by year-end 2000; (3) decrease manufacturing process waste disposal 25 percent by year-end 1994; (4) recycle 35 percent of its paper by year-end 1994; (5) reduce paper use by 15 percent by year-end 1994; (6) ensure that 100 percent of AT&T eligible manufacturing facilities gain acceptance into the OSHA Voluntary Protection program/AT&T equivalent program by year-end 1995 and that 50 percent gain STAR status. By year-end 1993, AT&T had virtually eliminated CFC air emissions from manufacturing operations; reduced manufacturing process waste disposal 57 percent; recycled 63 percent of its waste paper (24,000 tons); and reduced paper use by 28 percent. AT&T publishes an *Environment & Safety Annual Report.*

Company: AMP Incorporated
Industry: Manufacturing
Contact: Dale E. Kortze, associate director, Environmental Programs Department
Address: P.O. Box 3608, MS 81.05, Harrisburg, PA 17105-3608
Phone: (717) 561-6422 or general (717) 564-0100

What Company Does: AMP is the world's leading producer of electrical and electronic connection devices. Over 100,000 types and sizes of terminals, splices, connectors, switches, cable assemblies, touch screens, data entry systems, and related application tooling are supplied by AMP to more than 30,000 electrical and electronic equipment manufacturers. AMP has 25,000+ employees.

Environmental Programs: AMP has an environmental policy, training, and education program and a Hazardous Waste Management Evaluation Group. The company has developed an environmental policy that has a goal to move as quickly as possible toward zero discharge. AMP is working toward introducing more energy-efficient products, using recycling systems and collection facilities, and minimizing toxic waste, as well as performing environmental audits every six to twelve months.

Company: Anheuser-Busch Companies, Inc.
Industry: Diversified
Contact: Robert G. Couch, director, Environmental Communications
Address: Executive Offices, One Busch Place, St. Louis, MO 63118-1852
Phone: (314) 577-3291
Fax: (314) 577-9698

What Company Does: Anheuser-Busch is a diversified corporation with subsidiaries that include the world's largest brewing organization, the country's second largest producer of fresh-baked goods, and the second largest theme park operation in the United States. It also has interests in container manufacturing and recycling, malt production, rice milling, international brewing and beer marketing, snack foods, international baking, refrigerated and frozen snack foods, real estate development, creative services, rail car repair, transportation services, and metalized label printing.

Environmental Programs: Anheuser-Busch established Anheuser-Busch Recycling Corporation, which has grown to become the largest recycler of aluminum beverage cans in the world, recycling one aluminum can for every can that Anheuser-Busch uses. Anheuser-Busch is an industry leader in reducing, reusing, and recycling the by-products from its manufacturing operations. In 1993, it purchased more than $2 billion of packaging containing over one billion pounds of postconsumer waste. Through its Busch Gardens and Sea World operation, it works diligently to protect and preserve wildlife. Between 1978 and 1993, Anheuser-Busch pledged about $6 million to various conservation and wildlife organizations. The company supports groups that create innovative solutions to address environmental concerns.

Company: Apple Computer, Inc
Industry: Technology
Contact: Dani Tsuda, manager, Environmental Engineering Strategies
Address: 6 Infinite Loop, m/s 306-1JS, Cupertino, CA 95014
Phone: (408) 974-0476
Fax: (408) 974-5475

What Company Does: Develops, manufactures, and markets personal computers, servers, and personal interactive electronic systems for use in business, education, home, science, engineering, and government. A recognized pioneer and innovator in the personal computer industry, Apple does business in more than 120 countries around the world.

Environmental Programs: Apples environmental efforts are divided into four categories:

Green Computers. Following an international trend toward sustainable technology, Apple is making an effort to manage the environmental impacts of all Apple products throughout their life cycles—design, manufacture, operation, and obsolescence.

Community and Industry Affairs. Apple encourages corporate and employee giving to environmental groups and participates in industry and government consortia that are sharing information and resources to solve environmental problems.

Operations & Facilities. Apple has taken many steps toward total environmental responsibility in facilities management and improved manufacturing processes and procedures.

Empowered Employees. Because environmental management is a distributed function at Apple success depends on individuals throughout the organization being committed to environmental excellence. A sixty-two-page EH&S employee handbook encourages and advises all workers of their individual responsibilities to make Apple a safe and healthy workplace and to protect the environment. Periodic "brown-bag" lunch seminars feature speakers from local and national environmental groups.

Company: Appropriate Technology Transfer for Rural Areas (ATTRA)
Industry: Nonprofit, sustainable development
Contact: Teresa Maurer, assistant program manager
Address: P.O. Box 3657, Fayetteville, AR 72702
Phone: (800) 346-9140

What Company Does: Funded by a grant from the U.S. Fish and Wildlife Service, ATTRA is a nonprofit organization that is administered by the National Center for Appropriate Technology (NCAT). Free information and technical assistance is offered to farmers who want to farm in more environmentally sound ways and reduce their use of chemicals in farming while maintaining their profits. ATTRA's focus is on the dissemination of ecologically appropriate and efficient methods of farming based on protection of the environment.

Company: Armstrong World Industries Inc.
Industry: Manufacturing
Contact: John M. Scheldrup, manager, Public Relations
Address: P.O. Box 3001, Lancaster, PA 17604
Phone: (717) 396-2766 or general (717) 397-0611

What Company Does: Armstrong is an international manufacturer and marketer of interior furnishings, including floor coverings, building products, and furniture, plus specialty products for the building, textile, automotive, and other industries.

Environmental Programs: Armstrong has an environmental policy including source reduction, waste management, recycling, and hazardous waste management.

Company: Arrowhead Mills
Industry: Consumer products
Contact: Boyd M. Foster

Address: P.O. Box 2059, Hereford, TX 79045-2059
Phone: (806) 364-0730
Fax: (806) 364-8242

What Company Does: Arrowhead Mills is a natural food producer, purchasing grains, beans, seeds, and other agricultural products from certified organic growers to be used as raw materials.

Environmental Programs: All paper and cardboard in packaging are from recyclable materials, and no heavy metal inks are used. Arrowhead uses primarily organically grown products for its manufacturing of foods.

Company: Arthur D. Little, Inc., Center for Environmental Assurance
Industry: Consulting
Contact: Paul D. Mosher, human resources manager, Environmental, Health, and Safety Consulting
Address: Acorn Park, Cambridge, MA 02140-2390
Phone: (617) 498-5205
Fax: (617) 498-7019

What Company Does: Environmental, health, and safety consulting, management consulting, technology development.

Environmental Programs: Arthur D. Little has offered a full range of environmental, health, and safety consulting services for more than forty years. The company brings together technical, scientific, and management disciplines and helps companies manage their environmental, health, and safety programs more effectively. Areas of specific technical and management expertise include environmental auditing, environmental business and strategy analysis, risk and liability assessment, planning and policy development, compliance management, pollution prevention, environmental technology, environmental education and training, and environmental management information systems.

Company: Asian NGO Coalition for Agrarian Reform (ANGOC)
Industry: Nonprofit, sustainable development
Address: Angoc Regional Secretariat, 47 Matrinco Building, 2178 Pasong Tamo, Makati, Metro Manila, 1200 Philippines

What Company Does: ANGOC was founded in 1979 with the primary objective of promoting sustainable development and environmental action. The Sustainable Development Environment Action Program was formed by ANGOC to address the environmental concerns in developing countries that are inextricably linked with the problems of poverty, unequal access to wealth, and underdevelopment. Publishes *Alternatives*, *Grassroots Action in Natural Resources Management*, and *Bankwatch*.

Company: Atlantic Recycled Paper Company / NOPE
Industry: Consumer products
Contact: Daniel Jerrems, president
Address: P.O. Box 39179, Baltimore, MD 21228
Phone: (410) 747-7314 or (800) 323-2811
Fax: (410) 747-8778

What Company Does: Sells recycled paper products, including office paper, mailing labels, fax paper, envelopes, legal pads, facial tissue, and paper towels, as well as cotton shower curtains, rainforest crunch, and natural cleaners.

Company: Atlantic Richfield Company
Industry: Energy
Contact: Carolyn Ziegler-Davenport, communications representative
Address: 515 South Flower Street, Los Angeles, CA 90071
Phone: (213) 486-3690 or general (213) 486-3511
Fax: (213) 486-1986

What Company Does: An integrated energy company, the largest U.S. producer of low-sulfur coal and a leading oil refiner. It is the twenty-second largest corporation of the Fortune 500 industrials.

Environmental Programs: Atlantic Richfield (ARCO) has a board-level corporate Health, Safety & Environmental Committee that reviews policies and actions of more than 300 professionals. Through its operating division, ARCO Products Company, the company has led in the development of cleaner-burning reformulated gasoline. Its emission-control gasolines, EC-1 and EC-Premium, have significantly reduced vehicular emissions in Southern California. In 1996, an even cleaner gasoline, ARCOs EC-X, which is designed to meet the California Air Resources Board's Phase II standards—the toughest in the nation—will enter the market.

Company: Autumn Harp
Industry: Consumer products
Contact: Paul Ralston, president
Address: 61 Pine Street, Bristol, VT 05443
Phone: (802) 453-4807
Fax: (802) 453-4903

What Company Does: Autumn Harp, founded in 1977, manufacturers (high-quality) all-natural petroleum-free skin care products that contain vegetable- or beeswax-based raw materials and are not tested on animals. The company markets and distributes products under its own brand name and also develops and manufactures lip care products for The Body Shop International.

Company: Aveda Corporation
Industry: Consumer products
Contact: Julie Bykowski, executive assistant
Address: 4000 Pheasant Ridge Drive, Blaine, MN 55449
Phone: (612) 783-4000
Fax: (612) 783-4110

What Company Does: Established in 1978, Aveda manufactures and develops complete collections of pure plant products including pure-fumes, hair care and skin care products, color cosmetics, and environmental care products. Aveda uses naturally derived ingredients in place of synthetic materials, petrochemicals, or animal derived or animal-tested ingredients. Aveda has a long history of environmental responsibility through product development, corporate practices, and charitable giving. Aveda was the first signatory to the Ceres principles. Aveda's corporate facility includes on-site child care, an organic cafeteria, exercise rooms, natural light, and is located on sixty-five acres. Aveda donates thousands of dollars each to environmental organizations and other types of charities including the Give to the Earth Foundation.

Company: Avon Products, Inc.
Industry: Consumer products
Contact: Brian T. Martin, vice president, Corporate Communications
Address: 9 West 57th Street, New York, NY 10019
Phone: (212) 546-6341 or general (212) 546-6015
Fax: (212) 546-6136

What Company Does: Avon is the world's largest-selling brand of cosmetics. Its products are sold by direct marketing in more than 100 countries. Products include toiletries, cosmetics, fragrances, costume jewelry, and gift items.

Environmental Programs: Avon's environmental health and safety policy commits the company to meet or exceed all environmental laws and regulations of the many communities and countries in which it operates. Avon will develop products, processes, and practices that improve environmental quality. Avon provides educational programs, emphasizing shared responsibility for sound environmental practices. In 1993, Avon Received a CAAT Recognition Award from the Johns Hopkins University Center for Animal Alternatives Testing for its "commitment and dedication to non-animal alternatives for products safety evaluation."

Company: **Aztec Harvests Coffee Company, Inc.**
Industry: Consumer products
Contact: David Griswold, general manager
Address: 1480 66th Street, Emeryville, CA 94608
Phone: (510) 652-2100
Fax: (510) 652-2636

What Company Does: Specialty coffee importer/distributor owned by Mexican small coffee cooperatives. Coffee is grown without chemical pesticides or fertilizers by Mexico's network of independent coffee farmer cooperatives. Green or roasted. Call about special projects.

Company: **Baker Hughes Incorporated**
Industry: Manufacturing
Contact: J. A. Curtis, director of environmental affairs
Address: 3900 Essex Lane, Suite 1200, P.O. Box 4740, Houston, TX 77210-4740
Phone: (713) 439-8600

What Company Does: Baker Hughes is a world leader in drilling equipment, production tools, and process equipment for the oil and gas industries. Its line of process equipment includes machinery for wastewater processing that is widely used in the chemical process industry as well as the municipal wastewater-treatment industry.

Environmental Programs: Baker Hughes has a corporate environmental policy that includes waste and emission reduction. The Baker Hughes Process Equipment Group manufactures equipment or municipal waste treatment facilities and industrial wastewater facilities. Other applications include solid-waste handling and solid/liquid separation equipment manufacturing.

Company: **BankAmerica Corporation**
Industry: Banking
Contact: Richard Morrison, senior vice president, Environmental Policies & Programs
Address: Department 5800, P.O. Box 37000, San Francisco, CA 94137
Phone: (415) 622-8144

What Company Does: BankAmerica Corporation was founded in 1904 as the Bank of Italy by A. P. Giannini. Today, it is one of the world's premier financial services institutions, with assets of about $200 billion, deposits of approximately $150 billion, branches in eleven states in the western United States and offices in thirty-four countries. BankAmerica offers a full range of consumer, business, wholesale, and institutional banking services.

Environmental Programs: BankAmerica Corporation's environmental program is guided by nine environmental principles and four high-level goals. For each goal there are specific actions to be taken. The objective is to try to make BankAmerica as environmentally responsible as it can be. Elements of the program include: (1) recycling paper, plastics, packaging material, technology equipment, glass, and aluminum; (2) purchasing recycled paper and other products with a recycled content; (3) taking into account environmental responsibility as a factor in loan decisions; (4) conserving energy and water; (5) encouraging ride sharing and use of public transit among employees; (6) educating employees, customers, and the public on environmental issues; (7) establishing a $6 million debt-for-nature swap to benefit Latin America rain forests and a $150,000 annual BankAmerica Foundation grant allocation; (8) encouraging employees to assist environmental projects in their communities; and (9) taking public stands on selected issues of economic and environmental consequence.

Company: **Barclay Recycling, Inc.**
Industry: Manufacturing
Contact: Tony Novembre, vice president, Operations
Address: 75 Ingram Drive, Toronto, Ontario M6M 2M2
Phone: (416) 240-8227
Fax: (416) 240-0114

What Company Does: Barclay Recycling is the largest manufacturer of backyard composters.

Environmental Programs: Hundreds of successful municipal programs worldwide.

Company: **BASF Corporation**
Industry: Chemicals
Contact: Abby Jane Brody, manager, Media Relations
Address: 3000 Continental Drive North, Mount Olive, NJ 07828-1234
Phone: (201) 426-2600
Fax: (201) 426-2610

What Company Does: BASF is the North American member of the BASF Group, one of the world's largest chemical manufacturers.

Environmental Programs: BASF has achieved a 90 percent reduction in reported releases and off-site transfers of the Emergency Planning and Community Right-to-Know Ad's list of "toxic" chemicals between the base year of 1987 and 1992. Through their voluntary participation in the EPA's Industrial Toxics Project, they reduced emissions of seventeen priority chemicals by 60 percent. They have been recognized by EPA as an "early achiever" for exceeding a 50 percent reduction commitment set for 1995.

Company: **Baxter International Inc.**
Industry: Health care
Contact: William R Blackburn, vice president, Corporate Environment Affairs, and chief environmental counsel
Address: One Baxter Parkway, Deerfield, IL 60015-4633
Phone: (708) 948-4962
Fax: (708) 948-3660

What Company Does: Baxter International Inc., through its subsidiaries, is the world's leading manufacturer and marketer of health-care products and services. Baxter sells more than 200,000 products in nearly one hundred countries.

Environmental Programs: Baxter is an active participant in U.S. EPA's 33/50 air toxics reduction program and Green Lights program. The company has accepted the Coalition of Northeastern Governors' challenge to reduce packaging and endorses the International Chamber of Commerce Charter on Sustainable Development. Between 1991 and 1993, Baxter cut 22.6 million pounds of packaging from its products and processes. As of the end of 1993, the company achieved 73 percent of its company-wide goal of reducing the average per-unit weight of its packaging 15 percent by 1995, from 1990 levels. Each year the company publishes an annual environmental performance report. Since 1993, its comprehensive environmental manual has been available to the public through Clark Boardman and Interharm Press publishers. The manual details the best demonstrated environmental practices. Baxter donates proceeds from manual sales to environmental organizations.

Company: **Beauty Without Cruelty (BWC)**
Industry: Nonprofit
Contact: Dr. Ethel Thurston, chairperson
Address: 175 West 12th Street, Suite 16G, New York, NY 10011
Phone: (212) 989-8073

What Company Does: A nonprofit membership organization that informs the public about animal suffering in the fashion, cosmetic, and household products industries and about substitutes that are cruelty-free. Publishes *Action Alert,* a newsletter that details news about animal rights issues, fur-free celebrities, designers, etc., and information for letter-writing campaigns to companies and magazines; and *The Compassionate Shopper,* a listing of more than 250 companies that offer cruelty-free personal and household items. Offers a recommended bibliography of books on animal testing. Also affiliated with American Fund for Alternatives to Animal Research (212-989-8073), which offers grants to finance development of alternatives to animal testing/nonanimal alternatives for laboratory testing.

Company: **Beehive Botanicals**
Industry: Health and beauty care products
Contact: Linda Graham, president
Address: Route 8, Box 8257, Hayward, WI 54843
Phone: (715) 634-4274
Fax: (715) 634-3523

What Company Does: Specializes in beauty care products that utilize royal jelly, honey, bee pollen, and propolis. All products are free from mineral oil and artificial colors. The company has over twenty-eight consumer goods consisting of skin care, hair care, and personal care products and health supplements utilizing bee products as an active ingredient. Beehive Botanicals was conceived twenty-two years ago with the idea of being an ethical, environmentally friendly, and socially responsible company offering natural health-care products. The company serves both domestic and international markets. Internships available on an individual basis; no program in place.

Company: **Ben and Jerry's**
Industry: Consumer products
Contact: Andrea Asch, manager of natural resources use
Address: Route 100, P.O. Box 240, Waterbury, VT 05676
Phone: (802) 244-6957
Fax: (802) 244-5944

What Company Does: Ben and Jerry's is a producer of a diverse range of super-premium ice cream and yogurt products.

Environmental Programs: The company's manager of Natural Resources Use is responsible for assessing the company's impact on the environment in all areas of operation. The company's goal is to be 100 percent involved in responsibly managing its solid-waste stream, conserving energy and resources, and exploring sustainable renewable energy sources.

Company: **Bethlehem Steel**
Industry: Manufacturing
Contact: Dr. A. E. (Gus) Moffitt, Jr., vice president, Safety, Health and Environment
Address: 1170 Eighth Avenue, Bethlehem, PA 18016-7699
Phone: (610) 694-2424
Fax: (610) 694-1524

What Company Does: Bethlehem Steel is the second largest steel producer in the United States, manufacturing hot and cold rolled sheets, galvanized and other coated sheets, tin mill products, steel plates, structural shapes, and pilings, rails, line pipe, forgings, and castings.

Environmenal Programs: Over the past five years the company has spent more than $250 million in environmental capital improvements. Costs to operate and maintain existing environmental control equipment total approximately $125 million a year. Although a very high level of environmental protection has already been achieved, the company remains dedicated to continuous improvement in this crucial area.

Company: **Betz Laboratories**
Industry: Water treatment
Contact: Peggy A. Shane, human resources manager
Address: 4636 Somerton Road, Trevose, PA 19047
Phone: (215) 355-3300

What Company Does: Betz Laboratories' business is the engineered chemical treatment of water, wastewater, and process systems operating in a wide variety of industrial and commercial applications, with particular emphasis on the chemical, petroleum-refining, paper, automotive, electrical utility, and steel industries.

Company: **Boeing**
Industry: Manufacturing
Contact: Kirk J. Thomson, director, Corporate Environmental Affairs
Address: P.O. Box 3707, MS 7E-HF, Seattle, WA 98124-2207
Phone: (206) 393-4780

What Company Does: Boeing is a diversified aerospace company that designs and manufactures military and commercial aircraft, missiles, helicopters, and parts. It is also a major exporter (over 50 percent of revenues).

Environmenal Programs: Boeing's goal is to prevent pollution and reduce the use of toxic and hazardous materials in its processes. Its Chemical Reduction Program identifies major technological breakthroughs to support changes and to support the company's goal of eliminating all toxic and hazardous materials.

Company: **Boise Cascade**
Industry: Paper products
Contact: J. Kirk Sullivan, vice president, Governmental and Environmental Affairs
Address: One Jefferson Square, P.O. Box 50, Boise, ID 83728
Phone: (208) 384-7680 or general (208) 384-6161 or (208) 384-4841

What Company Does: Boise Cascade is an integrated paper and forest products company whose activities include manufacturing and distribution of paper and paper products, office products, and building products and the management of timberlands to support these operations.

Environmenal Programs: Boise Cascade is a major paper recycler, processing corrugated container plant clippings in the manufacture of linerboard and postconsumer wastepaper and old magazines for use in various business and printing papers. Through a combination of on-site recycling capacity and purchased recycled pulp, the company produces a wide range of recycled papers at most of its paper mills. Boise Cascade expected to spend approximately $70 million, over 20 percent of its capital spending, on environmental projects in 1994.

Company: **Booz Allen & Hamilton**
Industry: Consulting
Contact: John Newman, senior vice president
Address: 4330 EastWest Highway, Bethesda, MD 20814
Phone: (301) 951-2700

What Company Does: Booz Allen is an international management and consulting firm that combines industry knowledge from more than twenty worldwide industry practices with consulting expertise in strategy, operations, and systems. The firm has been active in environmental management through years of direct involvement in helping to develop and implement key programs for government and industry. Booz Allen also offers a special report on corporate environmental management.

Company: **Borden, Inc.**
Industry: Consumer products
Contact: Nicholas R. Iammartino, director, External Communications
Address: 277 Park Avenue, New York, NY 10172
Phone: (212) 573-4131 or general (212) 573-4000
Fax: (212) 371-2659

What Company Does: Borden is the world's largest producer of pasta; a leader in U.S. dairy and grocery products (including milk, ice cream, sliced cheese, pasta sauce, sweetened condensed milk, lemon juice, and bouillon); and a major supplier of baked goods in Germany, dry soups and bouillon in Spain, and powdered milk worldwide. Among its nonfood operations, Borden is the world's largest wall coverings producer and also makes consumer adhesives, forest products, and foundry adhesives and resins, and plastic film and packaging materials.

Environmental Programs: With the adoption of the Borden Principles of Environmental Responsibility in 1990, Borden formalized a long-standing commitment to safeguard the environment through its handling and usage of raw materials, and its manufacture, packaging, and distribution of products. Source reduction and waste minimization are primary focuses—e.g., the company has installed systems to recycle virtually all process water at its ten North American forest products adhesives plants and has increased usage of recycled paperboard and other packaging materials.

Company: **Bristol-Myers Squibb Company**
Industry: Pharmaceuticals
Contact: Thomas Hellman, Ph.D., vice president, Environmental Affairs
Address: 345 Park Avenue, New York, NY 10154
Phone: (212) 546-5615 or general (212) 546-4000

What Company Does: Bristol-Myers Squibb is a highly diversified pharmaceutical/health care/consumer product corporation known for anticancer drugs and products such as Clairol and Bufferin.

Environmental Programs: Bristol-Myers has an environmental program based on the principles of product life-cycle management and continual improvement. The company is a signatory of the International Chamber of Commerce's Business Charter for Sustainable Development, a voluntary participant in the EPA's Industrial Toxics Project, and a member of the Advisory Committee to the Coalition of Northeastern Governors' Source Reduction Task Force.

Company: **Brookside Soap Company**
Industry: Consumer products
Contact: Sandie Ledray, president
Address: P.O. Box 55638, Seattle, WA 98155
Phone: (206) 742-2265
Fax: (206) 355-6644

What Company Does: The Brookside Soap Company manufactures all-natural bar soaps that contain no ingredients of animal origin and no synthetic fragrances or colorants. The company also offers bath oils, herbs, and accessories. It sells its products wholesale and through retail mail order. All packaging is 100 percent postconsumer waste recycled paper printed with soy-based inks. All of its formulations are environmentally responsible, biodegradable, and nontoxic.

Environmental Programs: The company's products are cruelty-free and contain nothing of animal origin. Products are packaged in minimal paper packaging.

Company: **Browning-Ferris Industries, Inc. (BFI)**
Industry: Environmental services
Contacts: Jon Greenberg and Richard E. Oakley, director of environmental policy and divisional vice president, Landfill Operations
Address: 1350 Connecticut Avenue NW, Suite 1101, Washington, DC 20036
Phone: (202) 223-8151 or (713) 878-8100
Fax: (202) 223-0685 or (713) 584-8043

What Company Does: Browning-Ferris Industries is one of the largest publicly held companies whose subsidiaries and affiliates collect, process for recycling, transport, and dispose of a wide range of commercial, industrial, medical, and residential solid wastes. BFI subsidiaries are also involved in resource recovery facilities, waste-to-energy plants, and portable restroom and sweeping services.

Environmental Programs: BFI's environmental programs are both internally and externally focused. Internally, its environmental programs are designed and implemented to better assure total compliance with all permits, rules, and laws that apply to the company's various operating facilities and to satisfy all of BFI's customers, which include the regulatory agencies and the public who host BFI's facilities. Externally, BFI is involved in numerous programs that foster a cleaner and safer environment worldwide. BFI is active in the Global Environmental Management Initiative, which is an organization of twenty-one companies dedicated to fostering environmental excellence worldwide. It is also involved in the creation of wildlife habitats at several of its locations in concert with the Wildlife Habitat Enhancement Council. BFI also provides Mobius, a public education program on recycling, which has been presented to thousands of school children and community groups around the world.

Company: **Burson Marsteller**
Industry: Consulting

Contact: Nancy Maloley, executive vice president and cochair, Worldwide Environmental Practice Group
Address: 1850 M Street NW, Suite 900, Washington, DC 20036-5890
Phone: (202) 833-8550

What Company Does: Burson Marsteller is a public affairs firm that provides issues management, crisis management, green marketing counseling, and environmental management consulting to a variety of clients.

Company: Burt's Bees, Inc.
Industry: Consumer products
Contact: Joe Coen, senior vice president, Sales and Marketing
Address: 308 West Hillsboro Street, Creedmoor, NC 27522
Phone: (919) 528-0064
Fax: (919) 528-4868

What Company Does: Manufactures and distributes a wide range of innovative, natural lifestyle products, including a broad assortment of personal care products, hand-crafted beeswax candles, flavored and fruited honey, pet snacks and grooming items, and apparel for adults and children.

Environmental Programs: Burt's Bees demonstrates its concern for the welfare of its customers and the environment by using only the finest ingredients and materials from sustainable resources in its products and by making every employee accountable for resource conservation in all aspects of operations. Burt's Bees is an active supporter of numerous environmental and animals rights groups in the United States and promotes trade with local artisans in Haiti.

Company: Business for Social Responsibility (BSR)
Industry: Nonprofit
Contact: Kathy Grimes, vice president
Address: 1030 15th Street NW, Suite 1010, Washington, DC 20005
Phone: (202) 842-5400
Fax: (202) 842-3135

What Company Does: BSR is a national business alliance providing leadership to address many of the enormous economic, social, and environmental problems that confront business and society. Among BSR's charter members are Reebok International, Ltd., Levi Strauss & Company, The Body Shop USA, Ben & Jerry's Homemade, and The Calvert Group. BSR operates at both the national and regional levels through state and local networks.

Environmental Programs: BSR members model a variety of environmental programs, from green design to sourcing decisions to manufacturing processes to waste reduction and energy-efficiency programs. The BSR Education Fund has initiated a national Eco-Efficiency Project that will create business and utility partnerships, promote development of more energy-efficient manufacturing technologies, and educate the general business community on a variety of environmental and energy programs.

Company: **California Certified Organic Farmers (CCOF)**
Industry: Nonprofit, agriculture
Contact: Diane L. Bowen, executive director
Address: 303 Potrero Street, Suite 51, Santa Cruz, CA 95060
Phone: (408) 423-2263
Fax: (408) 423-4528

What Company Does: A nonprofit, volunteer-based, grassroots organization composed of over 630 California organic farmers and food processors. The goal is to promote a healthy, ecologically accountable, and sustainable agriculture. Twenty years ago, a small group of organic farmers formed CCOF to define uniform organic farming standards and to establish a certification system for organic produce. It is now the largest statewide organization of organic producers in the nation, with fourteen local chapters across the state and a central office in Santa Cruz. The organization is the primary certification and trade association for organic farmers in California and a major representative for the organic foods industry.

Company: **Californians Against Waste Foundation (CAWF)**
Industry: Nonprofit
Contact: William Jones
Address: 926 J Street, Suite 606, Sacramento, CA 95814
Phone: (916) 443-8317
Fax: (916) 443-3912

What Company Does: A nonprofit organization formed in 1984 to help create a sustainable state economy for recycled products. CAWF promotes the reuse, recycling, and renewal of natural resources through public education, research, and development programs. It is affiliated with Californians Against Waste, which lobbies state and local government. Internships available. Contact Rick Best, policy associate.

Company: **Calvert Group**
Industry: Investments
Contact: Reed Gligorovic, product coordinator
Address: 4550 Montgomery Avenue, Bethesda, MD 20814

Phone: (301) 951-4815 or (800) 368-2748
Fax: (301) 654-2960

What Company Does: Calvert Group is one of the Washington area's largest mutual fund companies. Assets under management have grown to over $4.8 billion.

Environmental Programs: Calvert and its distributor, Calvert Securities Corporation, offer one of the nations largest families of socially and environmentally responsible mutual funds. With over $1.4 billion dollars in eight socially screened funds, including bond, money market, global, balanced, and equity options, Calvert is able to offer individual and institutional investors a variety of ways to accomplish responsible investment goals. Calvert's fund managers embrace a "double bottom line" approach to investing, combining traditional in-depth financial analysis with a dynamic screening process aimed at identifying the most responsible corporations. The funds that apply environmental criteria seek out those companies that appear to be outstanding in their environmental practices and have created new or innovative products that help sustain or enhance the environment.

Company: Carrying Capacity Network
Industry: Nonprofit
Contact: Monique Miler, executive director
Address: 1325 G Street NW, Suite 1003, Washington, DC 20005-3104
Phone: (202) 879-3044 or (800) 466-4866
Fax: (202) 879-3019

What Company Does: A nonprofit, nonpartisan activist network that facilitates cooperation and information dissemination among organizations working on carrying-capacity issues such as environmental protection, population stabilization, growth control, and resource conservation. "Carrying capacity" refers to the number of individuals that can be supported without degrading the natural, cultural, and social environment, i.e., without reducing the ability of the environment to sustain the desired quality of life over the long term.

Company: Catalyst Group
Industry: Financing and consulting
Contact: Blake Ross
Address: 139 Main Street, Brattleboro, VT 05301
Phone: (802) 254-8144
Fax: (802) 254-8591

What Company Does: Provides investment banking services for energy-efficiency and demand-side management industries, including vendor and end-user equipment leasing programs and performance contract (energy service agreement) financing. Catalyst is also a utility consultant, offering financing, design, training, and implementation services to utilities promoting energy efficiency. The company also offers financing services to the recycling, waste management, and natural food industries.

Company: Celestial Seasonings
Industry: Consumer products
Contact: Cindy Frakes, public relations manager
Address: 4600 Sleepytime Drive, Boulder, CO 80301-3292
Phone: (303) 530-5300
Fax: (303) 581-1249

What Company Does: Founded in 1970, Celestial Seasonings offers forty all-natural tea blends. The company is the largest importer of raw herbal tea ingredients in the United States.

Environmental Programs: Celestial Seasonings made a commitment to environmental responsibility when the company was founded in 1970. It had a source-reduction packaging approach from the start; its herb teas are made without wasteful packaging such as individual foil envelopes, strings, tags, or staples, resulting in a savings of 2 million pounds of packaging every year. The tea bags it uses are 100 percent oxygen-bleached. International programs include interaction with developing countries to establish sustainable agricultural programs and eliminate dependency use of chemicals. The company's internal programs include a corporate recycling program for paper, aluminum, metal, cardboard, and burlap; composting; and a grassroots environmental committee of employees.

Company: Center for Community Self-Help
Industry: Nonprofit, community development
Contact: Mary Mountcastle, development associate
Address: 409 East Chapel Hill Street, P.O. Box 3619,
Durham, NC 27702-3619
Phone: (919) 683-3016
Fax: (919) 688-3615

What Company Does: A nonprofit community development organization founded in 1980 to foster economic opportunity for nontraditional borrowers and residents of low-income and rural areas in North Carolina. The center is the umbrella organization for its financing arms—a credit union and a revolving loan fund—which were created in 1984 to provide access to capital for business and affordable housing loans for community residents. The three affiliates compose a statewide community development bank whose major guiding principles are ownership, public-private partnerships, and diversity. The center designs new programs, analyzes and advocates policies that create economic opportunities for residents, and advises policy makers. It also publishes a quarterly newsletter.

Company: **Center for Energy and Environmental Studies, Princeton University**
Industry: Nonprofit, energy
Contact: Robert H. Socolow, director
Address: The Engineering Quadrangle, Princeton University, Princeton, NJ 08544
Phone: (609) 258-5445
Fax: (609) 258-3661

What Company Does: Founded in 1971, the center works to find how new technologies may solve today's environmental problems.

Company: **Center for Global Change**
Industry: Nonprofit
Contact: Alan Miller, executive coordinator
Address: University of Maryland at College Park, The Executive Building, Suite 401, 7100 Baltimore Avenue, College Park, MD 20740
Phone: (301) 403-4165
Fax: (301) 403-4292

What Company Does: An interdisciplinary research group that studies environmental quality issues and their relation to energy use and economic growth, the center investigates technologies and policies to reduce environmental degradation and disseminates its research to the policy, science, and business communities through publications, conferences, and other educational activities.

Company: **Center for Global Education**
Industry: Travel
Contact: Sara Nelson-Pallmeyer, associate director
Address: Augsburg College, 2211 Riverside Avenue, Minneapolis, MN 55454
Phone: (612) 330-1159
Fax: (612) 330-1695

What Company Does: Conducts seven to twenty-one-day educational travel seminars and undergraduate study-abroad semester programs to Mexico, Central America, South Africa, and the Middle East, bringing North Americans face-to-face with the poor and others struggling for justice and human dignity. Free listing of upcoming trips and programs. Internships in Namibia and Mexico. Long-term staff in United States, Mexico, Central America, and Namibia.

Company: **Center for Marine Conservation**
Industry: Nonprofit
Contact: Denise Thomas, office administrator
Address: 1725 DeSales Street NW, Washington, DC 20036
Phone: (202) 429-5609
Fax: (202) 872-0619

What Company Does: A nonprofit environmental group specializing in marine policy. Major program areas are fisheries management, habitat protection, pollution prevention, recovery of endangered species, and marine biological diversity.

Company: **Center for Our Common Future (CCF)**
Industry: Nonprofit, sustainable development
Address: Palais Wilson, 52 rue des Paquis, 1201 Geneva, Switzerland

What Company Does: CCF was formed by Our Common Future, the report of the World Commission on Environment and Development (WCED), as a means to monitor their follow-up activities. The primary objective of the center is to promote the WCED report. In the future, the center will begin to become an objective information clearinghouse. Inspired by the United Nations Conference on Environment and Development (UNCED), CCF will also concentrate on creating ways to include public participation in sustainable development. Publishes *The Brundtland Bulletin* and *Network 92.*

Company: **Center for Policy Alternatives**
Industry: Nonprofit
Contact: Linda Tarr-Whelan, president and executive director
Address: 1875 Connecticut Avenue NW, Suite 710, Washington, DC 20009
Phone: (202) 387-6030
Fax: (202) 986-2539

What Company Does: Founded in 1975, the center is a technical assistance provider, an advocacy group, and a think tank for state-level public officials that serves as a catalyst for change through the promotion of "ideas that work." Its network of state leaders includes over 1,500 legislators and public officials and a core group of elected state officials known as Policy Alternative Leaders.

Environmental Programs: The center presents creative policy solutions on a wide range of economic, social, and environmental policy issues through policy research, trend-setting models, publications, and conferences and seminars. In the area of sustainable development, the center focuses on the critical issues of agriculture, energy/atmospheric protection, environmental justice, solid waste, toxics, trade, and transportation.

Company: Center for Resource Management (CRM)
Industry: Nonprofit
Contact: Paul Parker, vice president
Address: 1104 East Ashton Avenue, Suite 210,
Salt Lake City, UT 84106
Phone: (801) 466-3600
Fax: (801) 466-6800

What Company Does: A national, nonprofit organization founded in 1981. CRM's mission is to promote sustainable development that balances vital human needs with environmental stewardship. We must move beyond blame to integrate environmental and economic decision-making. The CRM creates alliances and builds bridges between the environmental, corporate, and governmental communities to solve today's problems without damaging the earth's capacity to provide for the needs of future generations.

Company: Center for Rural Affairs
Industry: Nonprofit, agriculture
Contact: Don Ralston, administrative director
Address: Box 406, Walthill, NE 68067
Phone: (402) 846-5428
Fax: (402) 846-5420

What Company Does: Founded in 1973, the center works to establish sustainable rural communities nationwide that respect social and economic justice as well as our role as stewards for the natural environment.

Company: Center for Safety in the Arts
Industry: Nonprofit
Contact: Angela Babin, director of information

Address: 5 Beekman Street, Suite 1030, New York, NY 10038
Phone: (212) 227-6220
Fax: (212) 233-3846

What Company Does: A national organization dedicated to researching hazards in the visual and performing arts and educating artists, school art programs, and museums. Membership is $24 and includes a subscription to *Art Hazards News,* which is published five times a year. Internships available. Contact Tom Russack, executive director.

Company: Center for Science and the Environment (CSE)
Industry: Nonprofit
Address: 807 Vishal Bhawan, 95 Nehru Place, New Delhi, India 110019
Phone: 91-11-643-3394/8109

What Company Does: A public-interest research and information dissemination not-for-profit group that was founded in 1981 by concerned journalists, engineers, environmentalists, and scientists. Its primary goal is to heighten the public's appreciation of vital environmental and development issues. In addition, it strives to strengthen relations between environmental NGOs and the media. CSE provides detailed reports on the state of India's environment, briefing workshops for journalists, and seminars and workshops on sustainable development. Publishes *The Green File* and *Towards Green Villages* and provides the Documentation Unit, a collection of 18,000 books, 1,000 video cassettes, and 400 maps and posters on the environment, plus a clipping service.

Company: Chambers Development Company, Inc.
Industry: Environmental services
Contact: John G. Rangos, Sr., chairman and CEO
Address: 10700 Frankstown Road, Pittsburgh, PA 15235
Phone: (412) 242-6327

What Company Does: Chambers is the fourth largest public environmental services company in the United States, involved in waste disposal management, collection, and hauling and recycling. The company provides comprehensive disposal services to hundreds of communities.

Company: Champion
Industry: Paper products
Contact: Lawrence A. Fox, vice president and secretary

Address: One Champion Plaza, Stamford, CT 06921
Phone: (203) 358-7000
Fax: (203) 358-2974

What Company Does: Champion is one of the largest domestic producers of pulp and paper. It manufactures paper for business communications, commercial printing, publications, and newspapers. In addition, the company has significant plywood and lumber manufacturing operations and owns or controls approximately 5.1 million acres of timberlands in the United States. Champion's Canadian and Brazilian subsidiaries also own or control significant timber resources supporting their operations.

Environmental Programs: Champion has invested hundreds of millions of dollars in facilities to control pollution and dispose of solid waste. Among other things, the company has implemented and is continuing to implement oxygen delignification and chlorine dioxide substitution—the preferred technology under the proposed regulations pursuant to the federal Water Pollution Act—at its bleached kraft mills. The company conducts a substantial reforestation program, planting tens of millions of trees each year.

Company: Chelsea Green Publishing Company
Industry: Publishing
Contact: Ian Baldwin, Jr., president and publisher
Address: P.O. Box 428, 205 Gates-Briggs Building, White River Junction, VT 05001
Phone: (802) 295-6300
Fax: (802) 295-6444

What Company Does: Publishes and distributes books on subjects ranging from nature and gardening to Native American culture to politics to energy and the environment; also distributes other small publishers' books in the United States. Books are made on acid-free recycled papers. Semiannual catalog is available to customers. Internships are available.

Company: Chesapeake Bay Foundation
Industry: Nonprofit
Contact: Evelyn Strand, employment contact, or William C. Baker, president
Address: 162 Prince George Street, Annapolis, MD 21401
Phone: (410) 268-8816
Fax: (410) 268-6687

What Company Does: Founded in 1966, the Chesapeake Bay Foundation is dedicated to the call, Save the Bay. It is the largest nonprofit conservation organization working to save the Chesapeake Bay, and its mission takes it into Maryland, D.C., Virginia, and Pennsylvania. It works through educational programs, environmental defense, and land management—and has over 85,000 members.

Company: **Chevron Research and Technology**
Industry: Energy
Contact: R. L. Arscott
Address: 1003 West Cutting Boulevard, Richmond, VA 94804
Phone: (415) 894-7700
Fax: (415) 894-0855

What Company Does: Chevron is the largest producer of natural gas and combined oil and gas in the United States. It refines crude oil and produces petroleum products, and conducts business from wellhead to filling station.

Environmental Programs: Chevron's Toxicology and Health Risk Assessment Unit undertakes rigorous toxicological analyses to determine if a product has toxic effects. Chevron developed oronite gasoline additives, a leading-edge technology widely used to control automobile exhaust emissions and promote fuel economy by improving and maintaining engine cleanliness. It also developed ICEBGON, an effective salt substitute for de-icing roads that has no harmful side effects.

Company: **Children's Alliance for Protection of the Environment (CAPE)**
Industry: Nonprofit
Contact: Ingrid Kavanagh, founder, or Pat Scharr, executive director
Address: P.O. Box 307, Austin, TX 78767
Phone: (512) 476-2273
Fax: (512) 476-2301

What Company Does: Works to change environmental attitudes and behavior through responsible conservation, preservation, and restoration activities of young people around the world.

Environmental Programs: This action-oriented global conservation organization has active members in more than thirty-five countries. CAPE sponsors events around issues such as beaches, rain forests, and habitat preservation and works with national and international organizations such as the U.S. Fish and Wildlife Service, U.S. Environmental Protection Agency, the United Nations Environment Programme, and the Neotropica Foundation. CAPE members communicate through the quarterly newspaper *Many Hands* and a pen pal program. CAPE develops educational materials, such as its *Program Guide*, and holds teacher workshops.

Company: **Church & Dwight Co., Inc.**
Industry: Consumer products
Contact: Bryan Thomlison, director, Environmental Programs
Address: Arm & Hammer Division, 469 North Harrison Street, Princeton, NJ 08543-5297
Phone: (609) 497-7230
Fax: (609) 279-7301

What Company Does: Church & Dwight is a supplier of sodium bicarbonate, a natural chemical compound that is used in its core business, consisting of Arm & Hammer Baking Soda and Carpet and Room Deodorizer, Arm & Hammer Dental Care Toothpaste, and Arm & Hammer Laundry Detergent.

Environmental Programs: Church & Dwight has had a history of environmental commitments since 1880 with its commission of environmental paintings, reproduced and packaged with its baking soda until 1966, to the first major phosphate-free laundry detergent in 1970, to a commitment in 1990 and beyond to create alliances between manufacturers, educators, environmental groups, and other shareholders for environmental education.

Company: **Ciba-Geigy Corporation**
Industry: Pharmaceuticals
Contact: Joseph T. Sullivan, senior vice president
Address: 444 Saw Mill River Road, Ardsley, NY 10502-2699
Phone: (914) 479-5000
Fax: (919) 479-2224

What Company Does: Ciba-Geigy is the U.S. arm of the Swiss pharmaceutical and chemical company of the same name, representing approximately a third of Ciba-Geigy's worldwide business with nearly $4 billion in sales and 15,000 employees in the United States.

Environmental Programs: Ciba-Geigy Corporation has an environmental policy that includes reducing and recycling waste at the source. Each plant facility has a goal of 10 percent emission reduction each year, and an environmental audit team reports to the CEO.

Company: **Citizens for a Better Environment**
Industry: Nonprofit
Contact: Terri Hershman, development director
Address: 501 Second Street, Suite 305, San Francisco, CA 94107
Phone: (415) 243-8373
Fax: (415) 243-8980

What Company Does: A nonprofit, statewide, urban environmental organization, founded in 1978, that employs technical research, legal action, grassroots organizing, policy advocacy, and public education to further goals of pollution prevention. Internships available. Contact Danny Larson, campaign director.

Environmental Programs: The mission is "to transform a vision of a healthy, sustainable future into effective advocacy and citizen action." Carries out programs to reduce and prevent environmental health hazards and toxic pollution in California. Issues *Environmental Review,* a quarterly publication.

Company: City Bikes
Industry: Transportation
Contact: Phil Koopman or Charlie McCormack, owners
Address: 2501 Champlain Street NW, Washington, DC 20009
Phone: (202) 265-1564
Fax: (202) 462-7020

What Company Does: City Bikes specializes in bicycles as transportation: "Most of our local customers are commuters, messengers, and police." Also sells parking racks, utility bikes, and fleets to organizations working in developing countries. In addition to advocacy work, provides support for cycling awareness and safety programs for the children in the area. Internships available.

Environmental Programs: Supports local, regional, and national bicycle and other nonmotorized transportation advocacy groups and events, maintains a comprehensive recycling program, and encourages distributors to use environmentally friendly packaging.

Company: Clean Harbors, Inc.
Industry: Environmental services
Contact: Dan McCoy, vice president, Employee Relations
Address: 1200 Crown Colony Drive, Quincy, MA 02269-9137
Phone: (617) 849-1800

What Company Does: Provides comprehensive environmental services in twenty-five states in the Northeast, Midwest, and Mid-Atlantic regions. From forty locations, Clean Harbors furnishes a wide range of hazardous waste management and environmental support services to a diversified customer base. The company's hazardous waste management services include treatment, storage resource recovery, and transportation and disposal of hazardous materials. Environmental remediation services include emergency response, surface remediation, groundwater restoration, and facility decontamination.

Company: **Clean Sites, Inc.**
Industry: Nonprofit, environmental services
Contact: Edwin H. Clark II, president
Address: 1199 North Fairfax Street, Suite 400, Alexandria, VA 22314
Phone: (703) 683-8522 or (703) 739-1240
Fax: (703) 548-8773

What Company Does: A nonprofit organization established in 1984 by a coalition of businesses, environmental groups, and senior EPA officials to help find ways of accelerating the cleanup of hazardous wastes, it emphasizes the use of dispute resolution and facilitation techniques in addressing complex environmental problems; and offers technical services in project design and management, peer reviews, environmental audits, and technical mediation. Other major program areas include facilitating public participation and conducting public policy analyses. The staff of sixty includes engineers, scientists, mediators, financial managers, and public policy experts. The organization works closely with all levels of government, private companies, and community and environmental groups on specific projects.

Company: **Clean Water Action, Inc.**
Industry: Environmental services
Contact: David Zwick, president
Address: 1320 18th Street NW, Suite 300, Washington, DC 20036
Phone: (202) 457-1286
Fax: (202) 457-0287

What Company Does: Works to advance the protection of our natural resources through managing toxic chemicals, safe solid wastes, and protection of wetlands, coastal and surface waters, and groundwater.

Company: **Clorox**
Industry: Consumer products
Contact: Sandy Sullivan, manager, Marketing and Environmental Communications
Address: 1221 Broadway, Oakland, CA 94612
Phone: (510) 271-7732
Fax: (510) 271-2946

What Company Does: Clorox develops, manufactures, and markets household products and food products including Clorox bleach, Soft Scrub mild abrasive cleaner, Hidden Valley Ranch salad dressings, Pine-Sol Cleaner, Kingsford Charcoal, Formula 409 all-purpose cleaner, and K.C. Masterpiece barbecue sauce.

What Company Does: Clorox has aggressive programs in place to minimize the environmental impact of its packaging, including source-reduction programs and the increased use of recycled materials in packaging. This includes the use of recycled (postconsumer) resins in its Clorox liquid bleach gallon bottles, Pine Sol, Soft Scrub, and Soft Scrub with Bleach products. Clorox has environmental audit teams to help ensure plant environmental safety.

Company: **Cloud Nine, Inc.**
Industry: Consumer products
Contact: Joshua Taylor, president
Address: 300 Observer Highway, 3rd floor, Hoboken, NJ 07030
Phone: (201) 216-0382
Fax: (201) 216-0383

What Company Does: Offers a line of twelve chocolate bars with nontraditional flavors such as Oregon Red Raspberry, Sun-dried Cherries, and Espresso Bean Crunch, plus a new tropical source brand of dairy-free, refined, sugar-free bars in four unique flavors.

Environmental Programs: Bar wrappers are produced from recycled paper and printed with vegetable inks. Company donates 10 percent of its profits to promote rain forest conservation through the Rainforest Alliance. Also utilizes recycled materials for marketing and shipping/packaging in corrugated boxes. Resource- and energy-conserving techniques applied in manufacturing.

Company: **Coca-Cola Company**
Industry: Consumer products
Contact: Robert Rivers
Address: P.O. Drawer 1734, Atlanta, GA 30301
Phone: (404) 676-5775 or general (800) GET-COKE
Fax: (404) 676-6260

What Company Does: Coca-Cola is the world's largest soft drink marketer and is also a leading U.S. producer of citrus products.

Environmental Programs: The Coca-Cola Company has a worldwide environmental management system in place, with a variety of programs operating to achieve overall environmental goals and objectives. In addition, the company works with communities throughout the world on recycling and anti-litter programs.

Company: **Coddington Environmental, Inc.**
Industry: Marketing

Contact: Walter Coddington, chairman
Address: 885 Third Avenue, New York, NY 10022
Phone: (212) 230-2570
Fax: (212) 230-2569

What Company Does: Coddington Environmental provides companies, environmental organizations, and government agencies with environmental marketing consultation and project management services.

Company: Committee for the National Institute for the Environment (CNIE)
Industry: Nonprofit
Contact: Peter Saundry, executive director
Address: 730 11th Street NW, Third floor, Washington, DC 20001-4521
Phone: (202) 628-4303
Fax: (202) 628-4311

What Company Does: CNIE is a national organization consisting of over 7,000 scientists, educators, environmentalist businesses, and other citizens. Its central mission is to improve the scientific basis for making decisions on environmental issues by creating an independent, nonregulatory federal agency for science for the environment.

Environmental Programs: Paid and unpaid internships available year round in environmental issues, congressional relations, grassroots organizing, and media relations.

Company: Commonwealth Edison Company (ComEd)
Industry: Energy
Contact: John T. Costello, manager of public affairs
Address: One First National Plaza, 38 FNW, P.O. Box 767, Chicago, IL 60690-0767
Phone: (312) 394-3059
Fax: (312) 394-8693

What Company Does: Generates, transmits, and sells electricity to customers in Chicago and northeastern Illinois. ComEd provided more than ninety million megawatt-hours of electricity in 1994.

Environmental Programs: Commonwealth Edison has committed to reduce discharge of contaminants and the production of waste by-products beyond the compliance level and to recycle materials used in operations to the greatest extent possible. It is company policy to support research directed to the solution of industry-related environmental problems through active participation and contributions of financial and other resources. ComEd conducts air- and water-related audits of all its facilities, as well as waste-related audits of all its disposal facilities. In addition, ComEd has pilot programs in place to reduce consumer demand for electricity.

Company: Commonwealth Films, Inc.
Industry: Communications
Contact: Thomas P. McCann, president
Address: 223 Commonwealth Avenue, Boston, MA 02116
Phone: (617) 262-5634
Fax: (617) 262-6948

What Company Does: Commonwealth Films is the leading international producer of educational videos about business ethics, information/computer security, and legal compliance. Included in seven video library collections is the Environmental Compliance Video Library, which serves as a cornerstone for thousands of corporate compliance initiatives covering generator responsibilities and liabilities; federal, state, and local law violations; disposal; litigation; management responsibility; investigation and prosecution; recordkeeping; labeling; and more. The company has more than 20,000 customers internationally, and 496 of the Fortune 500 use Commonwealth Films.

Company: Community Environmental Council (CEC)
Industry: Nonprofit, community programs
Contact: Jon Clark, executive director
Address: Gildea Resource Center, 930 Miramonte Drive,
Santa Barbara, CA 93109
Phone: (805) 963-0583
Fax: (805) 962-9080

What Company Does: A nonprofit research and education organization, founded in 1969, that works to design systems of environmental management and implement them to solve environmental problems. It links government, universities, the private sector, environmentalists, and the local community to address issues of resource management and policy, waste management, land-use planning, and urban growth. The CEC also publishes policy papers, research reports, manuals, and a biannual newsletter, *The Gildea Review*. It maintains a research library, holds seminars and conferences, and offers memberships.

Company: Community Service, Inc.
Industry: Nonprofit, community development

Contact: Jane Morgan, director
Address: P.O. Box 243, Yellow Springs, OH 45387
Phone: (513) 767-1461

What Company Does: A fifty-year-old nonprofit organization helping people to improve their communities. Books, annual conferences, workshops, consultation. Encourages land trust to preserve land. Sells books on this and other community-related subjects.

Company: Compost Patch
Industry: Environmental organization
Contact: Charles Leiden, president
Address: 306 Coleridge Avenue, Altoona, PA 16602
Phone: (814) 946-9291

What Company Does: Offers ideas and networking on groups and individuals that are transforming the world. Offers a newsletter, networking, a lending library, and a book service. Simple living, applied ecology, the importance of place and waste. Write for sample newsletter.

Company: CONCERN
Industry: Nonprofit
Contact: Darragh Lewis, field coordinator
Address: 1794 Columbia Road NW, Washington, DC 20009
Phone: (202) 328-8160
Fax: (202) 387-3378

What Company Does: A nonprofit organization that provides environmental information to individuals, community groups, educational institutions, public officials, and others involved with the environment, public education, and policy development in order that safe solutions to problems that threaten the environment and public health may be pursued. Internships available.

Company: Conservation International
Industry: Nonprofit
Contact: Don Wynne, office manager, or Lindsey Lambert, marketing director
Address: 1015 18th Street NW, Suite 1000, Washington, DC 20036
Phone: (202) 429-5660 or (202) 887-5188

What Company Does: A nonprofit organization, Conservation International focuses mainly on tropical ecosystems. Working in twenty-two countries, the organization provides technical and financial support for ecosystem conservation through local capacity building.

Company: Consultative Group on International Agricultural Research (CGIAR)
Industry: Sustainable development
Address: CGIAR Secretariat, c/o World Bank, 1818 H Street NW, Washington, DC 20433
Phone: (202) 473-8951
Fax: (202) 473-8110

What Company Does: The CGIAR supports a network of eighteen international agricultural centers that conduct research aimed at producing new technologies for sustainable agricultural development.

Company: Context Institute
Industry: Nonprofit, education
Address: P.O. Box 11470, Bainbridge Island, WA 98110
Phone: (206) 842-0216
Fax: (206) 842-5208

What Company Does: Founded in 1979, Context Institute has explored how human society can become sustainable and has served as a catalyst for voluntary cultural change toward a more humane and sustainable future. Projects and activities are grouped in three program areas: the Journal Program works to reach the public through the quarterly publication *In Context*, which discusses what a humane sustainable culture is; the Toolbox Program offers resources for sustainable development through the EcoTeam Workbook, which translates global goals into individual actions; and the *Eco-Village Report* publishes the results of a survey of ecovillages and sustainable communities throughout the world.

Company: Co-op America
Industry: Nonprofit, educational
Contact: Internship coordinator
Address: 1850 M Street NW, Suite 700, Washington, DC 20036
Phone: (202) 872-5307

What Company Does: A nonprofit organization helping people use their purchasing and investing power to support their social and environmental values. It offers the National Green Pages®, a magazine, social investment information, and boycott information.

Company: **Coopers & Lybrand**
Industry: Consulting
Contact: William G. Russell, director of environmental service
Address: 1301 Avenue of the Americas, New York, NY 10019-6013
Phone: (212) 259-1688
Fax: (212) 259-1301

What Company Does: Coopers & Lybrand is one of the world's largest accounting, financial advisory, and consulting firms. It offers advisory services in accounting, taxation, financial management, and employment benefits.

Environmental Programs: C&L has an environmental consulting practice that focuses on five primary services: CERCLA cost-recovery claim analysis and auditing and economic analyses of alternative remediation methods and evaluation of waste responsibilities; due diligence services for property transactions and mergers and acquisitions; valuation of contaminated properties, including assessments of "stigma" and costs of cleanup, using cash flow projections and market surveys; financial management and cost-control services for remediation and other corporate environmental activities; environmental management systems services including evaluation of environmental audits and internal controls, management information systems, environmental cost accounting, and related services.

Company: **Corning Incorporated**
Industry: Manufacturing
Contact: Tony Gallo, director, Energy, Environmental and Facility Services
Address: Corporate Engineering Division, HP ME-1 025, Corning, NY 14831
Phone: (607) 974-6411
Fax: (607) 974-6119

What Company Does: Corning Incorporated is an international corporation focused in four business segments: Specialty Materials, Communications, Laboratory Services, and Consumer Products.

Environmental Programs: Corning has an environmental policy with five-year goals that include reducing environmental incidents to zero; reducing wastes taken to landfills by 25 percent; reducing lead wastes by 15 percent; complying with relevant provisions of the new Clean Air Act amendments; and monitoring processes and operations around the world. Corning has an environmental board made up of senior company officials, an *Environmental Procedures Handbook*, and an Environmental Control Department, which is the operational hub of Corning environmental efforts.

Company: Council on Economic Priorities (CEP)
Industry: Nonprofit
Contact: Sean Moulton, environmental researcher
Address: 30 Irving Place, New York, NY 10003
Phone: (212) 420-1133
Fax: (212) 420-0988

What Company Does: CEP evaluates and encourages corporate social responsibility and good environmental practices and conducts policy studies on national security. The council is a membership organization and publishes a monthly research report.

Environmental Programs: Publishes *Shopping for a Better World*, which rates companies in environmental and other categories. CEP has also established the Corporate Environmental Data Clearinghouse, which profiles the environmental performance of hundreds of companies.

Company: Cousteau Society, Inc.
Industry: Nonprofit
Address: 870 Greenbrier Circle, Suite 402, Chesapeake, VA 23320
Phone: (804) 523-9335
Fax: (804) 523-2747

What Company Does: The Cousteau Society is a nonprofit, membership-supported organization dedicated to the protection and improvement of the quality of life for present and future generations. Founded in 1973 by Captain Jacques-Yves Cousteau, the society now has 300,000 members worldwide. The society believes that only an informed and alerted public can make the decisions necessary to protect and manage the world's natural resources.

Company: CPC International, Inc.
Industry: Consumer products
Contact: Gale L. Giffin, director, Corporate Communications
Address: International Plaza, Englewood Cliffs, NJ 07632-9976
Phone: (201) 894-4000
Fax: (201) 894-2186

What Company Does: CPC International is one of the largest U.S. consumer products and food processing companies, with operations in fifty-eight countries worldwide. Its products include sauces, soups and bouillons, mayonnaise, corn oil, peanut butter, jams, jellies, margarine, cheese, syrups, and desserts. Its corn-refining business produces sweeteners, including glucose, dextrose, and high-fructose corn syrup.

Environmental Programs: CPC has made substantial progress in reducing the amount of packaging materials used, consistent with the need to provide adequate product protection. Recycled materials are used whenever possible, and recycling programs have been instituted at the company's manufacturing, research, and headquarters facilities. CPC provides financial support for research on recycling.

Company: **Cracker Barrel**
Industry: Consumer products
Contact: DeAnna Fry, environmental affairs coordinator
Address: P.O. Box 787, Hartmann Drive, Lebanon, TN 37088-0787
Phone: (615) 444-5533

What Company Does: Cracker Barrel is a restaurant and retail chain country store, with facilities located along major exits of key interstate highways in the Southeast and Midwest of the United States.

Environmental Programs: Cracker Barrel has instituted a recycling program that is currently saving 3,700 trees each month. Recycling of cans and plastic containers has benefited the company as well as the environment by saving over $90,000 per year in reduced trash-hauling costs. The company has reduced unnecessary packaging, including 235,000 pounds of cardboard and 40,000 pounds of plastic, by working with its vendors. Additional packaging reduction is planned.

Company: **Cultural Survival Enterprises**
Industry: Nonprofit
Contact: Christina Croston, marketing director
Address: 215 First Street, Cambridge, MA 02142
Phone: (617) 621-3818
Fax: (617) 621-3814

What Company Does: Cultural Survival Enterprises helps indigenous peoples and ethnic groups expand their income through the gathering, processing, and sale of sustainably harvested rain-forest products. Cultural Survival Enterprises is the marketing project of Cultural Survival, Inc.

Company: **Deere and Company**
Industry: Manufacturing

Contact: Ralph Grotelueschen, director, Safety, Environment, and Engineering Standards
Address: John Deere Road, Moline, IL 61265-8098
Phone: (309) 765-5151 or (309) 765-5772

What Company Does: John Deere is the largest manufacturer of farm equipment in the world, a leading producer of lawn- and grounds-care equipment for golf, commercial, and residential lawn applications, and of industrial equipment for the construction and forestry industries. The company's credit and insurance operations rank among the top twenty-five operations in their industries.

Environmental Programs: Deere was one of the first companies to both practice waste minimization and lead public and private initiatives to facilitate waste minimization. Hazardous waste for landfilling has been reduced 93 percent since 1980. Total toxic chemical releases have been reduced 63 percent since 1987. Total energy used per ton of product has been cut 52 percent since 1972.

Company: Defenders of Wildlife
Industry: Nonprofit
Contact: Conservation Department will provide information
Address: 1101 Fourteenth Street NW, Suite 1400, Washington, DC 20005
Phone: (202) 682-9400
Fax: (202) 682-1331

What Company Does: Defenders of Wildlife is a national nonprofit citizens' organization working to preserve and protect wildlife and its habitat. The organization is forty years old and has 80,000 members.

Company: Deja Shoe
Industry: Fashion
Contact: Julie Lewis, founder and vice president of research and product concepts
Address: 7320 SW Hunziker, #305, Tigard, OR 97223
Phone: (800) 331-DEJA
Fax: (503) 624-2620

What Company Does: Founded in 1990, Deja Shoe is a manufacturer of environmental footwear made from recycled materials. Deja's goal is to create attractive footwear, apparel, and accessories that help the environment. The company gives 5 percent of its pretax profits to the Species Survival Commission, part of the World Conservation Union, which promotes the conservation of biological diversity and ecosystems and supports sustainable natural resource use.

Company: **Deloitte & Touche**
Industry: Environmental consulting
Contact: Gary Brayton, national director, Environmental Management Services
Address: 50 Freemont Street, Suite 2800, San Francisco, CA 94105
Phone: (415) 247-4039
Fax: (415) 247-4717

What Company Does: Serves client needs in environmental management assessment, environmental risk management, Superfund support services, environmental litigation support, environmental information services, independent environmental program review, and environmental legislative and regulatory tracking services.

Company: **Desert Mountain Tea Co., Ltd.**
Industry: Consumer products
Contact: Ross Baumstone, general manager, or Marilyn Baumstone, operations manager
Address: P.O. Box 328, Whitethorn, CA 95589
Phone: (707) 986-7286

What Company Does: Producers of Wild Desert Tea, herbal blends, teapots, and accessories. Mail-order catalog on request. "We are wildcrafters and tread lightly." Shop and computers run on solar power. "Organic by Nature."

Company: **Design Management Institute**
Industry: Design
Contact: Earl Powell, director
Address: 107 South Street, Suite 501, Boston, MA 02111-2811
Phone: (617) 338-6380
Fax: (617) 338-6570

What Company Does: The Design Management Institute is a leading international organization dedicated to improving the management and utilization of design. Membership provides information on the latest advances in design management, the fundamentals of design excellence in all areas of an organization, and integrating design as an essential part of an organization's competitive advantage. Also offers an exchange of information with design managers from around the world including information on design for the environment.

Company: **Development Alternatives**
Industry: Nonprofit, sustainable development
Contact: Dr. Ashok Khosla, president
Address: B-32 Institutional Area, New Mehrauli Road, Hauz Khas, New Delhi, India 11016
Phone: 91-11-66-53-70
Fax: 91-11-686-6031

What Company Does: Founded in 1983, Development Alternatives works to develop technologies and programs that benefit the poor. The not-for-profit organization puts out state-of-the-environment reports, monitors and evaluates sustainable development programs, and organizes environmentally focused workshops. Publishes a bimonthly newsletter.

Company: **Digital Equipment Corp.**
Industry: Technology
Contact: Corporate Information Group—Environmental Issues
Address: 146 Main Street, Maynard, MA 01754
Phone: (508) 493-5111
Fax: (508) 493-8780

What Company Does: Digital is one of the largest U.S. information systems suppliers and workstation manufacturers and a leader in networking and integrating computers. The company has the largest private electronic mail network with over 85,000 employee users.

Environmental Programs: Digital has an environmental policy that includes conserving energy, recycling materials, product stewardship, ergonomics, environmental management and audit systems, workplace safety, and controlling and minimizing air emissions, wastewater discharges, and waste generation.

Company: **Domini Social Equity Fund**
Industry: Finance
Contact: Angela Braman
Address: 6 St. James Avenue, Boston, MA 02116
Phone: (617) 547-7479 or (800) 762-6814
Fax: (617) 354-5353

What Company Does: The Domini Social Equity Fund is a no-load mutual fund specifically created for investors interested in integrating social concerns into their investment decisions. The fund's investment advisor, Kinder, Lyndenberg, Domini & Co., seeks out companies with positive records in the following areas: safe and useful products, employee relations, corporate citizenship, and the environment. The fund does not include companies deriving more than 2 percent of gross revenues from the sale of military weapons, or any revenues from the manufacture of tobacco products, alcoholic beverages, gambling operations, or nuclear power plants.

Company: R. R. Donnelley & Sons Company
Industry: Printing
Contact: James M. Ratcliffe, vice president, Corporate Relations
Address: 77 West Wacker Drive, Chicago, IL 60601
Phone: (312) 326-8030 or general (312) 326-8000

What Company Does: R. R. Donnelley is the largest printer in the world, producing books, magazines, directories, computer documentation, financial documents, and catalogs. It has 34,000 employees and more than 150 installations worldwide.

Environmental Programs: The company has a recycling history of over fifty years. It is involved in air emission control and recovering and recycling byproducts, including acid mist and ink solvents. It recycles both paper and scrap metal. R. R. Donnelley has an environmental policy and a senior environmental officer.

Company: Dow Chemical Company
Industry: Chemicals
Contact: Jerry Martin, director of corporate and North American environmental affairs for operations
Address: 2030 Dow Center, Midland, MI 48674
Phone: (517) 636-8790 or general (517) 636-1000
Fax: (517) 636-1254

What Company Does: Dow manufactures and supplies more than 2,000 products including chemicals and performance products, plastics, hydrocarbons and energy, and consumer specialties, which include agricultural products, pharmaceuticals, and consumer products. The company operates 183 manufacturing sites in thirty-three countries and employs about 55,400 people around the world.

Environmental Programs: Dow's U.S. plants have reduced chemical emissions to the air by 90 percent in the last twenty years. Dow also has committed to reduce its total emissions to air, land, and water—reportable under SARA Title III—by 50 percent from 1988 to 1995. In 1986, the company began a formalized pollution prevention program called Waste Reduction Always Pays (WRAP), in which employees identify and implement voluntary projects to reduce waste from the manufacturing process. The WRAP program continues to be successful, with millions of pounds of waste no longer emitted, treated, incinerated, or landfilled.

Company: Ducks Unlimited, Inc.
Industry: Nonprofit, wetlands conservation
Contact: Glenn D. Childs, director of communications and education
Address: One Waterfowl Way, Memphis, TN 38120-2351
Phone: (901) 758-3825
Fax: (901) 758-3850

What Company Does: Ducks Unlimited (DU) is a nonprofit organization founded by sportspeople in 1937 to preserve North American waterfowl and wetland habitat. It publishes a bimonthly magazine, *Ducks Unlimited.*

Environmental Programs: Ducks Unlimited conducts habitat conservation projects throughout the United States, Canada, and Mexico. It works to protect, enhance, restore, support, and help manage wetlands. Its Matching Aid to Restore States Habitat (MARSH) program provides states with funds for specific wetlands projects, and its Private Lands program provides equipment and advice to private landowners who voluntarily enhance waterfowl wintering habitat on their property. DU also operates a research institute and a fund-raising foundation.

Company: E.I. du Pont de Nemours and Company
Industry: Chemicals
Contact: Darwin G. Wika, leader of environmental stewardship, or Dr. Paul V. Tebo, senior vice president, Safety, Health and Environment
Address: Safety, Health and Environmental Excellence Center, 2516 Nemours Building, DuPont Company, 1007 Market Street, Wilmington, DE 19898
Phone: (302) 773-0966 or (302) 774-4060
Fax: (302) 774-3140

What Company Does: DuPont is the largest chemical manufacturer in the United States and also includes energy subsidiaries. Its products range from synthetic fibers to petroleum products. DuPont sells industrial products, fibers, polymers, petroleum, coal, agricultural products, electronics, imaging systems, and pharmaceuticals.

Environmental Programs: DuPont grants the DuPont Environmental Excellence Award, which recognizes employees who have taken environmental initiatives. The company's annual operating environmental expenditures are now approaching $1 billion. DuPont is investing more than $1 billion to develop alternatives to CFCs, eliminating or reducing wastes from manufacturing processes, recycling by-products or wastes from its manufacturing processes, and upgrading storage and waste disposal techniques and facilities.

Company: **Earth Action**
Industry: Nonprofit
Contact: Gayle Ann Kelly, executive director
Address: 143 West 29th Street, Suite 902, New York, NY 10001
Phone: (212) 563-5991
Fax: (212) 563-5994

What Company Does: Works in five areas including an elderly division to feed elder-bound residents in the New York area, children's education programs, workshops on values and environmental education, hands-on environmental projects, and an indigenous division currently working on a film entitled *A Circle of Women*, which highlights original instructions from female elders on how to take care of the earth. Works on fund-raisers with an arts focus—music, painting, and film. Internships available.

Company: **Earth Island Institute**
Industry: Nonprofit
Contact: John A. Knox or David Phillips, executive directors
Address: 300 Broadway, Suite 28, San Francisco, CA 94133-3312
Phone: (415) 788-3666
Fax: (415) 788-7324

What Company Does: Earth Island Institute was founded in 1982 and has more than 32,000 members. The institute publishes *Earth Island Journal* and other publications and supports development of innovative projects, currently numbering more than thirty, ranging from Baikal Watch to the International Marine Mammal Project to Urban Habitat Program.

Environmental Programs: Earth Island Institute's International Marine Mammal Project works to make oceans safe for marine mammals worldwide. It strives to eliminate dolphin mortality caused by the international tuna fishing industry, to end the use of driftnets, and to stop purse-seine vessels from encircling dolphins in their nets. In addition, it aims to stop the resumption of commercial whaling worldwide and to promote sustainable fishing.

Company: Earthwatch
Industry: Nonprofit, education
Address: 680 Mount Auburn Street, P.O. Box 403GW, Watertown, MA 02272
Phone: (800) 776-0188 or (617) 926-8200
Fax: (617) 926-8532

What Company Does: Earthwatch, a nonprofit organization founded in 1972, recruits 4,000 people a year to work side by side with scientists on two-week field research projects around the United States and in sixty countries. Participants can choose from 160 studies in over twenty disciplines; projects include preserving endangered sea turtles in St. Croix, studying maternal health in Zimbabwe, excavating medieval Moscow, and analyzing how global warming has affected the Chesapeake Bay. Volunteers support research and cover food and lodging expenses with tax-deductible fees. Minimum age is sixteen; no special skill needed. Membership is $25/year, which includes a bimonthly magazine listing all projects. Limited fellowships and scholarships available. Internships available at Earthwatch headquarters; contact the personnel director.

Company: Eastman Kodak Company
Industry: Manufacturing
Contact: James E. Blamphin, manager, Environmental News
Address: 343 State Street, Rochester, NY 14650
Phone: (716) 724-5036

What Company Does: Eastman Kodak Company manufactures and markets products and services in imaging (photographic films, papers, and chemicals), information management (copier-duplicators), health care (x-ray films, pharmaceuticals), and home care (do-it-yourself).

Environmental Programs: Kodak's main environmental focus is on source reduction of wastes, including extensive recycling at all levels of production through to marketing.

Company: Eco Expo
Industry: Environmental
Contact: Marc Merson, president

Address: 14260 Ventura Boulevard, #201, Sherman Oaks, CA 94123
Phone: (818) 906-2700
Fax: (818) 906-0367

What Company Does: A consumer/trade show and Green Business Conference that presents the largest gathering of environmental products and programs in the United States.

Company: Ecology & Environment, Inc.
Industry: Environmental consulting
Contact: Jennifer McDonough, Human Resources
Address: Buffalo Corporate Center, 368 Pleasantview Drive, Lancaster, NY 14086
Phone: (716) 684-8060
Fax: (716) 684-0844

What Company Does: Founded in 1970, Ecology and Environment (E&E) pioneered the multidisciplinary approach to environmental consulting. The company serves a wide range of industrial, government, and commercial clients. Its experience includes work in energy and resources development, pipelines and terminals, chemical and metal manufacturing, transportation, industrial parks, ports and harbors, power plants, and community development. It covers all project environmental considerations such as air, water, and groundwater pollution control; noise abatement; preservation of terrestrial, aquatic, and marine life; conservation; economic impact; and occupational and public health.

Company: EcoNomics, Inc.
Industry: Consulting
Contact: William O'Toole, president
Address: 832 Camino Del Mar, Suite 2, P.O. Box 2209, Del Mar, CA 92014
Phone: (619) 481-1980
Fax: (619) 481-2433

What Company Does: Offers multimedia environmental communication services and an on-line databank on business and environmental issues. For public sector clients the company provides comprehensive recycling and solid-waste services; for the private sector it provides strategic planning and implementation services for recycling, source reduction, buy-recycled, manufacture for recyclability, and product life-cycle analysis.

Company: **EcoTimber International**
Industry: Sustainable forestry products
Contact: Jason Grant, cofounder and vice president, Sales & Marketing
Address: 350 Treat Avenue, San Francisco, CA 94110-1326
Phone: (415) 864-4900
Fax: (415) 864-1011

What Company Does: EcoTimber International sources, distributes, and markets quality hardwoods from tropical and domestic forestry operations that are leading examples of ecosystem stewardship and community responsibility. EcoTimber is dedicated to helping preserve the worlds forests by building market support for sustainable forest products and fairly compensating the producers, thereby increasing incentives for ecologically sound forestry worldwide. EcoTimber markets its hardwoods and hardwood products under the brand name ecotimber®. EcoTimber is currently seeking internship candidates who are interested in contributing to the development of a catalytic environmental enterprise.

Company: **Educational Communications, Inc.**
Industry: Nonprofit, communications and activism
Contact: Leslie Lewis, coordinator
Address: P.O. Box 351419, Los Angeles, CA 90035-9119
Phone: (310) 559-9160

What Company Does: Nonprofit volunteer information and activist organization that specializes in environmental media programs for nonprofit groups. Covers ecological issues through the Ecology Center of Southern California; "Environmental Directions," a thirty-minute weekly environmental interview-format radio show that airs internationally; "Environmental Viewpoints," a news and information radio show; *Econews*, the nations longest-running weekly television series, airing weekly on cable and PBS stations; *The Compendium*, a bimonthly newsletter with a calendar of events, issue summaries and updates, book reviews, etc. Internships available; contact Nancy Pearlman.

Company: **Elmwood Institute**
Industry: Nonprofit
Contact: Zenobis Barlow, executive director
Address: 2522 San Pablo Avenue, Berkeley, CA 94702
Phone: (510) 845-4595
Fax: (510) 845-1439

What Company Does: The Elmwood Institute is an international think tank founded in 1984 to facilitate ecological views and considerations in the solution of social, economic, environmental, and political problems.

Company: EM Enterprises
Industry: Consumer products
Contact: Monika Paulson, vice president
Address: 41964 Wilcox Road, Hat Creek, CA 96040
Phone: (916) 335-7097
Fax: (916) 335-7087

What Company Does: Mail-order distributor that offers cruelty-free (no animal testing and no animal ingredients), environmentally friendly products for a variety of companies. Products range from household detergents and cleaners to pet products and insect repellents to personal products. Catalog is printed on recycled paper. All manufacturers represented have to qualify under criteria dictating no animal testing of products or ingredients from suppliers and no animal ingredients. Also must be safe and biodegradable.

Company: Energy Simulation Specialists, Inc. (ESS)
Industry: Consulting
Contact: Norma J. Dulin, manager, Marketing and Communications
Address: 64 East Broadway Road, Suite 230, Tempe, AZ 85282
Phone: (602) 967-5278
Fax: (602) 921-0892

What Company Does: ESS is a twenty-five-person firm that provides technical consulting for energy-efficient building design and utility company conservation programs. Its technical staff is made up of mechanical engineers, architects, and computer specialists. Using highly specialized software, the firm develops computer models of existing or proposed buildings, then evaluates the impact of alternative heating and cooling systems, lighting designs, and other building options on the buildings overall energy consumption and operating costs.

Company: Engelhard Corporation
Industry: Chemicals
Contact: Mark Dresner, director, Corporate Communications
Address: 101 Wood Avenue, Iselin, NJ 08830-0770
Phone: (908) 205-5000

What Company Does: Engelhard is a world-leading provider of specialty chemicals, engineered materials, and precious metals management services.

Environmental Programs: A key strategy for Engelhard is to capitalize on opportunities created by worldwide concern for the environment by being a leading source of cost-effective technologies that enable compliance with existing, as well as new and more stringent, regulations. Engelhard is a pioneer in auto-catalyst technology and develops and manufactures catalysts for pollution abatement from a variety of mobile and stationary sources. The company is aggressively developing new catalysts to enable petroleum refiners to produce the environmental gasolines required by the U.S. Clean Air Act. Engelhard also has developed and commercialized unique, patented technology for removing lead from water.

Company: Environmental Action Inc.
Industry: Nonprofit
Contact: Sheryl Harrison, administrative coordinator
Address: 6030 Carroll Avenue, Suite 600, Takoma Park, MD 20912
Phone: (301) 891-1100 or (301) 891-2218

What Company Does: Environmental Action is a national member-based organization that works for strong state and federal environmental laws and supports grassroots action to achieve these goals. It has a strong year-round internship program with emphasis on research and writing skills. No stipend is available. Publishes *Environmental Action* magazine quarterly. Subscriptions are $30.

Company: Environmental Advantage
Industry: Consulting
Contact: Eric Ingersoll, founder
Address: 305 West 20th Street, Suite 3, New York, NY 10011
Phone: (212) 255-7876
Fax: (212) 255-1308

What Company Does: Environmental Advantage (EA) helps companies build profitable businesses through market-based solutions to environmental problems. The company carries out this work in the areas of capital markets and investment strategy, forestry, energy, agriculture, and integrated solutions. EA helps its clients develop an in-depth understanding of how environmental forces are dramatically transforming its clients' markets. EA works with its clients to anticipate and take advantage of these shifts by identifying which of the environmental problems facing their industries present the most profitable business opportunities. Clients include corporations, solution-oriented start-up companies, government agencies and institutions, and nongovernmental organizations.

Company: **Environmental Careers Organization (ECO)**
Industry: Nonprofit, education
Contact: Kevin Doyle, national director of program development
Address: 286 Congress Street, Third floor, Boston, MA 02210-1009
Phone: (617) 426-4375
Fax: (617) 423-0998

What Company Does: Annually offers 400 to 550 paid, professional-level positions of three to twenty-four months with dozens of private, public, and nonprofit environmental employers for college students and recent graduates. ECO is a private, national, nonprofit organization that has helped over 5,500 people launch environmental careers since 1972. Offers one of the nation's largest programs of paid environmental internships for people of color, called the Diversity Initiative. Also offers environmental career aids such as *The New Complete Guide to Environmental Careers* (Island Press, 1993) and the Annual National Environmental Careers Conference, now in its eleventh year.

Company: **Environmental Communication Associates, Inc.**
Industry: Consulting
Contact: Andrea J. Grant, president
Address: 1881 9th Street, Suite 200, Boulder, CO 80302
Phone: (303) 444-1428
Fax: (303) 444-9128

What Company Does: Environmental Communication Associates (ECA) is a multidisciplinary, environmental consulting firm. Its team of specialists in communications, policy analysis, management consulting, science, and training works with businesses in mapping and implementing strategies to meet environmental challenges and opportunities. ECA is known for its work in community outreach, risk communication, strategic environmental planning, and corporate training.

Company: **Environmental Economics**
Industry: Research, publishing

Contact: Michael Silverstein, president
Address: Environmental Economics, 6347 Wayne Avenue (A-2), Philadelphia, PA 19144
Phone: (215) 844-5839

What Company Does: Environmental Economics is a think tank devoted to researching the environmental transformations taking place in industry today. Publications include the *Environmental Industry Yearbook, The Environmental Factor,* and *Mother Gaia's Book of Business and Investing.* Environmental Economics also operates the Environmental Business Book Club.

Company: Environmental Law Institute (ELI)
Industry: Nonprofit
Address: 1616 P Street NW, Suite 200, Washington, DC 20036
Phone: (202) 328-5002

What Company Does: Through its information services, training courses and seminars, research programs, and policy recommendations, the institute activates a broad constituency of environmental professionals in government, industry, the private bar, public interest groups, and academia. Central to ELI's mission is convening this diverse constituency to work cooperatively in developing effective solutions to pressing environmental problems.

Environmental Programs: Inter-American Environmental Program; Wetlands Program; Environmental Program for Central and Eastern Europe; Center for Public Health and Law; Center for State, Local and Regional Environmental Programs. Publishes *Environmental Forum.*

Company: Environmental Media Association (EMA)
Industry: Nonprofit, entertainment
Contact: Chris Chandler, program coordinator
Address: 3679 Motor Avenue, #300, Los Angeles, CA 90034-5701
Phone: (310) 287-2815

What Company Does: EMA's goal is to mobilize the entertainment community in a global effort to enlighten people about environmental problems and inspire them to act on those problems now. President of EMA is Andy Goodman.

Environmental Programs: Organizes annual awards dinner/fund-raiser to honor environmentally themed work in film, television, radio, music, and print media; provides research support to film, TV, and music productions with environmental themes; publishes bimonthly newsletter serving the entertainment industry as a resource for environmental information; conducts briefings for members of the entertainment industry to expand awareness of environmental issues.

Company: **Environmental Speakers International**
Industry: Public relations
Contact: Jeanine Anderson, president
Address: 8015 Holland Court, Suite C, Arvada, CO 80005
Phone: (303) 287-2212

What Company Does: A full-service speakers bureau that specializes in environmental topics. Produces programs, keynote addresses, seminars, and workshops designed to meet client needs.

Company: **Environmental Working Group**
Industry: Nonprofit
Contact: Internship coordinator
Address: 1718 Connecticut Ave. NW, Suite 600, Washington, DC 20009
Phone: (202) 667-6982
Fax: (202) 232-2592

What Company Does: An environmental research and policy analysis organization. Two major areas are agriculture and environment, including pesticides, food and water, and reform of the U.S. department of agriculture environmental programs and the Farm Bill. Internships available.

Company: **Envirotron, Ltd.**
Industry: Consulting, waste management
Contact: James H. Fitzgerald, president
Address: 685 Fifth Ave., 10th floor, New York, NY 10022
Phone: (212) 481-8900
Fax: (212) 371-8504

What Company Does: Envirotron is a small consulting firm that provides a variety of waste management services to commercial businesses. It has a client base of nearly twenty-five hotels, a few major retail chains, and a few office buildings.

Company: EOS Institute
Industry: Nonprofit, education
Contact: Lynne Bayless, executive director
Address: 580 Broadway, Suite 200, Laguna Beach, CA 92651
Phone: (714) 497-1896
Fax: (714) 494-7861

What Company Does: The EOS Institute is an educational nonprofit organization that promotes the exploration and understanding of how sustainable human environments function. Works in close relationship with other organizations with like interests. Ongoing development of comprehensive library on sustainable communities programs.

Company: Esprit
Industry: Apparel manufacturing
Contact: Cassie Hughes-Ederer, Public Relations, or Lynda Grose, Environmental Affairs
Address: 900 Minnesota Street, San Francisco, CA 94107
Phone: (415) 648-6900
Fax: (415) 550-3960

What Company Does: Esprit is a designer and manufacturer of apparel, accessories, and other lifestyle-related products.

Environmental Programs: Part of Esprit's corporate culture is an environmental audit of its own operations and those of suppliers. Esprit Ecocollection, a line of socially and environmentally responsible clothing, continues to lead the industry in reducing toxic chemicals in all phases of garment manufacturing.

Company: Ethical Investments, Inc.
Industry: Financial services
Contact: John E. Schultz, president
Address: 430 First Avenue North, #204, Minneapolis, MN 55401
Phone: (612) 339-3939
Fax: (612) 339-1315

What Company Does: Socially responsible investment counseling, asset management, and consulting for businesses and individuals. Free brochure and list of socially responsible mutual funds available. Internships available.

Company: **Fiddler's Green Farm**
Industry: Consumer products
Contact: Laine Alexander and Allen Ginsberg, proprietors
Address: P.O. Box 254, Belfast, ME 04915
Phone: (207) 338-3872
Fax: (800) 729-7935 and recorded message w/option to leave order

What Company Does: Fiddler's Green Farm is an organic farm that grows vegetables and offers by mail whole-grain baking mixes and hot cereals made from certified organic grains. It also offers honey, syrups, jams, organic granola, beans, coffee, and tea.

Environmental Programs: Fiddler's Green Farm uses organic farming methods and distributes organic food. Organic coffee orders support small-scale organic farming in Peru and Nicaragua.

Company: **First Affirmative Financial Network, Inc.**
Industry: Financial services
Contact: George Gay, chief operating officer
Address: 1040 South 8th Street, #200, Colorado Springs, CO 80906
Phone: (719) 636-1045 or (800) 728-3473
Fax: (719) 636-1943

What Company Does: Nationwide investment firm specializing in socially responsible investments. Co-op America's partner in providing financial services to its members. No structured internships in place, but contact for information.

Company: **Fish and Wildlife Service**
Industry: Biodiversity
Contact: Public Affairs
Address: U.S. Department of the Interior, 1849 C Street NW, Washington, DC 20240
Phone: (202) 208-5634
Fax: (202) 208-5850

What Company Does: Fish and Wildlife Service is a federal agency whose duties include managing the endangered species list and conserving and protecting America's fish and wildlife and their habitats.

Company: **Ford Motor Company**
Industry: Manufacturing

Contact: H. C. Grimm, supervisor, Recruitment and Placement
Address: The American Road, Dearborn, MI 48121
Phone: (313) 390-4627
Fax: (313) 390-6848

What Company Does: Ford manufactures, assembles, and sells cars, trucks, and related parts under the Ford, Mercury, and Lincoln labels.

Environmental Programs: Reducing emissions from facilities. Controlling air and water pollution and managing wastes from manufacturing facilities. Programs are directed not only at meeting legal requirements but also at pollution prevention and waste minimization.

Company: Found Stuff PaperWorks
Industry: Consumer products
Contact: Melissa Smedley, cofounder
Address: 744 G Street, Suite 201, San Diego, CA 92101
Phone: (619) 338-9432

What Company Does: Found Stuff PaperWorks is a micro paper mill creating handmade paper in the early American tradition—recycled. Papers are made from recycled junk mail; cotton, hemp, and linen fabric scraps; burlap coffee bags; and agricultural crops such as kenaf and garlic. In addition to stationery and postcards, papers are available in sheet form. The company also produces business cards and performs a wide range of custom work. Letterpress and offset printing are available on all papers with soy inks.

Company: Franklin Research and Development Corporation
Industry: Investments
Contact: Chitra Staley, senior vice president
Address: 711 Atlantic Avenue, Boston, MA 02111
Phone: (617) 423-6655

What Company Does: Franklin specializes in portfolio management and publishes a socially responsible investment newsletter, *Insight.* It monitors community-oriented investments, audits social performance of portfolios, and tracks socially responsible corporations, especially with regard to the environment.

Company: Fred Meyer, Inc.
Industry: Retail
Contact: Barry Naone, environmental affairs manager

Address: P.O. Box 42121, 3800 S.E. 2nd Avenue, Portland, OR 97242
Phone: (503) 232-8844 or (503) 797-5617(P.R.)

What Company Does: Fred Meyer, Inc., is a $2.98 billion retailer in the West, with a unique retail concept that features large, one-stop-shopping stores offering more than 225,000 food and nonfood products grouped into dozens of specialized merchandise sections.

Environmental Programs: Fred Meyer has been recycling since the 1960s. It was the first retailer to join EPA's Green Light program to promote energy efficiency. It has had a private pesticide-residue testing program for fruits and vegetables since 1988. And it was one of the first retailers to participate in the Green Cross product certification program.

Company: Future Fisherman Foundation
Industry: Nonprofit
Contact: Sharon Rushton, executive director
Address: 1033 North Fairfax Street, Suite 200, Alexandria, VA 22314
Phone: (703) 519-9691
Fax: (703) 519-1872

What Company Does: Promotes participation in and education about fishing as well as enhancement of aquatic resources. Includes the Hooked on Fishing—Not on Drugs program, which combines drug prevention, environmental education, and sportfishing into one powerful package. Program used by schools, churches, police departments, and youth organizations. Offers student and instructor manuals in sportfishing and aquatic resources.

Company: Garden Club of America
Industry: Nonprofit, agriculture
Address: 598 Madison Avenue, New York, NY 10022
Phone: (212) 753-8287
Fax: (212) 753-0134

What Company Does: The purpose of the Garden Club of America is to stimulate the knowledge and love of gardening; to share the advantages of association by means of educational meetings, conferences, correspondence, and publications; and to restore, improve, and protect the quality of the environment through educational programs and action in the fields of conservation and civic improvement.

Company: Gardener's Supply Co.
Industry: Gardening

Address: 128 Intervale Road, Burlington, VT 05401
Phone: (802) 660-3500
Fax: (802) 660-3501

What Company Does: An employee-owned company carrying organic fertilizers and pest controls, composting supplies, water-saving irrigation equipment, and lots more. Free catalog.

Company: Gauntlett Group, Inc.
Industry: Consulting
Contact: Suwanna B. Gauntlett, president
Address: 5900 Hollis Street, Suite G, Emeryville, CA 94608
Phone: (510) 658-9013
Fax: (510) 658-3834

What Company Does: The Gauntlett Group, based in San Francisco, provides strategic environmental management services to industry and government worldwide. It specializes in corporate program development and implementation, focusing on improved and environmental performance and bottom-line profits.

Company: GE Plastics
Industry: Manufacturing
Contact: Dan Adamus, manager, Press Relations
Address: 1 Plastics Avenue, Pittsfield, MA 01201
Phone: (413) 448-7487

What Company Does: GE Plastics is the world's leading supplier of engineering thermoplastic resins.

Environmental Programs: GE Plastics has initiated a cooperative venture with Digital Equipment, Nailite, and McDonald's to establish the feasibility of plastics recycling. Panels made from a recycled grade of NORYL® resin from GE Plastics were manufactured by Nailite Corporation with reclaimed computer housings collected by Digital Equipment for reuse in roof panels for McDonald's restaurants.

Company: General Mills
Industry: Consumer products
Contact: Robert L. Esse, director and senior principal engineer, Packaging
Address: 9000 Plymouth Avenue North, Minneapolis, MN 55427

Phone: (612) 540-2910
Fax: (612) 540-4959

What Company Does: General Mills produces breakfast cereals, dessert mixes, flour and dry mixes, yogurt, frozen seafood, fruit snacks, microwave popcorn, and ready-to-make dinners. It also owns Red Lobster and the Olive Garden restaurants, making the company the fifth largest food service company in the United States.

Environmental Programs: General Mills source-reduced packaging by 4.8 million pounds and utilizes 52 percent postconsumer material in packaging. The company also supports four carton-recycling initiatives in an effort to determine the possibility of recycling packaging made out of the clay-coated board used for dry-shelf food products.

Company: General Motors Corporation
Industry: Manufacturing
Contact: Dennis Minano, vice president, Environmental Activities Staff
Address: 30400 Mound Road, Box 901E, Warren, MI 48290-4015
Phone: (313) 556-5000
Fax: (313) 947-0063

What Company Does: GM produces cars and trucks worldwide under a variety of nameplates including Buick, Cadillac, Chevrolet, GMC Truck, Oldsmobile, Pontiac, and Saturn. It is also a specialist in information systems, telecommunications, and defense electronics through its subsidiaries.

Environmental Programs: GM has improved the fuel efficiency of its products 128 percent since the mid-1970s. It offers the most fuel-efficient production vehicle sold in America, the Geo Metro XFi. The company has produced fifty Impacts, its electric-powered vehicle, and will invite customers to drive them as part of a nationwide PreView drive. GM has had a broad corporate policy on environmental matters for more than three decades; this policy reaches further than compliance with the law and provides guidance to employees worldwide. GM also endorsed the Ceres Principles this year.

Company: Gillette Company
Industry: Consumer products
Contact: Joan Gallagher Fitzgerald, director of corporate public relations
Address: Prudential Tower Building, Boston, MA 02199-3799
Phone: (617) 421-7000
Fax: (617) 421-7123

What Company Does: The Gillette Company is an international company that develops, manufactures, and sells a wide range of personal-care and -use products such as razors and blades, toiletries, cosmetics, stationery products, electric shavers, small household appliances, and oral care products.

Environmental Programs: Since 1973, Gillette has achieved worldwide reductions in energy consumption of over 35 percent and water-use reductions in a range of 30 to 96 percent. Since 1986, hazardous waste generated by Gillette's U.S. units has been reduced by 3 percent; and since 1987, emissions to the environment have been reduced by more than 91.2 percent in the United States.

Company: Global Environment Fund, L.P., and GEF Management Corporation
Industry: Investments
Contact: Sumner Pingree, vice president
Address: 1201 New York Avenue NW, Suite 220, Washington, DC 20005
Phone: (202) 789-4500
Fax: (202) 789-4508

What Company Does: GEF Management Corporation is an investment advisor that specializes in investments that promote environmental improvement in growth-oriented businesses created by the growing demand for pollution control, waste minimization, resource recovery, and efficient use of energy. Formed in 1989, the company has grown to be one of the leading firms in the global environmental arena, with more than $130 million in assets under management at the end of January 1994. Limited partnership investments range from liquid stocks to private placements and venture capital. GEF's newest investment fund, Global Environment Emerging Markets Fund, closed January 14, 1994, with $70 million in committed capital. It will emphasize clean energy and clean water as investment themes for the rapidly growing developing countries.

Company: Global Environmental Management Initiative (GEMI)
Industry: Nonprofit
Contact: Andrew Mastrandonas, executive director
Address: 2000 L Street NW, Suite 710, Washington, DC 20036
Phone: (202) 296-7449
Fax: (202) 296-7442

What Company Does: GEMI is a nonprofit organization formed in April 1990 by the private sector to support environmental excellence on the part of business. Twenty-seven member corporations donate staff, money, and other resources to GEMI projects.

Environmental Programs: GEMI encourages corporations to share processes and approaches to sound environmental management, including health and safety issues.

Company: **Global Tomorrow Coalition**
Industry: Nonprofit
Contact: Alison Hayes, communications assistant
Address: 1325 G Street NW, Suite 1010, Washington, DC 20005-3104
Phone: (202) 628-4016
Fax: (202) 628-4018

What Company Does: A nonprofit coalition of organizations engaged in programs to preserve resources and maintain sustainable development. It has over one hundred U.S. organizations as members. The coalition disseminates materials from members to the public, sponsors conferences and forums, acts as an information resource and clearinghouse, and engages in global education on issues and policy.

Company: **W. R. Grace & Co.**
Industry: Chemicals
Contact: Dr. Alden Pierce, corporate director, Environment, Health and Safety
Address: One Town Center Road, Boca Raton, FL 33486-1010
Phone: (407) 362-1511
Fax: (407) 362-1865

What Company Does: Grace is the world's largest specialty chemicals company and holds a leadership position in specialized health care. It employs more than 40,000 employees in forty-eight states and fifty countries.

Environmental Programs: Grace's environmental, health, and safety functions are consolidated under the leadership of the corporate director of EHS. An EHS steering committee functions as the policy-making body and acts in an advisory capacity to the corporate director. Comprised of the senior most EHS managers from all core products lines and world regions and the chief EHS counsel, it is chaired by the corporate director. Grace is a voluntary signatory to two major EPA initiatives: Green Lights and the 33/50 program.

Company: **Grand Canyon Trust**
Industry: Nonprofit, conservation
Address: Route 4, Box 718, Flagstaff, AZ 86001
Phone: (602) 774-7488
Fax: (602) 774-7570

What Company Does: A nonprofit conservation organization, founded in 1986, which works for the preservation of the natural and cultural resources of the Colorado Plateau. The trust works to foster a long-range vision for conservation of the region and studies issues and policies and practices preservation and balance management. The trust monitors agencies overseeing protection and use of the region's public lands and resources. It promotes dialogue between the area's land owners, land users, and community and state leaders, and it advocates legislative and legal change. The trust publishes a quarterly journal, the *Colorado Plateau Advocate.*

Company: Greater Yellowstone Coalition
Industry: Nonprofit, conservation
Contact: Clare Duysters, program assistant and intern coordinator
Address: 13 South Willson, P.O. Box 1874, Bozeman, MT 59771
Phone: (406) 586-1593
Fax: (406) 586-0851

What Company Does: The Greater Yellowstone Coalition (GYC) is a nonprofit organization founded in 1983 to preserve and protect the Greater Yellowstone ecosystem and the quality of life it sustains. GYC advocates consideration of the long-term integrity of the entire ecosystem in management and protection of wilderness and wildlife. Its work includes research, regional and resource planning, public education, policy analysis, and legislative action. GYC has published an environmental profile of the Greater Yellowstone ecosystem and plans to issue a blueprint for the overall protection of the area. GYC conducts field trips, conferences, and workshops and publishes a quarterly journal, *Greater Yellowstone Report.* Internships available.

Company: Green Century Capital Management, Inc.
Industry: Finance
Contact: Mindy S. Lubber, president
Address: 29 Temple Place, Suite 200, Boston, MA 02111
Phone: (617) 482-0800
Fax: (617) 422-0881

What Company Does: The Green Century Funds are a family of no-load, environmentally responsible mutual funds that arose as a response to many individuals and organizations who were concerned about the environment and the potential impact of their investments on the world. The Green Century Funds provide individual investors and institutions with the opportunity to make financially responsible and environmentally conscious investments and puts 100 percent of the investment advisors' own net profits into supporting environmental advocacy. Internships available.

Company: **Greens**
Industry: Nonprofit, education and political action
Contact: Amy J. Belanger, coordinator, Greens Clearinghouse
Address: P.O. Box 30208, Kansas City, MO 64112-7336
Phone: (800) 257-7336
Fax: (816) 931-0014

What Company Does: A grassroots action and political group formed to work on a global vision that is supported by political candidates and by local community-based activism. Based on ten key values of ecological wisdom: social justice, grassroots democracy, nonviolence, decentralization, community-based economics, feminism, respect for diversity, personal and global responsibility, and future focus. Membership is $10 for students, $25 regular. Has a clearinghouse for green literature and merchandise; organizes conferences as well. Internships available.

Company: **Greenworking**
Industry: Nonprofit, environmental networking
Contact: Michelle Conant, program director
Address: 19 Marble Avenue, Pleasantville, NY 10570
Phone: (914) 741-2088
Fax: (914) 741-2336

What Company Does: Greenworking is a nonprofit environmental networking organization that focuses on fostering collaboration and facilitating information sharing by providing a link between environmentally concerned organizations and individuals. Greenworking maintains current information on environmental groups in New York State, publishes regional and statewide directories, and produces a bimonthly newsletter called *The Green Drummer*. The main objective of the newsletter is to provide a forum within which environmental organizations can communicate. *The Green Drummer* includes a calendar of events, an activist of the month, and featured topics. Related organizations and interested individuals are encouraged to submit ideas, announcements, letters, and articles.

Company: **Griesinger Films**
Industry: Film and video
Contact: Peter R. Griesinger, producer and director
Address: 7300 Old Mill Road, Gates Mills, OH 44040-9637
Phone: (216) 423-1601

What Company Does: Produces and distributes films and videos on sustainable development, featuring organic agriculture, ecological economics, and global structures. Videotapes include *Changing US Farm Policy, An Introduction to Ecological Economics, Investing in Natural Capital* and *Conversation for a Sustainable Society.*

Company: Growing Connections
Industry: Nonprofit, education
Contact: Irene K. Sassoon, director of public education
Address: 2123 East Grant Road, Tucson, AZ 85719
Phone: (602) 325-7909
Fax: (602) 325-7961

What Company Does: Educates children through gardening-based instruction. Nutrition and environmental education for lower-income, minority schoolchildren and their families, emphasizing intake of fresh vegetables and reduced intake of dietary fat, sugar, and salt; promotes awareness and practice approaches, with special emphasis given to gardening and to appreciating unity and diversity in partnership with and toward empowerment of children, families, schools, and communities. Environmental focus was added in 1990. Internships may be available.

Company: GSD&M
Industry: Advertising
Contact: Glenda Goehrs, vice president, Environmental Affairs
Address: 1 Cielo Center, 1250 Capital of Texas Highway, 4th Floor, Austin, TX 78746
Phone: (512) 327-8810

What Company Does: GSD&M is the third largest advertising agency in the Southwest, with 1993 billings of $210 million. Current clients include: Coors Brewing Company, Southwest Airlines, RC Cola, Fannie Mae, Chilis Restaurants, Pearle Vision, Texas Lottery, Texas Tourism, and Wal-Mart.

Environmental Programs: GSD&M publishes *The Green Reader,* a monthly environmental newsletter distributed free to companies and organizations all over the country. The firm recycles newsprint, office and computer paper, plastic and aluminum cans and glass, and video cassettes. It purchases recycled office supplies and has a silver recovery system for its darkroom to filter toxic chemicals before they go into groundwater. GSD&M helps clients develop responsible environmental marketing strategies that work in the marketplace.

Company: **Hazardous Materials Control Research Institute (HMCRI)**
Industry: Education and research
Contact: Christine Holmes, membership coordinator
Address: 1 Church Street, Suite 200, Rockville, MD 20850
Phone: (301) 251-1900
Fax: (301) 738-2330

What Company Does: HMCRI is concerned with all facets of prevention, control, and remediation of hazardous materials to, in, and from commerce and the environment. It promotes dialogue with professionals in the field via conferences and publications.

Company: **Hewlett Packard**
Industry: Technology
Contact: Employment Management System
Address: 3000 Hanover Street, Palo Alto, CA 94304
Phone: (415) 857-1501

What Company Does: Hewlett Packard is an international manufacturer of measurement and computation products and systems recognized for excellence in quality and support. The company's products and services are used in industry, business, engineering, science, medicine, and education in approximately 110 countries. HP has 93,000 employees and generated revenues of $20.3 billion in its 1993 fiscal year.

Environmental Programs: HP surpassed both goals of the U.S. EPA's 33/50 program; In 1991, HP's 33/50 releases were cut by 88 percent. These releases were further reduced in 1992, for a cumulative reduction of 91 percent since 1988. HP recycles customers' used cartridges from printers and has introduced a remanufactured toner cartridge for LaserJet printers. HP has introduced approximately twenty models of enery-efficient personal-computer products. It has begun marking plastic parts with codes describing the type of plastic used, which makes the parts easier to recycle.

Company: **Hoechst Celanese Corporation**
Industry: Chemicals
Contact: Susan Engelman, vice president, Environmental, Health, and Safety Affairs
Address: Route 202–206, P.O. Box 2500, Somerville, NJ 08876-1258
Phone: (908) 231-4479 or general (908) 231-2000
Fax: (908) 231-2896

What Company Does: Hoechst is one of three German firms leading the world in chemical sales. Its diversified product lines include basic and agricultural chemicals, dyes, fibers, plastics, and pharmaceuticals (in which it is sixth in the world). The firm operates in 140 countries with 169,295 employees. It bought Celanese in 1987. Its 1990 sales were $5.9 billion.

Environmental Programs: Hoechst has a comprehensive environmental policy, including standards for contractors, risk management, and risk assessment.

Company: **IMCO Recycling, Inc.**
Industry: Environmental services
Contact: Ralph L. Cheek, chairman and chief executive officer
Address: 5215 North O'Connor Boulevard, Suite 940, Williams Square Central Tower, Irving, TX 75039
Phone: (214) 869-6575

What Company Does: IMCO is one of the largest recyclers of aluminum and other scrap metals. It processes aluminum for Alcoa, Reynolds Metals, Kaiser, ALCAN, and others at six different plants in the United States.

Company: **INFORM**
Industry: Nonprofit, research and education
Contact: Jerri McDermott, associate director of communications
Address: 120 Wall Street, 16th floor, New York, NY 10005
Phone: (212) 689-4040
Fax: (212) 447-0689

What Company Does: INFORM, founded in 1974, is a national nonprofit environmental research and education organization that examines business practices contributing to environmental deterioration, assesses changes business and government are making to prevent or reduce this damage, and identifies practical ways to protect natural resources and public health. Research reports and outreach focus on solid- and hazardous-waste management and alternative vehicle fuels, with an emphasis on prevention rather than treatment or disposal. Publishes *Tackling Toxics in Everyday Products: A Directory of Organizations*, a directory of more than 250 public, private, and nonprofit organizations in the United States and abroad working to study, solve, and prevent problems related to toxic chemicals in consumer products (health effects, regulations, and labeling).

Company: **Institute for African Alternatives (IFAA)**
Industry: Nonprofit, sustainable development
Contact: Dr. Mohamed Suliman, director
Address: 23 Bevenden Street, London N1 6BH, England
Phone: 071-251-1503
Fax: 071-253-0801

What Company Does: IFAA works to advance research on environmental concerns, create alternative policies that will help reverse Africa's environmental decline, and coordinate the work of African and international NGOs and other organizations working on sustainable development issues. Publishes *IFAA Catalogue*, *IFAA Eco News*, and *IFAA Newsletter.*

Environmental Programs: IFAA's research and awareness program focuses on ecological degradation, development, and armed conflict in Africa. Five reports have been published on the state of war and peace in Africa.

Company: **Institute for Biodynamic Shelter**
Industry: Nonprofit, design
Contact: Eric Thompson
Address: 86 Washington Road, Waldoboro, ME 04572
Phone: (207) 832-5157
Fax: (207) 832-7314

What Company Does: The shelter's mission is to influence the structures that influence behavior; to remove the boundary between the indoor and outdoor environments to help forge a vital reunion between earth and spirit; and to design, build, and demonstrate biodynamic shelters and conduct ongoing research in supportive technologies.

Company: **Institute for Community Economics**
Industry: Nonprofit
Contact: Mike Kusek, development officer
Address: 57 School Street, Springfield, MA 01105-1331
Phone: (413) 746-8660
Fax: (413) 746-8862

What Company Does: Publishes newsletter called *Community Economics* three times a year. Also has resources available on community land trusts, community loan funds, and related institutions. Operates a revolving loan fund.

Company: **Institute for the Development of Earth Awareness (IDEA)**
Industry: Environmental organizations

Address: P.O. Box 124, Prince Street Station,
New York, NY 10012-0003
Phone: (212) 741-0338
Fax: (212) 807-8384

What Company Does: A nonprofit 501(c)(3) organization that addresses the causes—rather than the symptoms—of the problems currently facing the earth and its inhabitants. IDEA's mission is to help our society reestablish a harmonious relationship with the natural world. To accomplish this, it endeavors to help people understand the cultural, behavioral, and spiritual roots of our relationship with nature. It provides in-depth information about the earth's ecology and how to live and work with the earth instead of in opposition to it.

Company: Institute of Gas Technology (IGT)
Industry: Nonprofit
Contact: Martin Wise, manager, Human Resources
Address: 3424 South State Street, Chicago, IL 60616
Phone: (312) 949-3874 or general (312) 949-3650

What Company Does: Founded in 1941, the institute's primary functions are to perform sponsored R&D, provide educational programs and services, and disseminate scientific and technical information. IGT's environment-related R&D programs include the application of biotechnology to environmental protection and remediation, hazardous waste cleanup, the desulfurization of fossil fuels, the development of low-emission high-efficiency burners and waste combustion systems, the conversion of solid feedstocks, renewables, and waste into environmentally benign gaseous and liquid fuels, waste minimization, and the development of fuel cells.

Company: Institute for Global Communications
Industry: Computer networks
Contact: Michael Stein, EcoNet program officer
Address: 18 De Boom Street, San Francisco, CA 94107
Phone: (415) 442-0220
Fax: (415) 546-1794

What Company Does: Links peace, environmental, and social activists in ninety-two countries through nonprofit PeaceNet, EcoNet, ConflictNet, and LaborNet computer networks. The networks provide a low-cost way to access hard-to-get information with a credit card and a modem. Call (415) 322-0162 and log in as "new." Internships available; contact Jilliane Smith.

Company: **Institute for Global Ethics**
Industry: Nonprofit, research and education
Address: P.O. Box 563, 21 Elm Street, Camden, ME 04843
Phone: (800) 729-2615
Fax: (207) 236-4014

What Company Does: The Institute for Global Ethics was established to encourage and facilitate a new sort of ethical thinking. It publishes *Insights on Global Ethics,* which discusses ethical issues analyzed through a global lens. Also available to members is *Update,* a newsletter covering institute activities. In addition, books and tapes are available at a special members' discounted rate.

Company: **Institute for Local Self-Reliance (ILSR)**
Industry: Nonprofit, sustainable development
Address: 2425 Eighteenth Street NW, Washington, DC 20009-2096
Phone: (202) 232-4108
Fax: (202) 332-0463

What Company Does: ILSR works with nonprofit organizations, businesses, and government toward self-reliance through pollution prevention, efficiency, citizen participation, recycling, renewable resources, and materials and waste management. It offers technical assistance, organizes conferences, conducts research, analyzes public policy issues, and disseminates information through technical reports and other publications. ILSR also serves as a link between diverse constituencies in national and regional networks.

Company: **Institute for Social Ecology (ISE)**
Industry: Education
Contact: Claudia B. Maas, associate director
Address: P.O. Box 89, Plainfield, VT 05667
Phone: (802) 454-8493
Fax: (802) 454-8017 (shared with Goddard College; must be marked ISE)

What Company Does: Offers summer courses, including: Design for Sustainable Communities; Ecology and Community; Social Ecology and Higher Education; and Women and Ecology. College credit available. Course descriptions free. Internships available.

Company: **Interfaith Center on Corporate Social Responsibility**
Industry: Finance

Contact: Diane Bratcher, director of communications
Address: 475 Riverside Drive, Room 566, New York, NY 10115
Phone: (212) 870-2936

What Company Does: ICCR is made up of a coalition of 250 Protestant, Jewish, and Roman Catholic institutional investors including denominations, religious communities, agencies, pension funds, dioceses, and health care corporations. These members use investments and other resources to promote economic justice and development in low-income and minority communities. ICCR publishes *The Corporate Examiner,* which analyzes corporate responsibility issues and trends. Ten-issue annual subscription: $35. ICCR also coordinates shareholder resolution and other challenges to corporations on issues such as the environment, equal employment opportunity, and tobacco abuse. Write for more information. Internships available; contact Timothy Smith.

Company: Interlock Media Associates
Industry: Communications
Contact: Jeanie Clarke, associate producer
Address: 19 Arrow Street, Cambridge, MA 02138
Phone: (617) 354-3584
Fax: (617) 547-4711

What Company Does: With a focus on community-based efforts, the firm documents through video, sound, design, writing, and research the impact of development on indigenous communities and the environment. Specializes in "cross-cultural productions linking third world organizations with one another and environmental, media, and human rights agencies in North America and Europe." Also consults on communications, educational programming, and media facility design. "Exchange of information between communities and across borders." Internships available.

Company: International Alliance for Sustainable Agriculture
Industry: Nonprofit
Contact: Joseph Barisonzi, managing director
Address: 1701 University Avenue SE, Minneapolis, MN 55414
Phone: (612) 331-1099

What Company Does: A nonprofit organization created in 1983 to foster worldwide development of sustainable agriculture that is ecologically sound, economically viable, socially just, and humane. Publishes resource guides and a quarterly newsletter, *Manna.* Also offers other publications, operates a Resource and Information Center, and gives public presentations.

Company: International Center for the Solution of Environmental Problems (ICSEP)
Industry: Nonprofit
Address: 535 Lovett Boulevard, Houston, TX 77006
Phone: (713) 527-8711

What Company Does: ICSEP's work focuses on rural and urban atmospheric-related problems, with some projects dedicated to habitat design. Typical project examples include: soil erosion; hazardous waste disposal; climatic response to city design; transportation; African famine and drought; preservation of rural life; flood control; land subsidence; habitat design; air pollution; effect of temperature on agricultural growth; atmospheric release of noxious chemicals; and herbicide distribution from agricultural spraying. ICSEP clients include: EPA, Shell Oil Company, Exxon, and Texas Instruments.

Company: International Fund for Agriculture Research (IFAR)
Industry: Agriculture
Contact: Richard L. Sawyer, president
Address: 1611 North Kent Street, Suite 600, Arlington, VA 22209
Phone: (703) 276-1611
Fax: (703) 522-8077

What Company Does: IFAR works to increase public awareness that permanent solutions to the problems of human hunger, malnutrition, and environmental degradation are to be found through enhanced agriculture and associated research. IFAR is a North American support organization to the global network of international agricultural research centers, those funded by the Consultative Group on International Agricultural Research (CGIAR) and those funded independently.

Company: International Institute for Sustainable Development (IISD)
Industry: Nonprofit
Contact: 161 Portage Avenue East, 6th floor, Winnipeg, Manitoba,
Address: R3B OY4, Canada
Phone: (204) 958-7700
Fax: (204) 958-7710

What Company Does: IISD is a nonprofit private corporation established and supported by the governments of Manitoba and Canada. Its mandate is to promote sustainable development in decision-making within government, business, and the daily lives of individuals. IISD engages in policy research and communications, including a focus on international trade, business strategy, and national budgets.

Company: **International Society of Tropical Foresters, Inc.**
Industry: Nonprofit, forestry
Contact: Warren Doolittle, Ph.D., president
Address: 5400 Grosvenor Lane, Bethesda, MD 20814
Phone: (301) 897-8720 ext. 4
Fax: (301) 897-3690

What Company Does: A membership organization open to all persons interested in tropical forestry. Works as a communications network amoung tropical foresters and others concerned about forest conservation. Publishes a quarterly newsletter with editions in Spanish, English, and French.

Company: **Investor Responsibility Research Center (IRRC)**
Industry: Finance
Contact: Jonathon Naimon, research analyst
Address: 1755 Massachusetts Avenue NW, Suite 600, Washington, DC 20036
Phone: (202) 833-0700
Fax: (202) 332-8570

What Company Does: Publishes newsletter called the *Investor's Environmental Report*. Also has an Environmental Information Service (EIS). EIS products include the newsletter, corporate profiles detailing the environmental activities of major U.S. companies, and other studies. Contact IRRC for information on membership. Internships available; contact Charine Adams.

Company: **Investors' Circle**
Industry: Finance
Contact: Susan Davis, executive director
Address: 2400 East Main Street, Suite 103, St. Charles, IL 60174
Phone: (708) 876-1101
Fax: (708) 876-0187

What Company Does: The Investors' Circle is a group of key accredited investors who come together to promote their common goals of developing the industry of socially responsible investing without sacrificing economic returns. Circle members' individual interests are broad ranging, including environmental protection and conservation, energy reduction, technologies to improve the environment, sustainable agriculture, and sustainable forestry.

Company: Susan B. Irving, Inc.
Industry: Entrepreneurial
Contact: Susan B. Irving, president
Address: 249 West 29th Street, 5N, New York, NY 10001-5231
Phone: (212) 239-9719
Fax: (212) 564-8523

What Company Does: In 1991 Susan Irving started work projects with Zulu tribespeople in KwaZulu in Natal, South Africa, that produce *imbenge* or "scooby" baskets made from recycled or scrap telephone wire. These work projects help preserve the Zulu heritage of weaving and bring in much-needed income. Salvaged telephone wire is sent from the United States, or is taken from Johannesburg industry to the craftspeople's remote villages in Natal.

Company: ISCO, Inc. (Environmental Division)
Industry: Environmental services
Contact: Sheryl Wright, director of human resources
Address: 531 Westgate Boulevard, Lincoln, NE 68528
Phone: (402) 474-2233

What Company Does: The Environmental Division of ISCO, Inc., manufactures and markets scientific and water monitoring instrumentation. The company is the world's market leader in the manufacture of wastewater samplers and one of the market leaders in the manufacture of flow meters.

Company: ITW-HiCone Division of Illinois Toolworks, Inc.
Industry: Manufacturing
Contact: James Cathcart, director, Environmental Affairs
Address: 1140 West Bryn Mawr Avenue, Itasca, IL 60143
Phone: (708) 773-9300 or (708) 773-3015

What Company Does: ITW-HiCone produces six-pack rings used to hold soft drink and beer cans together.

Environmental Programs: ITW has developed a ring carrier that is photodegradable when exposed to direct or indirect sunlight and can also be recycled. The company has recapture and recycling programs. Its latest innovation is a new tear tab-ring carrier that allows consumers to break the ring when removing a can; this carrier is also photodegradable.

Company: Jantz Design
Industry: Clothing and furniture
Contact: Eliana Jantz, president
Address: P.O. Box 3071, Santa Rosa, CA 95472
Phone: (800) 365-6563
Fax: (707) 823-0106

What Company Does: A small company in Northern California, Jantz Design makes the highest-quality natural bedding of wool and cotton. Products include layered beds, cotton batting, sleep pillows, and wool comforters, flannel robes, house slippers, towels, sleep/lounge wear, custom pillows, bedlinens, and furniture. Jantz uses natural wool and cotton and is committed to supporting the market for new agricultural practices that are better for the environment. Call or write for catalog.

Company: Japan Committee for the Global Environment
Industry: Nonprofit, sustainable development
Address: Environmental Information Center, Toranomon First Building Minato-ku, Tokyo 105, Japan
Phone: 81-3-3595-3992

What Company Does: The committee was founded to promote global environmental awareness in Japan. This is accomplished in two ways: first, within Japan by building a coalition between the people and the government on ways to protect and preserve the global environment and to develop an environmentally friendly and sustainable society; second, by working abroad to encourage worldwide cooperation with developing countries to achieve sustainable development and promote active involvement in protecting the global environment.

Company: Johnny's Selected Seeds
Industry: Agriculture
Contact: Barbara Kennedy
Address: Foss Hill Road, Albion, ME 04910
Phone: (207) 437-4301
Fax: (207) 437-2165

What Company Does: Johnny's is a mail-order home-garden and market-grower seed company that produces completely untreated seeds. All varieties offered are untreated. Several corn varieties are sold both untreated and treated for market growers who require seed treatment. Johnny's maintains an environmental commitment to providing high-quality organic seed strains for growers.

Company: **Johnson & Johnson**
Industry: Consumer products
Contact: Jeffrey J. Leebaw, assistant director, Corporate Communications
Address: One Johnson & Johnson Plaza, WT-205, New Brunswick, NJ 08933
Phone: (908) 524-3350
Fax: (908) 524-3621

What Company Does: Johnson & Johnson is the world's largest and most comprehensive manufacturer of health care products. It serves the consumer, pharmaceutical, and professional markets. Its well-known consumer products include Band-Aid brand adhesive bandages, the Tylenol brands of pain relievers, and the line of Johnson's baby toiletries such as Johnson's Baby Shampoo and Johnson's Baby Oil.

Environmental Programs: Johnson & Johnson is actively pursuing a series of initiatives aimed at addressing present-day environmental challenges. Overall goals range from reducing waste emissions to developing smaller, lighter, recyclable products and packaging. To help its packaging engineers measure annual source-reduction progress, Johnson & Johnson developed PackTrack software. This computer program helps users to develop environmentally neutral packaging designs and to calculate packaging reductions. In an eighteen-month, PackTrack pilot program, twenty-five participating Johnson & Johnson companies reported 5.5 million pounds of annual packaging reductions with savings of $2.8 million in raw materials alone. The company has eliminated the use of all heavy-metal inks that traditionally had been used for domestic distribution. And since 1973, Johnson & Johnson has reduced energy usage worldwide by 35.5 percent.

Company: **S. C. Johnson and Son, Inc.**
Industry: Consumer and commercial products
Contact: Jane M. Hutterly, vice president, Environmental Safety & Actions Worldwide
Address: 1525 Howe Street, Racine, WI 53403-2236
Phone: (414) 631-2000
Fax: (414) 631-2183

What Company Does: S. C. Johnson is one of the largest privately held consumer and commercial product companies, with products including Raid, Off, Pledge, Windex, and Vanish.

Environmental Programs: In 1975, S. C. Johnson eliminated CFC propellants from its aerosols, three years prior to the 1978 U.S. ban. The company has adopted an environmental mission statement and principles that highlight its commitment to protecting the environment through the proper design and manufacture of products and services, research, reduction and disposal of waste, and sustainable use of natural resources. Included is the protection of the biosphere, public policy, education that will improve the environment, and a commitment to internal policy assessment. S. C. Johnson is the recipient of the 1994 World Environment Center's Gold Medal for Environmental Stewardship.

Company: **Keep America Beautiful, Inc. (KAB)**
Industry: Nonprofit
Contact: Becky Lyons, director, Planning & Administrative Services
Address: Mill River Plaza, 9 West Broad Street, Stamford, CT 06902
Phone: (203) 323-8987
Fax: (203) 325-9199

What Company Does: A national nonprofit organization dedicated to improving waste-handling practices in American communities. Founded in 1953, KAB has 500 local affiliates in forty-one states, including twenty-one official statewide affiliates. Limited internships available.

Company: **Kellogg**
Industry: Consumer products
Contact: Tim Knowlton, government community affairs manager
Address: One Kellogg Square, P.O. Box 3599, Battle Creek, MI 49016-3599
Phone: (616) 961-2000
Fax: (616) 961-2871

What Company Does: Kellogg produces breakfast cereals and other food products, including granola bars, Eggo waffles, Pop-Tart toaster pastries, and stuffings. Kellogg has the largest share of the U.S. dessert market and owns Ferns International, Whitney Foods, and Le Shake.

Environmental Programs: Kellogg has used recycled packaging since the new company was founded in 1906. One hundred percent of all packaging used for Kellogg's cereal and products produced in the United States is manufactured from recycled carton board. The company has developed a waste management and recycling program to recycle millions of pounds of paper, wooden pallets, and scrap metal, as well as thousands of gallons of used motor oil. In addition, it recycles waste food by sending it to food processors and farmers for use as animal feed.

Company: **Kemper National Insurance Companies**
Industry: Insurance
Contact: Gary Slettum, employment manager
Address: 1 Kemper Drive, Long Grove, IL 60049
Phone: (708) 320-2174 or general (708) 320-2000

What Company Does: This is a property/casualty insurance mutual company. Kemper offers insurance and insurance-related services in all fifty states, for both commercial and personal lines of insurance.

Environmental Programs: Kemper has an Environmental Conservation Policy concerned with recycling, use of recycled products, waste reduction, energy conservation, and environmental pollution. The company has been recycling for over nineteen years. Kemper also has an environmental committee.

Company: **Kerr-McGee Corporation**
Industry: Energy
Contact: Donald F. Schiesz, corporate vice president and head of Safety and Environmental Division
Address: P.O. Box 25861, Oklahoma City, OK 73125
Phone: (405) 270-1313

What Company Does: Kerr-McGee is an energy and chemical company based in Oklahoma City, with operations and exploration activities in the United States, Canada, and six other countries. Its 1994 sales were $3.35 billion.

Environmental Programs: Kerr-McGee has an Environment and Health Management staff and an Executive Environmental Committee. Its corporate environmental policy focuses on waste reduction and management.

Company: **Keystone Center**
Industry: Nonprofit
Contact: Robert W. Craig, president
Address: Box 8606, Keystone, CO 80435
Phone: (303) 468-5822
Fax: (303) 262-0152

What Company Does: The Keystone Center is a nonprofit public policy, scientific, and educational organization headquartered in Keystone, Colorado, with a satellite office in Washington, D.C. Through the Science & Public Policy Program, the center provides neutral conflict management and mediation services on national and international policy disputes in seven major areas. The program also mediates site and issue-specific conflicts on local, regional, and state levels. The staff provides training and technical assistance to organizations desiring a more effective process for decison-making and the management of internal disputes.

Company: Kimberly Clark
Industry: Consumer products
Contact: Kenneth A. Strassner, vice president, Environment and Energy
Address: 1400 Holcomb Bridge Road, B-200, Roswell, GA 30076-2199
Phone: (404) 587-8634
Fax: (404) 587-7093

What Company Does: Kimberly Clark makes paper and nonwoven products including Huggies ultratrim diapers, Kleenex tissue, Kotex and New Freedom tampons and pads, and Depend incontinence protection products. Its commercial products include commercial grade tissue, business paper, tea-bag papers, and newsprint.

What Company Does: Since 1872, when Kimberly Clark went into business by recycling linen and cloth rags into newsprint, the company has been responsive to environmental issues. Kimberly Clark has an environmental protection policy, and was one of the first American companies to establish an internal environmental auditing program. Annual environmental capital expenditures are $60 million. An additional $75 million is spent on environmental operating costs.

Company: Kinder, Lydenberg, Domini & Co., Inc.
Industry: Finance
Contact: Steven D. Lydenberg, research director
Address: 129 Mt. Auburn Street, Cambridge, MA 02138-5766
Phone: (617) 547-7479
Fax: (617) 354-5353

What Company Does: Registered investment advisory firm that provides social research on publicly traded U.S. companies to the financial community. Also serves as a consultant to money managers and institutional investors on social investing—develops social screens and monitors managers' implementation of clients' social objectives. Develops company reviews and social investment databases; an on-line computer service that offers access to all reviews produced by KLD.

Environmental Programs: Created and maintains the Domini 400 Social Index, a listing of 400 stocks of publicly traded firms that pass broad-based social screens, that is both a benchmark for manager performance and a resource for the social investment community. Also publishes *Monthly Update.*

Company: Kmart Corporation
Industry: Retail
Contact: Susan M. England, environmental marketing specialist
Address: International Headquarters, 3100 West Big Beaver Road, Troy, MI 48084-3163
Phone: (810) 643-1077
Fax: (810) 643-5513

What Company Does: Kmart is a general merchandise retailer with operations in both discount and specialty stores.

Environmental Programs: Kmart Corporation organized an environmental task force at its corporate headquarters to address the environmental concerns of its stores and business. Kmart is a member of the National Recycling Coalition and Buy Recycled Business Alliance. It supports environmental education and habitat preservation programs through corporate contributions to environmental nonprofit organizations.

Company: Knight-Ridder, Inc.
Industry: Communications
Contact: Polk Laffoon, vice president, Corporate Relations
Address: One Herald Plaza, 6th floor, Miami, FL 33132-1693
Phone: (305) 376-3838 or general (305) 376-3800

What Company Does: Knight-Ridder is an international information and communications company engaged in newspaper publishing; business news and information services; electronic retrieval service; news, graphics, and photo services; cable television; and newsprint manufacturing.

Environmental Programs: Knight-Ridder has a Statement of Environmental Principles. The company engages in newsprint recycling and hazardous waste and other waste management programs.

Company: Kroger Company
Industry: Manufacturing and retailing
Contact: Paul Bernish, director, Public Relations
Address: 1014 Vine Street, Cincinnati, OH 45202-1119
Phone: (513) 762-4000

What Company Does: Kroger is the nation's largest food retailer; it also manufactures a number of food products.

Environmental Programs: Kroger recycles much of the paper, cardboard, plastic, and other materials used in its business, providing national leadership within its industry in developing public policy on solid-waste issues. The company instituted a Bag Sense program, which provides customers with a two to three cent incentive for each bag they bring back for reuse. In Cincinnati, Kroger estimates that 20,000 fewer bags each week are used as a result of this effort. Kroger offices recycle millions of pounds of computer paper and office stationery.

Company: **L&F Products**
Industry: Consumer products
Contact: Patricia A. Jones, associate director, Communications & Public Relations
Address: 225 Summit Avenue, Montvale, NJ 07645
Phone: (201) 573-5700
Fax: (201) 573-5858

What Company Does: L&F Products is a leading worldwide consumer goods manufacturer and marketer of quality household, personal care, professional, and do-it-yourself products. Some of L&F's leading brands include Lysol cleaners and disinfectants, Resolve cleaners, d-Con rodenticides, Chubs thick baby wipes, Ogilvie home permanents, Minwax wood finishes, Thompson's exterior stains, and Red Devil enamels. L&F is an independent operating unit of Eastman Kodak Company.

Environmental Programs: L&F's environmental activities range from extensive internal recycling programs to external initiatives to reduce solid waste in both its packaging and its manufacturing processes and minimize the impact its products have on the environment. Each division of L&F incorporates an environmental strategy into its yearly marketing plan to include packaging, communication, and community outreach.

Company: **Lake Michigan Federation**
Industry: Environmental education and advocacy
Contact: Kathy Bero, SE Wisconsin director
Address: 647 West Virginia Street, Suite 307, Milwaukee, WI 53204
Phone: (414) 271-5059
Fax: (414) 271-0796

What Company Does: In 1995, the Lake Michigan Federation (LMF) celebrates twenty-five years of promoting citizen action to protect and restore the Great Lakes ecosystem. Program activities are focused in three different areas: shoreline/habitat, toxics, and energy. LMF continues to work at the international level with groups and individuals from Canada, the United States, and tribal communities.

Company: **Lakeshore Enterprises**
Industry: Nonprofit, wildlife control
Contact: Penny Iverson, sales representative
Address: P.O. Box 238, Benzonia, MI 49616
Phone: (800) 968-9453
Fax: (616) 882-5242

What Company Does: Produces Green Screen, a line of high-quality wildlife deterrent products that discourage deer, rabbits, and raccoons from browsing on a variety of vegetation year round. Pesticide-free and safe to use up to the day of harvest. Nonprofit organization, employing persons with disabilities. Other products include habitats for birds and bats and recycled, handprinted gift wrap products. Lakeshore's products are environmentally benign.

Company: **Land Trust Alliance**
Industry: Nonprofit, conservation
Contact: Jean Hocker, president
Address: 1319 F Street NW, Suite 501, Washington, DC 20004
Phone: (202) 638-4725
Fax: (202) 638-4730

What Company Does: The Land Trust Alliance (LTA) is a nonprofit organization formed in 1982 to strengthen the land trust movement and ensure that land trusts have the information, skills, and resources they need to save land. LTA acts as an umbrella and an information clearinghouse for independent, often geographically isolated, land trust organizations across the nation. It operates a national database for land trust information, maintains a reference library, and organizes national conferences. LTA promotes public awareness and advocates public policy that supports land trusts. It publishes a quarterly professional journal, *Exchange*, and offers books, guides, and other educational materials that focus on conservation, land trusts, and related issues. Among these is LTA's annual *National Directory of Conservation Land Trusts*. Internships available.

Company: **League of Conservation Voters (LCV)**
Industry: Nonprofit
Contact: Kelly Jones, internship coordinator
Address: 1707 L Street NW, Suite 550, Washington, DC 20036
Phone: (202) 785-8683
Fax: (202) 835-0491

What Company Does: LCV, founded in 1970, is the bipartisan political arm of the U.S. environmental movement. The league's goal is to change the balance of power in the U.S. Congress to reflect the proenvironment concerns of the American public.

Company: **Lever Brothers, Inc.**
Industry: Consumer products
Contact: Melinda Sweet, director, Environmental Affairs
Address: 390 Park Avenue, New York, NY 10022
Phone: (212) 906-4571
Fax: (212) 318-3680

What Company Does: Lever Brothers is a leading consumer household products company headquartered in New York City and the maker of such brands as Wisk, Surf, All, and Sunlight detergents; Snuggle fabric softener; Dove Beauty Bar and Lever 2000 and Caress soaps. Lever is an operating company of Anglo/Dutch Unilever PLC/NV, one of the world's leading consumer products concerns with major food, personal product, soap and detergent, fragrance, and industrial businesses with annual sales of $44 billion.

Environmental Programs: Lever's award-winning environmental programs focus on community and youth education at the grassroots level. In 1993, Lever worked with eight cities nationwide to build playgrounds made with recycled materials; in 1994, the company worked with the National Park Foundation to donate recycled plastic lumber to ten national parks; both programs are designed to highlight the need to find markets for recyclables—beyond packaging—to ensure the success of recycling. Lever is a member of the Keep America Beautiful board of directors and has partnered with KAB affiliates around the country to sponsor community cleanup events and environmental education programs.

Company: **Levi Strauss & Co.**
Industry: Manufacturing
Contact: Elissa Sheridan, Corporate Affairs and Global Environmental Council
Address: 1155 Battery Street, San Francisco, CA 94111
Phone: (415) 544-6000
Fax: (415) 544-3939

What Company Does: Levi Strauss & Co. (LS&CO.) is the worlds largest manufacturer of branded apparel. It markets jeans, jeans-related products, and casual sportswear in more than sixty countries. It employs a staff of about 2,200 people in its San Francisco headquarters and approximately 36,000 people worldwide. It operates forty-one production facilities, nine finishing centers, and sources product globally.

Environmental Programs: In 1992, LS&CO. set forth its Environmental Philosophy and Guiding Principles, a far-reaching document that articulated the company's environmental vision. In 1994, the company established the Global Environmental Council (GEC), which will work to develop appropriate global environmental priorities, requirements, and standards for the company; coordinate and monitor compliance; and promote responsible environmental stewardship. Working closely with the GEC are four Regional Environmental Committees, one each in Asia, Europe, North America, and South America.

Company: Lighthawk—The Environmental Air Force
Industry: Nonprofit
Contact: Julia Bergen, education director
Address: P.O. Box 8163, Santa Fe, NM 87504
Phone: (505) 982-9656
Fax: (505) 984-8381

What Company Does: Publishes an excellent newsletter that keeps people current on environmental topics. The organization's goal is to protect biological diversity and natural ecosystems by bringing together the power of flight and research, community organizing, and action to the international conservation movement. Lighthawk uses its airplanes to fly key decision makers, media, and activists over endangered lands in order to give them the information they need to take action. It also performs aerial monitoring of key environmental areas. Internships available.

Company: Marcal Paper Mills, Inc.
Industry: Manufacturing
Contact: Peter Marcalus
Address: One Market Street, Elmwood Park, NJ 07407
Phone: (201) 796-4000
Fax: (201) 796-0470

What Company Does: Marcal is a paper manufacturing company.

Environmental Programs: Marcal processes over 150,000 tons of recyclable paper a year and gives new life to materials that might otherwise contribute to the solid-waste stream. The company has been recycling for over forty years. All Marcal brand bath, facial, napkin, and towel products are made from 100 percent recycled paper: "Paper from paper, not from trees."

Company: Marine Biological Laboratory (MBL)
Industry: Nonprofit
Contact: Pamela Clapp, director of communications
Address: Water Street, Woods Hole, MA 02543
Phone: (508) 548-3705
Fax: (508) 457-1924

What Company Does: The MBL was established in 1888 as a nonprofit institution devoted to research and education in basic biology. It has been called "the uniquely national center for biology in this country." Scientists and students throughout the world come to the MBL to conduct research, teach, study, and collaborate with other scientists. They use the diverse and abundant organisms found in surrounding waters as model systems in their research.

Company: MarketPlace: Handwork of India
Industry: Nonprofit, clothing
Contact: Lyndon Rego, assistant director
Address: 1455 Ashland Avenue, Evanston, IL 60201
Phone: (708) 328-4011
Fax: (708) 328-4061

What Company Does: Nonprofit organization providing employment to unskilled women and handicapped people in India. Unique 100 percent cotton clothing features patchwork and embroidery accents. Internships available.

Company: Martin Marietta Corporation
Industry: Manufacturing
Contact: Charles E. Carnahan, vice president, Corporate Environmental Management
Address: 7921 Southpark Plaza, Suite 210, Littleton, CO 80120
Phone: (303) 977-5033
Fax: (303) 971-5056

What Company Does: Martin Marietta Corporation designs, manufactures, integrates, and operates systems and products in leading-edge technologies, including aerospace, electronics, information management, materials, and energy.

Environmental Programs: Martin Marietta has in place a comprehensive system of reviewing all aspects of its operation for environmental compliance through its Corporate Environmental, Health and Safety Department. The corporation was recently commended by EPA for its exemplary performance with respect to the reduction of hazardous waste generation, ozone-depleter reduction, and the release of toxic chemicals.

Company: Mary Kay Cosmetics, Inc.
Industry: Consumer products
Contact: Randall Graham, marketing publicity
Address: 8787 Stemmons Freeway, Dallas, TX 75247-3794
Phone: (214) 630-8787
Fax: (214) 905-5721

What Company Does: Mary Kay Cosmetics, a Fortune 500 company, is the largest direct seller of skin care products in the United States. It manufactures more than 200 products, which are distributed through a sales force of more than 325,000 independent beauty consultants in twenty-one countries worldwide.

Environmental Programs: Mary Kay has a three-tiered recycling program, which includes corporate recycling of office paper and other recyclables; employees bringing recyclables from home; and recyclable and recycled product packaging. More than 11 million pounds of glass, aluminum, paper, and plastic have been collected. More than $29,000 in proceeds from Mary Kay's recycling program has been donated to the Nature Conservancy of Texas.

Company: McCaw Cellular Communications, Inc.
Industry: Telecommunications
Contact: Bob Ratcliffe, Corporate Communications
Address: 5400 Carillon Point, Kirkland, WA 98033
Phone: (206) 827-4500 or (206) 828-8476

What Company Does: McCaw Cellular has ownership positions in over 100 cities across the country, representing over 110 million potential customers or "pops." Approximately 80 percent of the "pops" owned by McCaw and LIN Broadcasting Corporation, which is 52 percent owned by McCaw, are in the nation's thirty most populous markets and their contiguous service areas. McCaw Cellular operates major regional systems in California, Florida, Texas, the Pacific Northwest, the Midwest, the Rocky Mountain states, and the Northeast, currently offering service primarily under the name Cellular One. LIN Broadcasting holds significant interests in cellular systems in New York, Los Angeles, Philadelphia, Dallas, and Houston, and operates seven network-affiliated television stations.

Environmental Programs: McCaw Cellular has organized internal recycling of office paper, cans, and bottles. Recycling monies are used to support the Seattle Drug and Narcotics Program, which enables adults to reenter the community with training. The company has an employee transportation coordinator who serves as a representative to the Seattle Mass Transit Association.

Company: McDonald's Corporation
Industry: Food service
Contact: Beth Petersohn, manager, Customer Satisfaction Department
Address: Kroc Drive, Oak Brook, IL 60521
Phone: (708) 575-3000
Fax: (708) 575-6942

What Company Does: McDonald's is the largest food service organization in the world.

Environmental Programs: McDonald's is known for its conversion from plastics to paper and recycled paper products. The company works with environmental groups such as the Environmental Defense Fund to deal with environmental imaging and customer satisfaction. McDonald's has also spent more than $600 million in recycled materials for use in building and remodeling its restaurants. This program is called McRecycle USA, and was established to create end markets for recycled materials and to encourage manufacturers to develop products containing recycled materials.

Company: Mead Corporation
Industry: Forest products
Contact: Wallace O. Nugent, vice president, Purchasing and Logistics
Address: World Headquarters, Courthouse Plaza Northeast, Dayton, OH 45463
Phone: (513) 495-4005
Fax: (513) 461-2424

What Company Does: Mead is one of the world's largest manufacturers of paper for printing and business use. It is the largest maker of paper-based school and office supplies and the developer of the world's leading electronic information retrieval service for law, patents, accounting, finance, news, and business information.

Environmental Programs: Mead has established water pollution control groups and invested in company-wide installations of pollution control technology. It is committed to the environmental education of children and supports an educational program for grades four through six to introduce solid-waste issues to students.

Company: Mercedes-Benz of North America, Inc.
Industry: Transportation
Contact: A. B. Shuman, director, Public Relations
Address: One Mercedes Drive, P.O. Box 350, Montvale, NJ 07645-0350
Phone: (201) 573-2238
Fax: (201) 573-0117

What Company Does: Mercedes-Benz of North America is a distributor of passenger cars.

Environmental Programs: All Mercedes-Benz models have air conditioning systems without ozone-depleting CFCs and utilize CFC-free urethane foams. Mercedes-Benz has eliminated CFC solvents during production. It has designed components for easy recycling; the plastics it uses are labeled to show their composition. Mercedes installed the first activated charcoal filter, together with an electrostatic filter, to help prevent airborne pollutants from entering the passenger compartment. Its cars also use advanced emission controls. In addition, all S-Class and SL models use water-borne paints. The company has also been active in working with outside companies to develop pilot projects to develop more efficient recycling of scrapped vehicles.

Company: Merck & Co., Inc.
Industry: Pharmaceuticals
Contact: Valerie Carter, Public Affairs
Address: 1 Merck Drive, P.O. Box 100, Whitehouse Station, NJ 08889
Phone: (908) 423-7226

What Company Does: Merck is a worldwide research-intensive health products company that discovers, develops, produces, and markets human and animal health products and specialty chemicals.

Environmental Programs: Merck's corporate environmental goals have been: (1) 90 percent reduction of air emissions of carcinogens and suspected carcinogens by 1991; (2) total elimination of these air emissions or application of best available technology by 1993; (3) 90 percent reduction worldwide of all environmental releases of toxic chemicals by 1995. The first two goals have been met. Further, Merck's public objectives include a commitment to minimizing the release of any chemical into the environment that could affect health, deplete the ozone layer, or contribute to acid rain, the greenhouse effect, or any other global environmental problem.

Company: Mervyn's
Industry: Retail
Contact: Kathy Blackburn, public affairs manager
Address: 25001 Industrial Boulevard, Mailstop CO7F, Hayward, CA 94545
Phone: (510) 786-7723
Fax: (510) 786-7791

What Company Does: A subsidiary of Dayton Hudson Corporation, Mervyn's is a moderate-price promotional department store offering trend-right apparel and home fashions. As of March 1994, there were 279 Mervyn's stores and over 40,000 employees in fifteen states.

Environmental Programs: Mervyn's recycles thousands of tons of cardboard each year. Merchandise is shipped to stores in cardboard boxes, and after they're emptied, these boxes are sent back to the distribution centers, where they're baled and sold to a recycler. The company is continually working with vendors to reduce excess merchandise packaging.

Company: Miranda Productions, Inc.
Industry: Film and video
Contact: Abagail Wright, producer
Address: P.O. Box 4624, Boulder, CO 80306
Phone: (303) 546-0880
Fax: (303) 546-0990

What Company Does: Committed to making documentary films about social and environmental issues. "We hope to contribute to positive change in the world by using film and television to generate public awareness." Internships available.

Company: Modern World Design
Industry: Industrial design
Contact: Wendy E. Brawer
Address: 157 Ludlow Street, 4th floor, New York, NY 10002
Phone: (212) 674-1631
Fax: (212) 674-1631

What Company Does: Modern World Design takes an ecological approach to the design of resource-efficient products and services. This industrial design consultancy combines environmental compatibility factors and traditional design considerations to improve its clients' global impact. In addition to promoting source reduction, renewable energy, recycled-content materials, and other sustainability strategies, their design solutions promote public involvement with the environment, such as site-specific recycling bins with unique features for Times Square, NYC, and King County, Washington, and the Green Apple Map that charts NYC's ecology and showcases the interconnection between the natural and the constructed environments.

Company: Mohawk Paper Mills, Inc.
Industry: Manufacturing
Contact: George Milner, assistant vice president, Environmental Affairs
Address: P.O. Box 497, 465 Saratoga Street, Cohoes, NY 12047
Phone: (518) 237-1740
Fax: (518) 237-7394

What Company Does: Mohawk Paper Mills is an independent producer and distributor of premium papers.

Environmental Programs: Mohawk Paper Mills offers product lines of state-certified recycled paper that contain various percentages of postconsumer waste. Mohawk follows a voluntary program of waste reduction that aims to "generate less waste and avoid the use of hazardous substances." Among other initiatives, it has switched to environmentally safer dyes, conducts a program where waste oils are fuel blended or recycled, and carries on an internal office recycling program.

Company: Monsanto Corporation
Industry: Chemicals
Contact: Michael A. Pierle, vice president, Environment, Safety, & Health
Address: 800 N. Lindbergh Boulevard, St. Louis, MO 63167
Phone: (314) 694-8882 or general (314) 694-1000
Fax: (314) 694-8957

What Company Does: Monsanto is a global enterprise comprising Monsanto Company and its subsidiaries. Monsanto Agricultural Company makes high-value agricultural products such as Roundup and Lasso herbicides. Monsanto Chemical Company makes high-performance materials such as synthetic fibers for WearDated carpet and Saflex interlayer for laminated glass. The NutraSweet Company makes food products such as NutraSweet brand sweetener and Simplesse all-natural fat substitute. Searle makes pharmaceutical products such as Calan for hypertension and Cytotec for prevention of certain types of ulcers. Fisher Controls International, Inc., makes industrial process-control equipment.

Environmental Programs: Monsanto has begun an employee awards program to recognize outstanding environmental accomplishment, with up to $100,000 per year going to environmental causes or organizations designated by the winners. To report publicly on its progress in fulfilling the Monsanto Pledge, the company publishes an annual environmental review.

Company: Moore Recycling Associates, Inc.
Industry: Consulting
Contact: Carey R. Moore, communications specialist
Address: P.O. Box 136, Main Street, Hancock, NH 03449-0136
Phone: (603) 525-4916
Fax: (603) 525-6611

What Company Does: Moore Recycling Associates is a consulting firm that can provide up-to-date information on a variety of recycling technologies and equipment. It provides recycling services in project planning, project management, research, program operations, and training.

Company: Mother Hart's
Industry: Consumer products
Address: 3300 South Congress Avenue, No. 21, P.O. Box 4229, Boynton Beach, FL 33424-4229
Phone: (407) 738-5866

What Company Does: Mother Hart's produces a catalog of natural products for home and body. For the past twelve years the company's goal has been to offer pure and simple natural fiber home essentials that are long lasting, comfortable, and affordable, along with great service and prompt delivery. Products range from bedding to baby items to backpacks and duffels to hairbrushes and soaps.

Company: Motorola Corporation
Industry: Manufacturing
Contact: Thomas Ott, senior staff environmental engineer
Address: 1303 East Algonquin Road, Schaumburg, IL 60196
Phone: (708) 576-0785

What Company Does: Motorola is one of the world's leading providers of electronic equipment, systems, components, and services for worldwide markets. Products include two-way radios, pagers and telepoint devices, cellular telephones and systems, semiconductors, defense and aerospace electronics, automotive and industrial electronics, computers, data communications, and information processing and handling equipment.

Environmental Programs: Recognized in 1988 with the Malcolm Baldrige Award, Motorola's quality culture of continuous improvement and Total Customer Satisfaction is applied directly to environmental proactiveness.

Company: Mountain Rose Herbs
Industry: Consumer products
Contact: Julie Bailey, owner
Address: P.O. Box 2000, Redway, CA 95560-2000
Phone: (707) 923-7867

What Company Does: Traditional and beverage teas; handcrafted body, bath, and hair products; organic and wildcrafted herbs; essential oils, containers, and ingredients; books; baby care; unique gift items; natural pet care. Cruelty free. Internships may be available.

Company: Nabisco Foods
Industry: Consumer products
Contact: Mark L. Gutsche, senior director, Corporate Communications
Address: 7 Sylvan Way, P.O. Box 311, Parsippany, NJ 07054-0311
Phone: (201) 682-5000

What Company Does: Nabisco Foods Group manufactures and markets cookies, crackers, margarine, cereals, desserts, sauces and condiments, egg alternatives, nuts, hard roll candies, gum, and pet foods under brand names such as Oreo, Chips Ahoy!, Ritz, Teddy Grahams, Fig Newtons, Fleischmann's, Blue Bonnet, Ortega, A-1, Gray Poupon, Egg Beaters, Planters, Lifesavers, Milk Bone, College Inn, and Vermont Maid.

Environmental Programs: Nabisco has been reducing the weight of the plastic tubs and lids for Fleischmann's and Blue Bonnet margarines, which has reduced plastics usage by 2.2 million pounds, and has saved more than 1.1 million pounds of glass. The company uses more than 233 million pounds of recycled materials—more than 50 percent of all its packaging by weight. Nabisco also uses more than 20.4 million pounds of recycled corrugated cardboard. Each of its twenty-two major production facilities has active recycling and conservation programs in place.

Company: National Association of Environmental Professionals (NAEP)
Industry: Nonprofit
Contact: Susan Eisenberg, executive director
Address: 5165 MacArthur Boulevard NW, Washington, DC 20016
Phone: (202) 966-1500
Fax: (202) 966-1977

What Company Does: NAEP has nearly 4,000 members representing government, consulting, academe, industry, and the private sector in the United States and abroad, working in all areas of air, water, noise, waste, ecology, and education and providing access to the latest trends in environmental research, technology, law, and policy. Membership includes: quarterly peer-reviewed journal, *The Environmental Professional;* bimonthly newsletter, *NAEP News;* and discounts on publications and meeting registrations. Internships available; contact the NAEP national office.

Company: National Audubon Society
Industry: Nonprofit
Contact: Human Resources
Address: 700 Broadway, New York, NY 10003
Phone: (212) 979-3000

What Company Does: The Audubon Society is a nonprofit membership organization focusing on environmental public policy and education.

Company: National Coalition for Marine Conservation (NCMC)
Industry: Nonprofit
Contact: Ken Hinman, executive director
Address: 3 West Market Street, Leesburg, VA 22075
Phone: (703) 777-0037
Fax: (703) 777-1107

What Company Does: Founded in 1973, NCMC works to stop overfishing and preserve coastal habitat through education, research, and support for conservation. A leading voice for marine conservation, NCMC also puts on symposia.

Company: National Environmental Development Association (NEDA)
Industry: Nonprofit

Contact: Rob Murchinson, administrative associate
Address: 1440 New York Avenue NW, Washington, DC 20005
Phone: (202) 638-1230
Fax: (202) 639-8685

What Company Does: A coalition of organized labor, agriculture, and industry. Works toward creating national environmental policy with the premise that it is possible to have a clean environment and a strong economy. Communicates with Congress, regulatory agencies, the media, and the general public on key issues such as air and water pollution control, waste management, and groundwater. Publishes a newsletter entitled *Balance* three times a year. Sponsors a Distinguished Service Award and Balance in Journalism Award.

Company: National Geographic Society
Industry: Nonprofit
Contact: Human Resources
Address: 1145 17th Street NW, Washington, DC 20036
Phone: (202) 857-7000
Fax: (202) 828-6141

What Company Does: With nearly 10 million members, the National Geographic Society is the largest nonprofit scientific and educational organization in the world. Its mission is to increase geographic knowledge. Continuing a historic commitment to conservation, its flagship magazine, *National Geographic,* regularly features articles on environmental problems around the world. The society publishes three other magazines, as well as books, atlases, maps, and educational materials, and produces top-rated television documentaries, many available on videotape. The Geographic Education Program and the National Geography Bee encourage and support the teaching of geography in the nation's schools. The Committee for Research and Exploration directs society funds into scientific research.

Environmental Programs: Nature is one of the major subjects explored in Geographic books, television programs, and magazine articles. The society has supported more than 4,000 scientific research projects, many related to the environment. In American classrooms, the Geography Education Program demonstrates the link between knowledge of geography and environmental stewardship. The society's editorial offices and production facilities have recycling programs in place.

Company: National Trust for Historic Preservation
Industry: Nonprofit
Address: 1785 Massachusetts Avenue NW, Washington, DC 20036

Phone: (202) 673-4000
Fax: (202) 673-4038

What Company Does: The National Trust for Historic Preservation, chartered by Congress in 1949, is a nonprofit organization with over 250,000 individual members. The mission of the National Trust is to foster an appreciation of the diverse character and meaning of our American cultural heritage and to preserve and revitalize the livability of our communities by leading the nation in saving Americas historic environments. It has seven regional offices, owns eighteen historic house museums, and works with thousands of local community groups in all fifty states.

Environmental Programs: The trust provides technical advice and financial assistance to nonprofit organizations and public agencies engaged in preservation, as well as to the general public; sponsors educational programs, technical workshops, and an annual preservation conference; advocates for protection of the country's heritage in the courts and with legislative and regulatory agencies; sponsors programs to demonstrate how preservation can stimulate community revitalization and economic development; owns and operates historic house museums. It publishes a bimonthly magazine, *Historic Preservation;* a monthly newspaper, *Historic Preservation News;* a legal quarterly, *Preservation Law Reporter;* a bimonthly journal for professionals, *Historic Preservation Forum;* and books and brochures on a variety of related topics.

Company: National Wildlife Federation (NWF)
Industry: Conservation
Contact: Human Resources
Address: 1400 16th Street NW, Washington, DC 20036-2266
Phone: (202) 797-6680
Fax: (202) 797-6646

What Company Does: Founded in 1936, the National Wildlife Federation is the largest American conservation group. Through advocacy, lobbying, publications, education, and grassroots networks it works to advance and disseminate information on biodiversity, energy and water resources, public lands management, and sustainable development. NWF has forty-seven state affiliate organizations and operates eight regional Natural Resource Centers. Also publishes *National Wildlife,* a bimonthly magazine focusing on biodiversity, endangered species, illegal wildlife trade, and habitat on a national level. Also publishes *The Conservation Directory.*

Company: Native Seeds / SEARCH
Industry: Nonprofit
Contact: Mahina Drees, director

Address: 2509 North Campbell Avenue, #325, Tucson, AZ 85719
Phone: (602) 327-9123

What Company Does: Nonprofit conservation organization preserving seeds of crops grown by Native Americans in the Southwest United States. Over 200 varieties of vegetables including corn and squash. Promotes the use of traditional desert foods to prevent and control diabetes. Internships available (limited to Native Americans).

Company: Natural Baby Co.
Industry: Consumer products
Contact: Dan and Jane Martin, owners
Address: 816 Silvia Street, 800B-PR, Trenton, NJ 08628
Phone: (609) 771-9233
Fax: (609) 771-9342

What Company Does: Offers baby products through a mail-order catalog. Products range from organic herbal remedies to books to organic teething biscuits to a range of cloth diapers and mothers' and children's clothing made of natural fibers and organically grown cotton.

Company: Natural Cotton Colours, Inc.
Industry: Textiles
Contact: Sally Fox, president
Address: P.O. Box 66, Wickenburg, AR 85358
Phone: (602) 684-7199
Fax: (602) 684-7299

What Company Does: Founded in 1982, Sally Fox and her company, Natural Cotton Colours,™ have used traditional breeding methods to develop lines of naturally colored cotton with fiber quality, spinnability, and color intensity that can be processed with modern textile equipment. FoxFibre cottons require no dyes or bleaches and whenever possible are organically grown.

Environmental Programs: Natural Cotton Colours is currently working on improved cottons with much greater natural pest tolerance and improved fibers with beautiful new shades and colors. It is the only cotton breeding program in the United States that stresses organic production. In 1993, Natural Cotton Colours won the first ever United Nations Environmental Programme Award for its contribution to the future of the environment and the agricultural and textile industries, the Edison Award for the Most Innovative Company of 1993, the *Good Housekeeping* magazine's 1993 Green Award, and the 1993 IFOAM Organic Cotton Recognition Award.

Company: Natural Resources Defense Council (NRDC)
Industry: Nonprofit
Contact: Jack Murray, director, Development
Address: 40 West 20th Street, New York, NY 10011
Phone: (212) 727-2700
Fax: (212) 727-1773

What Company Does: A nonprofit organization with over 170,000 members dedicated to protecting natural resources, NRDC concentrates its activities in areas of air and water pollution, land use, toxic chemicals, the urban environment, public health, and wildlife and resource protection in the United States and internationally. It is known for its leading-edge research in energy conservation, and its office space has been renovated to be among the most energy efficient in the country. NRDC is a professional organization whose staff members are primarily lawyers and scientists. Publishes *Amicus Journal.*

Company: Nature Conservancy
Industry: Nonprofit
Contact: Vance Blankenbaker, member relations program coordinator
Address: 1815 North Lynn Street, Arlington, VA 22209
Phone: (703) 841-5300
Fax: (703) 841-5373

What Company Does: A nonprofit membership organization established in 1951, dedicated to protecting land where endangered species and threatened ecosystems exist. Purchases land for preservation purposes; maintains the world's largest system of private nature preserves. Internships available.

Company: Neighborhood Open Space Coalition (NOSC)
Industry: Nonprofit
Contact: Anne McClellan, executive director
Address: 72 Reade Street, New York, NY 10007
Phone: (212) 513-7555
Fax: (212) 385-6095

What Company Does: NOSC is a working partnership of over 125 member organizations dedicated to expanding and enhancing parks and open-space opportunities through research, planning, and advocacy. Recognized on local, state, and national levels for innovation and leadership, the coalition assists neighborhood, borough, and citywide open-space efforts to improve the city's quality of life through a wide array of greening projects. Provides technical assistance, develops master plans and specific site designs, leverages financial resources, and provides services to its members. Internships available; contact Mara Kasler.

Company: **Nestlé USA, Inc.**
Industry: Consumer products
Contact: Environmental Affairs Department
Address: 800 North Brand Boulevard, Glendale, CA 91203
Phone: (818) 549-6000

What Company Does: Nestlé is a food manufacturer known for brand names such as Taster's Choice, Nestlé's Quik, Toll House Chocolate Morsels, Carnation, and Lean Cuisine. It is also a major manufacturer of pet food and pet care products.

Environmental Programs: Nestlé has a strong energy-efficiency and resource management program in place. The company practices solid-waste reduction and control through packaging reduction, recycling, and packaging technology. It is the largest user of recyclable aluminum food cans in the United States, and the majority of its other product packaging is either recyclable or made from recyclable materials (including glass, paper, and steel).

Company: **New Forests Project**
Industry: Nonprofit
Contact: Stuart Conway, director
Address: 731 8th Street SE, Washington, DC 20003-2866
Phone: (202) 547-3800
Fax: (202) 546-4784

What Company Does: Founded in 1981, the project works to initiate agroforestry, reforestation, and sustainable development projects in rural villages throughout Africa, Central and South America, and Asia.

Company: **Northeast Sustainable Energy Association (NESEA)**
Industry: Energy
Contact: Michelle Vaillancourt, office manager
Address: 23 Ames Street, Greenfield, MA 01301
Phone: (413) 774-6051
Fax: (413) 774-6053

What Company Does: A nonprofit membership organization founded in 1974 that promotes renewable and sustainable energy sources and energy conservation. Organizes conferences, seminars, and events such as a solar and electric car race. Operates a bookstore and publishes the *Northeast Sun*, a quarterly magazine. Also offers a Resource Referral Service, which promotes members' professional services. Internships available.

Company: Northrop Grumman Corporation
Industry: Manufacturing
Contact: James Hart, Public Affairs
Address: 1840 Century Park East, Los Angeles, CA 90067-2199
Phone: (310) 553-6262
Fax: (310) 553-2076

What Company Does: Northrop Grumman Corporation is a Los Angeles–based, advanced-technology company that designs, develops, and manufactures bombers, fighters, and surveillance aircraft; commercial and military aerostructures; electronic systems; and information systems.

Environmental Programs: Northrop Grumman is committed to pollution prevention. It has an electronic photography system that captures images on a floppy disk, eliminating the hazardous waste associated with conventional photography. It was the first company to participate in a program to reclaim and recycle halon, a fire suppressant that scientists have linked to ozone depletion.

Company: Northwest Coalition for Alternatives to Pesticides (NCAP)
Industry: Nonprofit
Contact: Norma Grier, executive director, or Carrie Swadener, information services coordinator
Address: P.O. Box 1393, Eugene, OR 97440-1393
Phone: (503) 344-5044

What Company Does: NCAP is a grassroots, nonprofit, regional organization dedicated to the reduction of pesticide use through provision and distribution of information on the hazards of pesticides and alternatives to their use. NCAP publishes a quarterly magazine, the *Journal of Pesticide Reform*, focusing on pesticides and pest management.

Environmental Programs: NCAP offers opportunities for a wide variety of volunteer and internship projects in the area of pesticide reform.

Company: NRH Associates, Inc.
Industry: Environmental consulting
Contact: Nancy Holmes, president

Address: P.O. Box 178, Swanton, VT 05488-0178
Phone: (802) 868-5015

What Company Does: Environmental and energy consultants. Programs for waste reduction, reuse, and recycling. Guidance in producing environmentally sound products, packaging, and marketing. Sustainable forestry, tree planting programs, biomass/wood energy consulting.

Company: Occidental Petroleum Company
Industry: Energy
Contact: Catherine deLacy, vice president, Health, Environment and Safety
Address: 10889 Wilshire Boulevard, Suite 1500, Los Angeles, CA 90024
Phone: (213) 208-8800 or general (213) 879-1700
Fax: (213) 443-6934

What Company Does: Occidental is a diversified company engaged in oil exploration and production, chemicals production, and natural gas transmission.

Environmental Programs: Occidental has spent $110 million to meet government compliance requirements at both domestic and foreign facilities. It has reserves of $742 million as of 1993 for remediation efforts at a number of sites. This includes monies budgeted to anticipate future environmental costs for problems at past operating sites, including Love Canal.

Company: OHM Corporation
Industry: Environmental services
Contact: Robert E. McGregor, director, Corporate Human Resources
Address: 16406 U.S. Route 224 East, P.O. Box 551, Findlay, OH 45840
Phone: (419) 423-3526

What Company Does: OHM provides on-site remediation and emergency response services for hazardous and industrial wastes. These services include engineering and design of environmental treatment equipment in combination with technologies, asbestos abatement, implementation, and operation of systems for on-site treatment projects, as well as emergency response to oil and chemical spills, explosions, and industrial accidents. Its revenues were $245 million in 1993. The company has twenty-six locations in the United States.

Company: Organic Wine Company, Inc.
Industry: Sustainable agriculture
Contact: Veronique Raskin, president
Address: 54 Genoa Place, San Francisco, CA 94133
Phone: (800) 477-0167 or (415) 346-5332
Fax: (800) 477-0167, push * key: (415) 346-5332

What Company Does: A producer of wines made from French organic grapes, which means that the grapes were grown without the use of any synthetic pesticides, herbicides, fertilizers, or growth enhancers. For more information on French organic wines and the Organic Wine Company, call the above number or the affiliate Paul Chartrand of Chartrand Imports at (800) 473-7307.

Company: Orion Society
Industry: Nonprofit, environmental education
Contact: Mr. Laurie Lane-Zucker, managing director
Address: 136 East 64th Street, New York, NY 10021
Phone: (212) 758-6475
Fax: (212) 758-6784

What Company Does: The Orion Society is a nonprofit environmental education organization with a constituency that includes many of the country's leading nature writers, artists, scientists, and environmental educators. The society produces publications, model curricula, and national reading series that strive to integrate the humanities and sciences and cultivate nature literacy in people of all ages.

Company: Ortho-McNeil Pharmaceutical
Industry: Pharmaceuticals
Contact: Sandy Yee, manager, Environmental Affairs
Address: Welsh and McKean Roads, Spring House, PA 19477-0776
Phone: (215) 628-5000

What Company Does: Ortho-McNeil's parent company is Johnson & Johnson, a leading manufacturer of pharmaceuticals for prescription use.

Environmental Programs: Ortho-McNeil has internal recycling, waste reduction, and tank upgrade programs and monitors its wastewater. Its cafeteria uses silverware and dishes, which are washed and reused. The company uses recycled paper whenever possible and tries to reduce packaging while meeting FDA requirements, and it recycles glass, cans, and plastic. It also provides environmental leadership training.

Company: **J. Ottman Consulting**
Industry: Environmental consulting
Contact: Jacquelyn Ottman, president
Address: 1133 Broadway, Suite 1211, New York, NY 10010-7903
Phone: (212) 255-3800
Fax: (212) 255-5480

What Company Does: J. Ottman is a marketing resource for consumer products companies looking to develop and promote environmentally sound products. Services include marketing and product positioning, new-product development including concept generation via the firm's proprietary "Getting to Zero"® brainstorming workshops on source reductions, communications, and other topics. Internships available year round. Ms. Ottman is the author of *Green Marketing: Challenges and Opportunities* (NTC Business Books, 1993).

Company: **Overseas Private Investment Corporation (OPIC)**
Industry: Finance
Contact: Christina Kunek Halpern, credit analyst
Address: 1100 New York Avenue NW, Washington, DC 20537
Phone: Corporate information: (202) 336-8799; Jobs: (202) 336-8682

What Company Does: The Overseas Private Investment Corporation is a U.S. government agency that encourages American private business investment in developing countries, newly emerging democracies, and fledging free-market economies. OPIC assists American investors through financing of business through loans and loan guaranties; insuring investments against a broad range of political risks; and providing a variety of investor services. OPIC supports, finances, and insures projects that have a positive effect on U.S. employment, are financially sound, and promise significant benefits to the social, economic, and environmental development of the host country.

Environmental Programs: OPIC has supported the formation of a $70 million privately owned and privately managed equity investment fund, which is managed by the Global Environmental Fund Management Corporation. It has developed environmental assessment standards that have become the model for other multilateral institutions. OPIC conducts an environmental assessment of every project proposed for financing or insurance and regularly declines support for projects that, in its judgment, would have an unreasonable or major adverse impact on the environment of the host country. (The corporation is currently developing forestry standards for Russia.) Lastly,

OPIC sponsors environment-related investment missions and initiatives to various developing countries.

Company: **Oxfam America**
Industry: Nonprofit
Contact: Carolyn Walden
Address: 26 West Street, Boston MA 02111-1206
Phone: (617) 482-1211

What Company Does: Oxfam America is a nonprofit, international agency that funds self-help development and disaster-relief projects in poor countries in Africa, Asia, Latin America, and the Caribbean. They also produce and distribute educational materials for people in the United States on issues of hunger and development. Unlike many international aid agencies Oxfam America neither seeks nor accepts U.S. government funds. In its most recent fiscal year, revenues totaled more than $13 million, most of which were donations from individuals and private religious, student, and civic groups. Internships available.

Environmental Programs: Oxfam development projects provide: seeds and tools to help people get started; wells, irrigation systems, and clean drinking water; credit for farmers too poor to get land on their own; training in marketing, accounting, and agricultural methods; training in organizing techniques to empower local people; and training in literacy and numerary. Publishes the *Oxfam America Trading* catalog, which is helping to initiate, nurture, and implement a global system of fair trading.

Company: **Ozarks Resource Center**
Industry: Nonprofit
Contact: Janice Lorrain, director
Address: Box 3, Brixey, MO 65618
Phone: (417) 679-4773

What Company Does: The Ozarks Resource Center is a nonprofit, federally tax-exempt organization working to promote: appropriate technology, sustainable agriculture and forestry, environmentally responsible practices, economic development, and self-reliance for the family, community, and bioregion.

Company: **Parnassus Income Fund**
Industry: Finance
Address: 244 California Street, San Francisco, CA 94111
Phone: (800) 999-3505 or (415) 362-3505

What Company Does: The Parnassus Income Fund takes into consideration the following factors for investment in a company: fair treatment of employees, sound environmental policies, a good equal-employment opportunity policy, quality products and services, sensitivity to the community where it operates, and ethical business practices. Internships available.

Company: Patagonia, Inc.
Industry: Outdoor apparel
Contact: Stephanie Smith, corporate recruiter
Address: P.O. Box 150, Ventura, CA 93002
Phone: (805) 643-8616

What Company Does: Patagonia is a designer and distributor of clothing for outdoor sports such as climbing, fishing, kayaking, skiing, and sailing. The company also produces sportswear and functional, durable children's clothes.

Environmental Programs: Patagonia has begun a comprehensive environmental review process to examine all the materials and methods used in making its products. All catalogs are printed on recycled paper. Patagonia's catalog includes a statement of the company's philosophy to live within limits and to focus on making long-lasting, high-quality products. The company is committed to donating 1 percent of sales in the form of monetary donations, products, and employee resources to preserving and restoring the natural environment.

Company: Pathmark (a division of Supermarkets General)
Industry: Retail
Contact: John Shipton, senior vice president, Marketing & Public Affairs
Address: 301 Blair Road, Woodbridge, NJ 07095
Phone: (908) 499-3000 or (908) 499-4105
Fax: (908) 499-6805

What Company Does: Pathmark operates combination grocery and drug stores. Its parent company, Supermarkets Holdings Corp., also owns Rickel Home Centers and employs 33,556 associates.

Environmental Programs: Pathmark Stores, Inc., engages in significant internal recycling. The company also leases space to "We Can" for bottle recycling and Pathmark pays customers $.02 for each shopping bag they reuse. Supermarkets Holdings Corp. is concerned with solid-waste management.

Company: PAX Analytics, Inc.
Industry: Consulting, computer systems

Contact: David Greenberg, president
Address: 227 West Leyden Road, Colrain, MA 01340
Phone: (413) 624-5557

What Company Does: Designs environmental monitoring systems for lay environmentalists utilizing a Macintosh computer. Ideal for citizens' groups involved in local campaigns to monitor industrial polluters, nuclear powerplants, etc. Brochure on request.

Company: PAX World Fund
Industry: Investments
Contact: Luther E. Tyson, president
Address: 224 State Street, Portsmouth, NH 03801
Phone: (603) 431-8022

What Company Does: The PAX World Fund is a twenty-five-year-old mutual fund specializing in socially responsible investing.

Environmental Programs: The fund emphasizes investment projects with third world implications for development or conservation.

Company: Pennzoil Company
Industry: Energy
Contact: Thomas C. Powell, vice president, Administrative Affairs
Address: Pennzoil Place, P.O. Box 2967, Houston, TX 77252-2967
Phone: (713) 546-8686

What Company Does: Pennzoil is engaged in exploration, development, and marketing of oil and natural gas; manufacture and marketing of petroleum products; mining and marketing of sulfur; operation of quick lube centers and transportation components.

Environmental Programs: Pennzoil has ninety full-time employees involved in either the corporate Environmental Safety and Health Affairs Department or in direct field support for environmental, safety, and health activities at manufacturing, service, and production facilities. A corporate environmental safety and health policy, issued by the CEO and a comprehensive set of environmental, safety, and health principles provide the authority and guidance to implement regulatory requirements and voluntary programs.

Company: People for the Ethical Treatment of Animals (PETA)
Industry: Nonprofit
Contact: Michael Rodman, personnel director
Address: P.O. Box 42516, Washington, DC 20015-0516

Phone: (301) 770-PETA
Fax: (301) 770-8969

What Company Does: People for the Ethical Treatment of Animals is a non-profit animal protection organization founded in 1980 to promote the rights and improve the lives of animals. PETA works through public education, research and investigations, special events, campaigns and demonstrations, and legal and political action. It publishes a quarterly news magazine, *PETA News,* as well as a catalog of cruelty-free products. Internships available.

Company: PepsiCo
Industry: Consumer products
Contact: Elaine Franklin, manager, Corporate Relations
Address: Purchase, NY 10577
Phone: (914) 767-7150 or general (914) 253-2000
Fax: (914) 253-2203

What Company Does: PepsiCo is known for its operations in three different markets, including soft drinks (Pepsi, Diet Pepsi, Mountain Dew, Slice), restaurants (Pizza Hut, Kentucky Fried Chicken, Taco Bell), and snack foods (Frito-Lay, Ruffles, and Doritos).

Environmental Programs: Because of its size and various businesses, PepsiCo stresses environmental action at the division level. The divisions work on joint solutions in a number of areas, such as source reduction, packaging, and recycling. Their programs are as varied as the number of facilities they have—a system including some 24,000 restaurants, 44 snack-food plants, and 95 bottling plants. Each division has an officer or function that handles environmental issues.

For more information contact: Sal Porazzo, director of environmental affairs, Pepsi-Cola Company, One Pepsi Way, Somers, NY 10589, (914) 767-7150; Mary Staples, manager of government affairs, Frito-Lay, Inc., 7701 Legacy Drive, Plano, TX 75024-4099, (214) 334-2125; Steve Provost, vice president, Public Affairs, Kentucky Fried Chicken, 1441 Gardiner Lane, Louisville, KY 40213, (502) 456-8434; Christopher Townsend, director of government and community affairs, Taco Bell Corporation, 17901 Von Karman, Irvine, CA 92714, (714) 863-5296; Larry Whitt, vice president, Public Affairs, Pizza Hut, Inc., 9111 East Douglas, Wichita, KS 67207, (316) 681-9234.

Company: Philips Electronics North American Corporation
Industry: Manufacturing
Contact: Ann C. Pizzorusso, director of environmental affairs

Address: 100 East 42nd Street, New York, NY 10017-5699
Phone: (212) 850-5472 or general (212) 850-5000
Fax: (212) 850-5515

What Company Does: Philips markets its products under the Norelco, Sylvania, and Magnavox brand names. Philips makes compact discs, televisions and video equipment, semiconductors, appliances, and light bulbs.

Environmental Programs: Philips introduced the Earth Light SLX18 Lamp, considered revolutionary for its economic and environmental benefits, and won first place in the environmental category of the *Discover* magazine awards for technological innovation. Philips semiconductor facility received the EPA's Regional Administration Award for the fourth consecutive year for consistently meeting federal and state requirements of the Resource Conservation and Recovery Act. Philips is working on new technology to reduce the use of CFCs in its operating divisions.

Philips has also won the National Development Association's award for environmental communication and outreach and six Green Flag awards for environmental compliance at its plants in the Mexican Border Zone.

Company: Planned Parenthood
Industry: Nonprofit
Contact: Barbara Snow, vice president for communications
Address: 810 Seventh Avenue, New York, NY 10019
Phone: (212) 541-7800
Fax: (212) 765-4711

What Company Does: The world's oldest and largest voluntary reproductive health care organization, founded in 1916. Has more than 22,000 volunteers and staff members nationwide and provides medical, educational, and counseling services to meet family planning needs of nearly 5 million Americans each year. Its political arm, the Planned Parenthood Action Fund, works actively on lobbying efforts and voter identification to preserve the right of reproductive choice. It also has an international division, which assists developing countries. For information on Planned Parenthood's resource catalog, including information on birth control, reproductive health and rights, and sexuality, contact the Marketing Department at the address above or call (212) 261-4656. Volunteer opportunities available; contact Lois A. Mirabella.

Company: Population Council
Industry: Nonprofit
Contact: Margaret Catley-Carlson, president

Address: 1 Dag Hammarskjold Plaza, New York, NY 10017
Phone: (212) 339-0500
Fax: (212) 755-6052

What Company Does: The Population Council seeks to improve the well-being and reproductive health of current and future generations around the world, and to help achieve a humane, equitable, and sustainable balance between people and resources. The council, a nonprofit, nongovernmental research organization established in 1952, has a multinational board of trustees; its New York headquarters supports a global network of regional and country offices.

Environmental Programs: The council publishes two scholarly journals, *Population and Development Review* and *Studies in Family Planning*, and disseminates information on population issues through publications, conferences, seminars, and workshops. It also grants fellowships for advanced degree training in population-related studies and sponsors postdoctoral training in biomedical research related to human reproductive physiology.

Company: Population Reference Bureau (PRB)
Industry: Nonprofit
Contact: Peter J. Donaldson, president
Address: 1875 Connecticut Avenue NW, Suite 520, Washington, DC 20009
Phone: (202) 483-1100
Fax: (202) 328-3937

What Company Does: The Population Reference Bureau is a nonadvocacy educational organization that gathers, interprets, and disseminates information on population trends and their public policy implications, globally and in the United States. PRB works in four program areas: publications, information and education, international programs, and U.S. policy studies. Services include publications, seminars, training, technical assistance, and media outreach. Internships available.

Company: PPG Industries, Inc.
Industry: Manufacturing
Contact: Paul M. King, Environment, Health, and Safety Department
Address: One PPG Place, Pittsburgh, PA 15272
Phone: (412) 434-3703
Fax: (412) 434-3490

What Company Does: PPG is the world's largest automotive and industrial coatings supplier. It produces flat and fabricated glass products, fiberglass, chlorine and caustic soda, and various specialty chemicals.

Environmental Programs: PPG is committed to waste reduction and enhancement of the health, safety, and environmental performance of all its operations. It has had an independent, worldwide compliance assurance program since 1983. As part of its environmental efforts, PPG's company units are working diligently to reduce emissions, even permitted and reported emissions. From 1988 to 1993, PPG's operations reduced by 66 percent those air, water, and solid-waste emissions that are reported yearly to the U.S. EPA.

Company: Premark International, Inc.
Industry: Consumer products
Contact: Isabelle Goossen, manager, Public Relations
Address: 1717 Deerfield Road, Deerfield, IL 60015
Phone: (708) 405-6218
Fax: (708) 405-6311

What Company Does: Premark International, Inc., consists of: Tupperware, the world's leading manufacturer and marketer of premium-quality plastic products for food; the Food Equipment Group, which manufacturers, sells and services commercial products worldwide for food preparation, cooking, weighing, wrapping, baking, refrigeration; Ralph Wilson Plastics Co., the largest manufacturer of decorative laminates in the United States; Tibbals Flooring Co., a maker of prefinished hardwood flooring products; Florida Tile, a leading U.S. ceramic tile manufacturer; the West Bend Company, a manufacturer of small electric kitchen appliances and direct-to-the-home stainless steel cookware; and Precor, a maker of aerobic fitness equipment.

Environmental Programs: The company has a Corporate Responsibility Committee, which oversees its environmental policies. It also employs a director of regulatory affairs responsible for environmental compliance and a senior environmental council. Premark has a long-standing worldwide, annual environmental and safety audit program.

Company: Price Waterhouse
Industry: Accounting
Contact: Jonathan Bellis, partner
Address: 1177 Avenue of the Americas, New York, NY 10036
Phone: (212) 596-7570

Price Waterhouse is a public accounting firm and a leader in providing environmental auditing and accounting guidance to major corporations across the country. Services include: design of audit procedures that enable audit engagement teams to report to management, audit committees, or other interested parties on the adequacy of a client's financial accounting and disclosure practices in the environmental area; comparative analysis of client environmental accounting and disclosure policies against prevalent industry practice; industry- or company-specific accounting, disclosure, and tax guidance for environmental matters, with presentation in either written or seminar form; assistance to clients involved in merger and acquisition transactions in understanding and quantifying major financial risks in the environmental area; and assistance in environmental function management reviews, benchmarking, and information systems.

Company: **Procter & Gamble Company**
Industry: Consumer products
Contact: Deborah D. Anderson, vice president, Environmental Quality Worldwide
Address: 2 Procter & Gamble Plaza, Cincinnati, OH 45202-3314
Phone: (513) 983-1100

What Company Does: The Procter & Gamble Company is a major developer, manufacturer, and marketer of consumer goods in a broad range of product categories worldwide. Primary product categories include soap, paper, food and beverages, and health and beauty aids. Some of its best-known brands are Crest, Pampers, Tide, Oil of Olay, Vicks, Crisco, and Ivory. The company employs over 103,000 people in more than fifty-five operations located throughout North America, Europe, Canada, the Far East, and South America and has begun to expand into the Eastern European market. Brands are marketed in over 140 countries.

Environmental Programs: Procter & Gamble's policy is to ensure that its products, packaging, and operations are safe for employees, consumers, and the environment. The company is committed to reducing the environmental impact of its products and packaging in its design, manufacturing, distribution, use, and disposal whenever possible. P&G created a $20 million fund to help develop the infrastructure worldwide to advance composting of leaf and yard waste, food waste, and paper/paperboard packaging and products that are otherwise not recovered from municipal solid waste.

Company: **Progressive Asset Management, Inc.**
Industry: Finance
Contact: Thomas Van Dyck, vice president
Address: 1814 Franklin Street, Seventh floor, Oakland, CA 94612

Phone: (510) 834-3722 or (800) 786-2998
Fax: (510) 836-1621

What Company Does: Progressive Portfolio Services is a division of Progressive Asset Management, the first and largest full-service investment brokerage in America to specialize in socially responsible investing. Progressive Portfolio Services is designed to assist individuals and institutions in implementing socially responsible investment policies and identifying investment managers who can perform while applying social screens. Services provided include assistance in developing social and financial objectives, selection of investment managers capable of utilizing social screening, social screening of current investment managers.

Company: **Progressive Securities Financial Services Corporation**
Industry: Finance
Contact: Carsten Henninsen, president
Address: 2435 SW Fifth Avenue, Portland, OR 97201
Phone: (503) 224-7828 or (800) PRO-GRESS (776-4737)
Fax: (503) 224-5633

What Company Does: Founded in 1982, Progressive Securities is one of the oldest money management firms in the country specializing in socially and environmentally responsible investing. Investment research incorporates the following social concerns into its analysis: environment, energy, employee relations, weapons production, corporate citizenship, repressive regimes, product quality and safety, animal testing, tobacco, alcohol and gambling, and community development. Internships available.

Company: **Public Citizen**
Industry: Nonprofit
Contact: Julia Lyman, director of communications
Address: 2000 P Street NW, #610, Washington, DC 20036
Phone: (202) 833-3000

What Company Does: Nonprofit membership organization founded by Ralph Nader, representing consumer interests. Fights for safe products, clean energy, corporate and government accountability. Publishes a magazine, health letter, and books.

Company: **Quaker Oats Company**
Industry: Consumer products

Contact: Laura V. Jackson, coordinator, Media Relations
Address: Quaker Tower, 321 North Clark Street, Chicago, IL 60610
Phone: (312) 222-7372
Fax: (312) 222-8304

What Company Does: Quaker's brands respond to the desire of today's consumers for an active, healthy lifestyle by providing good nutrition and convenience. Hot cereals, ready-to-eat cereals, Gatorade thirst quencher, Rice-a-Roni and Noodle-Roni, Aunt Jemima breakfast products, Quaker Rice and Grain Cakes, and even premium and high-nutrition pet foods are a few of the products that meet those criteria. Internships available; contact Reva Hank, (312) 222-2852.

Environmental Programs: Quaker has a long-standing, well-documented commitment to protection of human health and the environment and is continually seeking to reduce its utilization of natural resources and emissions. The company's fundamental policy is to conduct its businesses responsibly and in a manner designed to protect its employees, consumers, public health, and the natural environment.

Company: Rachel Perry, Inc.
Industry: Consumer products
Contact: Melinda Rubin, marketing director
Address: 9111 Mason Avenue, Chatsworth, CA 91311
Phone: (818) 888-5881
Fax: (818) 882-1005

What Company Does: Rachel Perry is a natural cosmetics company dedicated to the health and beauty of the skin.

Environmental Programs: Rachel Perry is committed to preserving and maintaining the rain forests of the world. The company participates in a donation program designed to benefit those valuable resources. Products emphasize natural and renewable ingredients. Rachel Perry uses recycled boxes and paper and reusable silverware, glassware, and plates. Cans and bottles are recycled. The company supports animal rights, does not test on animals, and contributes to many animal welfare groups.

Company: Rainforest Action Network (RAN)
Industry: Nonprofit
Contact: Delaine McCullough
Address: 450 Sansome Street, Suite 700, San Francisco, CA 94111
Phone: (415) 398-4404

What Company Does: RAN is a nonprofit activist organization working to save the world's rain forests. It works with other environmental, indigenous, and human rights organizations in tropical countries. The network uses a variety of interns with computer, marketing, and communications skills. These internships are available for university credit in campaigns, RAN's information department, membership, and other areas.

Environmental Programs: RAN has served campaigns focused on rain forest issues including its Ecuador Oil campaign, Amazonia campaign, Mitsubishi Boycott, and Tropical Timber campaign.

Company: **Rainforest Alliance**
Industry: Nonprofit
Contact: Karin Kreider, director of finance & administration
Address: 65 Bleecker Street, New York, NY 10012
Phone: (212) 677-1900
Fax: (212) 677-2187

What Company Does: The Rainforest Alliance is an international nonprofit organization dedicated to conservation of the world's endangered tropical forests. Our primary mission is to develop and promote economically viable and socially desirable alternatives to tropical deforestation. Current activities include the Smart Wood and Eco-O.K. Banana certification programs, the Natural Resources and Rights Program, the Amazon Rivers Program, the Conservation Media Center, and the Catalyst Grants Program.

Company: **Rainforest Crunch / Community Products, Inc.**
Industry: Consumer products
Contact: Martha Broad, comanager
Address: RD 2, Box 1950, Montpelier, VT 05602
Phone: (802) 229-1840 or (800) 927-2695

What Company Does: Ben Cohen of Ben & Jerry's launched Community Products with the idea of using "business as a force for social change." The company buys Brazil and cashew nuts as a small step to saving the rain forest and helps finance a worker-owned nut shelling coop in the Amazon so that they can increase its profits and reduce costs. Rainforest Crunch is a Brazil- and cashew-nut butter-crunch candy; and 40 percent of company profits go toward saving the rain forest and other environmental projects.

Company: **Rainforest Foundation International, Inc. (RFI)**
Industry: Nonprofit
Contact: Larry Cox, executive director

Address: 270 Lafayette Street, Suite 1205, New York, NY 10012
Phone: (212) 431-9098
Fax: (212) 431-9197

What Company Does: The Rainforest Foundation works with Indians in Brazil to protect the rain forest and the human rights of its indigenous peoples through public awareness, political action, and practical assistance. RFI publishes a quarterly journal with updates on the foundation's programs, projects, and activities, including national and international campaigning, fund-raisers, and events. Updates on the environment and different indigenous groups are also given. RFI produces and circulates an annual report of activities, press releases, and letter writing campaigns.

Company: RCI Environmental
Industry: Environmental services
Contact: Greg Upah, president
Address: 17772 Preston Road, Suite 202, Dallas, TX 75252
Phone: (214) 250-6608

What Company Does: RCI Environmental provides indoor air pollution consultancy services, including residential, commercial, and industrial site evaluations and self-test kits for environmental hazards in the home. The company also publishes environmental guidebooks on residential health hazards and works with medical professionals on environmental health problems.

Company: Real Goods Trading Corporation
Industry: Alternative energy products
Contact: Helen Sizemore, executive assistant
Address: 966 Mazzoni Street, Ukiah, CA 95482-3471
Phone: (707) 468-9292
Fax: (707) 468-0301

What Company Does: Real Goods offers alternative energy systems, tools and appliances, and water-conserving plumbing devices. Catalog also merchandises environmental products ranging from toys and books to personal products and gifts. Publishes and sells *Alternative Energy Sourcebook*, and publishes a quarterly newsletter for customers, *Real Goods News*, which highlights new products and developments in technology. Also offers technical assistance and customer support. Real Goods, through its Institute for Independent Living, offers workshops dedicated to the study of all aspects of self-sufficent and sustainable lifestyles. For information and registration, call the registrar at (800) 762-7325. Internships are considered.

Company: Regional Environmental Center for Central and Eastern Europe
Industry: Nonprofit, sustainable development
Contact: Winston Bowman, public relations manager
Address: Miklos ter 1, Budapest, Hungary 1035
Phone: 36-1-250-3401
Fax: 36-1-250-3403

What Company Does: The center was established in 1990 to address the issues of regional environmental management and to provide a way to increase public access to environmental information. The staff has created a comprehensive base of environmental information, which includes electronically accessed sources. A not-for-profit organization, it also gives grants to environmental NGOs in the region and offers policy guidance to government officials.

Company: René Dubos Center for Human Environments
Industry: Nonprofit
Contact: William R. Eblen, president
Address: 100 East 85th Street, New York, NY 10028
Phone: (212) 249-7745 or (212) 772-2033

What Company Does: The René Dubos Center for Human Environments is an independent education and research organization founded by the eminent scientist and humanist René Dubos to focus on the humanistic and social aspects of environmental problems. The center's mission is to help decision-makers and the general public formulate policies for the resolution of environmental conflicts and for the creation of new environmental values.

Environmental Programs: The René Dubos Center launched the Decade of Environmental Literacy in 1990 in cooperation with the United Nations Environmental Program to develop materials for both formal and nonformal education that respond to the need for basic knowledge and skills for dealing with environmental problems and issues in order to improve environmental literacy in the schools, in the workplace, and in the community.

Company: Resource Recovery Systems, Inc. (RRS)
Industry: Environmental services
Address: 36 Plains Road, Essex, CT 06426
Phone: (203) 767-7057
Fax: (203) 767-7069

What Company Does: RRS provides an innovative waste disposal alternative to municipalities and waste haulers by cooperating with them to build and operate recycling systems. Services offered by RRS include design and building of recycling systems; operation of RRS recycling facilities; consulting on system and program design; and system sales. The company has over fifteen years of experience building and operating recycling facilities using its own proven technology.

Company: **Resources for the Future**
Industry: Nonprofit, research and policy analysis
Contact: Debra Montanino, director of external affairs
Address: 1616 P Street NW, Washington, DC 20036
Phone: (202) 328-5000
Fax: (202) 939-3460

What Company Does: Nonprofit think tank founded in 1952 to provide impartial and independent research and policy analysis about natural resources and the environment. Conducts research, policy analysis, and outreach on development, conservation, and use of natural resources and on the quality of the environment. Offers internship program, fellowship program, small grants program, and dissertation award, and appoints university fellows.

Company: **Reynolds Metal Company**
Industry: Manufacturing
Contact: Ronald N. Thomas, Public Relations
Address: Richmond, VA 23261
Phone: (804) 281-3987

What Company Does: Reynolds Metal Company is a global corporation employing 29,000 men and women at more than 100 locations worldwide. Through its wholly owned operations and others in which it has varying interests, Reynolds conducts business in twenty-two countries throughout the world. The company produces, fabricates, distributes, sells, and recycles aluminum in various forms from ingot to brand name consumer products.

Environmental Programs: Reynolds began recycling more than fifty years ago by reprocessing scrap that was left over from fabricating operations. In March 1968, the company created the Reynolds Aluminum Recycling Company (RARCO), which offers to pay individuals or organizations cash for aluminum cans or other clean household aluminum. This material is shredded, sent to a Reynolds reclamation plant, and melted to be used to make useful aluminum products once again. During the 1980s Reynolds recycled almost 100 percent of the cans it manufactured. It has recycled more than 171 billion all-aluminum cans and has paid recyclers more than $1.7 billion.

Company: **Rocky Mountain Institute (RMI)**
Industry: Nonprofit, energy
Contact: Amory Lovins, president
Address: 1739 Snowmass Creek Road, Snowmass, CO 81654-9199
Phone: (303) 927-3851
Fax: (303) 927-4178

What Company Does: A nonprofit resource policy center, RMI was founded in 1982 by Hunter and Amory Lovins who worked in over fifteen countries as consultants in the field of energy efficiency and as policy advisors to Friends of the Earth. A staff of thirty researchers and support personnel oversees dissemination of research findings through publications, educational programs, and consulting. The institute focuses its work in seven areas—agriculture, economic renewal, energy, security, transportation, green development, and water—and carries on international outreach and technical exchange programs. The *Rocky Mountain Newsletter* is published three times a year.

Company: **Rogers Environmental Management, Inc. (REM)**
Industry: Environmental services
Contact: James A. Rogers, president
Address: 16-01 Broadway, Fair Lawn, NJ 07410
Phone: (201) 791-7377
Fax: (201) 797-3059

What Company Does: Rogers Environmental Management provides specialized technical consulting services to industry in the areas of compliance management, pollution prevention, comprehensive facilities permit programs, occupational health and safety, and site remediation. With over twenty years' professional experience in the markets of New Jersey and other states in the Northeast, REM has assisted hundreds of clients in navigating the regulatory high seas of federal, state, and local programs. REM listens to manufacturers and communicates their process to the regulators. REM also has projects in Mexico, Italy, Canada, and other international venues.

Company: **Ruder-Finn**
Industry: Communications

Contact: Ellen Schaplowsky, executive vice president and founder, Marketing for the Environment
Address: 301 East 57th Street, New York, NY 10022
Phone: (212) 593-6400
Fax: (212) 715-1662

What Company Does: Ruder-Finn, founded in 1948, is one of the world's largest independent public relations agencies. It is headquartered in New York, with offices in Boston, Chicago, Los Angeles, Raleigh, North Carolina, and Washington D.C., and international offices in London, Paris, and Stockholm.

Environmental Programs: The agency has a long history of involvement in environmental issues, dating from 1963 and its work with President Kennedy to create a massive public information program that helped win public support for the Nuclear Test Ban Treaty. Ruder-Finn's Marketing for the Environment Group was founded in 1990 to formalize the agency's longstanding experience and expertise in developing and implementing environment-related communications strategies for corporations, brand businesses, and nonprofit organizations.

Company: Sacred Earth Network
Industry: Nonprofit, communications
Contact: Bill Pfeiffer, executive director
Address: 267 E Street, Petersham, MA 01366
Phone: (508) 724-3443
Fax: (508) 724-3436

What Company Does: The Sacred Earth Network is an international nonprofit organization that provides outreach, training, technical support, and information services for an international electronic mail network that facilitates communication links between environmental organizations, educators, and activists. Internship available. Contact through the mail preferred.

Company: Safe Designs, Inc.
Industry: Advertising
Contact: Irene Marshall, vice president
Address: 541 Taylor Way, Suite 2, Belmont, CA 94002
Phone: (415) 508-2377
Fax: (415) 591-3095

What Company Does: Safe Designs is a certified woman-owned enterprise providing promotional items since 1981. Its Environmental Division has a line of products made with recycled material or with an environmental message. In 1992 the firm received a Special Commendation for Environmental Innovation from the Peninsula Conservation Center. A warehouse is available for inventory programs. Also available are incentive award programs, tradeshow giveaways, safety and motivational programs, mailing inserts, wearables, and holiday gifts.

Company: Safety-Kleen
Industry: Environmental services, recycling
Contact: Robert Burian, senior vice president, Human Resources
Address: 1000 North Randall Road, Elgin, IL 60123
Phone: (708) 697-8460

What Company Does: Safety-Kleen is a large-scale recycler of solvents and waste oil with markets in the United States, Europe, Asia, and Australia. The company provides cleaning-solvent services to hundreds of thousands of businesses, including small auto repair, dry cleaning, and industrial companies. Its services include working with solvents, lubricants, paint thinners, and coolants in various industries.

Company: Safeway, Inc.
Industry: Retail
Contact: Melita Elmore, vice president, Environment, Health and Safety
Address: 4th and Jackson Streets, Oakland, CA 94660
Phone: (510) 891-3670 or general (510) 891-3000

What Company Does: Safeway is a major retail grocer, owning and operating 1,080 U.S. and Canadian grocery stores, of which 44 percent are "superstores." Safeway also operates plants that supply various private-label grocery products.

Environmental Programs: Safeway has an active Environment, Health and Safety Division, which offers in-house technical consulting and training to employees. Also, it has an educational program directed to customers in stores. It highlights environmentally benign products and packaging, offers reusable bags at cost, and provides environmental tips. It also has energy management and recycling programs in place.

Company: Save America's Forests
Industry: Environmental
Contact: Carl Ross, codirector and founder

Address: 4 Library Court SE, Washington, DC 20003
Phone: (202) 544-9219

What Company Does: A coalition of businesses, groups, and individuals around the country working to make ecological values and forest protection the top priority for America's publicly owned national forests. Free *Citizen Action Guide*. Internships available; contact Jason Halbert.

Company: Save the Children
Industry: Nonprofit
Contact: Lee Mullane, communications director
Address: 54 Wilton Road, Westport, CT 06680
Phone: (203) 221-4130 or general (203) 221-4000
Fax: (203) 222-1067

What Company Does: A nonprofit, nonpolitical, and nonsectarian organization dedicated to improving the quality of life and ensuring the rights of disadvantaged children through programs in health, education, economic opportunity, and emergency relief. Some internships available.

Environmental Programs: Save the Children helps families and communities devise locally appropriate ways to improve their children's lives while preserving the environment. Projects include community and school woodlots and gardens, reforestation projects, intercropping, water catchments, and environmental education.

Company: Save-the-Redwoods League
Industry: Nonprofit
Contact: John B. Dewitt, secretary and executive director
Address: 114 Sansome Street, Room 605, San Francisco, CA 94104
Phone: (415) 362-2352
Fax: (415) 362-7017

What Company Does: Save-the-Redwoods League is a national nonprofit conservation organization, founded in 1918, that acquires coast redwood and giant sequoia forest land for protection in the California Redwood State Parks and in other public parks and preserves. The league purchases available Redwood forestland at its fair-market value. The land is then incorporated into one of the California Redwood State Parks or other public redwood parks and natural preserves. The league's program is based upon expert determination of the optimum area required to preserve the finest redwood forests in their natural state as complete watersheds. The league also publishes a number of informational pamphlets and booklets about redwoods and the redwood state parks.

Company: Scenic Hudson
Industry: Nonprofit
Contact: Cara Lee, environmental director
Address: 9 Vassar Street, Poughkeepsie, NY 12601
Phone: (914) 473-4440
Fax: (914) 473-2648

What Company Does: An organization founded to preserve, restore, and enhance the scenic, historic, and ecological recreational resources of the Hudson River and broaden understanding and appreciation of the Hudson Valley in the nation. Publishes quarterly newsletter entitled *Scenic Hudson News*. Internships available.

Company: Schering-Plough Corporation
Industry: Pharmaceuticals
Contact: Linn Weiss, staff vice president, Corporate Communications
Address: One Giralda Farms, Madison, NJ 07940
Phone: (201) 822-7000
Fax: (201) 822-7447

What Company Does: Schering-Plough is a research-based company engaged in the discovery, development, manufacture, and marketing of pharmaceutical and health care products worldwide. Pharmaceutical products include prescription drugs, vision care, and animal health products. Health care products include over-the-counter foot care and sun care products sold primarily in the United States.

Environmental Programs: As part of its corporate responsibility, Schering-Plough is committed to protecting the quality of the environment. It has an established environmental auditing program to ensure that all worldwide facilities comply with a comprehensive corporate environmental policy. Active in recycling programs, Schering-Plough is also playing a lead role in a New Jersey pilot program on pollution prevention. The company spent nearly 44 million in 1994 on environmental improvements, approximately 16 percent of total capital projects.

Company: Schultz Communications
Industry: Communications
Contact: Randall D. Schultz, president
Address: 9412 Admiral Nimitz NE, Albuquerque, NM 87111
Phone: (505) 822-8222
Fax: (505) 822-9122

What Company Does: A full-service advertising, public relations, and marketing company. Publishes *The Consumer's Guide to Planet Earth*, a handy resource for companies that offers a wide range of earth-friendly products and services, updated every six months. To purchase copies of the *Consumer's Guide*, send $7 to the above address.

Company: EF Schumacher Society
Industry: Nonprofit
Contact: R. Swann
Address: Box 76A, RD 3, Great Barrington, MA 01230
Phone: (413) 528-1737
Fax: (413) 528-4472

What Company Does: Research and application, and publication of books regarding tools for building sustainable communities. Conducts annual lecture program, maintains library and resource center.

Company: Scientific Certification System (SCS)
Industry: Consulting
Contact: Stanley P. Rhodes, president and founder
Address: The Ordway Building, Suite 901, One Kaiser Plaza, Oakland, CA 94612-2113
Phone: (510) 832-1415 or (510) 832-0359

What Company Does: Scientific Certification Systems is an independent certification organization that provides manufacturers, retailers, policy-makers, and consumers with scientific documentation of environmental and food safety claims appearing on products. SCS has issued dozens of Environmental Report Cards to companies undergoing full "cradle-to-grave" analysis. The report card provides a comprehensive environmental analysis of a product and its packaging.

Company: Seeds of Change
Industry: Agriculture
Contact: Nina Simons, director of marketing and public relations
Address: 621 Old Santa Fe Trail, #10, Santa Fe, NM 87501
Phone: (505) 983-8956 ext.1218, or for catalog (800) 95-SEEDS
Fax: (505) 983-8957

What Company Does: Seeds of Change collects and grows out heirloom and traditional seeds to reintroduce the best varieties of garden seeds saved by generations of ancestors. It was founded in 1988 to become the only company nationally to sell only certified organic, open-pollinated seeds. Retail distribution has grown by over 50 percent per year to include over 800 retailers in the United States and Canada. Free award-winning catalog, with lots of valuable growing information and essays, and the company's book, *Seeds of Change: The Living Treasure*, the definitive work on biodiversity, organics, and nutrition, are available through the company. Write for information on internships.

Company: Seventh Generation, Inc.
Industry: Consumer products
Contact: Oren Kronick, executive assistant
Address: Colchester, VT 05446-1672
Phone: (802) 655-6777, ext. 799
Fax: (802) 655-2700

What Company Does: Seventh Generation offers over 300 products for a healthy environment, including "green" cotton clothing and linens, recycled and unbleached paper products, and vegetable-based cleaners.

Environmental Programs: Seventh Generation assesses the impact that its business has on the environment with an annual environmental audit. The company uses the audit to set goals and develop programs that help lessen that impact.

Company: Sharons Finest
Industry: Consumer products
Contact: Judy Bowhall, office administrator
Address: P.O. Box 5020, Santa Rosa, CA 94502-5020
Phone: (707) 576-7050
Fax: (707) 545-7116

What Company Does: Offers and distributes plant-based cheese-alternative products.

Environmental Programs: Marketing materials are printed on recycled paper with soy inks. Ecological products and recycling are part of company philosophy. A portion of profits is donated to groups working to protect rain forests. Cheese alternatives are made from organic soybeans (TofuRella and Zero-Fat Rella), almonds (AlmondRella), and Brazil nuts (VeganRella).

Company: Shell Oil Company
Industry: Energy
Contact: Renata Karlin, senior staff specialist

Address: One Shell Plaza, P.O. Box 2463, Houston, TX 77252
Phone: (713) 241-6161 or (713) 241-4095

What Company Does: Shell is a worldwide producer of oil and gas and a leading U.S. marketer of gasoline. It is also a leading competitor in chemical products, including polymers, catalysts, and detergents.

Environmental Programs: Shell Oil Company consolidated health, safety, and environmental activities into a corporate department headed by a vice president in 1976. In 1990, it introduced an environmentally enhanced, unleaded fuel, SU2000E, designed to help reduce hydrocarbon vapor and carbon monoxide emissions. The company is also involved in research programs to investigate the effects of alternative fuels on air quality. Shell has joined the California Energy Commission in a ten-year program to study and market M85 fuel, a blend of methanol and gasoline. In addition, the company markets natural gas for vehicles through selected California service stations.

Company: J. L. Sherwin & Associates, Inc.
Industry: Consulting
Contact: John Sherwin, president
Address: 23 Diamond Spring Road, Suite 3, Denville, NJ 07834
Phone: (201) 625-0600
Fax: (201) 625-7505

What Company Does: J. L. Sherwin & Associates is an environmental management consulting firm that incorporates environmental issues into the day-to-day and long-term management of business operations. One key area of focus is helping companies reduce, reuse, and increase recycled content in their packaging. The results of its audit and planning process have enabled companies to improve established cost-savings programs, prepare for pending "rates & dates" legislation, and enhance their public image.

Company: Sierra Club Legal Defense Fund, Inc.
Industry: Nonprofit, legal
Contact: Tom Turner, staff writer
Address: 180 Montgomery Street, Suite 1400, San Francisco, CA 94104-4209
Phone: (415) 627-6700

What Company Does: The Sierra Club Legal Defense Fund is an independent nonprofit environmental law firm established in 1971. It represents individuals, nonprofit environmental organizations, community groups, and Native American tribes in environmental cases. The Legal Defense Fund conducts both national and international programs and offers advice on proposals for new laws. It publishes *In Brief*, a quarterly newsletter on environmental law. Also, Sierra Club publishes *Sierra—The Natural Resource*.

Company: Signature Marketing / The Environmental Promotion Company
Industry: Advertising
Contact: Evelyn Golden or Jonas Strimaitis, owners
Address: 134 West Street, Simsbury, CT 06070
Phone: (203) 658-7172
Fax: (203) 651-8376

What Company Does: Signature Marketing provides its clients with creative promotional products made from the clients own recycled or raw materials, or has custom-designed inserts and combination products such as clipboards and pads made from recycled paper. Products are developed on an individual basis.

Company: Smith & Hawken
Industry: Gardening
Contact: Ted Tuescher, environmental director
Address: 117 East Strawberry Drive, Mill Valley, CA 94941
Phone: (415) 383-4415, ext. 7629

What Company Does: Smith & Hawken is a mail-order and retail company specializing in botanical and garden supplies. Retail stores are now located in California and soon will be in several other states as well.

Environmental Programs: Smith & Hawken gives a percentage of its earnings to community and therapeutic gardens. The company plants two seedlings for each tree it uses for paper pulp in its catalogs and prints its catalogs on recycled paper. It does not use synthesized chemicals, pesticides, or sprays on its nursery plants and specifies organically grown materials for its catalog items. The company also recycles cans, glass, newspapers, cardboard, and wooden pallets, and fluorescent lights are recycled so mercury can be reclaimed.

Company: J. M. Smucker Company
Industry: Consumer products
Contact: Vickie Limbach, communications manager
Address: Strawberry Lane, Orrville, OH 44667-0280
Phone: (216) 682-3000
Fax: (216) 684-3475

What Company Does: J. M. Smucker is best known for its diverse selections of jams and preserves.

Environmental Programs: Smucker's has an environmental program that looks to preserve natural resources through source reduction, conservation, reclamation, and disposal. Smucker's is reducing the weight, volume, and thickness of its packaging, using recyclable materials, coding plastic to facilitate recycling, and avoiding heavy-metal pigments in printing; it also has an in-house recycling program.

Company: Smurfit Recycling Company
Industry: Recycling
Contact: Terry Moore, manager, Corporate Marketing
Address: 8182 Maryland Avenue, St. Louis, MO 63105
Phone: (314) 746-1255
Fax: (314) 746-1276

What Company Does: JSC, parent company of Smurfit Recycling Company, is one of the largest and broadest-based paper and paperboard packaging companies in the world, with over 180 facilities in the United States, Canada, Mexico, and Puerto Rico.

Environmental Programs: Smurfit Recycling is the nation's largest recycler of paper. The company also consults with businesses to design recycling programs.

Company: Social Investment Forum
Industry: Financial services
Contact: Carla Morteusen, executive director
Address: P.O. Box 57216, Washington, DC 20037
Phone: (202) 833-5522 or (617) 451-3369

What Company Does: Membership provides partnership in a national network of over 1,000 members; a directory of forum members; a guide that lists mutual funds, venture capital fund managers, individual and institutional investors; research providers; community development banks and loan funds; and brokers, advisors, and planners. The forum newsletter covers developments in the field and provides a clearinghouse through which members can track the performance of socially invested assets and get the latest information on socially responsible investing.

Company: Society of American Foresters
Industry: Nonprofit

Contact: William F. Banzhaf, executive vice president
Address: 5400 Grosvenor Lane, Bethesda, MD 20814
Phone: (301) 897-8720
Fax: (301) 897-3690

What Company Does: Founded in 1900, the society works to further the cause of professional forestry for the benefit of the nation.

Company: Solar Box Cookers International
Industry: Nonprofit
Contact: Beverly Blum, executive director
Address: 1724 11th Street, Sacramento, CA 95814
Phone: (916) 444-6616
Fax: (916) 444-5379

What Company Does: Works with grassroots organizations worldwide to develop training, educational materials, and promotion projects to promote solar cooking to benefit people and environments worldwide. Free brochure of products, which include solar cookers, water pasteurization indicator, plans to build and use a simple solar cooker, teaching materials. Internships available.

Company: Solar Works
Industry: Energy and design
Contact: Leigh Seddon, president
Address: 64 Main Street, Montpelier, VT 05602
Phone: (802) 223-7804
Fax: (802) 223-8980

What Company Does: Distributor of high-quality solar energy equipment. Solar Works designs, sells, and installs solar electric systems and carries a complete line of solar-related products that includes hot water systems, lighting, pumps, motors, and refrigeration. Solar Works also offers consulting services on passive-solar and energy-efficient building design.

Company: South End Press / Institute for Social & Cultural Change
Industry: Nonprofit, communications
Address: 116 Saint Botolph Street, Boston, MA 02115
Phone: (617) 266-0629

What Company Does: South End Press is a nonprofit, collectively run, political book publisher established in 1977. It is committed to producing and distributing books that encourage critical thinking and social action. The press has published manuscripts on environmental issues ranging from social ecology theory to wilderness preservation to community organizing to economic conservation as a green strategy for change. It has also established a fund to help those who cannot afford to buy its books.

Company: **Southern Exposure Seed Exchange**
Industry: Gardening
Contact: Jeff McCormack, owner
Address: P.O. Box 170, Earlysville, VA 22936
Phone: (804) 973-4703
Fax: (804) 973-4703 (after 1st ring push 1, then fax)

What Company Does: Offers 500 varieties of seeds, free of chemical treatment and many organically grown, of open-pollinated, heirloom, and traditional vegetables, sunflowers, and herbs. Catalog and gardening manual include information on disease and insect control and seed saving.

Company: **Southern Utah Wilderness Alliance (SUWA)**
Industry: Nonprofit
Contact: Mike Matz, executive director, or Ken Rait, issues coordinator
Address: 1471 South 1100 East, Salt Lake City, UT 84105-2423
Phone: (801) 486-3161
Fax: (801) 486-4233

What Company Does: Dedicated to the wise management of public lands on the Colorado River Plateau, SUWA seeks to give the people of southern Utah a voice in deciding the fate of America's most magnificent landscape. Through the allied efforts of SUWA's professional staff, local Utah activists, and concerned citizens across the United States, this grassroots organization advocates wilderness preservation for qualifying federal lands in Utah's priceless canyon country.

Environmental Programs: SUWA offers internships throughout the year to students interested in wilderness legislation, wild and scenic rivers, and public land policy.

Company: **SRI International**
Industry: Environmental consulting
Contact: Robert D. Shelton, director, Technology and Environmental Management Practice
Address: 333 Ravenswood Avenue, Menlo Park, CA 94025

Phone: (415) 859-3469
Fax: (415) 859-3437

What Company Does: SRI helps examine the environmental chain as it applies to various businesses, strengthen the weak links, and make sure that all the elements are connected and integrated into the normal business process.

Company: Stanley Works
Industry: Manufacturing
Contact: Scott E. Schaffer, director, Employee Relations, Health and Environmental Affairs
Address: 1000 Stanley Drive, New Britain, CT 06053
Phone: (203) 225-5111

What Company Does: Stanley Works is a worldwide manufacturer and marketer of tools, hardware, and specialty hardware products for consumer, industry, and professional use.

Environmental Programs: Stanley Works has a corporate environmental department headed by a director of environmental affairs and an environmental coordinator at each manufacturing location worldwide. The company has office recycling and manufacturing-waste minimization programs at virtually all its U.S. operations. It is associated with the World Environment Center in New York City, and has adopted Environmental Operating Standards that all divisions adhere to worldwide.

Company: Stone Container Corporation
Industry: Manufacturing
Contact: Ira N. Stone, senior vice president
Address: 150 North Michigan Avenue, Chicago, IL 60601-7568
Phone: (312) 580-4608
Fax: (312) 580-4650

What Company Does: Stone Container is a multibillion dollar international paper company, focusing principally on the production and sale of commodity paper and packaging products.

Environmental Programs: Stone Container operates one of the largest recycled newsprint mills in the world; 44 percent of all the newsprint the company produces contains approximately 65 percent de-inked and recycled fibers. Stone Container's pulping process employs a closed-loop system that enables its mills to recover and reuse or sell over 98 percent of all chemicals used.

Company: **Stony Brook–Millstone Watershed Association**
Industry: Environmental organization
Contact: Pat Pizzini, office manager
Address: 31 Titus Mill Road, Pennington, NJ 08534
Phone: (609) 737-3735
Fax: (609) 737-3075

What Company Does: A community-supported environmental organization located on a 585-acre nature reserve in Hopewell Township. Operations include environmental education, monitoring of issues concerning land use and water quality, operating an organic farm, and much more. Internships available; contact Jeff Hoagland, environmental educator, (609) 737-7592.

Company: **Stonyfield Farm**
Industry: Consumer products
Contact: Nancy Hirshberg, environmental coordinator
Address: 10 Burton Drive, Londonderry, NH 03053
Phone: (603) 437-4040
Fax: (603) 437-7594

What Company Does: Founded in 1983, Stonyfield Farm is a manufacturer of yogurt products. Environmental programs include in-house recycling; plastics recycling; energy conservation; Adopt-a-Cow program to teach consumers about the importance of family farms; a visitor's center and tour program to teach health, nutrition, agriculture, and how yogurt is made, and to promote sustainable agriculture; and a biannual newsletter called *Moos from the Farm* that is distributed to over 40,000 people nationwide and educates readers about important agricultural and environmental issues. Internships available to assist environmental coordinator with projects, including solid-waste minimization and recycling, plastic recycling, environmental auditing, and developing the sustainable premium program.

Company: **Student Conservation Association**
Industry: Nonprofit
Contact: Lesley Schuler, recruitment director
Address: P.O. Box 550, Charlestown, NH 03603
Phone: (603) 543-1700

What Company Does: A nonprofit organization that fosters life-long stewardship of the environment by offering expense-paid one- to three-month positions for students and adults to work in national parks, forests, and wildlife refuges. Internships available; contact Resource Assistant Program. Publishes *Earth Work* magazine, which features environmental and green jobs.

Company: Student Environmental Action Coalition (SEAC)
Industry: Education
Contact: Miya Yoshitani, director
Address: P.O. Box 1168 Chapel Hill, NC 27514
Phone: (919) 967-4600
Fax: (919) 967-4648

What Company Does: SEAC is a student and youth coalition that is organized by young environmental activists. Over 2,000 groups have been formed in all fifty states.

Company: Sun Company, Inc.
Industry: Diversified energy
Contact: Bob Banks, vice president, Health, Environment, and Safety
Address: Ten Penn Center, 1801 Market Street,
Philadelphia, PA 19103-1699
Phone: (215) 977-6301
Fax: (215) 977-3902

What Company Does: Sun Company is principally a petroleum refiner and marketer that operates refineries in Pennsylvania, Ohio, Oklahoma, and Puerto Rico. Sun markets fuel products under the Sunoco brand in eighteen states. It also markets lubricants and chemicals throughout the United States and in thirty-nine foreign countries.

Environmental Programs: Sun Company maintains a corporate code of conduct, which provides guidance to all employees regarding business ethics and health, environmental, and safety policies. These policies include basic compliance, pollution prevention, emergency preparation and response, and energy conservation. Sun Company endorsed the Ceres Principles in February 1993.

Company: SunFeather Herbal Soap Co.
Industry: Manufacturing
Contact: Sandy Maine, owner
Address: HCR 84, Box 60A, Potsdam, NY 13676
Phone: (315) 265-3648
Fax: (315) 265-2902

What Company Does: SunFeather, a manufacturer of soaps, bar shampoos, bath herbs, and fragrant salts, was founded in 1979 with the mission of sharing the beauty and joy of Mother Nature's medicinal and fragrance herbs in hopes that people would come closer to and appreciate more fully the wonderful gifts of the earth. Its line of personal care items consists of all-natural, long-lasting products handcrafted in small, 100-pound batches.

Environmental Programs: SunFeather donates preprofit income to over eight different environmental and peace groups that are working hard for earth, animal, and human well-being. It also shares profits with employees and offers an enjoyable "human scale" workplace; makes every effort to minimize the ecological impact of its daily work; and uses the vast network of business to promote global, local, and inner consciousness toward an economically and ecologically sustainable future for all.

Company: **SuperValu, Inc.**
Industry: Retail
Contact: Sara Reimers, communications assistant
Address: P.O. Box 990, Minneapolis, MN 55440
Phone: (612) 828-4007 or general (612) 828-4000
Fax: (612) 828-4495

What Company Does: SuperValu is a food wholesaler to a network of more than 4,300 independent grocery retailers in forty-seven states; the company has twenty-seven divisions.

Environmental Programs: SuperValu has adopted an environmental policy statement and has created a program to communicate its environmental policies to retailers. The company also has an extensive recycling program.

Company: **Synergy Marketing**
Industry: Environmental services
Contact: David Silberkleit, president
Address: 123 Harbor Drive, Suite 706, Stamford, CT 06902
Phone: (203) 325-4844
Fax: (203) 325-9662

What Company Does: Synergy Marketing's mission is to recycle 100 million tons of otherwise landfill-bound garbage through unparalleled support for diverse companies dedicated to influencing environmental and social issues. Synergy provides the following services for green companies: marketing support, public relations, recycled product merchandising, strategic planning, financial analysis, forecasting and budgeting, and planning and management of corporate giving programs.

Company: **TATA Energy Research Institute (TERI)**
Industry: Nonprofit, sustainable development
Address: 102, Jor Bagh, New Delhi, India 110003

Phone: 91-11-462-5296
Fax: 91-11-462-1770

What Company Does: TERI was established to train civil servants on energy and the environment. It has recently formed the Information and Research Center on Global Warming and Climatic Change, which collects and disseminates information through publications, audio-visual materials, and research. The new center plans to work with the Indian government on issues related to global warming.

Company: Tenneco, Inc.
Industry: Diversified industrial
Contact: Thomas J. Slocum, executive director, Corporate Communications
Address: 1010 Milan Street, P.O. Box 2511, Houston, TX 77252-2511
Phone: (713) 757-3430 or general (713) 757-2131
Fax: (713) 757-2777

What Company Does: Tenneco is a diversified industrial corporation with major business interests in natural gas pipelines, farm and construction equipment, automotive parts, shipbuilding, packaging, chemicals, and minerals.

Environmental Programs: Tenneco created a Department of Industrial Ecology, now called Environmental Affairs, which reports directly to senior management on the company's environmental compliance. Tenneco uses 50 to 100 percent postconsumer fiber in its packaging division.

Company: Thanksgiving Coffee Co.
Industry: Consumer products
Contact: Paul Katzeff, CEO
Address: P.O. Box 1918, Fort Bragg, CA 95437
Phone: (707) 964-0118 or (800) 462-1999
Fax: (707) 964-0351

What Company Does: A family-owned business that custom-roasts coffee for over 300 of the finest restaurants and country inns as well as 200-plus grocery stores and gourmet shops throughout California's wine country. All the coffees are certified organically grown through the Organic Crop Improvement Association (OCIA). Coffees are grown in Peru, Guatemala, and Mexico. Originator and manufacturer of Inca, Mayan, and Aztec Harvest ("Not just a cup, but a just cup") socially responsible coffee project.

Environmental leaders in the coffee industry. Vacuum valve packed. Free catalog.

Company: Third World Network (TWN)
Industry: Nonprofit, sustainable development
Address: 228 Macalister Road, 10400 Penang, Malaysia
Phone: 60-4-373511, 373612
Fax: 60-4-368106

What Company Does: TWN was formed in 1984 to bring about a better understanding of the needs and rights of people in the third world. In addition, it strives to create an equitable distribution of world resources and forms of development that both meet people's needs and are ecologically sound. Publishes *Third World Economics*, *Third World Resurgence*, *Third World Network Features*, *SUNS Bulletin.*

Company: Thorne Ecological Institute
Industry: Nonprofit
Contact: Susan Q. Foster, executive director
Address: 5398 Manhattan Circle, Suite 120, Boulder, CO 80303
Phone: (303) 499-3647

What Company Does: The Thorne Ecological Institute promotes positive change by encouraging individual behaviors—based on ecological principles—that achieve environmental, economic, and social harmony. Publishes newsletter and calendar of events in local area. Volunteer internships only.

Environmental Programs: Runs a natural science field school for children during the summer months. Also, organizes and hosts conferences for cooperative efforts with business, government, and individuals on environmental issues.

Company: 3M
Industry: Manufacturing
Contact: Dr. Robert P. Bringer, staff vice president, Environmental Engineering and Pollution Control
Address: 3M Environmental Engineering & Pollution Control, P.O. Box 33331, St. Paul, MN 55133-3331
Phone: (612) 778-5189/4335 or general (612) 733-1110/736-8261

What Company Does: 3M comprises three business segments: Industrial & Consumer; Information, Imaging & Electronics; and Life Sciences. The company is known for its culture of innovation. It has 87,584 employees.

Environmental Programs: 3M's environmental programs are very comprehensive, including policies and procedures affecting acquisitions and divestitures, asbestos, air emissions, corporate marketing claims, underground tanks and piping, and ozone-depleting chemicals. Environmental Engineering and Pollution Control offers summer internships with selected engineering schools and technical aid (half-time) positions.

Company: **Threshold, Inc.**
Industry: Nonprofit
Contact: John P. Milton, executive director
Address: Drawer CU, Bisbee, AZ 85603
Phone: (602) 432-7353

What Company Does: Threshold is a nonprofit "window" organization that acts as a delegator. Individuals or groups donate money to Threshold, which gives it to people who want to work on a project to help save rain forests, animals, natural resources, etc. Threshold created the Environmental Crisis Fund (ECF) to help heal major ecological threats now affecting planet earth. To make the projects of the ECF most effective, the fund commits itself to protecting critically endangered ecosystems; seeks to directly fund local environmental action and study groups; emphasizes building coalitions of like-minded groups to resolve environmental issues; restricts internal organization and administrative overhead costs to 20 percent of income.

Environmental Programs: Threshold has a partner program called Sacred Passage, an intensive awareness training and solo wilderness experience designed to attune the inner pace of one's life with nature's rhythms through ancient principles and teachings. Renew, a 5-day program for corporations and individuals, is conducted in Colorado, West Virginia, Arizona, Hawaii, the Baja Peninsula of Mexico, and Utah.

Company: **Time, Inc.**
Industry: Publishing
Contact: Connie Cosner, director, Facilities, or David Refkin, director, Environmental Affairs
Address: Time-Life Building, Rockefeller Center, New York, NY 10020
Phone: (212) 522-1212

What Company Does: Time, Inc., is a wholly owned subsidiary of Time Warner, Inc. Time is the world's leading media and entertainment company, with interests in magazine and book publishing, recorded music and music publishing, films and entertainment, cable television, and cable television programming.

Environmental Programs: Sierra Club awarded Henry Muller, managing editor for *Time* magazine, its David Brower Award for outstanding work in the area of environmental journalism. Time has started recycling "high-grade" white paper as well as bottles and cans at its corporate headquarters. It has also switched seven of its magazines to recycled paper.

Company: Times Mirror Magazines
Industry: Communications
Contact: Linda W. Boff, director, Public Relations
Address: 2 Park Avenue, New York, NY 10016
Phone: (212) 779-5222 or general (212) 779-5000
Fax: (212) 213-3540

What Company Does: Times Mirror Magazines is the nation's leading publisher of special interest, leisure-oriented magazines. Its publications include *Field & Stream, Golf Magazine, Home Mechanix, Outdoor Life, Popular Science, Salt Water Sportsman, Ski, Skiing, Skiing Trade News, The Sporting Good Dealer, The Sporting News,* and *Yachting.*

Environmental Programs: With over 30 million readers, Times Mirror Magazines reach more people actively involved in the outdoors than any other magazine company in America. Because of its editorial concentration on outdoor recreation and leisure activities, its publications have always been outspoken champions of conservation. To that end, the Times Mirror Magazine Conservation Council was formed in early 1990.

Company: Tom's of Maine
Industry: Consumer products
Contact: Community Life Department
Address: Lafayette Center, P.O. Box 710, Kennebunk, ME 04043
Phone: (207) 985-2944
Fax: (207) 985-1196

What Company Does: Tom's of Maine is the leading maker of natural personal care products, including toothpaste, deodorant, flossing ribbon, natural-bristle toothbrushes, mouthwash, shave cream, and shampoo.

Environmental Programs: Tom's of Maine was founded on the principles of "respect for people" and "respect for nature." The company donates 10 percent of is pretax profits to the common good, encourages employees to use 5 percent of their paid work time to volunteer in the community, and strives to create packaging that is environmentally sensitive.

Company: Toucan Chocolates, Inc.
Industry: Consumer products
Contact: Michael Goldman, president
Address: P.O. Box 72, Waban, MA 02168
Phone: (617) 964-8696
Fax: (617) 964-8381

What Company Does: Offers a line of gourmet chocolates using rain-forest nuts. Carried in retail stores across the country, as well as in mail-order catalogs.

Environmental Programs: Purchases nuts from rain-forest peoples through Cultural Survival, Inc., and donates approximately 20 percent of profits from chocolate sales to Cultural Survival in support of sustainable native economic development through harvested rain-forest products (to increase demand for renewable rain-forest resources). Boxes and booklets are made from 100 percent recycled paper (with 15 percent postconsumer content); stickers are printed on recycled stock; only vegetable-based inks, solvent-free adhesives, and natural fibers are used; and no plastics are used in packaging.

Company: TreePeople
Industry: Nonprofit, urban planning
Contact: Rena Kilmor, staffer, or Andy Lipkis, president
Address: 12601 Mulholland Drive, Beverly Hills, CA 90210
Phone: (818) 753-4600
Fax: (818) 753-4625

What Company Does: Urban forestry organization that focuses on tree planting, environmental education, and individual empowerment. Trains volunteers as urban foresters in its Citizen Forester Program (planting, care, and appreciation). Supports local grassroots organizations with education, training, and support for community activity. Publishes *Seedling News*, a quarterly newsletter.

Company: Trees for Life, Inc. (TFL)
Industry: Nonprofit
Contact: Balbir S. Mathur, executive director
Address: 1103 Jefferson, Wichita, KS 67203
Phone: (316) 263-7294
Fax: (316) 263-5293

What Company Does: Trees for Life, organized in 1984, is a nonprofit movement dedicated to planting fruit trees worldwide. These trees protect our environment and provide a self-renewing source of nutrition for people in need. The TFL program is now operating in India, Guatemala, Nepal, and Costa Rica with affiliate offices in Austria and Canada. Today more than 20 million trees have been planted. Plans call for the planting of 100 million fruit trees during this decade. In the United States, TFL makes available a trees adventure planting kit and educational materials for elementary students to promote ecological awareness, to encourage the planting of trees, and to learn the relationship between trees and hunger in the world. Since 1987, more than 2 million children in the United States have participated in this program. Internships only are available.

Company: Trianco Corporation
Industry: Consumer products
Contact: Loretta Wieting, ecopreneur
Address: 14 Buchanan Road, Salem, MA 01970
Phone: (508) 745-9766
Fax: (508) 745-8621

What Company Does: With its sister company, All-Natural Soap, Inc., in Ontario, Canada, Trianco Corporation produces and offers by mail a variety of environmentally safe specialty soaps called Babycakes and St. Davids Aromatherapy Soaps.

Environmental Programs: Soaps are biodegradable, cruelty-free, and have an all-vegetable base, and all ingredients are food grade or edible. Has researched, updated, and uses traditional, nonpolluting methods of production.

Company: Trout Unlimited
Industry: Conservation
Contact: Neal D. Emerald, grassroots coordinator
Address: 1500 Wilson Boulevard, Suite 310, Arlington, VA 22209-2310
Phone: (703) 522-0200
Fax: (703) 284-9400

What Company Does: Trout Unlimited was founded over thirty-five years ago and has been America's leading trout and salmon conservation organization. It is dedicated to conserving, protecting, and restoring coldwater fisheries and their watersheds. Members are actively engaged in such activities as planning and building stream improvement projects, working with government to secure fish-friendly legislation, and teaching young people the importance of protecting wild fish and their habitat.

Company: Trust for Public Land
Industry: Nonprofit
Contact: Susan Ives, vice president
Address: 116 New Montgomery Street, 4th floor, San Francisco, CA 94105
Phone: (415) 495-4014
Fax: (415) 495-4103

What Company Does: The Trust for Public Land (TPL) is a national nonprofit organization founded in 1972 to help public agencies and communities acquire and protect land of recreational, ecological, and cultural value for the public. Specializing in urban open space, TPL shares knowledge of nonprofit land acquisition processes, negotiates complex land transactions, and pioneers methods of environmentally sound land use. Publishes *Land and People.*

Company: 20/20 Vision National Project
Industry: Nonprofit environmental organization
Contact: Robin Caiola, codirector
Address: 1828 Jefferson Place NW, Washington, DC 20036
Phone: (800) 669-1782 (recording only) / (202) 833-2020
Fax: (202) 833-5307

What Company Does: Sends members a brightly colored postcard every month with the most effective twenty-minute actions you can take to preserve peace and protect the environment, and every six months sends you a report on the results of the suggested actions. Free action card and information. Internships available.

Company: Ultimo, Inc.
Industry: Design
Contact: Clare Ultimo, president
Address: 41 Union Square, New York, NY 10003
Phone: (212) 645-7858
Fax: (212) 989-2836

What Company Does: Provides graphic design capabilities, including corporate identity, logos, posters, sales and media kits, points of purchase, capability brochures, catalogs, books, ads, internal corporate media, publications, and direct sales media.

Environmental Programs: Ultimo applies a conscious design perspective that takes people and the environment into account. It makes a concerted effort to work for companies that have social and environmental concerns. Ultimo encourages clients to use recycled papers and soy-based inks. Internally, all applicable office waste is recycled or reused, including cans and plastic.

Company: **Union Carbide Corporation (UCC)**
Industry: Chemicals
Contact: F. L. Moore, assistant director, Environment
Address: 39 Old Ridgeberg Road, Danbury, CT 06817-0001
Phone: (203) 794-2400

What Company Does: UCC is the fourth largest chemical company in the United States. It is the world's largest producer of the chemical building block ethylene oxide and its derivative ethylene glycol, used for automotive antifreeze, polyester fiber, and other products. The company is a leading polyethylene producer and produces the widest range of oxygenated solvents of any U.S. company. UCC is also a leading marketer of specialty chemicals, and its worldwide chemical trading business serves industry in more than 100 countries.

Environmental Programs: UCC employs worldwide environmental standards that are often more stringent than those of the country in which it operates. A worldwide audit program functioning independently of line management provides objective assessments of HS&E performance.

Company: **United Nations Environment Programme (UNEP)**
Industry: Nonprofit
Contact: Noel J. Brown, director, Regional Office for North America
Address: Room DC2-0803, United Nations, New York, NY 10017
Phone: (212) 963-8138
Fax: (212) 963-7341

What Company Does: UNEP is the environmental conscience of the UN. Its mission is to provide leadership and encourage partnership in caring for the environment by inspiring, informing, and enabling nations and peoples to improve their quality of life without compromising that of future generations. Founded in 1972 as a result of that year's Stockholm Conference on the Human Environment.

Environmental Programs: UNEP acts as one of the implementing agencies of the Global Environment Facility, along with the World Bank and UNDP (United Nations Development Program), and serves as the secretariat for several international environmental conventions, dealing with ozone depletion, hazardous wastes, biological diversity, and trade in endangered species. Resources include: news releases, feature articles, fact sheets; *Our Planet* (periodical); *Annual Report of the Executive Director;* regional and specialized newsletter; special global environment reports; photographic collection; radio programs and television and video coproductions; electronic conferencing and bulletin boards.

Company: United Nations Population Fund (UNFPA)
Industry: Population
Contact: Nafis Sadik, executive director
Address: 220 East 42nd Street, New York, NY 10017
Phone: (212) 297-5000
Fax: (212) 557-6416

What Company Does: The United Nations Population Fund assists developing countries at their request in dealing with their population problems and plays a leading role in the UN system in promoting population programs. Publishes a population monthly *Populi,* its annual report *The State of World Population,* and other publications and produces videos for promotion of population awareness.

Company: Unocal Corporation
Industry: Energy
Contact: George A. Walker, vice president, Health, Environmental, and Safety Department
Address: 1201 West Fifth Avenue, Los Angeles, CA 90017
Phone: (213) 977-7600

What Company Does: Unocal explores for, develops, and produces crude oil and natural gas resources in the United States, Canada, and overseas. The company is the world's largest producer of geothermal energy. It also manufactures and markets a wide variety of refined petroleum products, agricultural chemicals, fertilizers, and specialty carbon products.

Environmental Programs: Unocal employs over 100 environmental professionals, located in Corporate Environmental Sciences, Division Environmental Affairs, and in various facilities. Unocal also maintains a staff of over 100 engineers and scientists to address soil remediation projects around the country. Unocal's environmental accomplishments include the first fully lead-free slate of gasolines, world leadership of development of low-impact geothermal resources, world leadership of sulfur removal technology in refineries, the highly successful and awarded South Coast Recycle Auto Program (SCRAP) (a revolutionary demonstration of the effectiveness of car crushing to remove air pollutants in a cost-effective program), installation of new reformulated gasoline manufacturing facilities at refineries, and major participation in the development of RECLAIM (Regional Clean Air Incentive Market), which is a revolutionary scheme to bring the power of market-based incentives to the control of air pollution in Los Angeles.

Company: Upjohn Company
Industry: Pharmaceuticals
Contact: Peter J. Maas, Community Relations and Legislative Affairs
Address: 7000 Portage Road, Kalamazoo, MI 49001
Phone: (616) 323-7183

What Company Does: The Upjohn Company is a worldwide, research-based provider of human health care products, animal health products, agronomic and vegetable seed, and specialty chemicals. The company has been dedicated to improving health and nutrition for more than a century.

Environmental Programs: Upjohn is nearing completion of an aggressive emission-reduction program, investing $68.5 million in air emission-control improvements. These are expected to reduce air emissions by about 95 percent from 1987 levels. Other efforts include a relatively new Pollution Prevention Program, which requires waste reduction in each division worldwide, recycling programs that collected 56,000 tons in 1992, and seeking alternative packaging materials that include recyclable packaging and shipping alternatives. Other initiatives include reforestation projects, development of remediation technologies, and organizational realignments directed at achieving optimum environmental performance.

Company: Urban Ecology, Inc.
Industry: Nonprofit
Contact: Stephen Wheeler, program director
Address: P.O. Box 10144, Berkeley, CA 94709
Phone: (510) 549-1724
Fax: (510) 841-0192

What Company Does: Urban Ecology is a nonprofit, international membership organization dedicated to bringing together diverse groups of people to build ecologically and socially healthy and sustainable cities and towns through application of principles of ecology in urban planning and development, and communicate and develop innovative alternatives to the ways we build.

Environmental Programs: Publishes *The Urban Ecologist*, a quarterly newsletter with a circulation of 4,000. Urban Ecology, Inc., structures projects in the areas of land use and planning, transportation, restoration, international education, and ecocity research.

Company: **USG Corporation**
Industry: Manufacturing
Contact: Matt Gonring, vice president, Corporate Communications
Address: 125 South Franklin Street, Chicago, IL 60606-4385
Phone: (312) 606-4124
Fax: (312) 606-5301

What Company Does: USG is the largest manufacturer of gypsum building materials.

Environmental Programs: USG is expanding its efforts to reclaim and reuse internal waste in its manufacturing processes. Its wallboard is made entirely from 100 percent recycled paper. The company accepts discarded phonebooks at their Jacksonville, Florida, plant to use in wallboard manufacturing. USG has developed its own natural gas supply, which meets the needs of its Oakland, New York, plant and also supplies excess energy to the local utility. The company recycles heat to conserve and maximize efficiency. USG Interiors uses slag, a by-product of iron ore reduction, in making commercial ceiling and insulation products. The Greenville, Mississippi, plant buys newspapers from the Boy Scouts for recycling into ceiling products. In certain processes the company uses cornstarch as a binder; cornstarch is less harmful to the environment than many chemicals and is more easily "renewable" than materials such as trees.

Company: **Vegetarian Resource Group**
Address: P.O. Box 1463, Baltimore, MD 21203
Phone: (410) 366-VEGE

What Company Does: Publishes *The Vegetarian Journal*, which offers nutrition and new product information, networking opportunities, recipes, articles, scientific updates, and book reviews and does not accept paid advertising. Also offers mail-order book list. Internships available; contact Charles Stahler.

Company: **Volkswagen AG**
Industry: Manufacturing
Contact: Maria Leonhauser, public relations manager
Address: Volkswagen United States, Inc., Public Relations Mail Code 3002, 3800 Hamlin Road, Auburn Hills, MI 48326
Phone: (810) 340-5053
Fax: (810) 340-5540

What Company Does: Volkswagen AG is the fourth largest automaker in the world, producing some 3.5 million vehicles a year.

Environmental Programs: Volkswagen's environmental policy is based on conservation, reduction, and recycling. By limiting the use of natural resources and avoiding the use of environmentally hazardous materials, the need to recover, recycle, and dispose of those materials is lessened. For those materials that are used, great care is taken to recycle wherever possible. VW's manufacturing facility in Wolfsburg, Germany, recycles nearly 88 percent of its industrial wastewater. VW operates a recycling plant in Germany that dismantles and recycles the entire car. VW guarantees that all 1992 Golfs sold in Germany will be taken back free of charge for recycling. The company has produced and sold about 2.2 million alternative-power vehicles, ranging from diesel to ethanol and methanol to electric. Most recently, Volkswagen and Audi entered into a joint project with Preussag Recycling to establish a nationwide recycling network for all VW and Audi scrapped vehicles.

Company: Volvo
Industry: Manufacturing
Contact: Nancy Fiesler, manager, Corporate Information
Address: Volvo North American Corporation, 535 Madison Avenue, New York, NY 10022
Phone: (212) 418-7432
Fax: (212) 418-7436

What Company Does: Volvo is the largest industrial group in the Nordic region. It began operations more than sixty-five years ago as a manufacturer of passenger cars. Today, the company is engaged in a broad range of activities in the transport vehicle field, with cars, trucks, and buses as its largest operating sectors. Other sectors include marine and industrial engines, and aerospace. Volvo's substantial industrial operations are supplemented by large shareholdings in associated companies within and outside Sweden.

Environmental Programs: The Volvo environmental policy is based on a holistic approach to the environmental impact of its products. The product companies are responsible for implementing the policy and taking the appropriate action. Environmental auditing is among the means used to monitor the effectiveness of the action programs. Volvo has taken the initiative in developing a sophisticated life-cycle analysis system, EPS (Environmental Priority Strategies in Product Design), which enables the adverse effects of pollutant emissions and the utilization of natural resources to be quantified in a single index describing the total environmental loading. All models in Volvo's new car range are CFC-free from 1994 on. In 1993 Volvo was the first automaker in the world to introduce a modification kit for converting used air-conditioned cars to the CFC-free refrigerant R-134a.

Company: **Henry A. Wallace Institute for Alternative Agriculture**
Industry: Agriculture
Contact: I. Garth Youngberg, executive director
Address: 9200 Edmonston Road, Suite 117, Greenbelt, MD 20770
Phone: (301) 441-8777
Fax: (301) 220-0164

What Company Does: The Institute for Alternative Agriculture uses advocacy, conferences, research, and education to promote and facilitate the adaptation of low-cost, resource-conserving, and environmentally sound farming techniques on a national basis.

Company: **Wal-Mart Stores, Inc.**
Industry: Retail
Contact: Steve Schwitters, environmental manager
Address: 702 SW 8th Street, Bentonville, AR 72716
Phone: (501) 273-4000 or (501) 273-8650

What Company Does: Wal-Mart is the fastest-growing chain of discount stores in the United States.

Environmental Programs: Wal-Mart has a commitment to the environment that includes its customers, vendor partners, and associates. The environmental initiative was started because of a request from Wal-Mart customers. The company challenges its vendor partners to improve their products so they are better for the environment. The home office recycles aluminum cans, white office paper, cardboard boxes, plastic milk jugs, plastic soft-drink bottles, and newspapers. Stores recycle cardboard at all locations, office paper at some locations, and plastic shopping bags at all locations where the store uses plastic bags. Wal-Mart participates in many local community cleanups and tree plantings.

Company: **Walnut Acres Organic Farms**
Industry: Agriculture
Contact: Paul Shaw, assistant general manager
Address: Penns Creek, PA 17862
Phone: (800) 433-3998
Fax: (717) 837-1146

What Company Does: Provides the safest, highest-quality foods available. Crops produced are independently certified by the Organic Growers and Buyers Association. Soil is free of synthetic fertilizers and other chemicals for nearly fifty years. Products sold in catalog that are purchased elsewhere are evaluated on principles of safety, quality, and sustainable agricultural practices. Call for catalog.

Environmental Programs: Supports organic farming. Offers rain-forest nuts, and a portion of proceeds from nut purchases supports sustainable economic development through a donation to Cultural Survival, Inc. Also offers environmentally conscious home supplies such as biodegradable, cruelty-free, phosphate-free cleaning products and water-saving devices. Signatory to the Ceres Principles, which commits Walnut Acres to environmental accountability. Sponsors of Penn ReLeaf, which organizes reforestation projects in Pennsylvania.

Company: Izaak Walton League of America (IWLA)
Industry: Nonprofit, fisheries
Address: National Office, IWLA Conservation Center, 707 Conservation Lane, Gaithersburg, MD 20879

What Company Does: Established in 1922 by a group of concerned anglers, the respected Izaak Walton League of America is a national nonprofit organization whose 53,000 members protect and enjoy the nation's soil, air, woods, waters, and wildlife. Members receive four publications: *Outdoor America*, *Outdoor Ethics*, *Splash*, and *League Leader*.

Environmental Programs: The league tackles such important conservation issues as clean water, clean air, wildlife habitat, public lands management, protection of natural areas, and enhanced outdoor recreation. In addition to its publications, the league uses television to spread its conservation message. As the longest-running weekly environmental program on television, the league's *Make Peace With Nature* airs stories about current national and international environmental issues.

Company: Warner-Lambert
Industry: Pharmaceuticals
Contact: E. Peter Wolf, director, Media Relations
Address: 201 Tabor Road, Morris Plains, NJ 07950
Phone: (201) 540-6696
Fax: (201) 540-3320

What Company Does: Warner-Lambert is a worldwide diversified company devoted to developing, manufacturing, and marketing health care and consumer products. In prescription pharmaceuticals, its research and development efforts are centered on cardiovascular, central nervous system, and chemotherapeutic agents. Warner-Lambert is the eleventh largest U.S.-based pharmaceutical company. Its consumer products include Halls cough tablets, Listerine antiseptic mouthwash, Benadryl antihistamine, Rolaids antacid, Trident and Dentyne chewing gums, Certs mints, and Lubriderm lotion. It has about 34,000 employees.

Environmental Programs: Warner-Lambert's internal efforts are concentrated on energy conservation, source reduction, recycling, and employee education. The company recycles over 1 million pounds of materials from the Morris Plains facility alone.

Company: Wellman, Inc.
Industry: Environmental services
Contact: Dennis Sabourin, vice president
Address: 1040 Broad Street, Suite 302, Shrewsbury, NJ 07702
Phone: (908) 935-7321
Fax: (908) 542-9344

What Company Does: Wellman is the largest recycler of plastic soft-drink bottles and fiber and film wastes in the United States. It uses those wastes to produce polyester and nylon fibers and plastic resins for a wide range of specialty markets in the United States and western Europe. The company employs approximately 3,700 people.

Company: Westinghouse Electric
Industry: Technology
Contact: Samuel R. Pitts, vice president, Law, Environmental Affairs and Insurance
Address: Westinghouse Building, 11 Stanwix Street, Pittsburgh, PA 15222-1384
Phone: (412) 642-3447
Fax: (412) 642-3923

What Company Does: Westinghouse is a diversified, global, technology-based corporation. The corporation's key operations include television and radio broadcasting, advanced electronics systems, environmental services, management services at government-owned facilities, services and equipment for utility markets, and transport temperature control.

Environmental Programs: The Westinghouse Government & Environmental Services Company includes the management of certain government-owned facilities and the U.S. naval nuclear reactors programs. It provides a variety of environmental remediation and toxic, hazardous, and radioactive waste-treatment services. Through Aptus, Inc., the corporation offers toxic- and hazardous-waste incineration, treatment, transportation, storage, and analysis services. Facilities performing these services are located in Kansas, Utah, and Minnesota.

Westinghouse Remediation Services, Inc., provides comprehensive toxic- and hazardous-waste remediation services, including mobile, on-site environmental treatment technologies. The Scientific Ecology Group, Inc., offers a broad range of on- and off-site services to manage radioactive materials and mixed wastes, including the only commercially licensed radioactive waste incinerator and the only recycling facility for radioactively contaminated metals in the United States. Through subsidiaries, Resource Energy Systems operates four waste-to-energy plants that convert municipal solid waste into clean electrical energy. Controlmatic, a group of affiliated indirect subsidiaries having principal operations in Germany, Switzerland, Austria, and Italy, offers products and services relating to control, monitoring, and industrial automation and instrumentation.

Company: Whirlpool Corporation
Industry: Manufacturing
Contact: Carol L. Sizer, manager, Media Relations
Address: Benton Harbor, MI 49022-2692
Phone: (616) 926-3231
Fax: (616) 926-5486

What Company Does: Whirlpool is the world's leading manufacturer and marketer of major home appliances. The company manufactures in eleven countries and markets products in more than 120 countries under major brand names such as Whirlpool, Kitchen Aid, Roper, Estate Phillips, Bauknecht, and others. Whirlpool is the principal supplier to Sears of major home appliances, marketed under the Kenmore brand name.

Environmental Programs: Whirlpool won the $30 Million Winner-Take-All Competition that pitted appliance manufacturers against each other in the race to develop a super-efficient, CFC-free refrigerator. It was the first U.S. appliance company to develop a process for recovering used CFCs from refrigerators and freezers, and it has completed a $3 million project to eliminate all electrical transformers cooled by PCBs, removing all underground storage tanks and replacing them with above-ground tanks for easier monitoring. The company also has a unique paper recycling program in place at its corporate headquarters that results in jobs for disabled adults.

Company: Wilderness Society
Industry: Nonprofit
Contact: Klara Podgorska, director of human resources

Address: 900 17th Street NW, Washington, DC 20006
Phone: (202) 429-3941 or general (202) 833-2300

What Company Does: The Wilderness Society is a nonprofit organization devoted to preserving wilderness and wildlife. Founded in 1935, it focuses on issues involving federal public lands, with an emphasis on economic analysis and biodiversity. Publishes *Wilderness*, a quarterly magazine.

Company: Wildlife Conservation Society (WCS)
Industry: Nonprofit
Contact: Dr. John Robinson, vice president, International Programs
Address: 185th Street & Southern Boulevard (Bronx Zoo), Bronx, NY 10460
Phone: (212) 220-5155

What Company Does: WCS is a wildlife and wilderness conservation organization with a full-time staff of ecologists and wildlife biologists conducting field research and training programs around the world. Its efforts are concentrated in many of the world's developing countries where biological diversity is greatest and the pressure on nature is most intense. Its unique strategy relies on long-term field studies to gather information on wildlife needs. The organization depends on familiarity with local conditions to translate results directly into conservation action and policy, train conservation professionals, and build public awareness.

Company: WMX Technologies, Inc.
Industry: Environmental services
Contact: Frank Moore, vice president
Address: 1155 Connecticut Avenue, Suite 800, Washington, DC 20036
Phone: (202) 467-4480

What Company Does: WMX Technologies is a world leader in environmental services, solid-waste hauling and disposal, and recycling.

Environmental Programs: WMX is involved in environmental services, recycling, solid-waste transfer, and groundwater monitoring. Its landfill gas recovery facilities in fourteen states can individually generate enough power to serve 10,000 households.

Company: Women's Environment & Development Organization (WEDO)
Industry: Nonprofit, policy advocacy

Contact: Barbara Ann O'Leary, program coordinator, Information and Database Resources
Address: 845 Third Avenue, 15th floor, New York, NY 10022
Phone: (212) 759-7982
Fax: (212) 759-8647

What Company Does: A nonprofit international membership organization empowering women to play an active role in decision-making on environmental and development policy. Organizes a women's caucus at major UN conferences. Volunteer opportunities available.

Environmental Programs: Organized the 1991 World Women's Congress for a Healthy Planet in Miami, where WEDO facilitated the development of World Women's Action Agenda 21, a blueprint for incorporating women's concerns about the environment and sustainable development into local, national, and international decision-making for the 1992 Earth Summit in Rio. WEDO advocates a woman- and development-oriented agenda at international conferences such as the UN World Summit for Social Development, the International Conference on Population and Development, and the UN Fourth Conference on Women.

Company: Wordwright Associates
Industry: Consulting
Contact: Susan K. Hughes, president
Address: 825 East Guenther Street, San Antonio, TX 78210-1237
Phone: (210) 532-2332
Fax: (210) 532-2023

What Company Does: Wordwright Associates is a marketing and communications firm that offers consulting services to a range of private, nonprofit, and public sector clients to "achieve goals encompassing and promoting sound environmental, social, ethical, and health practices."

Company: Working Assets Capital Management
Industry: Investments
Contact: Sophia Collier, president
Address: 111 Pine Street, Suite 1415, San Francisco, CA 94111
Phone: (415) 989-3200 or (800) 223-7010

What Company Does: Working Assets provides socially responsible investment services.

Environmental Programs: Working Assets seeks environmentally responsible investment opportunities in areas like renewable energy and energy efficiency, while avoiding investing in companies that have a record of EPA violations or that produce nuclear weapons. Also has a long-distance company and a credit card company that contribute a percentage of profits to environmental and socially responsible organizations.

Company: **World Resources Institute**
Industry: Nonprofit
Contact: J. Alan Brewster, senior vice president
Address: 1709 New York Avenue NW, Washington, DC 20009
Phone: (202) 638-6300
Fax: (202) 638-0036

What Company Does: The World Resources Institute is a nonprofit research and policy institute founded in 1982 to conduct research and develop policy options designed to promote economic growth while protecting natural resources and the environment worldwide. The institute has a staff of 110.

Company: **World Wide Fund for Nature**
Industry: Nonprofit
Address: Avenue du Mont-Blanc, CH-1196 Gland, Switzerland
Phone: 41-22-3649-111

What Company Does: Established in 1961, the World Wide Fund is one of the largest independent nature conservation and advocacy groups. It aims to conserve nature and ecological processes by preserving genetic, species, and ecosystem diversity; ensuring that the use of renewable resources is sustainable both now and in the longer term; and promoting actions to reduce pollution and the wasteful exploitation and consumption of resources and energy.

Company: **World Wildlife Fund, Inc.**
Industry: Nonprofit
Contact: Verity Stiff, human resources manager
Address: 1250 24th Street NW, Suite 500, Washington, DC 20037
Phone: (202) 293-4800
Fax: (202) 293-9211

What Company Does: The World Wildlife Fund is a U.S. nonprofit organization working worldwide to conserve nature. Its focus is on global conservation of natural resources. The fund supports scientifically based conservation projects, economic development, and public policy and education. It has twelve-week summer internships.

Company: **Worldwatch Institute**
Industry: Nonprofit
Contact: Carole Douglis, director of communications
Address: 1776 Massachusetts Avenue NW,
Washington, DC 20036-1904
Phone: (202) 452-1999
Fax: (202) 296-7365

What Company Does: The Worldwatch Institute is a nonprofit environmental research institute founded in 1974. It conducts research and publishes the annual *State of the World*, *World Watch* magazine, and *The World Watch Papers* emphasizing the interdependence of the world economy and its environmental support systems. It has a staff of thirty plus.

Company: **Wysong Corporation**
Industry: Consumer products
Contact: Jill Hubbard, personnel director
Address: 1880 North Eastman, Midland, MI 48640
Phone: (517) 631-0009
Fax: (517) 631-8801

What Company Does: Wysong focuses on human and animal nutrition, health care, and personal care by providing education, food products, medicines, and personal care products with an environmental, holistic focus. Cruelty-free.

Environmental Programs: Wysong has developed environmental education, research, product development, and philanthropic programs.

Company: **Xerox**
Industry: Technology
Contact: Abhay Blaushan
Address: 3400 Hillview Avenue, Palo Alto, CA 94304
Phone: (415) 813-7065
Fax: (415) 494-4000

What Company Does: Xerox is a leading manufacturer of copiers and duplicating equipment, including laser printing, scanning, and fax machines.

Environmental Programs: To ensure the environmental quality of all Xerox products and operations, Xerox developed a policy that places environmental considerations at the forefront of its business practice. Corresponding programs include Design for the Environment, waste-free factories, waste reduction and recycling, buying recycled products and materials, packaging reduction, pollution prevention, and CFC elimination. Results have been impressive, with averages of 60 percent recycling rates, the elimination or reuse of packaging in some applications, the development of innovative manufacturing processes that reduce or eliminate the use of hazardous substances, and recovery and reuse of metals, plastics, parts, and assemblies. Programs are estimated to have saved Xerox over $150 million in 1993 alone.

Company: **Yosemite National Institutes**
Industry: Nonprofit
Contact: R. Garrett Mitchell, president and CEO
Address: Golden Gate National Recreation Area, Building 1033, Sausalito, CA 94965
Phone: (415) 332-5776
Fax: (415) 332-5784

What Company Does: The Yosemite Institutes is a private, nonprofit corporation that encourages the growth and development of high-quality outdoor environmental learning programs for America's youth, families, teachers, and senior citizens. It currently oversees the work of the Marin Headlands Institute, the Yosemite Institute, and the Olympic Park Institute, which introduce about 20,000 students annually to hands-on, experiential "educational adventures in nature's classrooms."

Environmental Programs: The institute focuses on residential field science programs in various national park sites, using a proprietary environmental curriculum. It is seeking internship collaboration with business schools for new product/program development.

Company: **Zebra Group**
Industry: Environmental consulting
Contact: Carrie Collins, president
Address: 1445 New York Avenue NW, Suite 400, Washington, DC 20005
Phone: (202) 624-8311
Fax: (202) 737-0879

What Company Does: The Zebra Group is an environmental consulting and communications firm that helps companies and organizations market environmental products and services, communicate their environmental efforts to their customers and constituents, and adopt environmentally sound business practices.

Company: Zero Population Growth
Industry: Nonprofit
Contact: Dianne Sherman, communications director
Address: 1400 16th Street NW, Suite 320, Washington, DC 20036
Phone: (202) 332-2200
Fax: (202) 332-2302

What Company Does: Zero Population Growth (ZPG) is a national, nonprofit membership organization founded to achieve a sustainable balance between the world's population and its environmental resources. The organization works through public information, education, and political action to promote awareness of the environmental, social, and economic impacts of population growth. ZPG offers fact sheets, reports, and other materials, and it publishes the bimonthly newspaper, *The ZPG Reporter.*

Resource Directory

The Resource Directory is a new addition to *Green at Work*. Entries include books, directories, magazines, and organizations, and are arranged alphabetically by interest area. This directory is intended as a first step in actively exploring environmental questions, issues, and careers.

Organizations

Animal Rights

Animal Welfare Institute
P.O. Box 3650
Washington, DC 20007
(202) 337-2332

The Animal Welfare Institute has been working for over forty years to prevent needless suffering of animals. Areas of concern include: laboratory animals, trapping, the wildlife trade, whales, and farm animals.

National Anti-Vivisection Society
53 West Jackson Boulevard, Suite 1552
Chicago, IL 60604
(312) 427-6065

The society fights to abolish the use of nonhuman animals in biomedical research, product testing, and education, primarily through education and dialogue. Publishes the *NAVS Bulletin*. Subscription included with membership: life, $100; student/senior, $10; individual, $25.

Biodiversity

Association of Forest Service Employees for Environmental Ethics (AFSEEE)
P.O. Box 11615

Eugene, OR 97440
(503) 484-2692

Seeks the preservation of ecological values and biological diversity in our national forest through education and advocating for reform of U.S. Forest Service management practices.

Careers

Center for Respect of Life and Environment (CRLE)
2100 L Street NW
Washington, DC 20037
(202) 778-6133

CRLE is a division of the Humane Society of the United States. It develops ecologically sensitive academic curricula and sustainable campuses through programs in the arts, sciences, and applied professions, and through *Earth Ethics*, a quarterly publication. Also provides fact sheets with general information on careers that help animals and the environment.

Human Environment Center / The Environmental Consortium
1913 18th Street NW
Washington, DC 20009
(202) 588-8036

Minorities interested in working for environmental organizations are encouraged to contact this consortium of major environmental organizations.

Renew America
1400 16th Street NW, Suite 710
Washington, DC 20036
(202) 232-2252

Has paid internship programs for college and postcollege levels. Publishes reports on a broad range of environmental issues.

Children

Save the Rainforest
604 Jamie Street
Dodgeville, WI 53533
(608) 935-9435

This group operates through a network of 18,000 high schools and elementary schools, educating kids about the world's dwindling rain forests.

Students sometimes travel to see rain forests firsthand and often raise funds for conservation in the tropics.

Tree Musketeers
136 Main Street, Suite A
El Segundo, CA 90245
(800) 473-0263

A nonprofit corporation run by and for kids that is primarily focused on urban forestry. It has four program areas: young executive, administrative, network, and hometown forest. The young executive program helps the youth involved gain appropriate executive/management skills; the administrative program helps with carrying out of other programs; the network program handles outreach on a national level; and the hometown forest program includes tree plantings and an outdoor community classroom, Tree House.

Communications

Business Publishers, Inc.
951 Pershing Drive
Silver Spring, MD 20910-4464
(301) 587-6300
(301) 587-1081

Publishes twenty-three environmental newsletters in categories ranging from environmental health to green marketing to a *World Environment Report* on international resource management. Their *World Directory of Environmental Organizations* (not to be confused with the publication of the same name listed on p. 405 of the "Directory" section) provides 60,000 company, organization, agency, institution, and personnel listings worldwide, and includes environmentally related product manufacturers, equipment, services, and public interest groups.

Cutter Information Corporation
37 Broadway
Arlington, MA 02174-5539
(617) 648-8700 or (617) 641-5123

Publishes a dozen environmental newsletters for businesses.

Environmental Action Report (EAR)
P.O. Box 2002
Santa Rosa, CA 95405

(707) 584-4EAR
(707) 584-0442

A nonprofit, public benefit organization that "brings the environment home" through the power of radio.

Interior Concerns Publications
P.O. Box 2386
Mill Valley, CA 94942

Produces publications for environmentally concerned designers, architects, and builders, including *Resource Guide*, *Interior Concerns Newsletter*, and *Globuild-Net*.

New Society Publishers
P.O. Box 41029
Pasadena, CA 91114-8029
(215) 382-6543
(215) 222-1993

Publishes books on alternative economics, environmental activism, feminism, case studies, and education. Internships considered.

Wary Canary Press
P.O. Box 2204
Fort Collins, CO 80522
(303) 224-0083

Publishes *Environ, A Magazine for Ecologic Living and Health*, a quarterly magazine that publishes and reprints articles, reports, and news briefs on environmental health, book reviews, etc. and *The Wary Canary*, a newsletter dealing with and targeted to people suffering from environmental illness or multiple chemical sensitivity.

Community Development

Isles, Inc.
126 North Montgomery Street
Trenton, NJ 08608
(609) 393-5656

A community-developed corporation involved in affordable housing, community gardens and parks, neighborhood planning, and environmental education. Isles' self-help programs target lower-income neighborhoods in Trenton.

National Association of Community Development Loan Funds (NACDLF)
924 Cherry Street, 3rd floor
Philadelphia, PA 19107-2405
(215) 923-4754

The lending priority of the funds is to assist community-based projects that directly benefit low-income individuals.

Planet Drum Foundation
P.O. Box 31251
San Francisco, CA 94131
(415) 285-6556

Provides an effective grassroots bioregional approach to ecology that emphasizes sustainability, community self-determination, and regional self-reliance.

U.S. Environmental Protection Agency (EPA)
401 M Street SW
Washington, DC 20460
(202) 260-2090

Issues grants for environmental education and grassroots environmental programs.

Design

American Institute of Architects (AIA)
1735 New York Avenue NW
Washington, DC 20006
(800) 365-2724

Publishes a quarterly subscription service called the *Environmental Resource Guide (ERG)* on the environmental impact of building materials in addition to reports, case studies, and bibliographies on sustainable design. Call for other environmental publications.

Graphic Arts Technical Foundation (GATF)
4615 Forbes Avenue
Pittsburgh, PA 15213-3796
(412) 621-6941

Publishes *GATFworld* (subscription $90/year), a magazine that includes up-to-date coverage on graphic arts news and trends and features a column called "Environmental Alert." Office of Environmental Services provides members and nonmembers of GATF with a variety of services, such as environmental audits of printing plants and assistance in preparing air permit applications.

Green Builder Program
City of Austin, Environmental and Conservation Services Department
206 East 9th Street, Suite 17.102
Austin, TX 78701
(512) 499-7827

Publishes *The Green Building Guide*, a 55-page booklet that provides details about the program, guidelines for sustainable construction, and an extensive glossary. *The Sustainable Building Sourcebook*, 440 pages, is a reference guide containing more technical information, including where to find materials. The Green Builder Program is an educational arm for the Environmental and Conservation Services Department of the City of Austin, which provides resources on environmental building materials and design.

Education

Bullfrog Films
P.O. Box 149
Oley, PA 19547
(610) 779-8226

The nation's leading distributor of films and videos about the environment. Free catalog.

Hudson River Sloop Clearwater, Inc.
112 Market Street
Poughkeepsie, NY 12601
(914) 454-7673

The Hudson River Sloop Clearwater is a nonprofit, membership-supported, environmental education and action organization working toward the restoration and protection of the Hudson River and adjoining waterways.

Institute for Earth Education
Cedar Cove
Greenville, WV 24945-0115
(304) 832-6404

The institute is an international nonprofit, volunteer organization composed of individuals and member organizations. Offers workshops and speeches, and sourcebook/catalog offers by mail a variety of teaching materials, posters, books, and other paraphernalia.

Joyful Noise
Box 295
Norwich, VT 05055
(802) 649-3840
Produces multicultural concerts, workshops, and music recordings and songbooks that focus on the power of the arts to heal, inform, and inspire action for a healthy planet and a just and peaceful world. Write for catalog.

North American Association for Environmental Education
1255 23rd Street NW, Suite 400
Washington, DC 20037
(202) 467-8754
Coordinates efforts of environmental educators and students.

Energy

National Energy Foundation
5160 Wiley Post Way, Suite 200
Salt Lake City, UT 84116
(801) 539-1406
Creates and distributes instructional materials dealing with energy and all-natural resources. Materials available to teachers and educational departments only.

Environmental Services

Association of Foam Packaging Recyclers
1025 Connecticut Avenue NW, Suite 515
Washington, DC 20036
(202) 822-6424
Works with industries and retailers to establish a nationwide recycling infrastructure for the collection, reprocessing, and reuse of postconsumer foam packaging. Members are major polystyrene packaging manufacturers, raw material suppliers, and equipment manufacturers.

Center for Hazardous Materials Research
University of Pittsburgh Applied Research
320 William Pitt Way
Pittsburgh, PA 15238
(412) 826-5320
Training center that offers educational courses, seminars, manuals, information, fact sheets, and technical assistance in hazardous materials, waste

management, occupational health and safety, environmental compliance, and emergency response.

Citizens Clearinghouse for Hazardous Waste
P.O. Box 6806
Falls Church, VA 22040
(703) 237-2249

Provides technical support for waste disposal management, recycling, and organizing. Publishes *Everyone's Backyard.*

Environmental Business International, Inc.
4452 Park Boulevard, Suite 306
San Diego, CA 92116
(619) 295-7685

Serves the business development needs of environmental companies through dedicated market assessment, competitive analysis, professional insight, and an independent perspective on the environmental industry.

Environmental Hazards Management Institute (EHMI)
10 Newmarket Road
P.O. Box 932
Durham, NH 03824
(603) 868-1496

A nonprofit, nonpartisan organization dedicated to resolving environmental problems through education and relationship building. Among EHMI's publications are a quarterly newsletter, the *EHMI Re: Source*, a bimonthly tabloid environmental education newsletter, the *EHMI Earth Express*, the *Household Hazardous Waste Wheel*, the *Kids Wheel*, and much more.

Environmental Speakers International
8015 Holland Court, Suite C
Arvada, CO 80005-2468
(303) 431-2468
(303) 425-9652

A full-service speakers bureau that specializes in environmental topics. Produces programs, keynote addresses, seminars, and workshops designed to meet client needs.

Environmental Support Center
1825 Connecticut Avenue NW, Suite 220
Washington, DC 20009
(202) 328-7813

Helps local, state, and regional environmental groups to become more effective by subsidizing costs for training, and organizational assistance and advising them in areas ranging from financial management to computer applications to communications and public relations.

National Association for Plastic Container Recovery
100 North Tryon, Suite 3770
Charlotte, NC 28202
(704) 358-8882

Assists communities interested in establishing PET plastic recycling programs, offers information on recycling PET plastic, and publishes a quarterly newsletter, *PET Projects.*

National Solid Wastes Management Association
1730 Rhode Island NW, Suite 1000
Washington, DC 20036
(202) 659-4613

Publishes *Waste Age*, a monthly magazine, and *Recycling Times*, a biweekly newspaper, and also offers a selection of books, reports, and guides relevant to solid-waste management.

Northeast Recycling Council
139 Main Street, Suite 401
Brattleboro, VT 05301
(802) 254-3636

Focuses on regional market development and policy coordination for recycling, holds meetings and conferences, and offers a newsletter and information service.

Steel Recycling Institute
680 Andersen Drive
Pittsburgh, PA 15220-2700
(800) 876-7274

Publishes quarterly newsletter, *The Recycling Magnet*, and has developed a database (800-937-1226) for consumers seeking the nearest location to recycle steel cans.

Urban Ore
1333 6th Street
Berkeley, CA 94710
(510) 559-4454

Publishes *Salvaging for Reuse: Profits in Highest and Best Use*, which includes eighty slides, script, and technical paper ($155). Other publications include a report on composting yard waste into humus and *The Lone Recycler*, a comic book for kids.

Food and Agriculture

Agroecology Program—Working Toward Sustainable Agriculture
University of California
1156 High Street
Santa Cruz, CA 95064
(408) 459-4140

Publishes newsletter called *The Cultivar;* offers certificate program in ecological horticulture.

Alternative Farming Systems Information Center (AFSIC)
United States Department of Agriculture, Room 111
National Agricultural Library, 10301 Baltimore Boulevard
Beltsville, MD 20705-2351
(301) 344-3704

Provides up-to-date information on sustainable agriculture. Publishes *AFSIC Notes*, a periodical containing an overview of applicable topics and suggested readings.

Land Institute
2440 East Water Well Road
Salina, KS 67401
(913) 823-5376

Conducts sustainable agriculture research. Ten-month postgraduate internships. Publishes *The Land Report*, a newsletter covering book reviews, policy, and research focusing on genetic diversity, land stewardship, and alternative agriculture.

Northeast Organic Farming Association of Massachusetts
411 Sheldon Road
Barre, MA 01005-9252
(508) 355-2853

Certifies organic farms, conducts educational conferences and workshops, offers videos on organic production, and distributes a map of organic farms throughout Massachusetts. Publishes a quarterly regional journal, *The Natural Farmer*, and a bimonthly chapter newsletter.

General Interest

Environmental Alliance for Senior Involvement (EASI)
EASI Conference
P.O. Box 368
The Plains, VA 22171
(703) 330-5667

A national coalition of environmental, senior, and volunteer organizations and agencies established to provide opportunities for older people to conserve and protect our environment.

Government Accountability Project (GAP)
810 First Street NE, Suite 630
Washington, DC 20002-3633
(202) 408-0034

Provides legal and advocacy assistance to concerned citizens who witness dangerous, illegal, or environmentally unsound practices in their workplaces and communities. GAP works with hundreds of public and private employees and grassroots organizations to expose threats to public health and safety and the environment.

Infact
256 Hanover Street, 3rd floor
Boston, MA 02113
(617) 742-4583

Builds international campaigns for corporate accountability. Currently running a campaign to stop the tobacco industry from addicting new customers around the world.

Institute for Conservation Leadership
2000 P Street NW, Suite 413
Washington, DC 20036
(202) 466-3330

Offers leadership training and empowerment to the entire environmental community (volunteer leaders and institutions that protect and conserve the environment). Designed to assist conservation leaders in strategic planning, organizational development and management, and development of skills, networks, and resources.

Stop Junk Mail Association
c/o 3020 Bridgeway, Suite 150A

Sausalito, CA
(800) 827-5549

Gets members' names removed from major mailing lists; provides comprehensive membership kit to stop junk mail; lobbies and educates to protect old-growth forests and privacy rights. Free brochure. Lectures and consults nationally to schools, corporations, and government groups on ways to reduce mail.

Health

National Center for Environmental Health Strategies
1100 Rural Avenue
Voorhees, NJ 08043
(609) 429-5358

Serves as an information clearinghouse, maintains a library, and offers referral, support, and advocacy services related to environmental illness and chemical sensitivity. Publishes a newsletter, *The Delicate Balance*, and distributes books, reports, and other resources on chemical sensitivity.

National Environmental Health Association
720 South Colorado Boulevard, South Tower, Suite 970
Denver, CO 80222-1925
(303) 756-9090

Professional association incorporated in 1937 whose mission is to "advance the environmental health and protection professional for the purpose of providing a healthful environment for all." Deals with virtually all environmental issues.

International

Canadian Artic Resources Committee, Inc.
1 Nicholas Street, Suite 412
Ottawa, Ontario K1N 7B7 Canada
Publishes *Northern Perspectives*, a quarterly policy journal on Canada's north. Also publishes books.

Center for Environment & Development for the Arab Region (CEDARE)
21/23 Giza Street, Nile Tower Building, 13th floor
P.O. Box 52
Orman Giza, Cairo, Egypt
(202) 570-0979, 570-3473, 570-1859, or 570-3474

CEDARE is sponsored by the Arab Fund for Economic and Social Development (AFESD), the government of Egypt (GOE), and the United Nations Development Programme (UNDP). Its purpose is to enhance environmental management and influence accelerated development.

Global Forum of Spiritual & Parliamentary Leaders on Human Survival
304 East 45th Street, 4th floor
New York, NY 10017
(212) 953-7947

Publishes *Shared Vision* newsletter.

Greenpeace International
Keizersgracht 176
1016 DW Amsterdam, The Netherlands
31-20-523-6555

Works to end nuclear testing, stop and reverse the destruction of the biosphere, stop whaling, prevent dumping of toxic waste, and support disarmament.

International Association of Environmental Managers
243 West Main Street, P.O. Box 308
Kutztown, PA 19530
(215) 683-5098

International Chamber of Commerce
38, Cours Albert 1er
75008 Paris, France
33-1-49-53-28-28
33-1-42-25-86-63 or 32-81

A nongovernmental organization that helps the business community make useful contributions to solving environmental issues while ensuring that their business concerns are acknowledged by intergovernmental agencies who are concerned with the environment.

New Consumer Ltd.
52 Elswick Road
Newcastle upon Tyne NE4 6JH, England
44-91-272-1148

An organization in Britain patterned after Co-op America. Educates the public about a just economy, and provides products and services from responsible businesses.

World Bank (International Bank for Reconstruction and Development)
1818 H Street NW
Washington, DC 20433
(202) 477-1234

The Environment Department of the World Bank has allowed it to become a major source of ideas and case studies focusing on sustainable development. The bank works on special undertakings like the Global Environmental Facility, which funds projects that deal with a variety of global environmental problems and supports regional initiatives.

World Environment Center (WEC)
419 Park Avenue South, Suite 1800
New York, NY 10016
(212) 683-4700

WEC's goal is to contribute to sustainable development worldwide by strengthening industrial and urban environmental health and safety policy and practices. It functions as a link for the sharing of information and experience between governments and industry, as well as among NGOs and national and international organizations.

Policymaking

Americans for the Environment
1400 16th Street NW, Box 24
Washington, DC 20036-2266
(202) 797-6665

Assists groups and individuals to solve environmental problems through the political process. Offers workshops and seminars, technical assistance, campaign-skills training programs, public educational materials, and information guides about electoral activity.

Eco-Justice Project
Anabel Taylor Hall
Cornell University
Ithaca, NY 14853-1001
(607) 255-4225

Works to ensure that the basic values of sustainability, reverence, participation, sufficiency, and solidarity become the bedrock of future policy and practice.

U.S. Public Interest Research Group (USPIRG)
215 Pennsylvania Avenue SE

Washington, DC 20003
(202) 546-9707

Focuses on corporate reform, energy policy, and environmental protection and monitors the implementation of environmental legislation. Publishes *Citizens Agenda.* Has state run organizations as well, check state or call USPIRG for regional offices.

Union of Concerned Scientists
26 Church Street
Cambridge, MA 02238
(617) 547-5552

Dedicated to advancing responsible public policies in areas where technology plays a critical role.

Publications

Animal Rights

Animals' Agenda
P.O. Box 25881
Baltimore, MD 21224
(410) 675-4566

A bimonthly magazine dedicated to informing people about animal rights and cruelty-free living for the purpose of inspiring action for animals. Subscription: $22/year.

Biodiversity

Dolphin Alert
300 Broadway, Suite 28
San Francisco, CA 94133
(415) 788-3666

A quarterly newsletter that addresses marine issues, particularly endangered species and marine mammals.

Global Climate Change Digest
Elsevier Science Publishing Co., Inc.
655 Avenue of the Americas
New York, NY 10010
(212) 989-5800

A monthly newsletter that focuses on the science and policy of climate changes, such as global warming and ozone depletion.

Ocean Realm
Raku Inc.
342 West Sunset Road
San Antonio, TX 78209
(512) 824-8099

A quarterly magazine focusing on marine mammals and some of the various environmental elements facing them.

Understory—Sustainable Developments from the World of Wood
1 Cottage Street
Easthampton, MA 01027
(413) 586-8156

Published by the Woodworkers Alliance for Rainforest Protection (WARP).

Careers

Access: Networking in the Public Interest
30 Irving Place, 9th floor
New York, NY 10003
(212) 475-1001

Publishes *Community Jobs: The National Employment Newspaper for the nonprofit sector.* Job listings in nonprofits and public interest law. Database of 4,000+ nonprofit organizations. *Community Jobs: NY/NJ*, *Community Jobs: Washington DC.*

The Career Grapevine
Southern Illinois University at Carbondale
Woody Hall B-204
Carbondale, IL 62901
(618) 453-2391

Lists environmentally related jobs.

Earth Work—Advancing Your Conservation Career
Box 550
Charlestown, NH 03603-0550
(603) 543-1700

Published monthly by the Student Conservation Association.

Environmental Career Opportunities
P.O. Box 15629
Chevy Chase, MD 20825
(301) 986-5545

Published biweekly by the Brubach Publishing Company; lists over 300 entry- through senior-level positions in environmental fields across the United States and overseas. Covers positions in advocacy, communications, fund-raising, policy, legislation, regulation, conservation, resource management, environmental engineering, risk assessment, impact analysis, scientific education and research, and internship.

Environmental Careers
760 Whalers Way, Suite 100, Building A
Fort Collins, CO 80525-9802
A magazine that lists training and employment opportunities in the environmental services industry.

Community Development

GEO—Grassroots Economic Organizing Newsletter
P.O. Box 5065
New Haven, CT 06525
(203) 389-6194
Clearinghouse on community-based economic and ecological development.

Neighborhood Works
2125 West Avenue
Chicago, IL 60647
(312) 278-4800
Bimonthly magazine dealing with housing, energy, environment, and economic development affecting city neighborhoods. Leading magazine on sustainability issues in low- and middle-income neighborhoods.

Design

Environmental Building News
RR1, Box 161
Brattleboro, VT 05301
(802) 257-7300
A bimonthly newsletter on environmentally sustainable design and construction. Provides feature articles on a wide range of topics relating to environmental building practices, including products and materials, news and developments, and essays on aspects of environmental design.

Education

Green Teacher
95 Robert Street

Toronto, Ontario M5S 2K5, Canada
(416) 960-1244

For teachers wishing to promote global and environmental awareness in kids K–12: ideas from successful green educators, classroom activities, reviews of teaching resources, and announcements of events.

Energy

Home Energy—The Magazine of Residential Energy Conservation
2124 Kittredge Street, NO. 95
Berkeley, CA 94704
(510) 524-5405

Covers every aspect of residential conservation, from super-efficient appliances and lighting to indoor air quality and water conservation.

Independent Energy—The Industry's Business Magazine
620 Central Avenue North
Miliaca, MN 56353-1788
(612) 983-6892

A magazine of the independent power industry, a $100 billion industry devoted to providing clean, low-cost electricity. Independent Energy analyzes business trends and market strategies and focuses on competitive strategies for the power market rather than on engineering aspects of the power industry.

New Energy Report
84 Canyon Road
Fairfax, CA 94930
(415) 459-2383

A monthly newsletter that recommends companies whose products and services are aimed at improving the environment. Firms covered include areas such as alternative energy, waste management and recycling, nonpolluting transportation, natural foods and cosmetics, and innovative building methods.

Solar Today
2400 Central Avenue, Unit G-1
Boulder, CO 80301

A bimonthly national magazine published by the American Solar Energy Society, with articles on all solar technologies, including the latest advances in products, services, policies, and regulations.

Environmental Services

EI Digest—Industrial & Hazardous Waste Journal
Environmental Information, Ltd.
4801 West 81st Street, Suite 119
Minneapolis, MN 55437
(612) 831-2473

Published monthly. Explores the regulations, technology, and business issues affecting hazardous and nonhazardous industrial-waste management.

Environmental Business Journal—Strategic Information for a Changing Industry
P.O. Box 371769
San Diego, CA 92137-1769
(619) 295-7685

Excellent journal for information on the environmental industry.

Plastics Recycling Update
Resource Recycling, Inc.
P.O. Box 10540
Portland, OR 97210
(503) 227-1319
(503) 227-3864

A monthly newsletter that apprises readers on plastic recycling programs and markets.

Resource Recovery Report
5313 38th Street NW
Washington, DC 20015
(202) 362-6034

A monthly newsletter that focuses on recycling and solid waste on a national level. Sponsors conferences and special studies on recycling.

Food and Agriculture

American Journal of Alternative Agriculture
9200 Edmonston Road, Suite 117
Greenbelt, MD 20770
(301) 441-8777

Covers new books, organization activities, policy, and research about inexpensive, resource-conserving, and environmentally friendly farming techniques.

Journal of Sustainable Agriculture
Biology Department
Fairfield University
Fairfield, CT 06430-7524
(203) 254-4000, ext. 2542
A quarterly journal covering policy, research, and organization activities involving sustainable agriculture.

New Farm
222 Main Street
Emmaus, PA 18098
(610) 967-8995
A bimonthly magazine that "puts people, profit and biological permanence back into farming."

General Interest

The Boycott Quarterly
Center for Economic Democracy
P.O. Box 64
Olympia, WA 98507-0064
A quarterly magazine containing a comprehensive list of ongoing boycotts and products made by boycotted companies, extensive boycott news and updates, and in-depth coverage of numerous boycotts.

Business Ethics—The Magazine of Socially Responsible Business
Business Ethics (Mavis Publications)
52 South 10th Street, Suite 110
Minneapolis, MN 55403
(612) 962-4700
An excellent resource for people interested in business and social responsibility.

Calypso Log
The Cousteau Society, Membership Center
870 Greenbrier Circle, Suite 402
Chesapeake, VA 23330
(804) 523-9335

Common Boundary—Between Spirituality and Psychotherapy
The Common Boundary Magazine & Conference Office
4304 East-West Highway

Bethesda, MD 20814
(301) 652-9495 or (800) 548-8737 for subscriptions only

E Magazine—The Environmental Magazine
Earth Action Network
28 Knight Street
Norwalk, CT 06851
(203) 854-5559

Earth First! The Radical Environmental Journal
Earth First! Journal, Inc.
P.O. Box 5871
Tucson, AZ 85703
Focuses on community environmental policy and activism.

Ecologist
MIT Press Journals
55 Hayward Street
Cambridge, MA 02142
(617) 253-2889

EnviroAccount Software
605 Sunset Court
Davis, CA 95616
(800) 554-0317
EnviroAccount asks 115 questions about user's lifestyle in six areas: home energy, home water, transportation, consumerism, waste advocacy, and land use/demographics and then assigns Impact Points and Action Points based on answers. Helps user to visualize links to the environment and to set lifestyle goals.

Environment
Heldref Publications
1319 18th Street NW
Washington, DC 20036-5149
(202) 296-6267
Environment is a scholarly periodical dedicated to following policy issues.

Environmental Ethics
University of North Texas
Department of Philosophy, P.O. Box 13496
Denton, TX 76203-3496
(817) 565-2727

A journal that addresses all environmental topics but primarily conservation, wilderness, ecological ethics, and wildlife management, with a philosophical focus.

Garbage Magazine—The Practical Journal for the Environment
Dovetale Publishers
2 Main Street
Gloucester, MA 01930
(508) 283-3200

GreenDisk
P.O. Box 32224
Washington, DC 20007
(703) 788-9562
Paperless environmental journal. Contains newsletters of various environmental organizations; lists of environmental conferences, workshops, meetings, and a collection of action alerts.

Greenpeace Magazine
Greenpeace
1436 U Street NW
Washington, DC 20009
(202) 462-1177

High Country News
High Country Foundation
Grand Avenue, P.O. Box 1090
Paonia, CO 81428
(303) 527-4898
A biweekly newspaper covering natural resources in the West.

In Business—The Magazine for Environmental Entrepreneuring
The JG Press
419 State Avenue
Emmaus, PA 18049
(215) 967-4135

Trumpeter Journal of Ecosophy
Lightstar
P.O. Box 5853, Station B.
Victoria, British Columbia V8R 6S8, Canada

Provides a diversity of perspectives on environmental relationships and nature. It explores ecosophy (ecological harmony and wisdom).

Utne Reader
1624 Harmon Place
Minneapolis, MN 55043
Available on any newsstand.

The WIT Report
274 Madison Avenue, Suite 601
New York, NY 10016
(212) 696-2037
World Information Transfer is a nonprofit, international, nongovernmental organization dedicated to promoting environmental literacy among opinion leaders and concerned citizens around the world. Its expert speakers address companies, clubs, and organizations on various aspects of the environment. *WIT Report* is available in English, Russian, Spanish, Ukranian, Polish, and Arabic.

International

Alternatives—Perspectives on Society, Technology and Environment
c/o Faculty of Environmental Studies
University of Waterloo
Waterloo, Ontario N2L 3G1, Canada

Earth Times
280 Park Avenue
New York, NY 10017
(212) 297-0488
A UN publication that informs reader of UN conferences and upcoming UN events.

International Environmental Affairs
UPNE, 23 South Main Street
Hanover, NH 03755-2048
(603) 643-7100
Journal addresses environmental and conservation issues and international management and policy issues (in the field of international environmental diplomacy), such as pollution, species diversity, resource management and

preservation, development, climate change, and international environmental policy.

International Wildlife
National Wildlife Federation
8925 Leesburg Pike NW
Vienna, VA 22184
(202) 872-8840

A bimonthly magazine that addresses the issues surrounding endangered animals with an international scope.

Kagenna
P.O. Box 4713
Cape Town, South Africa 8000

A quarterly magazine about green values: ecology, politics, culture. The only green issues magazine in South Africa; published by a nonprofit co-op.

Management and Finance

Clean Yield Group
P.O. Box 1880
Greensboro Bend, VT 05842
(802) 533-7178

Monthly stock market newsletter about social investing and money management services.

Environment Week
King Communications Group, Inc.
627 National Press Building
Washington, DC 20045
(202) 638-4260

Provides up-to-date information on current issues, trends, business developments, and technology. Information on regulations, clean air, fuels, the greenhouse effect, ozone depletion, and CFCs.

environment risk
Euromoney Publications plc
Playhouse Yard
London, ECCC4V 5EX, England
44-71-779-8699

Investor's Environmental Report
Investor Responsibility Research Center

1755 Massachusetts Avenue NW, Suite 600
Washington, DC 20036

Outdoors

Dave Foreman's Books of the Big Outside
Ned Ludd Books
P.O. Box 85190
Tucson, AZ 85754-5190
(602) 628-9610

A catalog listing books of interest to wilderness defenders.

National Parks
National Parks and Conservation Association
1015 31st Street NW, 4th floor
Washington, DC 20007
(202) 944-8530

A bimonthly magazine that focuses on activities in our national park system. Covers such issues as endangered animals, use of public land, and important landmarks.

Directories

Conservation Directory
National Wildlife Federation
1400 16th Street NW
Washington, DC 20036-2266
(202) 797-6800 or (800) 432-6564

Listing of environmental organizations nationwide.

Consultants and Consulting Directory, 12th edition
Gale Research Company
835 Penobscot Building
Detroit, MI 48226
(313)961-2242

Includes environmental consultant listings.

Directory of Environmental Information Resources, 2nd edition
Government Institutes, Inc.
966 Hungerford Drive, #24
Rockville, MD 20850

Includes over 1,000 listings of federal and state agencies, associations, professional organizations, databases, and publishers.

Directory of Environmental Organizations
Education Communications
P.O. Box 351419
Los Angeles, CA 90035-9119
(310) 559-9160

Directory of more than 5,700 local, state, national, and international listings. Available in alphabetical subject or zip code order, in print for $30, on mailing labels for $200, or on diskette for $300. May contact organization to order copy of directory or to be listed free in directory.

Directory of State Environmental Agencies
Environmental Law Institute
1616 P Street NW
Washington, DC 20036
(202) 939-3800

Contains basic information about environmental protection and management agencies of every state.

EI Environmental Services Directory
Environmental Information, Ltd.
4801 West 81st Street, Suite 119
Minneapolis, MN 55437
(612) 831-2473

Over 2,000 pages of information on environmental services businesses, such as treatment and recycling firms, construction companies, and laboratories.

Encyclopedia of Associations: National Organization of the United States
Gale Research Company
835 Penobscot Building
Detroit, MI 48226
(313) 961-2242

Contains listings of all associations and nonprofit organizations in the United States.

Encyclopedia of Business Information Sources, 6th edition
Gale Research Company
835 Penobscot Building
Detroit, MI 48226
(313) 961-2242

Contains listings of environmental on-line databases, directories, handbooks, newsletters, and trade and professional associations.

Environmental Grantmaking Foundations
1655 Elmwood Avenue, Suite 225
Rochester, NY 14620-3426
(800) 724-1857 or (716) 473-3090

Annual directory published by the Environmental Data Research Institute. 1995 edition profiles 600 of the most significant independent, community, and corporate foundations that give environmental grants. Together these foundations gave over $425 million for environmental purposes in 1994.

Helping Out in the Outdoors
American Hiking Society
P.O. Box 20160
Washington, DC 20041-2160
(703) 255-9304

Directory of volunteer jobs and internships on U.S. public lands.

National Directory of Internships
3509 Haworth Drive, Suite 207
Raleigh, NC 27609-7229

A publication of the National Society for Internships and Experiential Education.

Public Interest Profiles
Foundation for Public Affairs
Congressional Quarterly, Inc.
1414 22nd Street, NW
Washington, DC 20037

Contains profiles of environmental organizations.

World Directory of Environmental Organizations, 3rd edition
California Institute for Public Affairs
P.O. Box 10
Claremont, CA 91711

Includes over 1,000 listings of government, independent, and national environmental agencies.

Additional Resources

Recommended Reading

The Artist's Way, A Spiritual Path to Higher Creativity by Julia Cameron. New York: Putnam Publishing Group, 1992.

Biologic: Designing with Nature to Protect the Environment by David Wann. Boulder: Johnson Books, 1994.

Bionomics: Economy As Ecosystem by Michael Rothschild. New York: H. Holt & Co., 1990.

Choosing a Career in Business by Stephen A. Stumpf, Ph.D. New York: Simon and Schuster, 1984.

The Complete Guide to Environmental Careers by the CEIP Fund. Washington, D.C.: Island Press, 1989.

Design for the Environment by Dorothy Mackenzie. New York: Rizzoli International Publications, 1991.

Do What You Love and the Money Will Follow by Marsha Sinetar. New York: Paulist Press, 1989.

The E Factor: The Bottom-Line Approach to Environmentally Responsible Business by Joel Makower. New York: Tilden Press/Times Books, 1993.

Earth in the Balance: Ecology and the Human Spirit by Albert Gore. Boston: Houghton Millflin, 1992.

The Ecology of Commerce: A Declaration of Sustainability by Paul Hawken. New York: HarperBusiness, 1993.

Edge City: Life on the New Frontier by Joel Garreau. New York: Anchor Books, 1992.

The Environmental Economic Revolution: How Business Will Thrive and the Earth Survive in Years to Come by Michael Silverstein. New York: St. Martin's Press, 1993.

A Fierce Green Fire: The American Environmental Movement by Philip Shabecoff. New York: Hill & Wang, 1993

How Much Is Enough? The Consumer Society and the Future of the Earth by Alan During. New York: W.W. Norton, 1992.

How Things Don't Work by Victor Papanek & James Hennessey. New York: Pantheon Books, 1977.

In the Absence of the Sacred: The Failure of Technology and the Survival of the Indian Nations by Jerry Mander. San Francisco: Sierra Club, 1991.

In Transition by Mary Lindley Burton and Richard A. Wedemeyer. New York: HarperBusiness, 1991.

The Perfect Resume for the 90s by Tom Jackson. New York: Anchor Books, 1990.

The Soul of a Business: Managing for Profit and the Common Good by Tom Chappell. New York: Bantam, 1993.

Sustainable Communities: A New Design Synthesis for Cities, Suburbs & Design by Peter Calthorpe and Sim Vander Ryn. San Francisco: Sierra Club, 1986.

Take This Job and Love It by Dennis Jaffe and Cynthia Scott. New York: Simon and Schuster, 1988.

The Three Boxes of Life and How to Get Out of Them by Richard Bolles. Berkeley, Calif.: Ten Speed Press, 1978.

Through the Brick Wall: How to Job Hunt in a Tight Market by Kate Wendleton. New York: Villard Books, 1992.

What Color Is Your Parachute? by Richard Bolles. Berkeley, Calif.: Ten Speed Press, annual.

What Makes the Crops Rejoice: An Introduction to Gardening by Robert Howard with Eric Skjei. Boston: Little, Brown, 1986.

Where Do I Go from Here with My Life? by John Crystal and Richard Bolles. Berkeley, Calif.: Ten Speed Press, 1974.

Wishcraft: How to Get What You Really Want by Barbara Sher. New York: Ballantine Books, 1988.

Work with Passion: How to Do What You Really Love for a Living by Nancy Anderson. New York: Carroll & Graf, 1984.

Zen and the Art of Making a Living: A Practical Guide to Creative Career Design by Laurence G. Boldt. New York: Penguin Arkana, 1991.

Environmental Information Providers

There are many sources of books on the environment. The following three are among the best:

Island Press, Box 7, Covelo, CA 95428, (800) 828-1302. Island Press has one of the most comprehensive catalogs of environmental books, with topics ranging from poetry to analyses of major environmental challenges.

Natural Resources Defense Council, 40 West 20th Street, New York, NY 10011. NRDC publishes books and position papers on the following topics: water and air pollution, hazardous- and solid-waste management, energy and lighting, rain forests, food safety, pesticide use, natural resource protection in

Alaska, and environmental education for children. The NRDC is an excellent resource for researching varied topics of environmental interest.

World Resources Institute, 1750 New York Avenue NW, Washington, DC 20006 Publishes on diversified environmental topics. (See "Company Directory.")

Watchdog Groups

The following organizations provide information on corporate environmental performance and additional corporate information:

Citizen's Clearinghouse for Hazardous Waste, P.O. Box 3541, Arlington, VA 22216, (703) 276-7070.

Coalition for Environmentally Responsible Economies, 711 Atlantic Avenue, Boston, MA 02111, (617) 451-0927.

Council on Economic Priorities, 30 Irving Place, New York, NY 10003. CEP is a research watchdog.

Environmental Defense Fund, 257 Park Avenue South, New York, NY 10010.

Franklin Research and Development, 711 Atlantic Avenue, Boston, MA 02111, (617) 423-6655.

Greenpeace, 1436 U Street NW, Washington, DC 20009.

Inform, 381 Park Avenue South, New York, NY 10016, (212) 689-4040.

International Chamber of Commerce, ICC/UN Liaison Office, 1212 Avenue of the Americas, 21st floor, New York, NY 10036, (212) 354-4480.

Natural Resources Defense Council, 40 West 20th Street, New York, NY 10011.

Sierra Club, 730 Polk Street, San Francisco, CA 94109.

U.S. Public Interest Research Group, 215 Pennsylvania Avenue SE, Washington, DC 20003, (202) 546-9707.

Index by Industry

Index by Geographic Location

Island Press Board of Directors